A COMMENTARY ON
THE NEW
CODE OF CANON LAW

By THE REV. CHAS. AUGUSTINE, O.S.B., D.D.
Professor of Canon Law

WITH AN INTRODUCTION BY
HIS EMINENCE CARDINAL GASQUET

VOLUME III

De Personis, or
Ecclesiastical Persons

Religious and Laymen
(Can. 487-725)

SECOND EDITION

B. HERDER BOOK CO.

17 SOUTH BROADWAY, ST. LOUIS, MO.
AND
68 GREAT RUSSELL ST. LONDON, W. C.

1919

INTRODUCTION BY HIS EMINENCE CARDINAL GASQUET

I have been asked to write a brief Introduction to this third volume of the *Commentary on the New Code of Canon Law*. The subject matter is so important and affects so many people that an Introduction would almost appear to be out of place; but I cannot refuse the request of an old friend like Father Augustine to write a few words to preface his Commentary.

The sections of the Code treated in this volume deal with two classes of persons, namely religious and lay people. The laws relating to the first naturally follow upon those which deal with clerics, and they are set forth in this Codex in 195 Canons, in which is given with clearness and precision the whole jurisprudence of the Church regarding the religious life. In some ways this portion of the new Codex may be regarded as perhaps the most useful and necessary part of the Codification of ecclesiastical law. Hitherto legislation in regard to religious has been in what may be called "a fluid state." It was mostly based upon special Pontifical Constitutions and deductions from the same, and had not hitherto been gathered together and coördinated officially. The marvellous growth of religious bodies and the variety, especially in modern times, of their scope and purpose, had rendered it difficult, to say the least, to set out the ecclesiastical law applicable to them.

After the Council of Trent, the advent of Congregations of Clerks Regular made necessary great changes in the old monastic legislation, and these again opened the way for other Congregations of simple vows, perpetual or temporary, which have proved useful and even necessary to meet the needs of the Church in modern times.

The codification of the laws relating to religious life has consequently not been the easiest portion of this great work, which has been accomplished in the present Codex. The most important change which has been introduced in this section — at least so far as the older Orders are concerned — is the law which imposes a period of three years of temporary simple vows after the noviciate, before perpetual vows, simple or solemn, can be taken. Hitherto the very ancient monastic principle of stability was safeguarded by the subjects taking simple vows for three years, which on their part are perpetual, before taking their solemn vows.

Another point in the present legislation to be noticed is the greater stress which is laid upon the element of " common life," as an essential condition for the religious life. Canon 487 makes this clear. One who leads an eremitical life, for example, cannot be called a religious, because the condition of " common life " is wanting. In the same way Canon 673 defines as improperly called " religious " those who, though living together in common life, are not bound by vows.

The second portion of this volume deals in two sections with matters regarding the laity and their associations. In the first the enrollment of the laity in pious associations is strongly recommended. Since these are recognized by the Church, they should be approved and established by competent ecclesiastical authority. The Ordinary always is to exercise his jurisdiction over such associations. In view of the great multiplication of these confraternities in modern times, it is obviously of the greatest importance that the principles which regulate them should be set forth and understood.

The second section of this part deals with particular pious associations, such as " Third Orders," Archconfraternities, Confraternities, Pious Associations, etc.

It will be seen from this bare statement that the Volume here given to the public contains much of great practical importance, and I have little doubt that the Commentary furnished by so competent a canonist as Father Augustine, O. S. B., will be found of great assistance to those who wish to understand the New Codex.

A. CARD. GASQUET

Rome, Nov. 10, 1918.

TABLE OF CONTENTS

BOOK II. PART II. RELIGIOUS

CONTENTS

CONTENTS

CONTENTS

THE NEW CODE OF CANON LAW

BOOK II—PART II
RELIGIOUS

HISTORICAL INTRODUCTION

Before starting this part of our commentary, we shall give a brief historical sketch of the origin of the religious state and its development into various branches, orders, and congregations. To this shall be added a paragraph treating of exemption.

§ I.   ORIGIN AND EARLY PROPAGATION OF THE RELIGIOUS STATE

The primitive form in which the religious state appears is *monasticism.* " Dwelling alone," in its concrete Christian [1] aspect, is a creation of the closing third century and owes its origin to *SS. Antony* and *Pachomius.* The former is the father of the Anchorites proper, whilst Pachomius gave to the monks the cenobitic rule. Undoubtedly the persecutions from Decius to Diocletian, violent and universal as they were, made more than one Christian tremble for his faith and life and caused many

---

[1] As to the Essenes, cf. *Cath. Encyclopedia,* V, 546; Montalem- bert, *The Monks of the West,* (Engl. ed.), 1896, I, 217.

to seek shelter in the desert.[2] Yet this extrinsic motive alone would scarcely account either for the multitude of solitaries or for the perseverance of their ascetic institutes after peace had been restored to the Church. Hence another element must necessarily be assigned in explanation of so singular a phenomenon: it is the desire of fervent Christians to follow more closely in the footprints of the Savior and His Disciples, and to imitate the great forerunners of monastic life, the prophet Elias and St. John the Baptist.[3] However, it was not only the voice of Christ bidding His loved ones to forsake everything and follow Him; it was not merely the promise of a full measure of bliss that attracted the multitudes, but we may truly say that this abandonment of a sin-steeped world was due to a deeply felt desire of appeasing the longing of a "naturally Christian" soul. Montalembert describes it thus: "In the depths of human nature there exists without doubt a tendency, instinctive though confused and evanescent, towards retirement and solitude. Its manifestations are found in all the epochs of history, in all religions, in all societies, except perhaps among savage tribes, or in the bosom of that corrupt civilization, which by its excess and over-refinement too often leads humanity back to a savage condition."[4] The novelty, too, and a certain chivalric tendency may have drawn not a few into the wilderness. But withal the Christian sentiment deeply impressed, and especially that bewildering echo of the second advent of Christ — the *parousia* of St. Paul's teaching — prompted many of those whose souls had been purified in the

---

[2] Thus St. Paul, the first hermit; cf. *Vita S. Pauli*, in *Acta SS.* (Boll.), X, Jan. I, 603; Bulteau, O.S.B., *Abrégé de l'Histoire de l'Ordre de S. Benoit*, Paris, 1684, I, 4.

[3] Cf. St. Jerome, *Proleg. Vitae S. Pauli*, Migne, P. L., 23, 17.

[4] *The Monks of the West*, I, 15.

waters of penance to shake off worldly fetters in order to contemplate more freely the "light divine." Thus, then, we see St. Antony the Great [5] bury himself in the mountains of the Thebaid at Pispir, and S. Pachomius lead his cenobitic army to the cloistral realms of Tabennisi in the upper Thebaid on the Nile.[6]

But if we speak of the life in common organized by Pachomius, we must not compare it to St. Benedict's Rule. It looked indeed somewhat like a congregation of modern times, with its superior general, visitations and chapters; but the essential feature of Benedictine life, the family ideal, could not be attained by reason of the great number of monks, 50,000 being mentioned in the preface of St. Pachomius' rule.[7] The brethren were divided according to their arts or trades, each group having its own provost or prior. In the month of August there was a general chapter at which all officials were appointed. A great deal of freedom was left to the individuals; thus, for instance, they could take their meals in common or privately in their cells. Two fast-days per week were prescribed except during Easter and Whitsuntide.[8]

Community life was more strictly defined by *St. Basil* the Great. The "father" of cenobitic life would have his monks work and pray seven times a day in common, besides placing all ascetic exercises under the control of a superior.

The East, therefore, presented two kinds of monks: the solitaires following Antony, and the cenobites following the rule of Pachomius and the great Cappadocian Bishop.

5 Cf. *Vita S. Antonii* in *Acta SS.* (Boll.), Jan. 17, II, 471 ff.

6 See C. Butler, O.S.B., *The Lausiac History of Palladius* in "Cambridge Texts and Studies," P. I, 1898, P. II, 1904.

7 Migne, *P. L.*, 23, 64, n. 6; n. 8; Butler, *l. c.*, I, 236.

8 Migne, *l. c.*, n. 5.

The wave of monasticism from the East soon invaded the Western Church, not like a great inundation, but gradually, gently, and steadily. This was due in part at least to the whirlwind of Arianism. The persecution set on foot by these fanatics caused Athanasius and other Alexandrian clergymen to seek the protection of the Apostolic See.[9] This happened between the years 339 and 341 A. D. On the other hand Italian bishops like Eusebius of Vercelli were banished from their native soil into Eastern regions. The same Eusebius, confessor of the Catholic faith (d. 371), on returning from his exile — which had lasted from 355 to 362, during which time he had been the guest of the Thebaid monasteries — transplanted the monastic institute to Italy.

But it may be safely said that the first impulse to Western monasticism came from Rome, primarily through the service of St. Athanasius and through the influence exercised by the noble *Marcella*. Her palace stood on the Aventine hill, consecrated by the presence of the Prince of the Apostles. She is praised by St. Jerome as the " *prima monacha Romae.*" The life of St. Antony, written about 365, was known to her, and when St. Jerome came to Rome (382) to renew those instructions and narratives by adding to them the example of his own life, Marcella, with her mother Albinia, and her sister Asella placed themselves at the head of that select number of illustrious matrons who took him for their guide and oracle. She died shortly after the sack of Rome by Alaric (410).[10] *Pammachius*, a man of consular birth, is celebrated by the hermit of Bethlehem as the " first and leader of the monks " in Rome, whose example drew

9 *Acta SS.* (Boll.), II, 1108; St. Jerome, *Ad Principiam* (Migne, P. L., 22, 1087 f.).

10 Cfr. *Studien u. Mitteilungen* O.S.B., 1898, 303 ff.

many noble, learned, and powerful men to the monastic life.[11] It is to be noted that among the great houses of Roman nobility the Anician family distinguished itself in a conspicuous manner. A grand-daughter of Proba, of the gens Anicia, devoted her life to Christ in *Africa* and is celebrated by St. Augustine.[12] From Africa we cross the Mediterranean Sea to Spain, but particularly to France, that fertile soil of monasticism.

The historical genesis of monasticism has now been briefly outlined. We have seen that in its beginnings it was of human origin, and we naturally ask ourselves if it had also a *divine sanction,* or whether it was completely a human invention. To answer this question properly we must make a distinction. Christ invited His Apostles to His fellowship. He tendered this call to the wealthy youth and urged that he sell whatsoever he had and follow Him. The precepts contained in the Decalogue and in the Sermon on the Mount were addressed to all alike; but it was not so with the counsels leading to a more perfect life. "*Qui potest capere, capiat.*" Yet, it must be evident that, as Christ gave these counsels, He intended them not for mere contemplation, but for practice. He aimed at gathering a "little flock" which would more closely follow the footprints He left on earth, and unswervingly walk that narrow path which He himself had traveled. This close imitation of the Saviour is more surely achieved by living according to the

---

11 St. Jerome *Ep. ad Pammach.,* says: "*Primus in primis, archistrategos monachorum*" . . . "*quis enim crederet ut consulum pronepos et Furiani germinis decus, inter purpuras senatorum, furva tunica pullatus incederet!*" (Migne, 22, 641 f.) which words indicate that the dress of the monks was black and of coarse material.

12 Montalembert, *l. c.,* I, 293. Besides these names, others might be mentioned, such as Melania the elder and younger, Paula, Eustochium, etc., as well as St. Paulinus of Nola, not to speak of St. Augustine and his monk-like clergy.

three counsels: poverty, chastity, and obedience, which embody the perfection proposed by Christ. Hence, wherever these three are put into practice, the religious state exists, and that by divine right. Monasticism, however, is not *the* religious state; it is but a form or part thereof, as a branch is part of a tree. It would not, therefore, be quite correct to assert that monasticism exists by divine right, unless it be identified with the religious state in general. In this latter sense we might, though improperly, say that its foundation is divine,— that it is " the philosophy introduced by Christ." [18]

If this is true of monasticism, which is not the concrete form of the religious state, it is even more applicable to single monasteries or congregations, which, as history teaches, may appear and disappear. On the other hand, the law of prescription must be quoted in favor of monasticism; despite all dislikes, derision and persecution from adversaries within and without the Church, it has always proved a solid rock amidst the storms of the sea, and a fertile spring of true civilization and learning, rendering untold services to the whole of humanity.[14]

§ 2.　THE RELIGIOUS STATE UP TO THE FOURTH LATERAN COUNCIL [15]

Our Code (can. 488) distinguishes the following categories of religious:

The *Religious State* consists of	1. *Orders of Regulars* with solemn vows and	a) Monastic Congregations b) Clerical or lay orders.	
	2. *Congregations* with simple vows.	a) Exempt — not exempt. b) Pontificial institutes. c) Diocesan institutes.	either clerical or lay

[18] St. John Chrys., *Hom. ad Popul. Antioch.* 17; Montalembert, *l. c.*, I, 218.

[14] Montalembert, *l. c.*, I, 9.

[15] Cf. Montalembert, *The Monks of the West*, Engl. ed., 1896; Heimbucher, *Ordensgeschichte*, 1896, 2 vols.

Monasticism, as we have seen, was the common form of the religious state in the early Middle Ages, up to the time of the IVth Lateran Council (1215). That this year marks an epoch in religious life is evident from the far-reaching decrees of the Council mentioned, as well as from the fact that soon afterwards orders of a somewhat different type made their appearance. We need not recall the *different rules* which were introduced by saintly men. Individualism was the keynote of the first centuries up to the time of Charlemagne, when the *Rule of St. Benedict* was made the monastic code, not by extrinsic forces merely, but chiefly by its intrinsic merit. Its organization is cenobitic, prescribing a life in common under the government of an abbot, elected by the brethren for lifetime. Its end is the *conversio morum,* or truly moral conduct based upon the Evangelical truths. To achieve this principal aim St. Benedict clothed it in the form of a vow or promise, which was supported by two more — obedience and stability. These three formed the contents of the formula of profession which every son of St. Benedict had to pronounce after a year's novitiate. There were no special spiritual works demanded beyond what the Gospel taught; — no flagellations, no special fasts except those prescribed by the rule and the regulations of the Church, no new-fangled devotions. The liturgical prayer was to be *the* prayer of the monks, in it they should live, from it they should draw inspiration and example. But *work,* too, was prescribed, no kind, either intellectual or manual, being excluded, though the latter was the principal form, until a distinction between *fratres barbati* (*conversi* or lay brothers) and monks proper was made, towards the end of the Xth century.[16] These are the two main fea-

16 *Conversi* or *barbati* occur in the "Customs" of Einsideln, com-

tures of the Benedictines: "*Ora et labora*," by which they cultivated the soil, trained the young, and brought truth and culture to tribes and races not yet in touch with the Church or civilized society.

The Rule of St. Benedict was the foundation of many other orders. Thus the founder of the *Camaldolese* (St. Romuald, 1027) and the founder of the *Vallombrosians* (St. John Gualbert, 1073) adopted the Code of the " Patriarch of Western Monasticism." [17] The most illustrious branch is that founded by St. Robert at Citeaux, Burgundy, in 1098. The name of one great abbot of Clairvaux, *St. Bernard*, has given to the *Cistercians* a lustre which shall never fade. St. Bernard is said to have received 200 novices, and in the middle of the 14th century his order counted no less than 700 abbeys. Their rule was that of St. Benedict, whilst the more detailed organization is contained in the *Charta charitatis*. The chief superior is the abbot of Citeaux, who is assisted by four " Father Abbots " and a general chapter held every year. The powers of the chapter were extensive. It could even depose the abbot of Citeaux, though the latter was elected by the monks of Citeaux and the abbots of the other monasteries. Besides, the general chapter elected twenty-five *Definitores*, who were entrusted with the affairs of the Order outside the time of the chapter-meeting. This is, if not a deviation from, at least a change of, the Benedictine rule, and, we be-

posed by Abbot Gregory, an Englishman, towards the end of the 10th century. They were distinguished from monks, probably by a different kind of profession, wearing the beard, and their chiefly outward occupation; they were not admitted to choir service.

[17] The order of *Grandmont*, and that of *Fontevrault*, founded by Robert of Arbrissels, in 1100, might also be mentioned, especially the latter, because placed under the jurisdiction of an abbess, whom monks and nuns obeyed.

lieve, a wholesome democratic one, which the orders of
the following period adopted.

Closely allied to the Benedictine rule, although with
traits of hermitical life, somewhat similar to the Camaldolese, are the *Carthusians*, founded by St. Bruno (1084)
at Chartreuse, near Grenoble.

More clerical than monastic were the orders which
followed the so-called *Rule of St. Augustine*,— a compilation from the writings of the great Bishop of Hippo.[18]
To this class belong all the branches of the *Canons Regular* who adopted the common life and pronounced the
three religious vows and were spread in different congregations. The *Praemonstratensians* or Norbertines,
founded by St. Norbert (1120), and the *Trinitarians*,
by John of Mortha and Felix of Valois (1198), may
also be counted among the followers of the Augustinian
rule.

§ 3.   FROM THE FOURTH LATERAN TO THE TRIDENTINE
COUNCIL

Whereas the first period bore an almost exclusively or
at least overwhelmingly monastic [19] character, the following epoch may, according to the saying " *a potiori fit
denominatio*," be styled clerical, or at least *monastico-
clerical.* On one side we see the Benedictine and Cistercian orders flourish, or revived through the medium
of newly formed congregations, like those of St. Justina
of Padua (1412), of Melk in Lower Austria (1418),

18 The Rule in its present form
did not originate with St. Augustine. It is a compilation from his
two sermons " On the Morals of
the Clergy," and a " Letter (109)
to the Nuns of Hippo." Particular
statutes were added to this compilation later on; cfr. Alzog, *Manual of*

Church History, Engl. Transl.,
1876, Vol. II, p. 693.

19 Even the Canons Regular followed a rule that was, in the
main, taken from the Rule of St.
Benedict; such was that of Chrode-
gang of Metz; cfr. Hefele, *Conc.·
Gesch.*, IV, 17 ff.

and of Bursfeld (1440); on the other hand the phenomenal rise and development of the *Mendicants,* who devoted themselves chiefly to the sacred ministry, marks a new epoch full of life and energy.

St. Francis, the humble poor man (*poverello*) of Assisi in Umbria, founded his "confederation," as he called it, in 1209. On Nov. 29th, 1223, his rule was approved by Honorius III, whose predecessor, *Innocent III,* had enacted at the Lateran Council that, to prevent too great a confusion of religious, no one should found a new order, but all who felt called to the religious state should enter one of the established institutes,[20] and those who wished to found a new religious house should accept a rule and institute already approved. Though this canon was enacted *after* Francis had laid the foundations of his marvelous society, the great Pope and canonist seemed to be slow, especially on account of the extreme poverty proposed by the Saint, in giving his permission. At length an oral leave was granted through the intervention of the Cardinal of St. Prisca, Colonna. Honorius III gave his formal approval to the rule after the order counted thousands of members.

The *Code of St. Francis* is simple. It comprises twelve brief chapters. The first treats of the three vows, of which the strictest is that of poverty. It also contains a clause of "obedience and reverence to the Pope." Noticeable and new is the insertion of a special addition to the twelfth chapter, which enjoins the minister general to ask the pope for a *cardinal protector* and superintendent, in order that the brethren may always be subject to the Holy Roman Church and remain unswerving in the Catholic faith. The *organization* has some similarity with that of the Cistercians, in as far,

[20] Cfr. c. 9, X, III, 36.

namely, as the *minister general* is elected by the general chapter, which may also, upon unanimous vote, depose him. Under the minister general are the provincials, and under these the custodes (cap. 8). Chapters 9 and 12 treat of preaching, which the brethren are to omit if the Ordinary forbids them. Preaching among the Saracens and infidels may, by special grace, be undertaken with the permission of the provincial. As to the *vow* of *poverty* (cap. 6) the Saint commands his brethren " to possess nothing for themselves, neither house, nor estates, nor anything," but to live entirely on alms. This latter point is specifically Franciscan and, like many other human institutions, has caused some disturbance because of divergent interpretations.[21] But not on that account may any slur be cast upon the holy Founder's intention, nor should the subsequent splits among the Friars Minor form a reason or pretext for casting aspersions on the institute as such, which has wrought miracles of spiritual reformation among the faithful and produced a great number of Saints.

The *division* of the Franciscan Order, which practically began towards the end of the 14th century, was completed and sanctioned by Leo X, " *Ite et vos,*" May 28, 1517. Henceforth two great branches were recognized: that of the *Observants* with the brown habit, and that of the *Conventuals* with the black habit, who were entitled to possess movable and immovable property, whilst the Observants claimed no right to own property nor any special indults.

A third, very popular and deserving branch of the great Franciscan Order is that of the *Capuchins,* founded by Matteo di Bassi and approved by Clement VII, May

---

21 Cf. Nicholas III, " *Exiit qui seminat,*" in c. 3, 6°, V, 12, de   verb. signif.; Clem., " *Exivit,*" c. 1, Clem. V, II.

18, 1528. After severe trials, lasting for many years
and threatening its very existence, this order was formally recognized by Paul V, in 1619, as autonomous with
its proper Minister Generalis. Since they proceeded
from the *Observants,* the Capuchins cling to the original
rule of St. Francis and observe absolute poverty. Similar to their rule is the one composed by St. Francis of
Paula for his order, called "*Minimi,*" approved A. D.
1474.

In 1217, Innocent III approved an order which has
gained universal admiration for its scientific pursuits and
high achievements, especially in speculative theology. It
is the Order founded by *St. Dominic,* known as that of
the Friars Preachers or Dominicans. The Pope enjoined
the holy Founder to assume, according to the decree of
the Lateran Council, a rule already approved. He
adopted that of St. Augustine, as it was then called.
The *organization* proper of the new Order was established at a chapter held at Bologna in 1220. The constitutions adopted there enacted that the general chapter,
to be held every three years (now held every twelfth
year) should enjoy legislative powers and elect the *Magister Generalis,*[22] who himself chooses his associates
(*socii*) in the government of the Order. The *provincials*
are elected by the provincial chapter for four years and
are assisted by *definitores* chosen by the same chapter.
A *prior* is set over every house for the period of four
years and is assisted by a subprior. Special attention
was given to studies, which should last at least eight
years, two of which are devoted to propaedeutics.

A *characteristic* of the Order of the Friars Preachers
is poverty. Together with the Franciscans they are
called *mendicants.* At first they depended entirely on

[22] Now elected for twelve years.

alms, but later papal constitutions (like that of Martin V, 1425) allowed the Dominicans to hold landed property and have a secure income. Another feature peculiar to this order is the office of preaching, for which they were chiefly founded (against the Albigenses), and which they performed with great zeal and success especially at the time of the Reformation. Most remarkable is the great number of accomplished scholars whom they produced and who held the Catholic world spellbound for centuries. The names of Albertus Magnus, Thomas Aquinas, and Cajetan suffice to show their merit and greatness.

The rule of St. Augustine was followed also by the *Mercedarians,* "the royal, military, and religious order of the Blessed Virgin for the ransom of slaves," founded in 1223 by Peter Nolascus; by the *Servites,* or "Servants of Mary," established by seven Florentine nobles in 1233; and by the *"Alexian Brothers,"* founded in the 14th century and allowed to make solemn profession by Pius II (1459). These latter are a lay order engaged in charitable work, and since 1870 the members take only simple vows. The so-called *Hieronymites* and *Bethlehemites* likewise followed the so-called rule of St. Augustine.

During that same period the Benedictine Order experienced not only a reformatory impetus, but also an increase of branches: *St. Sylvester,* of the Gozzolini family, in 1231 founded at Fano near Fabriano a monastery which became the mother-house of the Benedictines of the same name. Their constitutions, based on the rule of St. Benedict, were finally approved by Alexander VIII (1681). They now devote themselves to mission work in various countries, including the U. S. (Diocese of Wichita, Kansas). Another Italian foundation was

that of *Celestine V*, who as Peter Murone established a
congregation based on the Benedictine rule and known
as *Celestinians*. This order at one time counted about
150 monasteries, but is now nearly extinct. The last
Benedictine congregation founded in that period is that
of *Bl. Bernard Tolomeo*, who called it the order of the
Blessed Virgin Mary of Mount Olivet, wherefore its
members are named *Olivetans*. They still have some
monasteries.

A rule with Oriental traits, but modified by Eugene
IV in 1431, is that of the *Carmelites*, written by Patriarch
Albert of Jerusalem in 1208 and then transplanted to
the West. Particularly in Spain this order gained a
solid footing and received a fresh impetus through the
reformatory zeal of the great *St. Teresa* and *St. John
of the Cross*, in the middle of the sixteenth century.

§ 4. FROM THE TRIDENTINE COUNCIL TO OUR TIME

This period might be called *congregational* because,
although a few orders were started, yet the signature of
the whole epoch is that of religious congregations without solemn vows, or of merely pious societies without
vows proper.

First and deserving of particular mention is the *Society
of Jesus*,[23] founded by St. Ignatius Loyola in 1534 in
the crypt of St. Denis of Montmartre at Paris and approved as an order by Paul III ("*Regimini militantis
ecclesiae*," Sept. 27, 1540) fifteen years before the holy
founder's death. The code of this order is remarkable
for its detailed and elaborate regulations. It is contained

[23] Nothing can be said against
that title (cfr. *Cath. Encycl.*, XIV,
81); however, if a member of S. J.
(Cuvilhier, *Meditationes Brevis-
simae*) contrasts the humility of St.
Ignatius with that of the founders
of other orders in favor of the
former, as if these latter had given
their own names to their foundations, it sounds somewhat puerile.

in the "*Institutum Societatis Jesu*," [24] often printed, and therefore no secret. For our purpose the most important part of the Institute is the "Constitutions," from which we learn the internal and external organization of that illustrious corporation. The head of the Society is called *praepositus generalis,* or simply General of the Jesuits, although the chief authority is vested in the "General Congregation," which is similar to the General Chapter of other centralized orders. To that General Congregation belongs the supreme legislative power, whilst the fullness of administrative power and spiritual authority is vested in the General. He appoints the provincials (at present twenty-seven, four in the U. S.), and the local superiors: rectors of colleges, provosts of professed houses, and masters of novices. The General is aided by five assistants, who, however, enjoy only a consultive vote, and by an "admonitor." This organization is to some extent democratic, inasfar, namely, as the General Congregation is the legislative organ. We fail to see where the aristocratic element [25] enters. It is rather a constitutional monarchy, because the General of the Society has unlimited power within the Constitutions.

The *members* are: (1) *novices,* whose "probation" lasts two years; (2) *formed scholastics,* aspirants to the priesthood with simple but perpetual vows; (3) *formed coadjutors,* lay brothers or priests with simple but perpetual vows; (4) *professed members,* who besides the three usual solemn vows of religion, make a fourth to obey the Pope in the matter of missions and to go wherever they are sent. They also make certain additional, but non-essential, simple vows in the matter of poverty

24 Cfr. *Cath. Encycl., l. c.,* which we chiefly follow concerning this Society.

25 Cfr. Heimbucher, *l. c.,* II, 55.

and external honors, also regarding ecclesiastical dignities, if we mistake not.

The *object* [26] of the order is not limited to practising
any one class of good works, but to study, in the manner
of the Spiritual Exercises, what Christ would do if He
were living in our day, and to carry out that ideal.[27]
Hence elevation and largeness of aim. Hence also the
motto of the Society: "*Ad Maiorem Dei Gloriam.*"
Obedience is the characteristic of the order,— to be
ready for any call and to preserve unity in every variety of work. Hence, by easy consequence,[28] the omis-
sion of office in choir, of a specially distinctive habit, of
unusual penances. The *ministry* of the Society consists
in preaching, the administration of the Sacraments, and
teaching.

History has shown that the members of the Society
have carried out their noble purpose for the welfare of
the Church at large; their literary and missionary work
lives after them, and one of the greatest titles of honor
peculiar to the Society is perhaps that of being the most
calumniated order in the Catholic Church.

Of a charitable character, purposing to help orphans
and the poor, is the order founded by St. Hieronymus
Aemilianus, approved by Paul III in 1540, and declared
a religious order by Pius V in 1608. It is called the
order of *Somasco,* because this place (near Bergamo in
Italy) was its first settlement. The rule is that of St.
Augustine.

The same rule was adopted by the order of St. John

---

26 *Cath. Encycl.,* XIV, 84 f.

27 This is not specifically Jesuitic,
except in as far as the method is
"according to the Spiritual Exercises
of St. Ignatius," provided, of course,
these are the exclusive literary
product of the holy founder.

28 However, it is known that St.
Ignatius omitted choir service from
his Code only after long deliberations.

of God ("*Brothers Hospitallers*"), founded in 1540 at Granada in Spain and raised to the dignity of an order in 1570 by Pius V. It has a lay character, because only a few of its members, generally one in each house or hospital, are priests. These Brothers enjoy the privileges of mendicants, granted by Urban VIII in 1624. Their chief task is nursing the sick.

Very similar is the order founded by St. Camillus of Lellis in 1504, and approved as an order with the privileges of mendicants by Gregory XIV, in 1591. The members are named "*Fathers of a Good Death.*"

For the sacred ministry and the embellishment of the church service St. Cajetan and Caraffa, later pope Paul IV, founded the *Theatines*, in 1524.

The *Barnabites* were established by Antonius Maria Zaccaria in 1530 at Milan.

For school purposes chiefly was instituted the "Order of the Pious Schools," or *Scolopii*, by St. Joseph of Calasanza at Rome, in 1597.

Now we come to the *congregations* of men. Hither belong the *Christian Brothers*, founded in 1679 by St. John Baptist de la Salle, and approved by Benedict XIII, in 1724. They are a lay institute engaged mainly in the primary and middle-class education of youth. Their number is as great as the merits they have gained in the field of pedagogy in almost every country of the globe. Two priestly congregations of a clerical character, which are spread over the whole Church are those of the *Passionists*, founded by St. Paul of the Cross, in 1725, for mission work and the constant remembrance of the Passion of our Lord, and that of the *Redemptorists*, founded in 1735 by St. Alphonsus of Liguori, especially for the exercise of the sacred ministry among the poor and forsaken, which scope it carries out with astonishing success.

The congregation of *St. Sulpice,* founded in 1642 by Jean Jacques Olier, and that of the *Eudists,* founded in 1643 by P. Eudes, are devoted to the training of the clergy.

Among the many *pious societies* whose members take no special vows, are to be mentioned the *Oratorians,* established by the "Apostle of Rome," St. Philip Neri, in 1575; the *Lazarists,* founded by St. Vincent de Paul, in 1624, and approved by Urban VIII, in 1632; the *Oblates of the Immaculate Conception,* established in 1816 by Bishop Mazenod; the Marists, or *Fathers of the Society of Mary,* founded in 1816 by Abbé Colin; the *Fathers of the Precious Blood,* founded by Bl. Gaspar del Bufalo, in 1823; the *Pallottini,* founded by the Ven. Vincent Pallotti, in 1835; the *Fathers of the Holy Ghost,* founded in 1848; the *Salesians* of Don Bosco, founded in 1855; the *White Fathers,* founded by Cardinal Lavigerie, in 1868; the *Society of the Divine Word* (Steyl), founded by Arnold Janssen, in 1875; the *Society of the Divine Saviour,* founded by J. B. Jordan, in 1881; the *Fathers of the Holy Cross,* founded in 1841 at Notre Dame, Ind.; the *Paulists,* founded in 1859 as an offshoot of the Redemptorists; the brethren of *St. Viator;* the priests of the *Most Bl. Sacrament,* founded by Julien Eymard, in 1856, and others, among them many Tertiaries from older orders. The *Assumptionists,* founded in 1520, with the rule of St. Augustine, conduct schools and missions in various countries, especially in France, where they flourished before the iniquitous laws of 1905.

§ 5. FEMALE ORDERS AND CONGREGATIONS

The rules for nuns, or sacred virgins, as they were called, were sometimes nothing else but practical instructions given by renowned bishops. Thus St. Ambrose

composed his "Exhortation to the Virgins," (about
397). That the rite of veiling those who vowed virginity
dates to remote antiquity, perhaps to the beginning of the
fourth century, is unquestionable. The existence of
sacred virgins is testified to by Tertullian.[29] Monasteries
of nuns were early and numerous in Egypt, Cappadocia,
and Palestine. Later the *monachae* were also introduced
into the West. Rules were then written especially for
nuns. Thus St. Caesarius of Arles (542) wrote a rule
for virgins and monks,[30] St. Leander of Seville (603)
one for his sister Florentia.[31] But the *Rule of St. Benedict*, under which St. Scholastica lived, soon governed
most convents of nuns. In 742 a German national
council enacted that "monks and nuns should introduce
and observe the Rule of St. Benedict."[32] Besides the
Benedictines there were also *Cononesses,* as we learn
from a council of Mayence in 813.[33] However, it is safe
to say that to the beginning of the thirteenth century the
majority of nuns followed St. Benedict's rule, either
as "black" Benedictines, or as Camaldolese or Vallom-
brosian Sisters. This condition prevailed up to our time.
The branch of the Olivetans was instrumental in the
foundation of the noble society of the *Oblates of Tor de
Specchi,* whose holy foundress was St. Frances of Rome
(+ 1440). A congregation founded by the Ven. Mech-
tildis in 1654, and approved by Innocent XI in 1676, was
devoted to the perpetual adoration of the Bl. Sacrament.

In our country the Benedictine nuns, established within
the last 70 years, have grown in number and do meri-
torious work in parish schools and academies. But their

29 Cfr. Wilpert, *Die gottgeweih-
ten Jungfrauen,* 1892.
30 Migne, *P. L.,* 67, 1099 ff.; 1107
ff.
31 *Ibid.,* 72, 873 f.
32 Mansi, *Coll. Conc.,* XII, 366.
33 *Ibid.,* XIV, 64 (can. 73).

vows are, now at least, simple, though perpetual, and because of the nature of their work papal enclosure is not imposed on them. Outside of special Apostolic indults they are not under the jurisdiction of Benedictine abbots, but under that of the Ordinaries of the dioceses. Neither do they elect an abbess, but a mother superior.[84]

The great *Mendicant Orders* of St. Francis and St. Dominic also had sisterhoods following their respective rules. St. Clare was vested by the seraphic Saint himself with the tunic of the order, March 18, 1212. This was the beginning of the *second order* of the " Poverello " of Assisi, but the code proper of the Clarisses was that which combined the second (1247) and third rule (1253) and remained the fundamental constitution for all Franciscan nuns who take solemn vows and are subject to the Friars Minor. Besides these St. Francis established a rule for persons remaining in the world, who were called *Tertiaries*. Towards the close of the thirteenth century some of these Tertiaries commenced to live in common and were therefore called *Tertiaries Regular*. These were united with the first order of the Friars Minor by Leo X, in 1512, and are therefore an order of *moniales* with solemn vows. The same Pope allowed *Tertiaries* to exist *with simple vows* and in community. These follow the rule of St. Francis, as approved by Nicholas IV. Lastly there was a class of Tertiaries who did not live in common but with the permission of the bishop took one or three vows and wore the religious habit.

Pius V, by his Constitution " *Circa pastoralis,*" of May

---

84 The Catalogue O. S. B. of 1910, p. 710 f., gives the total number of " Black " Benedictine Sisters as 8360, of whom only 411 are exempt. Most of those not exempt (2214) live in the U. S. Most probably the number has, since 1910, increased to 3000.

29, 1566, compelled all nuns with solemn vows to live in enclosure, and furthermore decided that all Tertiaries, or "those who are called of the penance"—thereby striking a blow chiefly at the aforesaid Tertiaries of St. Francis — should make solemn vows and be obliged to observe the enclosure.[35] But conditions were stronger than the Pope. Despite all the penalties threatened, new congregations sprang up. For a long time the S. C. EE. et RR. was wont to approve the rules of such congregations with the clause: "without however approving the institute itself." [36] This custom was tenaciously followed up to the beginning of the 19th century, when so many deserving communities sprang up that Rome could no longer withhold formal approbation.

But to return to the Franciscan Sisters. It is astonishing to see how many branches sprang from that productive tree. One of them was that of the sisters of *St. Elizabeth,* which existed in great numbers in the 16th century. They wear sometimes a brown, sometimes a grey habit (*soeurs grises*). It is impossible to name them all, but we must mention at least the institute of Sisters founded by P. Theodosius Florentini under the name of "Holy Cross" or "*Mercy-Sisters of the Holy Cross,*" whose seat is at Ingenbohl,[37] and the "School Sisters of the Holy Cross," at Menzingen, both in Switzerland.

Similar to the orders mentioned, that of *St. Dominic* also had a *second* and *third* order for women. The former was probably founded in 1217 in Rome, whilst the latter was established by Munio di Zamora and ap-

35 Cfr. Pius V, "*Lubricum vitae genus,*" Nov. 17, 1568, which compelled male congregations to take solemn vows.

36 Bened. XIV, "*Quamvis iusto,*" April 30, 1749, § 5.

37 These Sisters enjoy some exemptions, for instance, in the choice of their confessors, etc.

proved by Innocent VII (1405) and Eugene IV (1439). Prominent among the Tertiaries of St. Dominic are the "*Mantellatae*" or Poor School Sisters of the Third Order of St. Dominic.

The rule of *St. Augustine* was followed by the order of nuns established by St. Birgitta of Sweden in 1344, the constitutions of which were approved by Urban V (1379). The *Ursulines* were founded by St. Angela Merici in 1535, and appear as an order with solemn vows under the rule of St. Augustine in 1612. The same rule is the foundation of the order founded by St. Francis de Sales and St. Francis de Chantal, in 1610, and known as *Visitation Nuns*. In our country they are the only nuns with solemn vows.

The congregation founded in 1635 by St. Vincent de Paul as *Filles de la Charité*, or *Sisters of Charity*, spread widely over the world and gained universal approbation by their works of charity. Of a very charitable character is also the order of the *Sisters of the Good Shepherd*, an offspring of an older sisterhood, the *Bon Secours*, founded in 1644.

Chiefly for educational purposes were intended the institute of the "*Sorores Anglicae*" or English Ladies, who had a peculiar fate, as may be seen from Benedict XIV's Constitution "*Quamvis iusto*," of April 30, 1749. Related to them are the *Loreto Sisters* (1822) and the "*Congregation of Irish Sisters of Charity*" (1836). To these may be added the *Notre Dame Sisters*, the *Sisters of St. Joseph* (1805), the *Sisters of the Precious Blood*, etc., etc.

Last, but by no means least, may be mentioned the "*Ladies of the Sacred Heart of Jesus*," founded by Bl. Magdalen Sophie Barat, in 1800, and approved by Leo XII, 1826. These "Ladies with the hearts of dragoons" have flourished in the U. S. in consequence of the zeal of Madame Duchesne.

If we omitted to mention the *military orders*,[38] it was for the obvious reason that they are no longer of importance.

After this brief summary notice may be taken of the differences between the various organizations. Up to the foundation of the Society of Jesus the *religious state* was considered to be founded on solemn vows or profession, and until the middle of the last century there was generally but one profession in the religious orders (except the Jesuits), and this a solemn one.[39] The religious state even now requires the *three vows* embodied in the formula of profession which binds the members to their community. Hence congregations in which only one vow, for instance, that of obedience, is taken, are not religious congregations, nor do they partake of the religious state.[40] On the other hand it is now immaterial whether they are congregations in which solemn or simple vows are made, either pontifical or diocesan institutes, as long as profession of the three essential vows is made in a community approved by ecclesiastical authority, either supreme or inferior (bishop). But it is not without reason that orders, *i. e.*, religious organizations with solemn vows, are of higher rank and more esteemed by the Church. For they are of a more stable nature and have a long-standing tradition in their favor. This we say, not to disparage the congregations, but as canonical truth. The very fact that the Church has granted to the regular

---

38 The *Order of St. John*, or Maltese Knights, was founded in 1048, that of the *Knights Templars* in 1119, that of the *Teutonic Knights* in 1190; others were established in different countries; cf. Funk, *Manual of Church History*, Engl. Trans., 1913, I, 375 f.

39 "*Neminem latet*," March 19, 1857; "*Perpensis*," May 3, 1902.

40 Can. 673, § 1.

orders exemption, which she has withheld from the congregations (except by special indult), shows her intention. A special indult was given to several important congregations, *v. g.*, the Redemptorists and the Passionists.[41]

§6. EXEMPTION

The Code tells us that " regulars are exempt from the jurisdiction of the Ordinary of the diocese," and that by the name of regulars must be understood religious of an order or religious organization in which solemn vows are taken.[42] In these words is contained the institute of exemption, which has a history of more than twelve centuries and an eventful development in a secular as well as in an ecclesiastical respect, which finally led to the legal recognition of singly granted privileges as a juridical entity. A brief historical review [43] may not be amiss and seems necessary to understand exemption.

1. Up to the beginning of the seventh century the general law of the Church may be said to be embodied in the words of the Council of Chalcedon: " No one is allowed to build or erect a monastery or oratory without the consent of the bishop of the city; all the monks living in that city or country should be subject to the bishops." [44] Whether this injunction was always carried out, we do not know; but it is certain that *Gregory the Great* (590–604) insisted upon the right of the diocesan bishop over monasteries and monks. For he emphatically states that the bishop is the competent judge in all causes of

---

41 Also to the Missionary Fathers of the Sacred Heart; cfr. Vermeersh in the *Cath. Encycl.*, XII, 758.

42 Cfr. can. 615; can. 488, 2, 7.

43 Cfr. Fabre, *Etude sur le Liber Censuum de l'Eglise Romaine*, 1892;

Archiv. für Kath. Kirchenrecht (Hueffner), 1906–1907; Schreiber, *Kurie und Kloster im XII. Jahrh.*, 1910 (in Stutz, *Kirchenrechtl. Abhandl.*, 65–68.

44 Can. 4, cf. c. 10, C. 18, q. 2.

monks and nuns, and that he has to watch over their conduct, punish and correct abuses, because he will have to
give an account to God for that part of his flock as well
as for the others.[45]

On the other hand he defends the rights of the monasteries and their superiors in a letter to Maximianus of
Ravenna,[46] where he says that the brethren have the right
to elect an abbot from among themselves, except in case
no one worthy of that office can be found in the monastery; that the bishop has no right to meddle in the temporal administration, revenues, property, documents, of
the monastery, and should not charge the monastery with
taxes nor invade it by any fraudulent action. The privilege of exemption we cannot find in Gregory's letters,
though some think it is there.[47] Gregory's rules on the
monastic life do not differ essentially from those laid
down in St. Benedict's Code.[48]

2. But we are approaching a period, and it is only
twenty-four years remote from the death of Gregory,
which foreshadows the beginning of real exemption.
Bobbio, a monastery founded by St. Columbanus on the
Trebbia, was apparently troubled and molested by the
Bishop Probus. Abbot *Bertulfus*, the second successor
of the holy founder, seeking protection against the vex-
atious bishop, betook himself to Rome, where Honorius I,
on June 11, 628, granted him a charter of freedom in
these plain terms, " No bishop shall rule, by whatever
right, in the aforesaid monastery." [49] This sounds like
real exemption and may justly be called the first privilege

---

[45] Gregory I, *Registrum Epp.*
(Ewald-Hartmann), 1891, IX, 203;
V, 4; VIII, 8; IX, 114; X, 3, 9;
XII, 6; XIV, 16.
[46] *Ibid.*, VIII, 17; cfr. V, 49;
III, 3; VII, 10.

[47] *Arch. f. K.-R.*, 1906, p. 314;
but Reg. IX, 16 is not to the point.
[48] *Reg.*, c. 64.
[49] Cfr. *Vita Bertulfi*, n. 6 (Migne,
87, 1063); Jaffé, *Regesta Pontiff.*,
ed. 2, n. 2017.

of its kind.   The number of such privileges from the beginning of the seventh to the middle of the ninth century is small, though some English and Frankish monasteries were given extensive exemptions. Weremouth and Melmesburg [50] received such from Sergius I (687–701) and Fulda [51] from Zachary I (741–752). The latter exempts the foundation of Sturmi from every foreign jurisdiction and subjects it to that of the Apostolic See.

3. The ninth century, and especially the pontificate of Nicholas I (858–867), witnessed an increase in the number of privileges granting exemption to monasteries. Forty-nine such privileges were given from 855 to 900 to different Frankish monasteries. As has justly been pointed out, there were good reasons for seeking and granting such papal exemptions.[52] For during that period of internal strife and feudal struggles the secular powers could offer but scanty security and protection, and the *advocati* or protectors whom Charlemagne set over the monasteries as lay-lawyers and guardians, often betrayed their protegés and ransacked the monastic property.   Furthermore, there was a feature peculiar perhaps to Frankish, or let us say, Germanic soil, viz.: the idea of *absolute landownership*, which claimed full and independent control over a church or altar built on the ground of the owner.   Hence more than one monastery was in the hands of the king or of a bishop or vassal upon whose land the monastic church with the monastery had been built.   Although this right claimed by the owner was directed chiefly to the temporal administration, yet it gradually led to interference in spiritual rights, especially the election of superiors, and thus jeopardized the free

50 Jaffé, *l. c.*, nn. 2106, 2140.
51 This privilege, formerly doubted, is now generally admitted as genu-
ine; it is contained in Migne, 89, 954.
52 *Arch. f. K.-R.*, 1906, p. 635.

election of abbots.[53] We said this feature was *perhaps* peculiar to Germanic soil. The Celtic race of *Ireland* shows a similar development,— namely, a dual system of tribal claims. For we find, says Bury,[54] " that in some cases the proprietor did not make over all his rights to the ecclesiastical community which was founded on his estate, but retained, and transmitted to his descendants a certain control over it, side by side with the control which the abbot exercised." Besides, there were monasteries in which a direct family right of inheritance to the abbey was established, so that the abbot could be chosen only from the founder's kin. Such a system was ill-fated and especially ill adapted to Benedictine government. Lastly, more than one bishop, either princely landlord or mere Ordinary of a diocese, who, being protected by the *brachium saeculare*, wielded almost absolute power, did not scruple to attack the property and quiet life of the monks,[55] who were esteemed by nobles and peasants alike. The history of Cluny bears out this statement.

4. Having mentioned these historical facts, we are ready to grasp the tendency of monastic bodies seeking the *protection of St. Peter* (*i. e.*, the Apostolic See),[56]— a formula occurring in papal privileges ever since the beginning of the tenth century. The regesta sometimes exhibit entries like this: " *monasterium tuendum suscipit, bona et privilegia confirmat, iura defendit.*" In most of these briefs a penal sanction is added against the violators of the papal injunction. Furthermore a *census* or tribute, five or two *soldi*,[57] or a *byzantinum*, or some other

---

[53] Loening. *Geschichte des deutschen Kirchenrechts*, 1878, II, 374 f.

[54] *Life of St. Patrick*, 1905, p. 174 f.

[55] Ancient monastic lectionaries contain Mass-formularies such as: "*Contra episcopos male agentes*," or simply: "*Contra malos episcopos.*"

[56] Jaffé, *l. c.*, n. 3466 and *passim*.

[57] The value of a *solidus*, if of

kind of money, was sometimes (not regularly) imposed on the monasteries which were placed under papal protection. The *ratification* of the monastic property was given both in general terms and by an enumeration of single possessions. Sometimes the briefs contain a description of the site and the name of the original donor.

As to the *privileges* granted by these papal constitutions, there is no uniform and constant tenor or formula, at least up to the time of Alexander III (1159–81). But it is safe to say that most of the privileges contained the *right of freely electing the abbot,* which was of paramount importance at a time when investiture became dangerous. Occasionally *exemption from the coercive power of the bishop* was explicitly stated in terms like these: "*ut nullus in ipsum monasterium audeat et praesumat sententiam excommunicationis inferre,*" or, "*a nullo possint interdici vel excommunicari nisi a Romano Pontifice.*" [58] Such a formula as this: "*ut monasterium in nullo alicui nisi tantum apostolicae ecclesiae respondere teneatur et ab omni alia jurisdictione et subjectione liberum sit et exemptum,*" must be taken to mean full exemption. In some privileges, *e. g.,* one granted by Pope Marinus (942–946), we also read of exemption from the duty of attending the diocesan synod.[59]

5. Fully to understand the sometimes heated controversies between bishops and abbeys we must consider two more features which bear more or less directly on the question of exemption: tithes and pontificals. Ever since the sixth century *tithes* were enforced and formed part

gold, would have been about $5.30, but others (Hodgkin, *Italy and Her Invaders,* I, 778) give it only as $3.00 or twelve shillings; cfr. also Du Cange, *Glossarium,* s. v. "*Solidus*"; the *byzantinum* introduced by Justinian, is nothing else but a gold solidus.

58 Jaffé, *l. c.,* nn. 3800, 4420; Migne, 137, 334; 143, 1327.

59 Jaffé, *l. c.,* nn. 3624, 3025; Gattula, *Hist. Cass.,* I, 94.

of the episcopal or ecclesiastical revenues which the faithful were obliged to pay to the church.[60] It is a very interesting canonical question whether they were paid to the church or to the altar. This was an issue at the time of Abbo of Fleury ($+$ 1004), as we learn from his writings. If these "*dimes*" were given to the churches, the monks, as proprietors of the same, could legally claim them, and were sometimes even authorized to do so in the papal briefs.[61] But if the donor's intention could be proved to be directed exclusively to the altar, the tithes were supposed to belong to the bishop, as its consecrator. This latter view was defended by Arnulf, bishop of Orleans, and some of his followers, but justly rejected by Abbo of Fleury, who calls the claim of the bishops a "modern heresy" and an "egregious pretext" for giving the offerings of the church to the horses and dogs of lay people, instead of to the monks. He also remarks, most reasonably, that a church without an altar is no church, but a common house.[62] Abbo gained his point with the Capets, and also with Pope Gregory V, a zealous promoter of Clunian reform. As noted above, the right to the tithes was often expressly defined in the bull of exemption.

The other bone of contention was the *pontificals*. The reader should remember that the abbots were at first, in fact for centuries, not endowed with the priestly character, and hence to speak of pontificals for the first three centuries, up to the beginning of the ninth, would be an anachronism. However, Pope Eugene I, in a synod held at Rome in 826, ordered that the abbots

60 The synod of Macon, 585, can. 5, ordered their payment under threat of censures, and later synods and royal capitularies enforced them.

61 For Cluny, cfr. Migne, 151, 291, 485 f.

62 *Ep. ad G.*, in Migne, 139, 440 ff.

should be priests in order that they might be able to
" heal the sins of their brethren." [63]　Here jurisdiction
in foro interno is plainly meant.　But Fleury received a
more extensive power from Pope Benedict VII (974–
983), *viz.*, that of absolving men and women of the
order.[64]　About the same time we hear of papal privileges directly touching the right of pontificals.　First,
indeed, negatively rather than positively.　Thus concessions were made that the diocesan bishop could perform
pontifical functions only at the direct invitation of the
abbot,[65] or that the abbot might invite any bishop to
perform them, provided he was no heretic or schismatic,
or that he might be blessed by any bishop.[66]

As to the right of *pontifical dress* we first read of
dalmatics and *sandals* being granted by John XIII (965–
972) to the abbot of St. Vincent of Metz.[67]　The gloves
or *chiroticae* were added in a privilege of Cielo d'Oro
(Pavia) for " the honor of St. Peter " and " the most
holy Augustine whose relics were there preserved."　The
Abbot of Brevnow (Bohemia) in 993 received the privilege of using mitre, gloves, sandals, maniple, and belt.[68]
The same right was granted to the abbot of Reichenau,
together with the prerogative of being consecrated *more
episcopali* by the Pope.[69]

Thus pontificals began to be given to abbots in the last
decades of the tenth century.　The privilege became more
frequent in the tenth and common in the twelfth century.
That the bishops were not too highly pleased with this
development we know from the chroniclers, one of whom,

---

[63] Can. 27, Mansi, *Coll. Conc.*,
XIV, 1000.

[64] Jaffé, n. 3803; Sackur, *Die
Cluniacenser*, 1892, II, 272 f.

[65] Jaffé, n. 3907 (Fulda, A. D.
999).

[66] Jaffé, n. 3826 (Cielo d'Oro,

Pavia, A. D. 986); 3764 (S. Salva-
tore, Pavia, A. D. 906).

[67] Jaffé, ed. 1, n. 2869, n. 2900.

[68] Jaffé, n. 3826, n. 2946 (1 ed.).

[69] Hermannus Contractus, *Chronica ad an.* 1032, Migne, 143, 253.

Herman the Lame of Reichenau, tells us [70] that the bishop of Constance, Warmannus, protested to the Emperor Conrad II so long and vigorously that the abbot was compelled to deliver the papal bull together with the pontifical insignia to be burnt on Holy Thursday, 1033. Cluny had a fight with the bishop of Macon for many years, and some bishops went so far as to deny the validity of such papal privileges.

6. However, all this resistance proved useless. In the XIIth century papal protection was granted not only to single monasteries, as had been the case in former centuries — Cluny being the sole " order " which was exempt as such — but also to entire congregations, for instance, those of Vallombrosa,[71] and Camaldoli.[72] This same century is perhaps the most important for the historico-canonical investigation into the meaning of exemption, which now enters the decretals. The subject is not free from controversy. It cannot be denied that the regulars sometimes stretched the papal protection further than the grantor had intended, wherefore the Roman Court was more than once asked what the papal protection included. Many monasteries which " delivered " [73] themselves to papal protection, generally, though not always, paid a certain tax or tribute (*census*), which was regarded as an indication (*indicium*) that they were under papal protection, but not that they were papal property, in the sense of private property. The relation between such monasteries and the papal Court was similar to that between a private proprietor and the State (eminent domain). In many briefs recurs the formula: " *ad indicium per-*

---

70 *Chronica* (Migne, 143, 235).
71 Migne, 200, 569, 1067; Jaffé, *l. c.*, nn. 4053, 8428.
72 Mittarelli, *Annal: Camaldul.*, II, App. 236.

73 This was called *traditio*, and the monasteries thus delivered were called *monasteria tradita* or *commendata*.

ceptae a Romana ecclesia libertatis (or *protectionis*, or
iuris or *proprietatis*), *bisancium unum quotannis Latera-*
nensi palatio persolvetis." What does that "*indicium*
libertatis" mean? was asked of Alexander III. He answered the question in a well-known decretal,[74] in which
he says that, as not all monasteries placed under the special jurisdiction (*iuris*) of Blessed Peter pay an annual
tribute, so neither are all the monasteries which pay that
tribute free from episcopal jurisdiction, and therefore
the wording of every privilege must be weighed, so that
every church which pays tribute and is under the special
jurisdiction of Bl. Peter and pays the annual tribute as
a token of the liberty received, may be looked upon as
exempt; whereas, on the other hand, a church which
simply pays the annual tribute as a token of the protection it receives is not *eo ipso* to be considered free from
the jurisdiction of the Ordinary." In order to understand this decision we must remember that in the XIIth
century a distinction was made at the Roman Court between *specialis tutela* and simple tutelage. The former
was connected with the clausula added in the privileges:
"*salva sedis apostolicae auctoritate*," whilst the privileges for simple tutelage had the clause: "*salva sedis*
apost. auctoritate et dioecesani episcopi canonica iustitia."
From this it follows that there were three kinds of religious bodies: (a) such as had no papal tutelage or brief
at all, and these were very few; (b) such as enjoyed the
papal protection, but were nevertheless more or less subject to the Ordinary's jurisdiction, and finally (c) such
as were under the special tutelage of the Apostolic See
and therefore exempt from the coercive power, especially of the diocesan bishop. The answer given by Alexander was authentic, but not novel, as some have

74 C. 8, f, V, 33; cf. c. 14, 1 b; c. 10, 6°, V, 7.

claimed.[75] For its obvious meaning is simply to warn
the religious not to read more into the text of the papal
brief than the legislator would naturally grant, and to
give the legates a key to the interpretation of papal documents. A similar decision is that of Boniface VIII, who,
instead of using the term *specialis,* says that the document
must treat "*principaliter*" of exemption.[76] This again
means that the whole tenor of the papal privilege must be
examined, not only the terms *tutela, protectio, libertas,*
etc.

7. Such is the theoretical aspect of exemption as we
find it in the Decretals, which, however, barely touch its
extent. The *First Lateran Council* (1123) laid down
general rules governing the relation between diocesan
bishops and regulars living in their territory. Three
canons especially regulate that matter. Abbots and
monks are not allowed to administer the Sacraments of
Penance and Extreme Unction, nor to visit the sick, nor
to say Mass publicly; the consecration of chrism, holy
oils and altars, and the ordination of clerics belong to
the diocesan bishop; religious priests in charge of souls
must be appointed by the Ordinary, to whom they must
give an account of their work and of what belongs to the
bishop; whatever services or tributes the monasteries
were wont to render to the Ordinary since the time of
Gregory VII, they must render also in future; nor does
the prescription of thirty years hold good for abbots or
monks.[77] In another canon (not found in all editions)
subjection and obedience to the bishops as their teachers
and pastors is inculcated for the monks as a paternal tra-

75 Schreiber, *l. c.,* I, 141 ff.; cfr.   76 C. 10, 60, I, 7.
Studien O. S. B., 1911 (Vol. 32),   77 Mansi, *Coll. Conc.,* cc. 17–19,
p. 693 ff., where a correct interpre-   Vol. XXI, 285 f.
tation is given.

dition.[78] This canon embodies the idea of St. Bernard, who was not inclined to favor exemption. Yet it was his order that some years after his death received most extensive privileges. Urban III granted the Cistercians of Clairvaux absolute freedom from the coercive power of the bishop, and other popes granted them the prerogatives of calling in any Catholic bishop for pontifical functions.[79] Similar privileges were granted to other monasteries.

It was but natural that the *military orders* (the Knights of St. John, the Maltese Knights, the Knights Templars, etc.), should, especially during the time of the Crusades, be greatly favored by the popes, who granted them extensive exemptions, in which even their oblates shared.[80]

8. Exemption became more widespread and hotly contradicted when the great *Mendicant Orders* arose. It lay in their very nature that their activity should extend to people and clergy alike, and that they should come into contact with the diocesan bishops. Their labors in the pulpit and in the confessional required approbation either by the Ordinary or by the Holy See. The latter decidedly favored the Orders because they were true reformers, and first granted them the old privilege of exemption from the coercive power of the Ordinary by deciding that no episcopal interdict was to touch the churches of the Mendicants,[81] that the excommunication of a religious by his superior was to be acknowledged by the bishop,[82] and that absolution from censures imparted by religious superiors to their subjects was valid without any further interposition.[83] These privileges, and especially that

78 *Ibid.*, col. 300.
79 Jaffé, nn. 9728, 9756.
80 *Archiv. für K.-R.*, 1907 (87), p. 270 ff.

81 Potthast, *Regesta Pont. Rom.*, 1874, I, n. 6808.
82 *Ibid.*, n. 7123.
83 *Ibid.*, n. 7901.

granted by Martin IV ("*Ad fructus uberes*," Dec. 13, 1281) provoked opposition on the part of the higher and lower clergy. This document [84] granted to the general and the provincials of the Franciscans and Dominicans the right to examine and approve by Apostolic authority their priests for preaching and hearing confessions, without interference from any bishop or parish priest. This general privilege was limited by Boniface VIII and Clement V to the provinces and cities where the Mendicants had settled, and required them to obtain the permission of the local prelate or pastor.[85] But the validity of confessions was nowhere affected.[86] The same decretal enacts the freedom of burial, not only for the Mendicants themselves, but also for those who wished to be buried from or in their churches or cemeteries, provided, however, that the *quarta funeris* was paid to the parish priest.

9. Thus, up to the *Council of Trent,* the chief aim of exemption may be described as *withdrawal of religious from the punitive or coercive power of the diocesan Ordinary.*[87] For the monasteries or congregations of the Benedictine Order another point was of paramount importance, namely, that the *freedom of election,* as enjoined by the Rule, should be guaranteed by the papal power, and we find this point insisted upon in nearly all the privileges. The exercise of *pontifical functions* and the *right of tithing* were also mentioned among the privileges granted by the Holy See, as well as the prerogative to call in *any* Catholic bishop to perform the pontifical functions of consecration and ordination.

However, these briefs of exemption were not always

84 *Ibid.,* Vol. II, n. 21821: "*generali et provincialibus.*"
85 Cfr. c. 12, X, V, 38.
86 C. 2, Clem. III, 7, de sepulturis.
87 Schreiber, *l. c.*

of the same extent; some were wider, some narrower, and hence the bearing of each had to be judged from the wording of the text. At first, as we have noted, such privileges were, as a rule, granted only to single monasteries. But the centralized organizations of Cluny, Camaldoli, Vallombrosa, and Citeaux paved the way for the still more centralized Orders of the Mendicants, who thus found the soil prepared for a fuller and more extensive exemption. But a " cut and dried " notion of exemption cannot be inferred from the papal documents of that period, as is evident from the quarrels between the secular clergy on the one hand and the regular clergy, especially the Mendicants, on the other, which arose everywhere in connection with the Constitution of Boniface VIII, "*Super cathedram*" (1300).[88] Bishops, parish priests and university professors tried to curtail the privilege of exemption, whilst the regulars vigorously fought for their rights. Both sides were guilty of excesses. The Council of Constance and Basle drew up a series of propositions aiming at a restriction of exemption, but without success. The same (fifteenth) century witnessed the rise of new monastic congregations devoted to reform of the religious life, and these were fully exempted by the popes. Thus Eugene IV granted to the brotherhood founded at St. Justina of Padua (1412) complete exemption from the jurisdiction of the Ordinaries, and from all charitable subsidies and other like obligations.[89] Sixtus IV, a former General of the Franciscans, showed great favor to the Mendicants,[90] especially the Friars Minor to whom, in the so-called "*Mare Magnum Minorum*"

---

[88] C. 2, *Extrav. Comm.*, III, 6, de sepulturia.
[89] June 30, 1436.

[90] *Arch. f. K.-R.*, 1907 (87), p. 626; Pastor, *Geschichte der Päpste*, II, 536.

(Aug. 31, 1474) he renewed and ratified all the privileges granted them by his predecessors.

10. The *Council of Trent* strove to cut off some exaggerated prerogatives, without, however, touching the substance of exemption. A distinction was, moreover, drawn between cases in which the regulars were subject to the Ordinary as such, and cases in which they were bound to obey him "as delegate of the Apostolic See." The former class comprises chiefly matters of ordination, hearing the confessions of seculars, the publication of censures and the observation of feast-days, the punishment of regulars who were scandalously delinquent outside their monasteries, preaching and the promulgation of indulgences.[91] There were but few cases in which the regulars were subjected to the Ordinary as delegate of the Apostolic See.[92] It is noteworthy that the Council refused to decide that all regulars, *i. e.*, religious with solemn vows,— only such existed at that time, with the exception of part of the Society of Jesus — were *ipso iure* exempt, or to define what exemption really implied. The Council seems to have taken for granted that most of the regulars were actually exempt and left the *quaestio iuris* untouched. As a consequence, the ancient controversies between bishops and monasteries about exemption continued after the Council. The Austrian bishops discouraged exemption, and the Bishop of Constance refused to acknowledge the written documents of Swiss monasteries which claimed exemption. Besides there are many small convents (*parvi conventus*) in which the regular discipline

---

91 Sess. 23, c. 2, de ref.; sess. 23, c. 15, de ref.; sess. 25, c. 12, de reg.; sess. 25, c. 14, de reg.; sess. 6, c. 3, de ref.; sess. 5, c. 2, de ref.; sess. 21, c. 9, de ref.; Bened. XIV, *De Syn. Dioec.*, IX, 15, 4 ff.

92 Sess. 5, c. 1, de ref.; sess. 25, cc. 5, 9, de reg.; sess. 6, c. 3, de ref.; cfr. Bachofen, *Compendium Iuris Reg.*, p. 327 f.

had declined and which, therefore, seemed to invite interference by the bishop.   Urban VIII and Innocent X
decreed that convents in which at least twelve religious
could not be maintained were subject to episcopal visitation, correction, and jurisdiction, the bishop in such cases
acting as delegate of the Apostolic See.[98]   However,
these papal decrees affected mostly houses existing in Italy
and the adjoining islands; elsewhere the houses of regulars continued to enjoy exemption, as far as the Tridentine laws permitted and the bishops did not interfere.
Leo XIII (" *Romanos Pontifices*," May 8, 1881.) allowed
the regulars living in England and the U. S., although
there be but two or three in a missionary residence, to
be exempt in all matters not pertaining to the care of
souls.

This, then, is briefly the history of exemption, which
has now received at last a formal acknowledgment for
all regulars, *i. e.*, members of religious orders who take
solemn vows and are, in the majority at least, of clerical
rank.

11. Before concluding this chapter it may be useful
to discuss the view of the glossators of Gratian's Decree
concerning *exemptio a lege dioecesana* and *exemptio a
lege iurisdictionis*.   The former was vindicated to the
monasteries, but not the latter.   Exemption *a lege dioecesana*, according to the glossators, comprises immunity
from taxation, cathedraticum or the third or fourth part
of the tithes, and freedom from being called to the diocesan synod, whereas the *lex iurisdictionis* comprises the
right of ordaining the clergy and consecrating altars,
churches, and virgins, the power of correction and of

---

[98] Urban VIII, June 21, 1625;
Innocent X, " *Instaurandae*," Oct.
15, 1652; " *Ut in parvis*," Feb. 10,
1654; Benedict XIV, *De Syn.*, III,
2, 1 ff.

suspending and judging criminal and civil cases.[94] The reader may judge for himself whether this distinction has any foundation in the privileges granted by the Apostolic See. These glossators (Huguccio, Ioannes Teutonicus, etc.) must have read very few papal briefs on that subject. Abbo of Fleury, for instance, never denied that the monasteries were obliged to pay the tithes established by law or custom for their churches, but his monastery was exempt in many other respects, especially from the obligation of having its clerics ordained by the diocesan Ordinary. Besides, the main element of all exemption privileges was freedom from the coercive power of the bishops. Nevertheless, the distinction explained above has been retained by later canonists,— a remarkable example of the power of imitation.

[94] Cfr. the Gloss on c. 1, C. 10, q. 1; on c. 34, C. 16, q. 1; c. 6, C. 18, q. 2; Benedict XIV, *De Syn. Dioec.*, I, 4, 3.

COMMENTARY

After these preliminary notes we now continue our commentary. The first five canons of Part II treat of the definition of the religious state, of the different terms occurring in the Code, and of the effect the Code has upon the rules and constitutions of religious and precedence among them.

DEFINITION OF THE RELIGIOUS STATE

Can. 487

Status religiosus seu stabilis in communi vivendi modus, quo fideles, praeter communia praecepta, evangelica quoque consilia servanda per vota obedientiae, castitatis et paupertatis suscipiunt, ab omnibus in honore habendus est.

Here we have both a *definition* and an *encomium* of the religious state. The religious state is a permanent mode of living in common, by which the faithful, besides obeying the commandments, also observe the evangelical counsels embodied in the vows of obedience, chastity, and poverty. The *encomium* or praise of that state is expressed in the words: *it is to be honored by all.*

To begin with the latter, it is but truth to say that it has been the *constant* and *universal teaching of the Church* ever since the religious state commenced to exist, that it is deserving of honor. St. Jerome calls the monks

40

and virgins " the flowers and ornaments of the Church." [1] His controversy with Jovinian is well known.[2] St. Augustine extols the monastic life as the best known in the universe.[3] Cassiodorius, the once powerful statesman under Theodoric the Great, says of it:[4] "A heavenly life upon earth, an imitation of the faithful angels, to live spiritually in the flesh, and not to love the vices of the world, a truly pleasant paradise, in which grow so many fruits of virtues." Alcuin (804) exclaims: "O happy life of the monks, pleasing and appeasing to God, and loved by the angels." [5] St. Bernard of Clairvaux compares the monastic orders to the angelic choirs and calls the religious life the shortest route to heaven.[6]

But there were also *dissentient voices.* One was that already noticed, of the heretic Jovinian. In the thirteenth century violent attacks were made on the religious state by a powerful and influential party, of which *William of St. Amour* was the recognized leader.[7] These new opponents, however, were, at least theoretically, silenced by *St. Thomas of Aquin,*[8] who wrote several smaller treatises against them and set forth the theological viewpoint with great force in his immortal " Summa " (Qa Qae). *St. Bonaventure* employed his truly seraphic pen against the adversaries of the Friars Minor.[9] *William's* errors were condemned by Alexander IV in more

1 Cf. Migne, P. L., 22, 489.

2 Ibid., 23, 211 ff.; however, exaggerations occur in St. Jerome's writings; cfr. Bardenhewer-Shahan, Patrology, 1908, p. 465.

3 Migne, P. L., 37, 372, 1277.

4 Ibid., 70, 734.

5 Migne, 100, 298.

6 Ibid., 182, 912; 183, 595.

7 Procter, O. P., The Religious State by St. Thomas Aquinas, London, 1902, p. III.

8 S. Thomas, Contra Retrahentes a Religionis Ingressu; Contra Impugnantes Dei Cultum (Paris ed., t. XX; English by Sands & Co., London, 1903).

9 Liber Apol. in eos qui Ordini Min. Adversantur; Expositio in Reg. Fratrum Min.; De Paupertate Christi contra Guil. (opp., Lugd., 1668, t. VII).

than one Constitution.[10]   The diabolical errors of Wiclif were reprobated by Martin V and the Council of Constance.[11]

The *Pseudo-Council of Pistoja* (1786) could not refrain from attacking the monastic or religious state, against which it issued several decrees, which were proscribed by Pius VI in his "*Auctorem fidei,*" Aug. 28, 1794.   The framers of these condemned decrees kindly permitted one order, *viz.*, that of St. Benedict, to exist, but pruned it to suit their Febronian-Josephinistic taste, allowing a certain amount of psalmody and a certain restricted capacity for the sacred ministry, abrogating the distinction between choir monks and others, rejecting the perpetual vow of stability, etc.[12]

We cannot help touching the attitude of certain followers of "*Americanism*" which was rejected by Leo XIII in his letter to Cardinal Gibbons, "*Testem benevolentiae,*" Dec. 25, 1898.   As this papal document clearly shows, the depreciation of the so-called *passive virtues,* such as obedience and humility, led the champions of that unecclesiastical tendency to belittle those congregations which are devoted to the contemplative life, and to underestimate the religious state as such, which, they maintained, is not in harmony with the spirit of our times, inasmuch as the vows restrict human liberty too much and are adapted more to weak than to strong minds.   All this, says Leo XIII, is opposed to the very nature of liberty, which is fostered by the religious vows and raised into a higher sphere; and contrary to the teaching of history. He calls attention to the fact that the first missionaries to the United States were religious, and that a statue has been publicly erected to one of them, Père Marquette.[13]

10 Denzinger, *Enchirid.*, n. 380.   12 Denzinger, *l. c.*, nn. 1443 ff.
11 *Ibid.*, 490–511; 520 f., 574, 665.   13 Cf. *Eccl. Review,* 1899, Vol.

The Code's *definition of the religious state* comprises three elements: stability, vows, and the common life. Before entering upon a discussion of these points we note that the Code says: *"quo fideles."* "Monks," solitaries or ascetics, were and are found in more than one pagan race, as among the Buddhists.[14] The essential difference between non-Christian and Christian asceticism lies, not so much in their extrinsic form,— for both tend to self-perfection by some kind of penance — but in the difference of their specific aims. Non-Christian asceticism aims at self-annihilation, Christian asceticism at love, as St. Thomas[15] so admirably states. "The Christian ideal is frankly an ascetic one, and monachism is simply the endeavor to effect a material realization of that ideal, or organization in accordance with it, when taken literally as regards its counsels as well as its 'Precepts.'"[16] Between counsels and precepts there is a difference of degree only, not of essence. For the end and aim of all Christians and, in fact, we may say, of every human being, is *perfection,* as Yahwe bade Abraham "walk before me and be perfect." This perfection consists in the love of God and men, which brings man to his eternal goal. However, aside from the love attained by the Blessed in heaven, there are diverse degrees of charity which we earthly pilgrims may arrive at; one is necessary for salvation, and therefore a matter of strict precept, whereas the other is merely a matter of counsel for those who desire to approach the ideal of perfection possessed by the Blessed. "Now it is in this effort that perfection

30, p. 406 f.; Card. Gasparri also refers to that document.

14 Cfr. Aiken, *The Dhamma of Gotama the Buddha and the Gospel of Jesus Christ,* 1900; *Idem* in the *Cath. Encycl.,* III, 32 f. Ascetica were found also among the Aztecs and Incas.

15 Procter, *l. c.,* Ch. II, p. 9.

16 *Cath. Encycl.,* X, 459 (Huddelston, O. S. B.).

in this life consists, to which we are invited by the counsels." [17]   This effort is a *striving* after perfection; but where and how is it to be made?

1. In a stable condition or *state,* for state implies a certain position which is not easily changed or moved, but quiet and favorably disposed.   This can be brought about in movable and changeable man only by assuming a voluntary obligation to remain in the state once chosen.[18] Therefore it is absurd to say that religious have abdicated their freedom and natural liberty.   The very act by which they enter the religious state is a voluntary one, performed with full deliberation.   But it is also unreasonable to deny, with Bouix,[19] the necessity of the obligation insisted upon by St. Thomas.   For no other tie is imaginable — except physical coaction, which has entirely ceased — that would bind a man to a state of life not prescribed by the Lord of life and death.

This state is called the *religious* state.   Religion signifies, not any kind of worship, but the worship of God. It is that virtue by which man offers service and homage to his Creator.   Therefore those are strictly called religious who give themselves entirely to the divine service, as a burnt offering so to speak,— a *holocaustum.*[20]

2. This offering is made by taking the *three vows* of poverty, chastity, and obedience.   A vow is a promise made to God of a thing or action which we are not obliged to offer at all, or at least not to the extent or in the form promised.   It has the character of a stable promise, and therefore is apt to produce or ratify the state chosen.   The object of a vow is something not

17 Procter, *l. c.*, Ch. 6, p. 17;   19 *De Iure Regularium*, 1857, I,
St. Thomas, *Summa Theol.*, 2a 2ae,   p. 7.
q. 184.   20 *Summa Theol.*, 2a 2ae, q. 186,
18 *Summa Theol.*, 2a, 2ae, q. 183,   a. 1.
a. 1.

merely good and lawful [21] in itself, but better or more noble. Lastly, a vow is something sacred because it partakes of the virtue of religion and has God himself for its direct aim and object. From these qualities follows the binding or obligatory character of a vow. It is a promise made to God with the special intention to do Him homage, and the man who makes this promise has the firm will to keep it unless prevented by unforeseen obstacles. That the three vows mentioned really and peculiarly belong to the religious state may be seen from what St. Thomas [22] says about them. They remove the obstacles that impede the road to perfection or love of God and men: (1) *poverty*, the disorderly inclination to gain and hold earthly possessions, (2) *chastity*, the impetuous aspirations of the flesh and human ties, and (3) *obedience*, the powerful love of oneself. Of the three, that of obedience belongs most peculiarly to the religious life, since by it man sacrifices his own will, and therefore everything, because obedience includes both poverty and chastity, for it is by his own free will that a man makes use either of his body or his goods.[23] From this we may understand why St. Benedict did not explicitly mention poverty and continence as special vows in his rule, for they are, partly at least, included in obedience.

3. But though a religious state which enjoins the three vows may and did exist among the ancient hermits, yet now-a-days the Church limits this state to a *life in common*, because a solitary life, unless assumed after due preparation or by a special divine grace, is full of dangers and illusions. Life in common, then, (cenobitic

---

[21] The vow of Jephta (Jud. 11, 30) was lawful in itself but too indiscriminately made, its fulfillment — the killing of his daughter — was simply unlawful.

[22] *Summa Theol.*, 2a 2ae, q. 186 (Procter, *l. c.*, Chs. 7-11, p. 18 ff.).
[23] *Ibid.*, q. 188, a. 8.

life), means a stable mode of living under the same rule and roof, although all the members may not be dwelling in the same convent or monastery or provincial house.

Canon 488

In canonibus qu⹀ sequuntur, veniunt nomine:

1.° *Religionis*, societas, a legitima ecclesiastica auctoritate approbata, in qua sodales, secundum proprias ipsius societatis leges, vota publica, perpetua vel temporaria, elapso tamen tempore renovanda, nuncupant, atque ita ad evangelicam perfectionem tendunt;

2.° *Ordinis*, religio in qua vota sollemnia nuncupantur; *Congregationis monasticae*, plurium monasteriorum sui iuris inter se coniunctio sub eodem Superiore; *religionis exemptae*, religio sive votorum sollemnium sive simplicium, a iurisdictione Ordinarii loci subducta; *Congregationis religiosae* vel *Congregationis* simpliciter, religio in qua vota dumtaxat simplicia sive perpetua sive temporaria emittuntur;

3.° *Religionis iuris pontificii*, religio quae vel approbationem vel saltem laudis decretum ab Apostolica Sede est consecuta; *iuris dioecesani*, religio quae ab Ordinariis erecta, hoc laudis decretum nondum obtinuit;

4.° *Religionis clericalis*, religio cuius plerique sodales sacerdotio augentur; secus est *laicalis;*

5.° *Domus religiosae*, domus alicuius religionis in genere; *domus regularis*, domus Ordinis; *domus formatae* domus religiosa in qua sex saltem religiosi professi degunt, quorum, si agatur de religione clericali, quatuor saltem sint sacerdotes;

6.° *Provinciae*, plurium religiosarum domorum in-

ter se coniunctio sub eodem Superiore, partem eiusdem religionis constituens;

7.° *Religiosorum*, qui vota nuncuparunt in aliqua
religione; *religiosorum votorum simplicium*, qui in
Congregatione religiosa; *regularium*, qui in Ordine;
sororum, religiosae votorum simplicium; *monialium*,
religiosae votorum sollemnium aut, nisi ex rei natura vel ex contextu sermonis aliud constet, religiosae
quarum vota ex instituto sunt sollemnia, sed pro
aliquibus locis ex Apostolicae Sedis praescripto sunt
simplicia;

8.° *Superiorum maiorum*, Abbas Primas, Abbas
Superior Congregationis monasticae, Abbas monasterii sui iuris, licet ad monasticam Congregationem
pertinentis, supremus religionis Moderator, Superior
provincialis, eorundem vicarii aliique ad instar pro-
vincialium potestatem habentes.

This canon explains the *terms* which are used in the
Code in connection with the religious life.[24] They are
the following:

1. *Religio* (institute) indicates a society, approved by
legitimate ecclesiastical authority, whose members strive
after evangelical perfection by observing the special laws
of that society and by making public vows, either perpetual or temporary, the latter to be renewed when the
time expires.

2. *Ordo* (order) denotes a religious organization in
which solemn vows are taken. *Congregatio monastica*
is a union of several independent monasteries under one
superior. *Religio exempta* means a religious organization of either solemn or simple vows that has been with-

---

24 The translation of this canon
is, on the whole, taken from the
Eccl. Rev., 1918 (Vol. 58), p. 141 f.,
by Very Rev. Fr. Stanislaus Woy-
wod, O. F. M.

drawn from the jurisdiction of the Ordinary of the diocese. *Congregatio religiosa*, or simply *Congregatio*, signifies a religious body in which only simple vows are taken; these simple vows may either be perpetual or temporary.

3. *Religio iuris pontificii*, or a religious pontifical institute, is a religious organization which has received from the Holy See either approval or at least a *decretum laudis*. *Religio iuris dioecesani*, or a religious diocesan institute, is a religious organization which has been instituted by the Ordinary and has not yet obtained a *decretum laudis* from the Holy See.

4. *Religio clericalis*, or clerical institute, means a religious organization most of whose members are priests; if they are laymen, it is called *religio laicalis*.

5. *Domus religiosa*, or a religious house, signifies the residence of a religious organization. *Domus regularis*, or house of regulars, is the house of an Order. *Domus formata* means a religious house in which reside at least six professed members, of whom, if there is question of a clerical organization, at least four must be priests.

6. *Provincia*, or province, is a combination of several houses of religious under one superior, constituting part of a religious Order or Congregation.

7. *Religiosi*, or religious, are those who have taken vows in any religious community; *religiosi votorum simplicium*, or religious with simple vows, are those who have taken vows in a religious Congregation; *regulares*, or regulars, are the professed members of an Order; *sorores*, or Sisters, are women who have taken simple vows; *moniales*, or nuns, are religious women with solemn vows, unless either by the nature or the context of the canons the term is to be interpreted otherwise. There are also nuns whose vows are by their rule solemn, but

have for certain countries been declared simple by the Holy See.

8. *Superiores maiores* are the Abbot Primate, Abbots who are superiors of monastic Congregations, Abbots of Monasteries that are independent though belonging to some monastic Congregation, the Superior General of any religious organization, the Provincial Superiors and their Vicars, and all others who have the same jurisdiction as Provincials.

Some notes seem required. *Religio* is here taken as part and parcel of the *Christian religion,* or religious state, as in a sense signifying preëminently what religion broadly implies, *viz.,* worship or service of God. The etymological derivation of *religio* is given by Cicero [25] and adopted by theologians is from diligently treating and, as it were, carefully rereading (*re-legere*) the things that pertain to the worship of God. Religion in the sense of religious state, therefore, is nothing else but a concrete and emphatic, nay, we may say, exclusive occupation with divine things or at least things that have reference to God, inasfar as man's perfection is thereby most securely achieved.

But, since it belongs to the whole Church, a *religio* is not to be thought of without the *approbation* of the *legitimate ecclesiastical authority.* True, we do not read of any formal approbation of the rules of St. Basil or St. Benedict,[26] but if they had not been in conformity with the spirit of the Church, their existence would have been not only precarious but short. In the eleventh and twelfth centuries the founders of religious institutes

[25] *De Natura Deorum,* l. II, c. 28: " *Qui autem omnia, quae ad cultum deorum pertinerent, diligenter retractarent et tanquam relegerent, sunt dicti religiosi ex relegendo.*"

[26] St. Gregory the Great (*Dial.,* II, 36) praises the rule of St. Benedict, but only as an ecclesiastical writer; the bull alleged by some is spurious.

thought it necessary to seek the formal approbation of the Holy See, and the fourth Lateran Council [27] and subsequent laws made this step imperative,— which does not, however, mean that ecclesiastical approbation is required by divine law.[28]

Approbation involves two elements: an authentic judgment and power conferred on the religious superior to accept vows and receive members. The *authentic judgment*, which is generally held to be infallible, at least concerning religious orders and in its final stage, implies nothing else but a declaration that the institute is becoming, licit, and useful; or, as Suarez [29] says, it is a kind of canonization, by which the institute is declared holy. The *faculty* is required, because the superior must act as a public person or in the name of the Church, wherefore the vows accepted by him are called *public* vows.

There are, however, *different degrees* of approbation. Before stating the mode by which the Roman Court is now wont to proceed, it is necessary to distinguish between orders and congregations. *Orders*, or organizations with solemn vows, are not easily approved now unless they accept the rule of one of the ancient orders as their fundamental code, to which they may add their own constitutions.

Rule means the sum-total of the regulations which the first founder gave to his community, whilst *constitutions* are additions or by-laws which modify or explain the original code. Thus the various (fourteen) Benedictine Congregations all obey the Benedictine Rule and, besides, each has its own constitutions. Later orders, *e. g.,*

27 C. 9, X, III, 36; c. un. 6°, III, 17; c. 1, Extrav. Comm., III, 11.

28 Suarez, *De Statu Religioso*, 1.

II, c. 15, n. 2 (ed. Paris, 1859, t. XV, 192).

29 *Ibid.*, n. 13 ff.

the Jesuits and Barnabites, call their original rule by the name of Constitutions.

Those modern *Congregations* which do not follow any of the ancient rules have Constitutions, not rules. But even if they follow a " rule," *e. g.*, that of St. Francis, they must have constitutions approved by the bishop or Holy See. As long as their constitutions are not approved by the Apostolic See, or have at least received the decree of recognition (*decretum laudis*) from the same authority, the institute is simply *diocesan*, subject to the jurisdiction of the Ordinary. And it matters nothing whether or not the members follow a rule already approved.

The Constitutions of a *monastic congregation* or of a branch of a clerical order require the papal *approbation*, but the procedure is not the same as for the approbation of religious congregations. For the former send their " Constitutions " to the S. C. Relig., which, after hearing one or more consultors, returns them with its remarks to the head of the monastic or clerical body concerned with the clause: " *ad triennium or quinquennium ad experimenti instar.*" When the time thus set has elapsed, application for a further trial or for final approbation must be made, whereupon the S. Congregation gives its decision.

In the case of *religious Congregations with simple vows* the procedure [30] is as follows:

1. If the institute has only one or two houses, and no constitutions properly so called, the sacred Congregation sometimes issues a *letter* praising the institution of the founder or the scope of the institute. This document is nothing else but a recommendation and does not make

---

[30] *Normae secundum quas S. C. EE. et RR. procedere solet in approbandis Novis Institutis votorum simplicium*, Rome, 1901.

the institute a papal one.   However, we would not deny
it the nature of a *religious* institute, provided episcopal
approbation has been obtained.

2. The *decree of recognition* or praise, *decretum laudis*,
is the first step by which the Holy See raises the institute
to papal rank.   This decree is granted after the institute has spread sufficiently and given proof of its spiritual
and material vitality.   To obtain the *decretum laudis*,

a) A *petition*[81] must be sent to the Sovereign Pontiff,
signed by the superior and his assistants, begging for
approbation.   This petition must be accompanied by

b) *Letters of recommendation* from the Ordinary or
Ordinaries in whose dioceses the congregation has houses.
These letters should contain the opinion of the Ordinary
concerning the nature, utility, and work of the congregation as well as a request for its approbation and suggestions as to desirable changes in the constitutions.   Each
letter must be signed and sealed by the bishop and addressed to the S. Cong. of Religious.[82]

c) An *accurate report* must be made to Rome on the
foundation of the institute and its present condition,—
personal, spiritual, and material.   The *personal report*
must state the number of professed members, novices and
candidates, and if there is a distinction between members
(*e. g.,* choir and lay members), how many there are of
each class; also the number of houses in the diocese or
dioceses.   The *spiritual* or disciplinary report concerns
the manner of, and progress in following the Constitutions,[33] the novitiate, and any serious difficulties that may
have arisen with regard to the Constitution.   The *mate-*

---

81 This must be written in Latin,
French or Italian.

82 See Bastien, *Directoire Canon-
ique,* translated by Lanslots, *Hand-
book of Canon Law,* 3rd ed., 1903.

83 A detailed statement of the
government is not required, because
this is supposed to be contained in
the constitutions.

rial or financial report must state the resources of the institute, whether a dowry (*dos*) be required and how much, whether there are any debts, etc. This report (under c) must be signed by the superior general, the treasurer, and the secretary general, and the Ordinary in whose diocese the mother house (*domus princeps*) is located must add his testimony as to the truthfulness and authenticity of the document.

d) Lastly, the *Constitutions* [84] as approved by the Ordinary must be included in either Latin, Italian, or French. At least twelve printed copies must be forwarded, because the various consultors are each entitled to a copy.

After the S. C. of Religious has issued the decree of recognition or praise, the Constitutions are not yet regarded as approved, but the institute is now under the jurisdiction of the S. C. Rel., and no change is allowed in the Constitutions. Before the Constitutions are approved, either on trial or definitively, the institute itself is *approved* and generally also the Constitutions receive an experimental approval; but this is granted only after a certain lapse of time, during which the Constitutions should be tried, and a faithful report made as to the practicability and efficiency of the same. During that time the changes and modifications inserted by the S. C. Rel. must be conscientiously followed and no changes should be made. Finally, after several experiments and a revision of the Constitutions according to the suggestions of the S. C. Rel., they are *approved,* whereupon neither the superiors of the institute nor the Ordinary of the diocese are allowed to change them. Note that any liturgical book, or directory, or calendar, or book of customs referred to in the Constitutions does not by vir-

[84] If the text is not printed, it should be typewritten. French is permitted because it is the diplomatic language of the Roman Court.

tue of that approbation become "canonized" or formally approved. For instance, a so-called "*Caeremoniale Monasticum*" is not sanctioned by the approval of the Constitutions. Books referring to the liturgy of the Latin Church require a special approbation by the S. C. of Rites.

It may be well to mention here what the "Normae" [35] wish to see *excluded* from Constitutions submitted for approval.

1. No preface or introduction is allowed, nor any historical notes or letters of endorsement or recommendation except such received from the Holy See.

2. No quotations must be made from the Bible, the Church councils, or from the works of the Holy Fathers or theologians, much less may dogmatical or moral questions be brought in or doctrinal decisions cited, especially in matters of vows. Ascetic instructions and exhortations, spiritual and mystical considerations, questions from manuals or ceremonials, are also to be eschewed.

3. No reference is to be made to the office of bishops and confessors, because the Constitutions are not written for these; neither is mention to be made of the order of study and life of the students, or of the detailed order of daily exercises.

4. No mention is to be made of civil laws or magistrates, nor of the approbation by the government.

5. Minute regulations about the lower offices, such as pertain to the kitchen, infirmary, or vestry, are to be omitted.

6. Every term or expression which applies to institutes with solemn vows must be avoided for congregations with simple vows, such as *regula, monasterium,*

[35] N. 26–33.

moniales, instead of which must be used: *constitutiones, institutum* or *domus, sorores,* etc.

These three stages: simple acknowledgment or recommendation of the intention of the founder and his scope, the decree of praise, and formal approbation, are not always insisted on by the S. C. Rel., but sometimes the first is omitted, because not asked for.[86] But the decree of praise and formal approbation of the institute or Constitutions — the two may be combined — are always required, as the Code plainly states.

c) Lastly, note the phrase: *vota publica, perpetua vel temporanea:* public vows, either perpetual or temporary. Here a *distinction between vows* is asserted, to which we may add the one between solemn and simple vows, as this occurs in n. 2 of the same canon.

1. A *vow* or promise made to God is *public* if accepted in the name of the Church by legitimate authority.[87] Such an authority may be any ecclesiastic who is empowered by the Church to accept vows, either bishops or religious superiors, acting with proper or delegated power. Hence " public " here means not precisely notorious (though this is generally implied, especially since tacit profession is no longer admitted), but public in the proper sense, as we speak of public authority. A *private* vow, for instance, to make a pilgrimage, or not to marry, is one made without the intervention of the Church. The vows of poverty, chastity, and obedience, taken in a religious congregation, are considered public.

2. Public vows may be either *perpetual* or *temporary.* They are perpetual if made without any time-limit and accepted as such by the legitimate superior. Note that the simple profession of members who pronounce their

86 *Normae,* n. 7.
87 Wernz, *Ius Decretalium,* III,   n. 572 (ed. 1, p. 586).

vows in a religious order involves only temporary (triennial)[38] vows. Temporary vows are such as are made for a certain limited term, for instance, three years. They must be promptly renewed, for a congregation with expired temporary vows would not constitute members in the religious state.

3. In number two of our canon, an *order* is called an organization in which *solemn* vows are taken, whereas a *congregation* is defined as a religious body whose members make only *simple* vows. Here we have the famous and controverted distinction between simple and solemn vows. Whence is it derived?

The distinction between solemn and simple vows was known to Gratian[39] and the canonists that followed him. Difficulties arose at an early date with regard to the bearing of vows upon the validity of marriage. The question was settled by Boniface VIII, who declared that the solemnity of the vow was introduced by ecclesiastical law, and what is called an invalidating impediment is produced only by the reception of sacred orders or by profession in a religious congregation approved by the Apostolic See.[40] This seems to mean that the authority of the Church determines which vows are simple and which are solemn. However, the Church would act blindly, as it were, if there were no *intrinsic distinction* between the two. Hence canonists[41] have endeavored to establish the precise difference between solemn and simple vows, with due regard always to the decision of Boniface VIII. St.

---

[38] Can. 574, § 1.

[39] Cfr. *dictum ad* c. 8, Dist. 27: those who simply take vows and those whose vows are endowed with the blessing of consecration, or who make religious vows; from which it may be inferred that all religious vows were considered solemn; cfr. c. 20, X, III, 32.

[40] C. un. 6°, III, 15.

[41] Cfr. *Cath. Encycl.*, *s. v.* "Vow" (Vol. XV, 512, by Vermeersch).

Thomas [42] places the solemnity of the vow in a certain spiritual blessing or consecration, in as far as this has special reference to the service of God. Hence we may say that the Angelic Doctor finds the difference between the two kinds of vows not in the ceremonies or the ritual as applied respectively in the administration of solemn and simple vows, but in the interior, more perfect and complete consecration to God, or, as a commentator [43] puts it, he does not speak of an accidental blessing or consecration, but of an internal consecration, which implies a more perfect and irretrievable surrender of one-self to God. If this is not a sufficient explanation, we doubt whether there is one. As regards the simple vows of the Jesuits, it required special papal constitutions [44] to render them productive of the truly religious state, to which, as the text says, their members belong because they devote themselves to the service of God,— but not irrevocably. Their's is a peculiar condition on account of the effects attached to their simple vows, and hence it must not be drawn into the question here at issue.

The general assumption of the Church up to the six-teenth and even nineteenth century was that a religious offers himself as a holocaust to God and thereby surren-ders himself entirely to the Church, who has the power to declare whether, considering the circumstances,[45] it is opportune to accept and declare the surrender to be ir-revocable to the whole extent or for all members and in-stitutes alike. The intention of the Church is identical

42 *Summa Theol.*, 2a 2ae, q. 88, a. 7.

43 Joh. a S. Thoma, *Cursus Theol.*, in II-II, ed. Lugd., 1653, p. 438.

44 Greg. XIII, " *Quanto*," Feb. 1, 1583; " *Ascendente*," May 26, 1584.

45 Pius IX, " *Neminem latet*," March 19, 1857 (Bizzarri, *Collect-anea*, 1885, p. 853 f.). The expla-nation given by Vermeersch (*Cath-Encycl., l. c.*) is less intelligible than that of St. Thomas, and we prefer the opinion of Wernz, *l. c.*, III, n. 572.

with that of the person who takes the vows, which is extensively and intensively just what the Church declares it to be.

A *monastic congregation* is a union of several autonomous or independent monasteries under the same superior. Such congregations sprang up after the IVth Council of the Lateran (1215), for instance, the congregation of St. Vannes, that of the Cassinese, and again after the Council of Trent, which renewed the decretal of Innocent III and insisted upon the formation of congregations.[46] At present there are fourteen Benedictine Congregations, two of them in this country; and if both were amalgamated, it would hurt neither Church nor State, nor their own efficiency.

An *exempt religious* order is one withdrawn from the jurisdiction of the Ordinary. Whilst all *regulars* who make solemn vows are *ipso iure* exempt, it needs a special Apostolic indult or privilege to exempt religious congregations, for instance, the Redemptorists, Passionists, etc.[47] A *religious congregation* is one whose members take simple vows only. They are either *papal institutes* or *diocesan institutes,* the difference between them lying in the manner of approbation or decree of praise. This distinction was canonized by the Constitution of Leo XIII, " *Conditae,*" Dec. 8, 1900.

A *clerical religion* is one the majority of whose members are priests. Note that " clerical " and " monastic " are no longer [48] adequate distinctions, as the Code plainly shows, for the clerical character may be possessed by monastic congregations as well. Historically speaking,

[46] Sess. 25, c. 8, de reg.; c. 7, X, III, 35.

[47] Both were declared exempt by Pius VI.

[48] Formerly this distinction was employed by canonists.

monastic congregations or orders belong to the contemplative orders, which were of a lay character. Since the tenth century [49] so-called *barbati* (bearded) or *conversi*, *i. e.*, lay brothers, were introduced and flourished especially among the Vallombrosians. Besides, after the eleventh century, many monasteries allowed their members to serve as pastors or curates at their chapels and churches, which thus became incorporated with the monastic bodies. This led to an increased number of monks with clerical character, and thus most of the monastic orders became clerical orders.

The division into *provinces* is due to the Mendicant Orders. St. Francis in 1217 divided his order into twelve provinces. The term *domus formata* is new and difficult to translate. It means a " canonically established house." Though the term is new, the object which it designates dates back to the decrees of Urban VIII and Innocent X, who subjected houses with less than twelve (or at least six) members to the jurisdiction of the diocesan Ordinary, which regulation has partly entered into the new Code.[50]

The *Abbot Primate* is mentioned first among the higher superiors or *superiores maiores*. This dignity was created by Leo XIII ("*Summum semper*," July 12, 1893) to foster and maintain the " fraternal confederation " established in the same year [51] among the " black " Benedictines. The Abbot Primate is not to be compared to the General of the Franciscans or the Jesuits, as our Code itself states.[52] We might call him a diplomatic representative of the Benedictines with limited power,

49 The abbey of Einsiedeln in Switzerland had such *barbati* already under Abbot Gregory in the last decades of the Xth century.

50 Cfr. can. 617, § 2.

51 *Studien* O. S. B., 1893 (Vol. 14), p. 279 ff.; p. 454 ff.

52 Can. 501, § 3.

accredited to the Holy See according to the Apostolic Brief of Leo XIII. His residence is at the College of St. Anselm [53] on the Aventine Hill, of which he is also abbot with ordinary jurisdiction. He is elected for a period of twelve years, but may be reëlected for twelve years more by the abbots presidents or by all the actual (not titular) abbots called to Rome. The election, in order to be valid, must be effected by a two-thirds' majority. This, in brief, is the history of a new creation which was wisely intended to produce a closer union among the Benedictines. Without a certain unity, now-a-days, in times of universal organization, any society appears to be doomed to failure.

CAN. 489

Regulae et particulares constitutiones singularum religionum, canonibus huius Codicis non contrariae, vim suam servant; quae vero eisdem opponuntur, abrogatae sunt.

CAN. 490

Quae de religiosis statuuntur, etsi masculino vocabulo expressa, valent etiam pari iure de mulieribus, nisi ex contextu sermonis vel ex rei natura aliud constet.

The rules and constitutions of all religious orders or institutes or congregations, provided they do not clash with any canon of this Code, remain in force; but any regulation or law or statute which is contraray to a canon of the Code, no longer binds either superiors or

---

[53] Innocent XI by his Constitution "*Inscrutabili*" (1687) erected a Benedictine college at St. Callisto in Trastevere, which was temporarily suppressed by reason of the revolutionary tendencies of 1834 and the following years, but reopened in 1888 and transferred in 1896 to the Aventine.

subjects. Thus elections must henceforth be held according to the Code,[54] and all special rules regarding the confession and communion of religious,[55] or the *causae fidei* belonging to the Holy Office,[56] or studies and ordinations [57] and profession are revoked.[58] As to privileges, see canon 613. The Code forbids what is *contrary* to the canons therein established. Hence whatever merely goes beyond the canons, or is a more explicit explanation thereof, may be lawfully retained. General and particular decrees are abrogated when they are opposed to the prescriptions of the Code. If no opposition exists, particular decrees given to an individual Congregation or Congregations, still continue to bind. On the other hand, in this same hypothesis general decrees, which are not explicitly or implicitly contained in the Code, have no longer any force. (See the *Irish Ecclesiastical Record,* 1918.)

Canon 490 lays down the general rule that whatever is enacted about religious, also binds religious women, even though the text may employ the masculine gender, except, of course, in matters not applicable to the female sex, or where the wording itself excludes them. A similar example is that of privileges, which, if granted to a male order, also apply to the nuns (second order), all other things being equal. It is evident that the regulations concerning studies or ordination or preaching or hearing confessions do not touch women. On the other hand, the expression " *si quis,*" though expressed in the masculine, obliges women.

54 Can. 507.
55 Can. 519 ff.; can. 595, § 2.
56 Can. 501, § 2.

57 Can. 587, § 2; can. 964-967; can. 2410.
58 Can. 572.

CAN. 491

§ 1. **Religiosi praecedunt laicis; religiones clerica-
les, laicalibus; canonici regulares, monachis; mona-
chi, ceteris regularibus; regulares, Congregationibus
religiosis; Congregationes iuris pontificii, Congregationibus iuris dioecesani; in eadem specie servetur
praescriptum can. 106, n. 5.**

§ 2. **At clerus saecularis praecedit tum laicis tum
religiosis extra eorum ecclesias atque etiam in eorum
ecclesiis, si agatur de religione laicali; Capitulum
vero cathedrale vel collegiale eisdem praecedit ubique
locorum.**

Religious precede laymen; clerical religious precede
lay religious; canons regular precede monks; monks precede the rest of the regulars; regulars precede religious
congregations; papal religious congregations precede diocesan congregations. Concerning precedence among re- ·
ligious of the same kind, the rule laid down in can. 106,
n. 5 must be observed.

With regard to the precedence between the *secular
clergy* and the regular clergy, the rule is that the secular
clergy precede laymen as well as religious,[59] but the latter
only in churches which do not belong to the religious,
unless a church belongs to a lay religious community; in
which latter case the secular clergy precede the religious
even in their own church. A cathedral or collegiate
chapter everywhere enjoys precedence over the religious.

Noticeable in this regulation is the fact that no distinction is made between monks and clerics regular, such as
the Barnabites, Theatines, Jesuites, etc. Only the canons

---

[59] The secular clergy, however, are supposed to wear surplice and biretta, if they claim precedence; S. C. EE. et RR., Dec. 3, 1847 (Bizzarri, *Collectanea*, p. 558).

regular,[60] such as those of the Lateran and the Premonstratensians (Norbertines), precede the monks, *e. g.*, Benedictines, Cistercians, Trappists (if these are priests), who in turn take precedence over all other regulars, if they are clerical orders. But among the other regulars — the Code makes no distinction between mendicants and non-mendicants — the rule laid down in can. 106, n. 5 must be observed.

This canon is taken from the Constitution of Gregory XIII, "*Exposcit,*" of July 15, 1583. It establishes that among regulars those precede who can prove quasi-possession of precedence in the place or city where a controversy has arisen; and if no quasi-possession can be proved, those who have first established a monastery or house in the controverted place precede those who came later. These are the rules the bishop should follow in settling controversies concerning precedence. The Friars Preachers (Dominicans) had precedence over the other Mendicants according to a decision of Pius V,[61] but since the Code takes the decision of Gregory XIII as the general norm for all regulars except monks, it is safe to say that the Dominicans must now follow the general rule.

Concerning the three families of the Friars Minor: the brown *Franciscans* (*Fratres Minores ab Unione Leonina*), the black Franciscans or Conventuals, and the Capuchins, the rule of precedence has been established as follows:

That family precedes which has been in a city or town for a longer time than another of the same order (O.

---

60 Pius IV, Sept. 23, 1563, settled the controversy between the Black Benedictines and Canons Regular in favor of the latter. Barbosa, *De Off. et Pot. Episc.*, P. III, alleg. 78, n. 29 (Vol. II, 322).

61 Barbosa, *l. c.*, n. 30; *Summa Apost. Dec.*, *s. v.*, "Praecedentia," n. 17.

F. M.), unless quasi-possession of precedence can be proved by the latter. However, since quasi-possession is often subject to controversies, the term of ten years, from Jan. 1, 1900, to Aug. 15, 1910, during which a family of Friars Minor has had actual possession of precedence before another family supplies proof of actual possession, unless there was no occasion to assert that precedence; in which latter case longer existence in city or town determines precedence. If a convent has been suppressed and ceased to exist in a city or town for fifty years, the date of return must be taken as the date from which existence is to be measured. If no convent of their own exists in a district outside the city or town, the general rule is that the Friars Minor of the Leonine Union (brown Franciscans) precede the Conventuals, and these in turn the Capuchins.[62]

We finally draw attention to the term *chapter*. A cathedral or collegiate chapter presenting itself in a body precedes all religious, even prelates and abbots, *e. g.*, in processions or on other ecclesiastical occasions. The text says *everywhere*, hence in the churches of religious [63] as well as on their own premises. The *vicar-general*, although appearing alone and not as a canon, precedes all the regular clergy, nay even abbots and prelates regular, because he represents the bishop.[64]

---

[62] Pius X, "*Seraphici Patriarchae*," Aug. 15, 1910 (*A. Ap. S.,* II, 713 ff.).

[63] But the abbot's choir stall must not be ceded to the first dignitary of the chapter, because that seat signifies, not only dignity, but jurisdiction.

[64] Can. 370; can. 106.

ERECTION AND SUPPRESSION OF RELIGIOUS CONGREGA-
TIONS, PROVINCES, AND HOUSES

CAN. 492

§ 1. Episcopi, non autem Vicarius Capitularis vel
Vicarius Generalis, condere possunt Congregationes
religiosas; sed eas ne condant neve condi sinant, inconsulta Sede Apostolica; quod si agatur de tertiariis
in communi viventibus, requiritur praeterea ut a supremo Moderatore primi Ordinis suae religioni
aggregentur.

§ 2. Congregatio iuris dioecesani, quamvis decursu
temporis in plures dioeceses diffusa, usque tamen dum
pontificiae approbationis aut laudis testimonio caru-
erit, remanet dioecesana, Ordinariorum iurisdictioni
ad normam iuris plane subiecta.

§ 3. Nec nomen nec habitus religionis iam constitutae assumi potest ab iis qui ad illam legitime non
pertinent aut a nova religione.

The text is silent about the foundation of new religious
orders, and only mentions (can. 497) the establishment
of religious exempt houses, supposing, perhaps, that there
is no need of a new religious order, or that a congregation may arise which may later develop into an order.
In § 1 the law permits *bishops,* and these only, to found
new religious congregations. Vicars-capitular and vic-
ars-general, even if endowed with a special mandate,
have no authority to make such foundations. As the

text says *bishops,* not Ordinaries, it seems logical to exclude also religious superiors, even though they enjoy quasi-episcopal jurisdiction. Abbots *nullius* or prelates *nullius,* on the other hand, would be allowed to found new congregations, because they have the same power as residential bishops.[1]

There is, however, a twofold *condition* attached to the leave of founding such communities:

· 1. The bishops must consult the *Holy See* and may not permit a foundation to be made without taking advice with the S. C. of Religious.

2. A congregation of tertiaries who live in common must be affiliated by the superior general of the first order to his own religion.

The first condition calls for special emphasis, since the Holy See has more than once insisted on it. Thus Leo XIII, by his Constitution "*Conditae,*" Dec. 8, 1900, and Pius X by his Motu proprio, "*Dei providentis,*" July 16, 1906, have regulated the foundation and juridical character of religious congregations. The substance of their precepts is as follows:

a) Before applying to Rome, in fact before admitting any religious sodality into his diocese, the Bishop must examine its constitutions as to their orthodoxy and moral character, and satisfy himself that they conform to the sacred canons, the decrees of the Roman Pontiffs, and the scope intended. This examination must also extend to the founders,— whether or not they are inspired by prudent zeal for the glory of God and for their own spiritual welfare and that of others. Sometimes it happens that personal spite and rancor, or the itch for honors, or a desire to wear a different habit causes separation. *Probate spiritus.*

1Can. 323, § 1.

(b) If possible, rather than permit the foundation of a new congregation, the bishop should call in members of a *congregation already approved,* if its purpose is the same.

(c) The *purpose* or aim of the new congregation *must be well defined* and not too *diversified,* which would be the case if the congregation should propose to devote itself to all kinds of charitable works.[2]

The "*Conditae*" as well as the "*Normae*" give some examples of occupations which are less suitable to Sisters.

(α) Sisterhoods who make it their special purpose to *nurse the sick in their homes by day and by night* are not entirely forbidden, but liable to be rejected by Rome, unless very solid reasons are given and certain precautions provided. The same is true concerning sisterhoods who take daily care, as quasi-domestic servants, of the families of poor laborers.

(β) Sisterhoods who conduct *hospitals open to both sexes* indiscriminately, or houses destined exclusively for infirm priests, must also provide conditions and means apt to prevent danger and avert scandal. The Roman Congregation is even stricter with sisterhoods who have for their (secondary) purpose the *management* of *clerical seminaries* or colleges of male students, or schools wherein co-education is practiced.[3]

(γ) Much less, say the *Normae,* should sisterhoods be approved whose scope is to *take direct care of babies* or of *maternity homes* (confinement cases) or similar occupations not befitting "virgins consecrated to God." The Constitution "*Conditae*" does not mention such congre-

---

[2] "*Conditae,*" I, 3; an exception is made in favor of missionary countries; cfr. *Normae,* n. 8.

[3] "*Conditae,*" I, 3; *Normae,* n. 13 f.

gations, and the *Normae* say "*direct* care." Hence, if hospital sisters keep a special department for such purposes and leave the immediate care of babies and women, especially assisting at operations or delivery, to physicians and trained nurses, the law would not be against them.[4] Circumstances of time and persons, especially in industrial centers, would seem to require a moderation of the former strictness.

Concerning "*mixed schools*," many parish schools would have to be closed in our country if the *Normae* would be put into effect. Here, too, circumstances must be considered. Finally, it must be added that, not only in America, but the world over it is charitable works of every kind that enkindle the flame of faith, attract non-Catholics, and confound bigots.

(d) Before approving any new congregation the bishops must also inquire into the *material and financial support* of these communities. The "*Conditae*" as well as the *Normae* justly insist upon the old law [5] that no approbation should be given to institutes which lack the resources necessary for a decent livelihood. Congregations which *live on alms* or go begging from door to door are scarcely to be approved,[6]— a point which will be more accurately determined later.

These, then, are a few points which the bishops should ponder before giving their approbation to any institute, or applying to Rome for that of the Holy See. The other condition touches *tertiaries, i. e.,* congregations which purpose to follow the rule of an ancient order, but with modified constitutions and simple vows. Note that

4 Bastien-Lanslots, *l. c.*, p. 46.
5 Cfr. c. 1, X, III, 1; c. 1, X, III, 7; c. un., 6°, III, 16; *Trid.*, seas. 25, c. 3 de reg.
6 "*Conditae,*" I, 3; "*Singulari quidem,*" March 27, 1896; cfr. can. 621–624.

in new congregations no distinction between rules and constitutions is admitted, but all are comprised by the name Constitutions.[7] Yet, if Franciscan Tertiaries frame their Constitutions, they must be, at least substantially, based on the Rule of St. Francis, and we believe that this Rule, together with the Constitutions, may be called the Code of their common life. Of course, approbation is given only to the Constitutions, which remain the chief, and, in fact, the only obligatory norm for such Tertiaries. These must then be *affiliated,* as the Code says, or aggregated by the superior general to the first order, whose name and habit they assume. Hence of the three Franciscan families the three respective superiors general are competent to affiliate Tertiaries. Thus also the Dominican, the Augustinian, the Carmelite and the Servite Generals. But what of the *Benedictine Sisters?* There is a difficulty here, arising from the peculiar position of the Benedictine Order. The Abbot Primate has not the same power as one of the Generals of the Orders above named. Besides, history records that monasteries of nuns were affiliated to single monasteries, not to Congregations, except perhaps that of Cluny. The case was different with the Cistercians, because of the jurisdiction of the Abbot of Citeaux. Until an authentic solution of the difficulty is given, we are at a loss to state who is empowered to affiliate the Benedictine Tertiaries. Since Benedictine Oblates are incorporated in the individual abbeys, we believe that the neighboring abbot should see to it that the Tertiaries are incorporated. There is no difficulty in incorporating them because the *aim of affiliation,* even with the Tertiaries of centralized orders, is only to make them capable of *partaking* of the *indulgences* and spiritual favors granted to the first

7 S. C. EE. et RR., March 2, 1861 (Bizzarri, *l. c.,* p. 791).

order.[8]   There is, then, no question of juridical incor-
poration, as if the jurisdiction of the Diocesan Ordinary
would thereby be curtailed.   For, unless a special Apostolic indult grants them exemption, all Tertiaries are
under episcopal jurisdiction.[9]

Therefore § 2 rules that *any diocesan congregation,*
although spread over several dioceses, remains a diocesan
institute subject to the jurisdiction of the Ordinaries according to canon law, until it has received pontifical approbation or the decree of recognition.   The *episcopal
approval,* which is absolutely required in order to make
the institute lawful and ecclesiastical, has another effect,
viz., to subject the members to the jurisdiction of the Ordinary or Ordinaries [10] with regard to the internal and
external administration, the election of superiors, though
these be chosen by the members, canonical visitation,
spiritual direction and discipline.[11]   In fact such an institute is no more than a parish consisting of members who
partake of the religious state and are considered by canon
law as ecclesiastical persons endowed with clerical privileges.   But they are not to be called corporations, in the
ecclesiastical sense, as they lack autonomy or independence.   Of course, civil law may give them corporative
character and class them among privileged societies.

The text says, furthermore, that if these diocesan institutions are spread over more than one diocese, the respective *Ordinaries* enjoy equal jurisdiction over them.
Hence no Ordinary may claim jurisdiction or direction
over houses in another diocese, because this would be
tantamount to reaching into the sphere of another bishop;

---

8 " *Normae,*" n. 16.

9 Some exemption was given to
the Sisters of the Holy Cross at
Ingenbohl in Switzerland.

10 Cfr. can. 495.

11 " *Conditae,*" I, 9–11.

nor is the bishop of the diocese in which the mother-house is situated, to be considered the quasi-spiritual director of the houses located in other dioceses.[12]

The last paragraph of our canon ordains that the *name and habit of a religious order* already established may not be assumed by persons who do not lawfully belong to said order, or by any religious order to be newly founded. A distinctive religious *habit* was certainly worn by the earliest religious, as historical documents prove. For the terms *velamen* and *velare* (*veil, to veil*) occur as early as the third century and were used for the act of consecrating virgins.[13] That the veil was given in church may be surmised from the fourth Council of Toledo (633). The tenth council of the same city (656) mentions, besides the dress given by the bishop or clergy-man, also a red or black cloth (*pallium*) worn on the head as a mark of distinction.[14] The religious habit was given by St. Francis to St. Clare. As to *monks*, it is known that St. Benedict in his rule speaks of the religious habit.[15] But even before that time a distinct religious habit was worn by Pammachius.[16] The synod of Gangrae (334) complains of the Eustathians (an Arian sect), for despising the common dress and wearing instead the *periboleion*, or mantle of the monks, in order to deceive the unwary.[17] Thus the religious habit appears of venerable antiquity. In the eighth and ninth centuries abuses crept into the monastic bodies,— a fact deplored and rebuked by St. Odo of Cluny.[18] St. Bede[19]

---

12 S. C. EE. et RR., March 23, 1860 (Bizzarri, *l. c.*, p. 778, and *passim*).

13 Cfr. Migne, 13, 1183; Bachofen, *Compendium Iuris Reg.*, p. 47.

14 Mansi, *Coll. Conc.*, X, 625 (can. 56); XI, 31 (can. 4).

15 *Reg.*, c. 58.

16 Cfr. above, p. 4 sq.

17 Can. 12; c. 15, Dist. 30.

18 *Vita Odonis*, III, 1; *Collatio*, II (Migne, 133, 75; 213).

19 *Hist. Eccl.*, IV, 25 (Migne, 95, 215 f.).

complains of fancy habits worn by English nuns. It seems that fashion played its part also in the later Middle Ages, for a well-known decretal of Clement V at the Council of Vienne determines the color (black, brown, and white) as well as the kind and measure of the religious habit, and admonishes the religious to be modest in their dress and to avoid costly vestments. A hood (*caputium*) and scapular are also mentioned, over which, the decretal says, the religious may wear an *almutium* or large cap of black cloth or fur. Monks as well as abbots and priors are allowed a cowl. Boots and shoes are also permitted.[20] A hat is not mentioned in the decretal, but we know that Benedict of Aniane (821) and later the Clunians allowed the monks to wear hats of felt or wool. The Clunians also insisted upon neatness and cleanliness.

The text then says that neither individuals nor new congregations may assume the habit of an established religious order to which they have no juridical relation. To permit this would be like letting a ship sail under a flag not its own, and would bring confusion into the Church. This danger is quite real.[21]

Here may also be inserted a few wise rules stated in the *Normae*.[22] Material, form, cut, and color of the habit should be in harmony with religious modesty and poverty. Gold or silver ornaments, except a cross or medal of silver, are not allowed, and the image on these crosses or medals, as well as their inscriptions, must be approved or at least tolerated by the Church. Silk dresses or other showy apparel which would cause talk

---

20 C. 1, § 1, Clem. III, 10 de statu monachorum.

21 When in Rome the author tried to count the different habits, but soon gave up the attempt as superhuman.

22 Nn. 66–70.

and ridicule must be entirely avoided. A distinction between the habit worn by the superior and the teaching or choir sisters, and between that of the latter and the habit worn by the lay sisters may be admitted, but the difference should not be so great that the habits make them appear as members of different congregations. This would be the case if the color were entirely different. A distinctive sign may be used in the habit of the professed sisters and that of the novices. The Constitutions which are sent to Rome should contain an accurate description of the habit. After the religious congregation has been approved or recognized, the habit may not be changed without the express permission of the S. C. Relig.

As to the *name* or title of new religious congregations, the "*Normae*" contain, besides the prohibition mentioned in the Code, some hints which may also find a place here. The title of an institute may be taken either from the attributes of God, or from the mysteries of our Holy Religion, or from the feasts of our Lord or His Blessed Mother or the Saints, or from the particular scope of the institute itself. For instance, Sisters of Divine Providence, Sisters of the Incarnation, Ladies of the Sacred Heart, Sisters of St. Joseph, School Sisters, etc. If the title or name of an existing congregation is taken, a characteristic addition must be made, for instance, Sisters of St. Francis of the Poor, or of St. Vincent de Paul of the Servants of the Poor. All titles should be simple, free from levity or sensationalism, and eschew reference to devotions not approved by the Holy See.

SUPPRESSION OF RELIGIOUS INSTITUTES

CAN. 493

Quaelibet religio etiam iuris dioecesani tantum, semel legitime condita, etiamsi unica domo constet, supprimi nequit nisi a Sancta Sede, cui etiam reservatur de bonis in casu statuere, semper tamen salva offerentium voluntate.

The first of the next three canons — all of which treat of the same subject, wherefore we connect canon 498 with the rest — has reference to the suppression of a religious congregation, or rather of a *religio* in general. Such a *religio*, lawfully established, though it may be only a diocesan institute and consist of but one house, may be *suppressed by the Holy See alone.* To the latter is also reserved the right of disposing of the property belonging to the suppressed *religio,* with due respect to the will of the donors.

The Code is undoubtedly somewhat stricter here than Leo XIII's "*Conditae,*" which permitted the bishops to suppress diocesan institutes. It is not difficult to see the reason for this stricter legislation. Joseph II, carrying out the teaching of Febronius, endeavored to "purify" the religious state, and his example has misled many others, so that Pius IX had to condemn the error that the civil government may suppress religious families at will,[28] and Leo XIII was compelled to raise his voice against the encroachments of France and Portugal. "The Church sighs, for besides being wounded in her vital rights, she also feels the drawback in her activity, which is developed by the concordant work of the secular and regular clergy; who touches these, touches the apple

---

28 "*Probe memineritis,*" Jan. 22, 1855; "*Cum saepe,*" July 26, 1855; *Syllabus,* n. 53.

of her eye." [24]　These reasons no doubt prompted Benedict XV to make the suppression of religious dependent on the Holy See, which ever protected and fostered them. If the *Apostolic See suppresses a religious institute*, it generally provides that the members who are in sacred orders be subject to the Ordinary, or permits them, if they so prefer, to choose another order or *religio*. But those who have no sacred orders, like the lay brothers, appear to be free from the obligations of the simple vows.[25]　As to the property of suppressed religious it is church and corporative property, and hence subject to the Holy See as the supreme administrator of all church property.　However, if the donors are still alive, their wishes must be respected.　The same is true if the donors are dead but have left special clauses in the legacy regarding the disposal of the property in such a case.　The Holy See will also take care that the members of the suppressed *religio* shall receive back their dowries, or an equivalent thereof.　But they can lay no claim to an equal share, as if they had been members of a stock company.　Neither may the Ordinary of the diocese demand a share, for the disposal of the whole rests with the Holy See.

On the *suppression of a religious house* the Code rules as follows:

Can. 498

Domus religiosa sive formata sive non formata, si ad religionem exemptam pertineat, supprimi nequit sine beneplacito apostolico; si ad Congregationem iuris pontificii non exemptam, supprimi potest a su-

---

[24] *Le Religiose Famiglie*, June 29, 1901 (*Analecta Eccl.*, 1901, IX), p. 281 f. (French text, *ibid.*, p. 283).

[25] We believe that this is the in-tention of the Holy See, who will mention that in the decree of suppression.

premo Moderatore, consentiente Ordinario loci; si ad Congregationem iuris dioecesani, sola Ordinarii loci auctoritate, audito Congregationis Moderatore, salvo praescripto can. 493, si de unica domo agatur, salvoque iure recursus in suspensivo ad Sedem Apostolicam.

This canon makes a distinction between a *religio* and a religious house. A religious house, be it one with at least six religious members (*formata*) or one with less than that number (*non formata*), if it belongs to an *exempt religio*, may not be suppressed without a papal indult.

This is the logical consequence of can. 497, § 1, which requires a papal indultt for the foundation.

If the house belongs to a *non-exempt papal institute*, it may be suppressed by the superior general of that congregation with the consent of the Ordinary. The latter has jurisdiction over both house and congregation, and is therefore interested in its suppression.

If a house belongs to a *diocesan institute,* and is not the only one of the congregation, the Ordinary himself may suppress it, after having heard the opinion of the superior of the congregation. Against this decision recourse may be had to the Apostolic See, but not *in suspensivo,* although Rome may reverse the decision of the Ordinary. The Holy See may suppress any house, even of exempt religious, without any reason, although we do not know of a case in which Rome proceeded arbitrarily. But the general rule holds good, because the Pope is the sovereign judge of his own actions in matters subject to him, and may suppress whole orders, as happened in the case of the Beguins and the Knights Templars.[26]

26 Cfr. c. un., 6°, III, 17; c. 1, *Clem.,* III, 11.

The Superior General needs the express consent (written or oral) of the Ordinary of the diocese, because, as was said, the latter is directly interested in the suppression, not only on account of his jurisdiction, but also by reason of the diminished service of God and the sacred ministry.

The Ordinary may suppress a house of a diocesan congregation, unless it be the sole house of that institute. In the latter case the matter belongs exclusively to the Holy See. The Ordinary in suppressing a house is not bound to the consent [27] of the Superior General of the congregation, but may proceed freely. Neither is the Ordinary of one diocese dependent on the consent of another in whose diocese the mother house is situated, for all Ordinaries have equal rights over diocesan congregations. However, an Ordinary should not suppress a religious congregation except for weighty reasons, suppression being an extreme measure. Such reasons would be, for instance, serious relaxation of religious discipline, abandonment or change of the purpose of the institute, financial troubles which could not otherwise be remedied, refusal to obey the common law as well as the injunctions of the Ordinary, etc.

It may be asked: What about the *inmates* of suppressed houses? The decisions of the Roman Court on this point may be summed up as follows:

(a) *Solemnly professed members* must, unless the papal Constitution of suppression has dispensed them, continue to observe their vows as well as they are able; if they can obtain admission into other houses of the same or some other *religio*, they are obliged to do so, if no dispensation from the vows has been granted either in

---

[27] "*Audito consilio*" means advice, not consent; cfr. can. 105, 1; "*Conditae*," I, 6.

general or in particular to those who asked for it.

(b) Members with *solemn vows,* who are in *sacred orders* and wish to remain in the diocese, may with the permission of the Ordinary take up their residence there and obtain incardination within six months from the date of suppression. They are subject to the Ordinary in virtue of obedience, and must, besides, observe their solemn vows, as far as their condition allows. This permission to stay in the diocese outside of a religious community is, of course, granted only by special indult, especially if the members of the suppressed institute cannot be gathered into other houses or if they do not wish to leave their native country.[28]

(c) Members of religious congregations with *simple vows,* we believe, are free from any obligation if the suppression was decreed by Rome. But if the suppression of one house was decreed either by the superior general with the consent of the Ordinary, or by the Ordinary of the diocese, where there is question of a diocesan institute, the members remain bound by their vows, especially that of chastity, from which they can be dispensed only by the S. C. of Rel., and therefore should seek other houses of the same institute, which must receive them.

If religious in sacred orders, *i. e.,* priests, after the suppression of their institute, remain in the diocese, the Ordinary may *compel* them to help in the sacred ministry, especially the care of souls.[29]

As to the vow of *poverty,* this remains in case of religious with solemn vows, and therefore their property

---

[28] Pius VI, Brief of April 13, 1782; S. Poenit., *Instructio* of June 28, 1866; *Declaratio* of April 18, 1867 and Sept. 12, 1872; S. C. EE. et RR., Aug. 15, 1861; S. C. super Statu Regul., Aug. 5, 1872; cfr. Piatus M., *l. c.,* I, 210 f.; Nervegna, *De Iure Practico Regul.,* 1900, p. 163; Bachofen, *Compendium Iuris Reg.,* p. 163.

[29] S. C. EE. et RR., July 30, 1881.

and whatever they may acquire after suppression, belongs to the order or congregation, unless the members have been secularized, or have obtained a dispensation from the Holy See to use their belongings for other purposes.[30] The vow of *obedience* also continues to bind the solemnly professed members of a suppressed institute, so far as their actual state permits them to observe it; but it may be transferred from the local to the immediate superior, provincial or general, to whose jurisdiction they are subject.[31] Therefore they also remain under the obligation of reciting the Breviary according to their own calendar and must follow the rite of their order if they say Mass in their own churches; elsewhere, of course, they have to follow the general rubrics.[32]

CHANGE OF PAPAL INSTITUTES

Can. 494

§ 1. Religionem pontificii iuris in provincias dividere, constitutas iam provincias coniungere vel aliter circumscribere, novas condere conditasve supprimere, monasteria sui iuris a monastica Congregatione separare et alii unire, ad unam pertinet Sedem Apostolicam.

§ 2. Exstincta provincia, de eius bonis statuere, salvis iustitiae legibus et fundatorum voluntate, spectat, nisi constitutiones aliud caveant, ad Capitulum generale vel, extra tempus Capituli, ad Moderatorem generalem cum suo Consilio.

By change of a religious institute is meant any alteration of the original or former condition of an order or

---

30 S. C. EE. et RR., Dec. 20, 1839; March 6, 1840; Piatus M., *l. c.*, I, 212.

31 S. C. EE. et RR., Aug. 5, 1872.

32 S. Poenit., April 18, 1867; Nervegna, *l. c.*

congregation. Our canon treats of such as have received the papal approbation or a decree of recognition. § 1 reserves to the Apostolic See the right of dividing such a *religio* into provinces, of amalgamating provinces, of changing their boundaries, of founding new provinces, of suppressing existing ones, and of severing one monastic congregation from, or uniting it to, another. Canonists, applying the Decretal [33] which prohibited the transfer and division of episcopal sees to Apostolic legates, deemed a papal indult necessary to effect a change in the existing order of a religious institute. Now this opinion is made law, and therefore any change of the kind set forth in the text is taken out of the hands of the general chapter and reserved to the Holy See.

However, § 2 allows the *general chapter* (unless the Constitutions should forbid the exercise of such power) to settle the property affairs of an extinguished province, with due regard to the rules of equity and the laws of foundation. If no general chapter is in session at the time of the change and settlement, the superior general with his council may take the necessary steps. *Equity* requires that the remaining property should be employed for purposes similar to that for which the province was founded, that the buildings should not be entirely alienate from their original object, and that the people should be recompensed for the loss they suffer by the departure of the religious. Equity also would seem to require that, if there remains a congregation or province of the same order or congregation in the country, this latter should first be benefited. This would no doubt coincide largely with the *will of the founders*. But, as has been said, the general chapter, or the superior gen-

---

[33] C. 4, X, I, 30, *de officio legati;* but the enactment of our canon is certainly new.

eral with his counsellors, is competent to decide that point. We believe the superior is dependent on the consent of his consultors, unless the Constitutions provide otherwise.

SPREAD OF DIOCESAN INSTITUTES

CAN. 495

§ 1. Congregatio religiosa iuris dioecesani in alia dioecesi domos constituere non potest, nisi consentiente utroque Ordinario, tum loci ubı est domus princeps, tum loci quo velit commigrare; Ordinarius autem loci unde excedit, consensum sine gravi causa ne deneget.

§ 2. Si ad dioeceses alias eam propagari accidat, nihil de ipsius legibus mutari liceat, nisi de consensu singulorum Ordinariorum quorum in dioecesibus aedes habeat, salvis iis quae, ad normam can. 492, § 1, Sedi Apostolicae fuere subiecta.

In order lawfully to found a house of a diocesan congregation the consent of both Ordinaries, *viz.*, that of the bishop in whose diocese the mother house is located, and that of the bishop in whose diocese the new house is to be founded, is required. However, the Ordinary of the diocese whence the foundation is made should not refuse his consent without a solid reason. Such a reason would be, *e. g.*, if in his prudent judgment either the members of the mother house were not sufficiently numerous to do justice to the work they wish to undertake in his diocese, *e. g.*, in schools or hospitals, or if the financial condition would not allow a division.

If new foundations are actually made in several dioceses, the respective Ordinaries in whose dioceses the houses are located are not allowed to change the constitutions of the congregation except by unanimous consent, and if the change involved is substantial, the Holy See must be consulted, for such a change is tantamount to founding a new congregation,— which right, according to can. 492, § 1, is reserved exclusively to the Holy See. This, at least, is our interpretation, and we believe, it is the only correct one. For it seems unnecessary to consult the Holy See, to which reference is made in § 2 of can. 495, regarding the foundation of a new house which is merely a branch of a diocesan congregation about whose foundation the Apostolic See has already been consulted, can. 492, § 2 mentioning congregations, not houses. Besides, there would be no distinction between congregations and houses if the foundation of both required papal consent, and this can. 495 would be entirely superfluous. However, if, as stated, *substantial changes*, especially such as affect the scope or government of an institute, are contemplated by the Ordinaries in whose respective dioceses houses of a diocesan congregation are to be erected, the Holy See must be consulted.

SUPPORT OF RELIGIOUS HOUSES

CAN. 496

Nulla religiosa domus erigatur, nisi iudicari prudenter possit vel ex reditibus propriis vel ex consuetis eleemosynis vel alio modo congruae sodalium habitationi et sustentationi provisum iri.

An early synod of Arles (813) enacted that no monastery or canonry should receive more members than could be decently supported from its revenues.[34] This law was renewed by the Decretals of Gregory IX, ex-

---

[34] Can. 8 (c. 1, X, III, 7).

tended to nuns by Bonitace VIII,[35] and adopted by the Council of Trent,[36] which ruled that no more religious should be admitted than could easily be maintained either from the revenues of property owned by the monastery or from the usual alms. This ruling was constantly upheld by the S. C. of Bishops and Regulars,[37] which always insisted that especially dowries should be invested in secure, stable, and remunerative goods, landed property, or securities.

Our canon provides that no religious house shall henceforth be founded unless there are good prospects and a sufficient guarantee that its members shall be decently lodged and supported either from some steady source of income, or from the usual alms, or from some other source. No exception is made and no distinction between exempt and non-exempt congregations, between mendicant and non-mendicant orders, between congregations of either sex. The canon simply says: " *nulla religiosa domus.*"

To the two traditional modes of income (revenues and alms) the Code adds a third by saying: *vel alio modo.* The income or revenues proper to a house are such as it owns in its own name (*reditus proprii*), and are stable and regular, whereas *alms* cannot be said to be property, especially since almsgiving is not prescribed by the virtue of justice.

Under the name revenues are comprised all kinds of regular income, such as movable and immovable property which renders fruits; shares and title deeds; civil or ecclesiastical pensions, capital as well as interest; legacies for perpetual masses; income from parochial and missionary work; dowries of nuns; tuition fees from

---

[35] C. un., § 1, 6°, III, 16.
[36] Sess. 25, c. 3, de reg.
[37] Bizzarri, *Collectanea*, p. 637, p. 644 f.

boarding and day scholars; royalties on books, patents, and copyrights. Manual stipends are not considered revenues, but alms, because they are neither regular nor dependable. Neither are the daily distributions among canons of a chapter regarded as revenues or *reditus*.[38]

What is the *other source* mentioned in the Code? Perhaps donations of a somewhat irregular and uncertain character, but still due for work done or by reason of a promise. Hospitals generally depend on such resources unless they are amply endowed; also orphanages, although these are more often maintained by alms, and sometimes by begging, if not beggary (chain letters, etc.), concerning which, as will be seen, the Code has laid down special rules. As to the *mendicant religious* who are acknowledged as such by the Church, their respective Constitutions will tell how far they are capable of possessing property, and to what extent they have to depend on alms.[39]

The Code further says that there should be good prospects and a reasonable guarantee that the religious will be decently supported. This judgment or verdict ("*prudenter iudicari possit*") must be given by the *bishop* in whose diocese the new house is to be founded. Hence he must investigate the material condition and prospects of the institute, and in order to obtain this information, study the character and scope of the institute. If the Congregation devotes itself to charitable works (schools, hospitals, etc.), or to the sacred ministry, its revenues may be regarded as assured. But if the members lead a contemplative life, to the exclusion of teaching and works of charity, its existence, especially in our

[38] Barbosa, *Tractatus Varii*, Appell. "reditus."
[39] Concerning the Friars Minor, see c. 3, 6°, V, 12; c. 1, Clem. V, 11; Richter, *Trid.*, p. 395 ff.; Reiffenstuel, III, 26, nn. 403, 435 ff.

country, is apt to be precarious, unless substantial donations are secured, or a sufficient fund is established, or sufficient dowries are demanded to guarantee support.

The bishop has also to consider the religious houses already existing in the city or town where a new house is to be erected. Concerning this point several constitutions have emanated from the Holy See which are still of practical value. The first point to be considered is whether the religious houses already existing are likely to be injured by the establishment of a new one. This is more likely in the case of such as live on alms, yet even in school and parish work and in charitable pursuits competition and rivalry may easily cripple an older institution. Therefore Clement VIII obliged Ordinaries to consult with the superiors of existing convents before giving permission for a new foundation.[40] Gregory XV commanded that the superiors and all others interested within a radius of 4000 paces of the new foundation should be consulted.[41] No exception was made in favor of any order, for while it is true that the houses of Mendicants are chiefly named in said Constitution, others are also mentioned. Neither are houses of female congregations exempt from these laws, especially now, after the Code is promulgated, as it simply says, " no religious house." The reasons are the same for both male and female institutes, as far as external works are concerned. Too many institutes within a limited space are, even now-a-days, not only a detriment to the material support one of the other, but a menace to the existence of religious institutes in general.

The Code lastly says that the law concerning sufficient

40 " *Quoniam*," July 23, 1603; Ferraris, *Prompta Bibliotheca, s. v.* " *Conventus*," art. I.

41 " *Cum alias*," Aug. 17, 1622 (Ferraris, *l. c.*).

provision has reference to both *habitation or dwelling place and support*. Hence the bishop, who is the first judge in the matter, must satisfy himself as to decent lodging. A decent lodging is one with which a man of modest aspirations, let us say of the middle class, would be content. The same may be said of material support. For not luxuries and dainties are to be sought in religious houses, but a moderate living, gauged by the amount and kind of work performed by the inmates, and the ordinary comforts to which a self-respecting human being is entitled. From this we may infer that if the new house to be established could live decently where older houses were suffering restrictions as to comfort, etc., this fact would be no reason for denying consent to the foundation. However, this consideration touches only the material aspect of the situation: peace and merit are factors that must also be reckoned with.

PERMISSION FOR FOUNDING A NEW RELIGIOUS HOUSE

CAN. 497

§ 1. Ad erigendam domum religiosam exemptam, sive formatam sive non formatam, aut monasterium monialium, aut in locis Sacrae Congregationi de Prop. Fide subiectis quamlibet religiosam domum, requiritur beneplacitum Sedis Apostolicae et Ordinarii loci consensus scriptis datus; secus, satis est Ordinarii venia.

§ 2. Constituendae novae domus permissio facultatem secumfert pro religionibus clericalibus habendi ecclesiam vel publicum oratorium domui adnexum, salvo praescripto can. 1162, § 4, et sacra ministeria peragendi, servatis de iure servandis: pro omnibus religionibus, pia opera exercendi religionis propria, salvis conditionibus in ipsa permissione appositis.

§ 3. Ut aedificentur et aperiantur schola, hospitium vel similis rationis aedes separata a domo etiam exempta, necessaria est et sufficit specialis Ordinarii scripta licentia.

§ 4. Ut constituta domus in alios usus convertatur, eaedem sollemnitates requiruntur de quibus in § 1, nisi agatur de conversione quae, salvis fundationis legibus, ad internum regimen et disciplinam religiosam dumtaxat referatur.

So far mention was made of the material requirements of a new foundation. Canon 497 further establishes the necessity of a *legal formality*, which consists in the consent of the proper authority.

1. To establish an *exempt religious house,* no matter whether it be *formata* (with at least six members) or *non-formata,* or whether it belong to regulars or nuns with solemn vows, a *papal indult* and the *written consent* of the *diocesan Ordinary* are required. The same requirements are demanded for the foundation of any house (whether exempt or not) in the territories subject to the S. C. Prop. Fide. For the foundation of a religious house which does not belong to exempt religious or nuns with solemn vows and which is not subject to the S. C. Prop. Fide, the permission of the Ordinary is sufficient. This decision definitively settles a controversy which existed among canonists [42] up to at least the publication of the Constitution, "*Romanos Pontifices*" of Leo XIII, May 8, 1881. Though the decretals [43] mention the Apostolic indult, it appeared to exclude or to supply the Ordinary's license. The Council of Trent [44] required only the Ordinary's consent. The decretals

---

[42] Cfr. Bouix, *De Iure Regul.,* 1857, I, 247 ff.; also Bizzarri, *l. c.,* p. 78.

[43] C. un., 6°, III, 17; c. un., 6°, III, 6.

[44] Sess. 25, c. 3, de reg.

were directly intended only for the Mendicants, and, as Bizzarri admits, there existed a controversy founded on no less an authority than Fagnani,[45] as to whether later papal constitutions were intended for the countries " beyond the Alps " (*ultra montes*). Benedict XIV was of the " opinion " that in as well outside of Italy both an Apostolic indult and the permission of the Ordinary were required. The controversy was settled for England by the above quoted constitution of Leo XIII, which was extended to our country in 1885, and has now entered the Code and consequently become binding everywhere. Hence a religious house in which members of an exempt order, or nuns with solemn vows, are to live habitually in common (be it called a monastery, or a convent, or an independent priory) if it conforms to the notion of a religious house, may no longer be founded without a papal indult and the written permission of the Ordinary. The same statement holds good concerning any religious house, whether exempt or not, to be founded in missionary territories subject to the Propaganda, which in 1901 demanded that all religious houses founded without such an indult should petition for a rectification of their status.[46]

Religious congregations, either of papal or of purely episcopal approbation, which are not subject to the S. C. Prop. Fide, need only the *permission,* written or oral, of the *Ordinary* in whose diocese they wish to found a new house. The reason for this difference undoubtedly lies in the exemption, which can be imparted only by the Holy See, and for houses subject to the S. C. Prop. Fide the reason must be sought, as a decree [47] of the same

---

45 *Comment.*, 1. III, tit. 7, cap. " *Non amplius,*" n. 55 ff.; Reiffen-stuel, III, 48, n. 38 f.

46 The S. C. Prop. Fide, Dec. 7, 1901 (*Analecta Eccl.*, X, 1902, p. 21) complained that Leo XIII's Constitution was not observed everywhere.

47 Dec. 7, 1901.

congregation insinuates, in the desire for an orderly and uniform regime.

§ 2 of canon 497 determines the *effect* and *consequence* of the legitimate permission, which carries with it (a) for all *clerical religious* the right to have a church or public oratory attached to their house and to exercise the sacred ministry, (b) for *all religious* the right to perform the pious works proper to them under the conditions laid down in the act of permission.

As to (a) the Code appends one special condition, *viz.*, that of obtaining another permission, *viz.*, from the Ordinary for building a church or public oratory.[48] It would follow that they need *two permissions* from the Ordinary: one for building a house, and another for building a church. This may at first sight seem to savor somewhat of bureaucracy or " red tape." It would be difficult to imagine a Benedictine community without a public oratory, and hence the permission for building a religious house of that order was always considered as including that of having a public oratory. However, the legislator probably felt that the parish organization might suffer from the multiplication of religious houses. Benedict XIV plainly hints at this obstacle, especially in cities,[49] but the chief obstacle he finds in the fact that the people are attracted by the celebrations held in the churches of religious orders and consequently often neglect to hear the word of God. Perhaps the great Pontiff had the Eternal City and Bologna in view. He also wished the hour of services in parish churches and the churches of religious to be so regulated that one should not interfere with the other. The Code therefore most reasonably prescribes that the special permission of the

---

48 Cf. can. 1162, § 4.
49 " *Etsi minime*," Feb. 7, 1742, § 15; *Id., Inst.*, 44; 105.

Ordinary be asked for the erection of churches by religious, thus enabling the bishop to regulate parish work so that it may not suffer from the building of churches and public oratories. The matter of financial support as well as the right of the parish priest to see his flock in his own church may have been another reason for demanding a special permission of the Ordinary.

The Code adds: *servatis de iure servandis,* which signifies, with due regard to that which is to be observed according to law. Hence religious are allowed to exercise the sacred ministry only in so far as it does not clash with the rights of others engaged in the same ministry. And here first of all the pastor's rights, as laid down in the Code,[50] are to be duly considered and respected. Note that the Code does not enumerate among the strict parochial rights the blessing of ashes on Ash Wednesday, and that of palms and candles,[51] nor has the parish priest any right to protest against or forbid religious saying low masses on feast-days before or at the same time he says *his* Mass.[52] The Code then establishes the right of *all religious* to pursue and exercise the pious works which they have assumed as their proper task. Therefore, if the Ordinary, when giving his permission, makes no restrictions (which he is at liberty to do) the religious may freely fulfill their obligations and pursue the end for which they were founded.

§ 3 contains a slight modification of Leo XIII's "*Romanos Pontifices.*" It declares that a special written permission of the Ordinary is required and suffices for building or opening a school or a hospice or similar building separate from a religious house, although the

50 Can. 462 f.
51 S. Rit. C., April 8, 1702 (*Decreta Authentica,* n. 2098).

52 S. Rit. C., April 21, 1635; March 23, 1641 (*ibid.*, nn. 620, 745), quoted also by Cardinal Gasparri.

latter may belong to exempt religious. Leo's above mentioned Constitution had commanded all religious to obtain the express permission of the Ordinary *and* of the Apostolic See for founding or opening a new college or school, but made a distinction between elementary or parish schools and colleges, which latter it exempted from the Ordinary's jurisdiction. Nevertheless in the next paragraph the same Constitution demanded the permission of both the Holy See and the Ordinary. The Code is satisfied with enjoining the latter's written special consent. *Special consent* here signifies one that is not included in the permission for building a religious house, but is directed explicitly to the school or hospice or similar building to be erected separately from the religious house. *Separated* seems to imply that the buildings mentioned must be distinct from the religious house, so that they are not under one roof with the latter, but form a distinct and independent entity, for instance, for fire insurance or taxation. How far they must be separated the Code does not explicitly state. They may be called separated or distinct even if connected by a covered hallway or corridor. But if a school were erected inside the monastery or convent walls there would be no separation, but simply a religious house, part of which is destined for a separate purpose. In this latter case the special permission of the Ordinary would not be needed.

What *school* means is quite evident and shall be further explained in Book III, Title 22, *De Scholis*. Here it may be noted that the Code does not distinguish between elementary schools, high schools, universities, etc., and hence all kinds of schools are included. *Hospitium* is taken from the Latin *hospes* (guest),[58] and therefore may mean a lodging-house for guests, or a hospice or

58 Du Cange, *Glossarium*, s. v. "*Hospitium*."

convent and refuge for travellers such as are kept by the canons of St. Maurice in Valais, Switzerland, on St. Gotthard and Great St. Bernard. But it may also mean a summer or health resort for religious, a mansion where they spend their vacation or sojourn for the sake of their health. These were the old *grangiae* [54] or country seats, villas which belonged to the religious and secular clergy as well as to laymen. Lastly by the name of hospice may also be understood a rural house inhabited by a lay brother who acts as superintendent or " farm boss " for the monastery. [55]

It may now be asked *why* the consent of the Ordinary is required for building or opening such houses. To answer this question is easy concerning schools, because the jurisdiction of the bishop extends to these and they are, moreover, institutions for the public welfare. But as to hospices a distinction was expected in favor of exempt religious, who are, however, expressly included in the text. [56] We may be permitted to observe that on the score of alienation exempt religious, with the exception of nuns and Sisters, are not bound to obtain the consent of the Ordinary. [57] Perhaps the reason for the law lies in the fact that hospices or similar buildings may have an oratory, for which, unless they are quasi-priories or dependencies of the main house, an Apostolic indult is needed, which is granted only after the bishop has inspected the chapel. [58] If a semi-public oratory is to be erected in such hospices the Ordinary's permission suf-

---

54 *Ibid., s. v. " Grangia."*

55 Piatus M., *Praelectiones Iuris Reg.*, II, p. 230.

56 Gasparri refers to *" Romanos Pontifices,"* but this constitution does not mention hospices.

57 Cfr. can. 534, Apostolic indult.

58 Benedict XIV, *" Magno cum*

animis," June 2, 1751, §§ 11, 18; can. 1195. The Jesuits have the privilege to erect private oratories in such hospices, if they are quasi-houses of their order and dedicated to divine worship; cfr. Piatus M., II, 231 (ed. 2).

fices.[59] In such cases, therefore, the intervention of the Ordinary is quite intelligible. But apart from the erection of a private or semi-public oratory in such hospices we fail to see the necessity of the Ordinary's permission; for such a house is neither a religious nor a sacred place.

§ 4 of can. 497 mentions the *formalities required for changing* a religious house, already established, into one devoted to a *different purpose*. They are the same as those prescribed in § 1 of the same canon: Apostolic indult and episcopal permission for exempt houses; the Ordinary's permission for other houses not subject to the S. C. Prop. Fide. The stress lies on *change*. What is the nature of the change that requires these formalities? A change may be local or material. No *local change* is here mentioned, which is somewhat surprising, since in the *"Romanos Pontifices"* a change from one place to another is made subject to the same formalities as are required for a new foundation. *Place* must be taken in the sense of a municipality, or at least township or parish; for a mere local change of site would not require the observance of these formalities.[60]

The text of the *"Romanos Pontifices,"* from which our Code is evidently taken, goes on to determine what *material change* in a religious house means. Such a change would take place if a school were converted into a church, a convent into a college or boarding school or hospital, and conversely. A change of this kind would fall under the regulations that require full solemnities, *viz.*, a papal indult and the written permission of the Ordinary, for it would be equivalent to a new foundation.[61] If the original destiny of the house is retained, and merely a secondary purpose added, for instance, a

59 Can. 1192.
60 Piatus M., *l. c.*, II, 279.
61 C. un., 6°, V, 6.

novitiate or junior department or house of studies for members of the congregation, the change would not transcend the purpose of the institute but be merely an act of administration and internal discipline requiring no formalities. If, on the other hand, the scope of the house should be widened, if, for instance, a school for interns or a scholasticate would be made a boarding school open to outsiders, the aforesaid formalities would have to be observed. The Code adds: *salvis fundationis legibus,* with due regard to the will of the founder, which means that if the house was endowed by a pious founder, his will must be respected, and a substantial change of its provisos would require the twofold permission of Pope and bishop, even though it would not exceed the limits of internal discipline. Of course, the last will must be in writing or at least testified to by two unimpeachable witnesses, else it is presumed that the founder has not laid down any specific conditions.

For can. 498 see *supra,* pp. 75 sqq.

TITLE X

CHAPTER I

SUPERIORS AND CHAPTERS

After dealing with the foundation and suppression of religious congregations and houses, the Code proceeds to treat of the organization or government of religious. Here, of course, no detailed enumeration of the different classes of superiors and their powers over the various institutes can be expected. Though the norms cover a wide range, they admit enough elbow space for the different constitutions, as far as these do not conflict with the new law. The superiors specially mentioned are: the Roman Pontiff, the Cardinal Protector, the Ordinary, the religious Superiors, the general Chapter and Counselors.

CAN. 499

THE ROMAN PONTIFF AND THE CARDINAL PROTECTOR

§ 1. Religiosi omnes, tanquam supremo Superiori, subduntur Romano Pontifici cui obedire tenentur etiam vi voti obedientiae.

§ 2. Cardinalis Protector cuiuslibet religionis, nisi aliud expresse cautum fuerit in peculiaribus casibus, iurisdictione in religionem aut in singulos sodales non pollet, nec potest se interiori disciplinae et bonorum administrationi immiscere, sed eius est tantummodo bonum religionis consilio et patrocinio promovere.

All religious are subject to the Roman Pontiff as their highest superior and must obey him also by virtue of the vow of obedience.

This general principle is based upon the ordinary, full, and universal power vested in the Pope, in virtue of which he is the *highest superior of all religious*.[1] This means that no religious order or congregation may lawfully exist without his sanction, even as human societies need the permission of higher authority for legal existence. Furthermore it implies that the papal ordinances and laws, as far as they touch religious, either in general as members of the Catholic Church and as a body, or in particular as single bodies, orders or congregations, must be complied with by all without exception. And this obedience must be offered to any and every legally elected pope, no matter what his personal qualities may be.[2]

But the same obedience is due also to the immediate *legal representatives of the Sovereign Pontiff*, and therefore religious must obey especially the S. Congregation of Religious and the tribunals of the Roman Court which are set up by papal authority, and also papal legates, if they have special faculties concerning exempt religious. Religious also owe obedience to general councils, and, during the vacancy of the Holy See, to the Cardinals who govern the Church in the meanwhile.

The *extent* of this *obedience* is partly personal, partly material. *Personally* it comprises all religious, exempt and not exempt, those with solemn and those with simple vows, as well as papal and diocesan institutes. For though the latter are only approved by the Ordinary, yet

---

[1] Sometimes the title "*abbas abbatum*" is given to the Pope to signify that he has jurisdiction even over abbots. In the XIIth century the abbots of Monte Cassino and Cluny contended for that title.

[2] Known is the attitude of Savonarola towards Alexander VI.

they would not belong to the religious state without at least an implied ratification by the highest superior of all religious. Hence no exception may be claimed by any religious. As to the *material extent* of this obedience a distinction must be made between that owing to the Pope as the supreme head of the Church, and that due to him in virtue of the vow of obedience.[3] The former reaches farther than the latter because the vow of obedience has its limits, as will be seen when we come to discuss the obligations arising from vows. In virtue of the *vow of obedience* religious are bound to obey the Pope as far as their rule and constitutions demand,[4] and no farther; for a religious has no intention to bind himself farther than the limits assigned by his rule and constitutions, wherefore he says: " According to that rule I promise," etc. The consequence is that where the rule stops, the vow of obedience also ceases, and even the Sovereign Pontiff cannot stretch it, because he himself has approved the rule or constitution. Hence the Pope could not, in virtue of the vow of obedience, command a religious to leave the order and accept secular dignities, or embrace the married state, or pass to a stricter or even a milder order,[5] although he has the power to dispense.

Nor could he, in virtue of the vow of obedience, command a Benedictine to pass from one congregation to another, because the vow of stability is made for the congregation, nay even (at least it was so in former times) for a particular monastery. Neither could the Pope command a member of the Minimi to accept the

3 Ferraria, *Prompta Bibliotheca,* s. v. "*Votum,*" art. II, n. 29; Bouix, *l. c.,* II, p. 434; Piatus M., I, 298; II, 367 (ed. 2).

4 Ferraris, *Prompta Bibliotheca,* s. v. *Votum,* art. II, n. 28.

5 Suarez, *De Statu Religioso,* l. 10, c. 10, nn. 1 ff.

mitigation of fasting, or force a Jesuit of the fourth
class of professed members to accept an ecclesiastical
dignity, because these have taken a special vow not to
accept dignities. But whatever is explicitly or implicitly
contained in rule and constitutions as falling under obedience to the religious superior, the Roman Pontiff is entitled to command in virtue of the vow of obedience.
*Still farther reaches his power as the supreme head of
the Church.* As such he may command any religious to
accept any ecclesiastical dignity or office for the utility or
necessity of the Church,[6] because the supreme jurisdiction in ecclesiastical matters rests with the Sovereign
Pontiff. Should any special vow be in the way of obeying the Pope's command, dispensation would be granted.
This, however, does not exclude the possibility and ad-
missibility of reverent remonstrances against acceptance.
As to civil or secular matters we do not believe that the
Pope should or would use his influence or power of command, because this sphere is not his. But in any matter
not against the rule or constitutions the religious must
obey the Pope in virtue of the vow of obedience.[7]

The next paragraph (§ 2) describes the *power* of the
Cardinal Protector. A Cardinal Protector is given to
every religious institute unless the Pope reserves the protectorate to himself. Leo XIII reserved to himself the
protectorate over the united Franciscans; Pius X over
the Benedictines. These are peculiar provisions which
entirely depend on the will of the Pope. Otherwise a
Cardinal Protector residing in Rome (*in curia*) is appointed for every religious order and congregation.
This custom was introduced by St. Francis of Assisi.

6 Suarez, *l. c.*, l. 11, c. 20, n. 21 f.
7 The Friars Minor have a special formula concerning obedience
to the Pope, but whether or not it
forms a special vow the authors
dispute. Cfr. Piatus M., I, 295
(ed. 2).

Bishops are not appointed for this office, in order that they may not assume authority over another diocese.[8] But the Cardinal Protectors appear to have usurped a jurisdiction over orders and congregations which prompted the Constitution of Innocent XII, "*Christi fidelium*," Feb. 16, 1694, which reduced the authority of the Cardinal Protector to a merely paternal and consultive one, forbidding him to interfere in official information, dispensations, favors and the execution of rescripts, all of which is directly communicated by the Roman Congregations to the respective religious superiors.[9] These laws have been embodied in the Code, which rules that the Cardinal Protector enjoys no jurisdiction over the religious as a body or over single members of the same and may not interfere with their internal discipline or administration of property. His duty consists merely in promoting the welfare of the congregation by his advice and protection. Of course the Pope may, for particular reasons, grant a certain amount of actual jurisdiction to a Cardinal Protector, as the Code says; but there are few cases that require such extraordinary interference, *e. g.*, serious trouble between the religious and the Ordinary, or relaxed discipline.

THE ORDINARY'S POWER

CAN. 500

§ 1. Subduntur quoque religiosi Ordinario loci, iis exceptis qui a Sede Apostolica exemptionis privilegium consecuti sunt, salva semper potestate quam ius etiam in eos locorum Ordinariis concedit.

§ 2. Moniales quae sub iurisdictione Superiorum

---

8 S. C. EE. et RR., Feb. 21, 1851 (Bizzarri, p. 590, n. 12).

9 S. C. EE. et RR., May 9, 1715 (Bizzarri, *l. c.*, p. 302 f.).

regularium ex praescripto constitutionum sunt, Ordinario loci subduntur tantum in casibus iure expressis.

§ 3. Nulla virorum religio sine speciali apostolico indulto potest sibi subditas habere religiosas Congregationes mulierum aut earum religiosarum curam et directionem retinere sibi specialiter commendatam.

After having determined the relation of the religious orders towards the Sovereign Pontiff and their respective Cardinal Protector, the Code regulates their relation to the Ordinary of the diocese. To him all religious of the diocese are subject, except those who have obtained the privilege of exemption from the Apostolic See, and these, too, in certain cases expressly provided by law.

The first paragraph states as a general principle that religious should by right be subject to the Ordinary of the diocese, because locally all religious belong to the diocesan organization. Of exemption, which in general means freedom from episcopal jurisdiction, enough has been said in the Introduction. Observe that the Code has done away with the Tridentine distinction between the Ordinary as such and the Ordinary as papal delegate, simply maintaining the right of the Ordinary. As to religious Congregations, the power of the Ordinary is more extended respecting diocesan institutes and less extended concerning papal institutes. The difference appears in the election of superiors, canonical visitation, administration of property, etc. Spiritual guidance and the administration of the Sacraments should not offer any great divergency.

As to *nuns, i. e.,* female orders with solemn vows, § 2 establishes that, if their constitutions subject them to the jurisdiction of regular superiors, they are withdrawn from the jurisdiction of the Ordinary, except in cases expressly stated in the Code. The only nuns of this class in the U. S., so far as we know, are those of five Visitation Convents, according to a decision of the S. Congregation of Bishops and Regulars in 1864,[10] which at the same time decreed that in all the monasteries to be afterwards erected the vows of these sisters should be simple only. We doubt very much whether the convents of the Visitation Sisters are actually exempt. They certainly are subject to the Ordinary, not to regular superiors. All other nuns in the U. S. take simple vows, unless otherwise decided by an Apostolic rescript.

The Code says, further, that *congregations of women* with simple vows may never, unless a special Apostolic indult is granted to that effect, be subjected to a religious order or congregation of men, nor is any such order or congregation allowed to retain the care and direction of such sisters as if specially entrusted to them. No male institute, exempt or not, may henceforth claim any jurisdiction, authority, or spiritual guidance over any sisterhood, for such power would curtail the bishop's rights and be tantamount to exemption. The Holy See has justly reserved to itself the appointment of such a spiritual director, and any jurisdictional or authoritative affiliation of a congregation of Sisters with a congregation of men is prohibited by common law and needs a special indult.[11]

Here it may not be amiss to mention what were called *double monasteries,* that is to say, religious communities of men and women living under the same rule and roof, or if not under the same roof, at least near together.

---

10 Bizzarri, *l. c.,* p. 735. The five convents are: Georgetown, Mobile, St. Louis (Kaskaskia), St. Aloysius (Frederick, Md.), and Baltimore.

11 S. C. EE. et RR., April 11, 1862 (Bizzarri, *l. c.,* p. 153 f.); "*Conditae,*" Dec. 8, 1900, I, 8: "In spiritual matters the congregations are subject to the bishops in whose dioceses they are established."

Ecclesiastical legislation opposed such institutes,[12] but notwithstanding we find double monasteries in France, England, and Germany. Whitby in England was a famous abbey ruled by Hilda, who enjoyed great fame.[13] In France Remirmont was a most renowned foundation, as was that of Robert d'Arbrissel ($+$ 1117), who subjected nuns and monks alike to the jurisdiction of an abbess.[14] Such institutes were, of course, possible only on a basis of strict discipline and complete separation of the sexes, and may be explained by the peculiar conditions existing under the feudal system. Not seldom they were founded by the abbess herself or her near relatives, and she was therefore looked upon as the proprietress or "lady" of the monastery.[15] The priests and clerics who supplied the spiritual wants of the nuns had to conform themselves to her "rule." Fountevrauld claimed to represent the beloved Disciple under the maternal guidance of the Blessed Virgin,— a rather mystic view. Benedict XIV seems surprised that the superioress of Fountevrauld should be exempt from the jurisdiction of the Ordinary, but he does not deny the fact.[16] Now-a-days it would hardly be advisable to found such monasteries. Only one affiliation, as stated under can. 492, § 1, is admissible, *viz.*, that of Tertiaries by the superior general of the first order, to enable them to participate in spiritual favors.

RELIGIOUS SUPERIORS

The Code now lays down some rules concerning the powers of religious superiors and chapters, their election and obligations.

12 Cc. 12, 23, C. 18, q. 2.
13 St. Bede, *Hist. Eccl.*, IV, 23 (Migne, 95, 209).
14 *Studien O. S. B.*, 1885, 2, 64 ff.
15 Cfr. Lingard, *Anglo-Saxon Church*, I, 194 f.
16 "*Quamvis iusto*," April 30, 1749, § 17.

CAN. 501

§ 1. Superiores et Capitula, ad normam constitutionum et iuris communis, potestatem habent dominativam in subditos; in religione autem clericali exempta, habent iurisdictionem ecclesiasticam tam pro foro interno, quam pro externo.

§ 2. Superioribus quibuslibet districte prohibetur quominus in causis ad S. Officium spectantibus se intromittant.

§ 3. Abbas Primas et Superior Congregationis monasticae non habent omnem potestatem et iurisdictionem quam ius commune tribuit Superioribus maioribus, sed eorum potestas et iurisdictio desumenda est ex propriis constitutionibus et ex peculiaribus Sanctae Sedis decretis, firmo praescripto can. 655, 1594, § 4.

A distinction is here made between domestic power and jurisdiction. The *domestic power* is granted to all superiors and Chapters over their subjects, but only in so far as their Constitutions and the common law permit; *ecclesiastical jurisdiction,* on the other hand, in the court of conscience as well as *in foro externo,* is possessed by the superiors of clerical exempt institutes only. Hence we have two kinds of superiors, namely (1) single persons and chapters; (2) such as are endowed with domestic power only, and such as enjoy jurisdiction proper.

1. *Single superiors* are either *maiores* or higher, or *inferiores,* lower or local. Among the *higher superiors* our Code enumerates the abbot primate, the abbot president of a monastic congregation, the abbot of an independent monastery, although the latter belongs to a mo-

nastic congregation, the superior general, the superior provincial and the latter's representatives, as well as those who enjoy a power similar to that of provincials. All these persons, if they belong to an exempt clerical order, are possessed of jurisdiction proper, and are therefore called *prelates*.[17] For a prelature is a dignity that combines precedence or preëminence — hence the name *prælatus*, from *praeferre*, to prefer — with jurisdiction. What jurisdiction means has been explained in the second volume of this work, to which we refer.[18] It implies public legislative, judiciary, and coercive power within certain limits. This is not the case with the *domestic power* (*potestas dominativa*), which consists in the authority of the superior to direct the members of a religious body to the end for which the institute was founded, and is therefore confined to the scope of the institute itself and limited by its constitutions and rules. This power is essential to any community for the reason that without authority no organization can attain its end. As S. Scripture says: "Where there is no governor, the people shall fall" (Prov. 11, 14). The extent, then, of the domestic power of the superiors is coterminous with the end of the institute as defined in its constitutions, and religious superiors are not at liberty to permit substantial deviations from the regular life.[19] To this right vested in the superiors corresponds the duty of *obedience* in the members, of which we shall treat under the heading of obligations.

This domestic power was for centuries the only one

17 Cfr. can. 488, 8; Suarez, *De Statu Rel.*, tr. VIII, l. II, c. 1, n. 1 ff. (ed. Paris, 1860, t. 16, pp. 77 ff.).

18 Can. 196; Suarez (*l. c.*, tr. VII, l. II, c. 18, n. 5, ed. Paris, 1859, t. 15, p. 218) says that the power of jurisdiction belongs to the power of the keys (*potestas clavium*); but so does the sacramental power, and yet it involves no jurisdiction proper.

19 *Trid.*, Sess. 25, c. 1, de reg.

religious superiors could wield. Gradually, especially
since the tenth and more largely since the eleventh century, there was added to it the power of jurisdiction,
which grew when certain orders attained exemption.
Hence, when St. Benedict speaks in his Rule [20] of excommunication, he means what we call monastic, not ecclesiastical excommunication, although the two are similar.

It remains to say something of *lower superiors*, for the
Code stops at the rank of provincials who are the last
in the series of higher (*maiores*) superiors. Are *guardians, conventual priors, rectors*, higher superiors? It appears that the affirmative opinion may safely be held.
Benedict XIV states that these are local superiors before ˙
whom trials concerning nullity of religious profession
must be instituted.[21] Besides they are in law looked
upon as dignitaries or at least such as may be appointed
legates.[22] Hence there seems to be little doubt that they
may be termed *superiors* in the sense of our Code. The
same may not be said of cloistral priors (*priores clau-
strales*), who do not fall under the category of dignitaries
(*in dignitate constituti*).[23]

The power of the superiors of exempt clerical religious orders is called *ordinary* because given in virtue of
their office. For the same reason the Code states that
these superiors are to be comprised under the name of
Ordinaries.[24] The jurisdiction of these superiors is
called *quasi-episcopal*, inasmuch as it extends to acts of
jurisdiction, though not all, proper to bishops.[25] The
Ordinary of the diocese has certain rights which these

---

20 *Reg.*, cc. 23 f.

21 " *Si datam*," March 4, 1748,
referred to by Gasparri, can. 488, 8.

22 C. 11, 6°, I, 3, *De Rescriptis;*
c. 2, Clem., I, 2; Piatus M., *l. c.,*
I, 493.

23 C. 2, Clem., I, 2; Reiffenstuel,
I, 29, n. 70 f.

24 Can. 198.

25 Suarez, *De Rel.*, tr. VIII, l. II,
c. 2, n. 14 (ed. Paris, 1860, t. 16,
p. 90 f.).

superiors must respect. Aside from this it is generally admitted that, as Pius V states, the religious superiors endowed with jurisdiction may exercise the same power over their subjects as the bishops over the clergy and faithful.[26] Hence when the Code speaks of "*Ordinarius*," without the addition "*loci*" (diocesan), the religious superiors are included, unless the wording or context plainly excludes them.

Superiors of religious orders which are *not exempt* enjoy only domestic power within the limits of their respective constitutions. Therefore ecclesiastical censures, dispensations from ecclesiastical laws, absolution from reserved cases, etc., are not within the range of their power, for in such matters the members and superiors of non-exempt religious are subject to the Ordinary, who may, however, communicate the necessary faculties to the superiors.[27]

Besides the superiors there are the *chapters* (*capitula*) of the orders and congregations, which are assemblies held for the purpose of treating matters pertaining to the institute. St. Benedict already inculcated the necessity of calling together either the whole community, or at least the seniors, that the Scriptural injunction might be followed: "Do nothing without counsel; and thou shalt not repent when thou hast done" (Eccles. 32, 24). He might also have alleged the text, Proverbs 11, 14: "There is safety where there is much counsel." But after all was said and done the abbot decided. Only in elections the constitutional element appears. Later, with the changed position of abbots endowed with jurisdiction and often with feudal powers, the legislation of the

[26] "*Romani Pontificis*," July 21, 1571, § 3, which explicitly mentions the Dominican Priors. [27] Cfr. "*Conditae*," II.

Church bound them not only to the advice, but to the consent, of the monks.[28] The English Benedictines set a good example and thereby helped to frame "the great charter" of a constitutional monarchy which was absolutely necessary to counteract the almost frightfully increased power of the abbots. If the rule of St. Benedict is cited against us, we answer that no rule, and no law of human origin is destined to last the same forever. Besides, if the abbots have been endowed with prerogatives not even hinted at in the Rule of St. Benedict, it is difficult to understand why the monks should be denied development of their capitular rights.[29]

The Cistercians, therefore, and the great Mendicant Orders, riding the wave of the times, introduced into their constitutions the institution of chapters, which later were approved, nay insisted upon by the Fourth Lateran Council as well as by that of Trent.[30]

Chapters are either *general,* or *provincial,* or *local,* according as they meet from the whole order, or from a province, or from one convent. The *convocation* of a *chapter* belongs to the superior who is empowered to call it by the constitution of the order; for there is a variety of rules which we cannot detail here.[31] The same is true concerning the *subject matter* to be treated in chapters. The *manner of procedure* may be defined by the constitutions; if it is not, the common law (see canon 101) must be followed. Whatever requires the *consent* (*consensus*) of the chapter affects the validity of the acts which the superior performs, and he would therefore act validly if he neglected the chapter's rights. But

---

[28] Cfr. cc. 2, 3, 6, X, III, 10, touching chiefly English monasteries.

[29] Molitor, *Religiosi Iuris Capita Selecta,* 1909, *passim,* would have us go back 1400 years!

[30] C. 7, X, III, 35; tit. 16 in 6°; tit. 10 in Clem.; *Trid.,* sess. 25, cc. 1, 8, de reg.

[31] Cfr. Piatus M., *l. c.,* I, 613 ff. (2nd ed.).

if the law or constitutions demand only the advice (*consilium*) of the chapter, transactions made by the superior without calling the chapter are valid.[32]

The power of a *General Chapter* is *supreme* in the respective order or congregation, not including the monastic congregations which are mentioned in § 3. It extends to the election, punishment and deposition even of the superior general, to the enactment and repeal of laws and statutes, unless these have been specifically ratified by the Pope. But the General Chapter may not enact laws or rules against the common law or against the rule of the order, either by making it stricter or relaxing its tenor, although mitigations may be introduced with the approval of the Holy See.[33] The power here described in general terms may, of course, be enlarged or restricted by the constitutions, which depend upon the approbation of the Holy See.

The *Provincial Chapter,* broadly speaking (for as to specified faculties the respective constitutions must be consulted), may enact laws touching the province, elect and depose provincial superiors, restrict and abolish privileges granted for the province, but not such as are granted to the whole order or congregation.

The *Local Chapter* is convoked for the consideration of matters touching the local community, especially novices and other affairs of importance. The monastic chapters are of greater authority than those of centralized orders whose convents generally consist of but a few members.

The *rights* of single *capitulars* in any religion are, habitually at least, granted by the first (simple) profession, although they may not be exercised during the time

[32] Can. 105.   [33] Piatus M., *l. c.*, 616 ff,

of simple or temporary vows.[34] But the Code has, as it were purposely, abstained from determining a more precise date for the exercise of capitular rights, evidently in order to avoid controversies. There is question about the requisite of sacred orders for the exercise of capitular rights in clerical religious. We can find no law text [35] whatever which requires a higher order for the right of voting, unless the chapters in question would be cathedral or collegiate chapters. It would, however, not contravene any law of the Church were the constitutions to prescribe a sacred order as a necessary condition of exercising capitular rights.

As to those who are *deprived* of that right consult can. 167, which excludes from the right of voting all who are incapable of a human act, minors, and censured and infamous persons.[36] Under can. 639 f. all those who are either temporarily or forever secularized are deprived of capitular rights.[37] The Code further mentions as liable to be deprived of capitular rights those who violate the rules of common life in a serious manner.[38] Finally the *lay brothers (fratres conversi)* are not admitted to the chapter rights; for although they are religious, they do not, according to the common law of the Church, belong to the clerical or hierarchic order properly so-called.[39] Besides the law was doubtless made in order to prevent dissensions, which were not rare in former times, especially on the occasion of elections, and to exclude undue lay influence in purely ecclesiastical matters.

---

[34] Can. 578, § 3.

[35] C. 2, Clem., I, 6, mentions churches of canons (collegiate chapters); *Trid.*, sess., 22, c. 4, refers to cathedral and collegiate churches only.

[36] Cfr. also can. 2331, 2336, 2342, 2360, 2368, 2385.

[37] Can. 639 f.

[38] Can. 2389.

[39] C. 32, § 1, 6°, I, 6; Engel, I, 6, n. 5.

MATTERS PERTAINING TO THE HOLY OFFICE

Religious superiors, according to § 2 of can. 501, are strictly forbidden to handle or interfere with cases belonging to the Holy Office. Although the synod of Toulouse in 1229 had enjoined exempt abbots who were not subject to the Ordinary's jurisdiction to proceed like bishops against heretics and their protectors and promoters,[40] this injunction was, it seems, not conducive to the end for which the Inquisition had been instituted. Hence, especially after the Council of Trent, the *causae fidei*, or matters of faith, which fell under the jurisdiction of the Holy Office, were exclusively assigned to the latter in places where it was able to exercise its power. But when heresy sprang up and spread far and wide, the bishops were the natural defenders of the faith and judges in such matters. Paul V excluded religious superiors from proceeding in matters strictly belonging to the Holy Office. [41] These matters are the following:

a) Whatever appertains to heresy and schism, as well as the persons (bishops, inquisitors) who proceed against these crimes, if they are impeded or disturbed in prosecuting the guilty;

b) Whatever savors of divination, witchcraft, sorcery, superstition, astrology, etc.;

c) Whatever touches the sacredness of the confessional; [42]

d) Persons, lay or clerical, who, though not priests, attempt to say Mass or hear confessions.

e) The Code adds another, *viz.*, religious who become

---

[40] Can. 2 (Hefele, *Concil.-Gesch.*, V, 873).

[41] "*Romanus Pontifex*," Sept. 1, 1606, § 2; H. O., May 15, 1901.

[42] Cfr. Santi-Leitner, *l. c.*, I, 31, n. 70; Bachofen, *Compendium Iuris Regul.*, 1903, p. 325; the sacredness of the confessional concerns *sollicitatio ad turpia* and refusal of absolution unless the name of the accomplice be revealed.

members of a Masonic sect or similar society must be denounced to the Holy Office.[43] These and similar matters, then, the religious superiors are not to prosecute, either criminally or judicially, by summoning witnesses or inflicting penalties, or in any way that would savor of inquisitorial procedure, but refer to the Holy Office if any proof is in their hands. They are not obliged to act on mere suspicion or rumor, because prudence and charity require an investigation; but they may administer fraternal correction or admonition. The culprits may be reported to the Ordinary or directly to the Holy Office.[44]

SUPERIORS OF MONASTIC CONGREGATIONS

These superiors, according to § 3, can. 501, have not the same power and jurisdiction as the higher superiors (*superiores maiores*), but only as much as they receive from their own constitutions and from special decrees of the Holy See. The same holds good also of the *Abbot Primate* of the Benedictine Order.

A special canon is devoted to the constitution of the Benedictines and their affiliated orders,— a deference for which these orders owe a debt to the sovereign legislator. To understand this the reader should consider that each Benedictine monastery deserving of that name is an autonomous or independent juridical person or corporation, whose head is from time immemorial called abbot (father). St. Benedict looked upon his communities as families over which the abbot was to rule with an authority similar to that of a Roman *paterfamilias*. He does not speak in his rule of an aggregation of the various monastic families, though it cannot be proved that the Benedictine Code excludes or condemns such amalgamation or confederation. To call the Cluniac Con-

---

[43] Can. 2336, § 2.   [44] H. O., May 15, 1901.

gregation or order, as it was styled, a distinct departure [45] from St. Benedict's rule seems to us a rather subjective judgment. And even granted — *dato, non concesso,*— that union in a stricter sense should be called a deviation from the primitive rule of St. Benedict, would it not be foolish to make even of a sacred Code a petrified thing impervious to any, even salutary changes, which do not touch the substance or nerve of the rule? Changed conditions require a change of rules. In England, France, Italy, and Germany, especially after the IVth Lateran Council,[46] congregations and chapters seem to have been a necessary requisite for maintaining discipline and order, as well as to exert influence in, and command the respect of, the outside world. It could not escape the farsighted Pope Leo XIII, who was so deeply interested in the Greek Union [47] and the Union of the Franciscans, that a closer confederation of the houses of the Order of St. Benedict would be productive of many advantages and benefits. With the coöperation of Cardinal Dusmet he succeeded in establishing a *" fraternal confederation of the Black Benedictines,"* over which he put an Abbot Primate, to be chosen for twelve years from any of the congregations. He resides in the College of St. Anselm in Rome, whose abbot with ordinary jurisdiction he is. But he has no jurisdiction over the single congregations or abbeys, or over the various abbots or members. No powers or rights are pointed out in the Apostolic brief [48]

45 Cfr. Alston in the *Cath. Encycl.,* IV, 73 f (*s. v.* " Cluny "); a more decisive deviation from the rule are temporary abbots. The author is correct insofar as the Cluniac system of priories was anything but Benedictine; but a union of abbeys is neither denounced nor recommended by the Rule.

46 C. 7, X, III, 35.

47 Cardinal V. Vanutelli reported to Leo XIII that the Benedictines would favorably impress the Orientals, and upon this report Leo XIII acted in supporting the new organization and reopening St. Anselm's College, Jan. 4, 1888.

48 " *Summum Semper,*" July 12, 1893: *Studien O. S. B.,* 1893, 454, 630 ff.

that created the new dignity, but some were granted in the
course of years by the Roman Court.[49]   Thus the Abbot
Primate may, leaving other faculties now dubious aside,
call the abbots presidents for a meeting in Rome at least
every six years.[50] But the decisions taken at such a
meeting are not to be considered laws for the order, for
no Order of St. Benedict, in the juridical sense, exists;
nor are the presidents entitled to make laws for the order,
or even for their congregations.

Chapters of each *congregation* are called by the presidents thereof, generally at stated times.   Those who
are to be present at the chapter are determined by the
Constitutions of each congregation, which greatly differ
from one another.   Thus the English Congregation admits the president, the actual abbots, the Cathedral Prior
of Newport, the delegates from single monasteries, the
procurator at the Roman Court, the master of the schools,
the assessor in judiciary matters and the inspector of the
temporalities.[51]   The American-Cassinese Congregation
calls abbots and independent priors as well as delegates.
The Swiss-American Congregation admits only abbots.[52]
The reason why these chapters enjoy no legislative power
for the congregation as such is because as long as a congregation is no juridically united body these authorities,
even under the presidency of one acting as abbot president, no matter how solemnly they may gather, are
merely single entities who represent their own communities, but not the whole congregation in the sense of an
ecclesiastical corporation.   We do not deny, however,

49 Cfr. *Annales O. S. B.,* 1908,
pp. 22, 46, 57; S. C. EE. et RR.,
Jan. 31, 1902; Dec. 2, 1906; Dec.
21, 1907; Pius X, May 30, 1908.
50 Such a meeting was held in
1907.

51 Leo XIII, " *Diu quidem,*" June
29, 1899 (*Bull. Cong. Ang. O. S. B.,*
1912, p. 125).
52 This is an anachronism, to be
removed like the *regium placet.*

that the Sovereign Pontiff could endow them with legislative power, in which case they would act as delegates of the Pope. The members of such chapters may propose and deliberate on matters of reform and regular discipline as well as mutual assistance and material support.[53] Precisely from this point of view it would be conducive to uniformity of discipline if not only abbots would be present at the so-called general chapters, but, according to the model of the English Congregation, also representatives of the communities with at least a consultive voice. The reason why our Benedictine Congregations, or at least most of them, are not a corporative unit is that profession, and especially the vow of stability, is made into the hands of the abbot, and is, at least intentionally, confined to the single monastery. Besides, although there may be a mutual promise of material help, yet the property of each monastery belongs to that monastery and not to the congregation as such. Whether two vital elements of the Benedictine "Order" should or may be changed, we leave to others to decide.

CAN. 502

Supremus religionis Moderator potestatem obtinet in omnes provincias, domos, sodales religionis, exercendam secundum constitutiones; alii Superiores ea gaudent intra fines sui muneris.

This canon enacts that the *superior general* is endowed with power over all the provinces, houses, and members of his institute within the limits of its constitutions, and that *other superiors* have as much power as their office requires.

The Constitution "*Conditae*" of Leo XIII had estab-

[53] Molitor, *l. c.*, p. 526; p. 339 ff.

lished the rule that the government of a religious congregation whose Constitutions are approved by the Holy See must not be tampered with by the Ordinary, but remains with the superiors, either general or local. Hence it empowered the supreme superiors to organize houses, to dismiss novices and professed members, etc., in accordance with the law as now set forth. But it also reserved to the Roman Pontiff the right to dispense from either temporary or perpetual vows.[54] How this is to be understood shall be explained under the title on *dismissal*. The *limitations* of the power granted to any superior, general or other, must be determined by the respective constitutions, which are supposed to be approved by the Holy See,— the supreme authority against which no inferior may act. It is not necessary to specify here because the different rights will be mentioned under various headings later. Only one point we will note. The domestic power includes the *right* of *punishing delinquent* members, but only in so far as no ecclesiastical censures or vindictive penalties are inflicted, because to mete out ecclesiastical penalties requires more than domestic power, *viz.*, jurisdiction. But from the infliction of a punishment which does not exceed the domestic authority of the superior no appeal in the proper sense can be made, although recourse may be had to a higher superior or to the S. Congregation of Religious.

CAN. 503

Superiores maiores in religionibus clericalibus exemptis possunt notarios constituere, sed tantum pro negotiis ecclesiasticis suae religionis.

Canon 503 grants the higher superiors of exempt cleri-

[54] " *Conditae*," II, 1 f.; Bastien-Lanslots, *l. c.*, p. 173.

cal orders the right of appointing *notaries* to act in ecclesiastical matters pertaining to their order. This, as history tells, is an ancient custom. Abbots chose their own notaries, who were recognized by the civil courts.[55] Under the new Code their office is purely ecclesiastical, and consists chiefly in keeping records, taking depositions, and authenticating documents.[56] Before they enter upon their office, notaries must take an oath to perform their functions faithfully. This oath is to be made into the hands of the superior who appointed them.[57] Such notaries may play an important role in ecclesiastical lawsuits, *e. g.*, such as concern the validity of the profession or expulsion of religious, also in cases of beatification and canonization, elections, the installation of religious superiors, etc.

QUALITIES OF SUPERIORS

CAN. 504

Firmis propriis cuiusvis religionis constitutionibus quae provectiorem aetatem aliaque potiora requisita exigant, ad munus Superioris maioris inhabiles sunt qui eandem religionem professi non sunt a decem saltem annis a prima professione computandis, non sunt ex legitimo matrimonio nati et annos quadraginta non expleverunt, si agatur de supremo religionis Moderatore aut de Antistita in monialium monasterio; annos triginta, si de aliis Superioribus maioribus.

This canon lays down the minimum *requirements* for the office of superior. (1) It leaves it to the respective constitutions of each institute to demand a higher age or

---

55 Reiffenstuel, II, 22, n. 260.
56 Authenticating relics would also belong to their office, but see can. 1283.
57 Can. 364.

more stringent requisites; (2) It rules that, to be elected higher superior, one must have been a member of the same institute for at least ten years from the date of his first or simple profession; (3) It demands that he must have been born of lawful wedlock; and (4) that the superior general of any religious institute and the superioress of nuns with solemn vows must have completed the *fortieth,* and every other superior the thirtieth year of age.

Concerning the first point note that while the religious constitutions may demand more extensive qualifications, they are not allowed to restrict the minimum determined by the Code; and hence all rules or constitutions contrary to canon 504 must be looked upon as abrogated.

The second point rules that the ten years during which one must have been a professed member of the religious institute of which he is to be elected superior are to be counted from the date of simple, not solemn, *profession,* that is to say from the date of that profession which is commonly made after the novitiate. Noteworthy is the phrase: "*the same institute.*" Clement V issued a decretal saying that the election of one who belongs to another *religio,* for instance, of a Franciscan as abbot of a Benedictine monastery, would be null and void.[58] The Code says "*religio,*" not congregation or province. From this point of view a religious of one monastic congregation of the same order may be validly elected abbot of a monastery of another congregation of the same order. However, a Cistercian could not legally be elected abbot of a monastery of Black Benedictines, because, though the original code of both is the same, yet they are justly called different orders.

The third requirement is *legitimate birth.* Various

[58] C. 1, Clem. I, 3, de electione.

councils, especially during the eleventh century, enacted
strict rules concerning such as were born out of lawful
wedlock; while admitting illegitimate children to religious profession, they excluded them from the higher
offices, especially prelacies.[59]   Sixtus V made still stricter
rules concerning such as were born from an incestuous
or a sacrilegious relation, entirely excluding them from
the religious state.[60]   A certain mitigation was introduced by the same pope by admitting such as were born
from parents between whom a legitimate marriage could
have existed at the time of birth, and who were legiti-
mated by the subsequent marriage of the parents.   The
whole question, therefore, falls rather under marriage
law, to which we refer.[61]

Of interest may also be that part of the declaratory
Constitution of Sixtus V which provides that among the
dignities from which religious of illegitimate birth are
debarred, are the following: provosts, abbots, priors
(conventual), guardians, *custodes*, provincials and generals.   The offices of professors (*lectores*), confessors,
doctors or masters of theology, preachers and rectors (of
seminaries) are not considered dignities.[62]

The last quality required in a superior is *age*.   The
Decretals [63] were somewhat less rigorous on this point
than is the Code, which extends the age limit, requiring
forty years for a superior general and thirty for all other
higher superiors, provincials, abbots, and local superiors.
This rule is just, for theory and practice, theological
knowledge and business abilities now-a-days require an
experience not necessary in former times.

59 C. 1, X, I, 17 (synod of Poit-
iers, 1078); Reg. Iuris 87 in 6°.

60 "*Cum de omnibus*," Dec. 1,
1587.

61 "*Ad Romanum spectat*," Oct.

21, 1588; cfr. can. 1015, 1114, 1116.

62 Bizzarri, *l. c.*, p. 845.

63 C. 43, 6°, I, 6 (abbess = 30
years); c. 1, Clem. III, 10, required
only twenty-five years for a prior.

Inhabiles means that the lack of one of these requirements constitutes a canonical impediment.

DURATION OF OFFICE

CAN. 505

Superiores maiores sint temporarii, nisi aliter ferant constitutiones; Superiores autem minores locales ne constituantur ad tempus ultra triennium; quo exacto, possunt ad idem munus iterum assumi, si constitutiones ita ferant, sed non tertio immodiate in eadem religiosa domo.

The text plainly betrays the preference of the legislator for temporary over permanent superiors. Unless the respective constitutions determine otherwise, the *higher superiors* should be elected for a *certain limited term*. As to *minor local superiors* the Code, setting aside the constitutions, simply rules that their term of office should not last more than three years, after the expiration of which they may be re-appointed for another term of the same length, provided the constitutions are not opposed to reëlection. But no one may serve three successive terms as superior of the same house.

The question whether it is *more expedient* to have temporary or permanent superiors is not without interest. That opinions upon it are divided is, we believe, due to more or less subjective prepossessions and perhaps to circumstances. It may be well to state the reasons for permanent superiors first. Superiors, like bishops, ought to be permanent, because permanency of tenure produces a stronger bond of charity between governor and governed. Besides, a perpetual superior is apt to take better care of his flock and to acquire experience which will benefit the subjects as well as the government itself.

Against perpetual superiors the following reasons are alleged: humility and zeal are promoted by short terms; experience teaches that temporary superiors do not repeat the mistakes of their predecessors. If the predecessor has been a bad or incapable ruler, the evil produced is neither so intensive nor so extensive, and can be more easily remedied. Corruption is not so apt to become rooted during a short regime. When perpetual superiors grow old, their government is also apt to grow old and rusty.[64] Lastly, favoritism does not grow so strong and pernicious under temporary superiors. It is not necessary to develop this argument further, but one thing is certain, *viz.*, that the Congregations of the Roman Court have never been in favor of perpetual superiors for *female* orders and congregations. In Italy they do not even allow abbesses to remain in office more than three years, or to be reëlected for a third term, unless there is "a strict necessity" and a unanimous vote of the Sisters.[65] As to the *Benedictines* it is known that, under their rule, abbots are elected for life, and the Code permits this custom, if enacted by the Constitutions,[66] to continue.

Minor local superiors are not henceforth allowed to hold office for more than six years. Who are these superiors? All who are inferior in rank and power to the "provincials and their vicars and all others who have the same powers as the provincials." Therefore, conventual priors, guardians, *custodes* and similar superiors, who enjoy the same power in their houses as provincials,

---

[64] Cfr. Piatus M., *l. c.*, I, 491 (ed. 2). An expedient for counteracting the evils attendant upon old age is the election of a coadjutor, as was done in several instances, in these latter years, in the O. S. B.

[65] There is a great number of decisions on this point in the regesta of the S. C. EE. et RR.

[66] The Cassinese Congregation had triennial abbots, the English Congregation elects its abbots for eight years.

do not fall under this prohibition.[67] But we do believe that all local superiors who are not endowed with jurisdiction but enjoy only domestic power, as in congregations of non-exempt religious, are affected by the law. Neither are superiors of diocesan institutes which have only one house exempt from the law of a triennial term. The mystic argument that a superior, like a mother, should not be removed from his family, has no juridical value.

ELECTION OF RELIGIOUS SUPERIORS

CAN. 506

§ 1. Antequam ad Superiorum maiorum electionem deveniatur in religionibus virorum, omnes et singuli e Capitulo iureiurando promittant se electuros quos secundum Deum eligendos esse existimaverint.

§ 2. In monasteriis monialium, comitiis eligendae Antistitae praesit, quin tamen clausuram ingrediatur, Ordinarius loci aut eius delegatus cum duobus sacerdotibus scrutatoribus, si moniales eidem subiectae sint; secus, Superior regularis; sed etiam hoc in casu Ordinarius tempestive moneri debet de die et hora electionis, cui potest una cum Superiore regulari per se ipse vel per alium assistere et, si assistat, praeesse.

§ 3. In scrutatores ne assumantur ipsarum monialium confessarii ordinarii.

§ 4. In mulierum Congregationibus electioni Antistae generalis praesideat per se vel per alium Ordinarius loci, in quo electio peragitur; cui, si agatur de Congregationibus iuris dioecesani, peractam electionem confirmare vel rescindere integrum est pro conscientiae officio.

67 Pius V, " Romani Pontificis," July 21, 1571; Sixtus V, "Ad Romanum spectat," Oct. 21, 1588.

Can. 507

§ 1. In electionibus quae a Capitulis fiunt, servetur ius commune de quo in can. 160–182, praeter cuiusque religionis constitutiones eidem non contrarias.

§ 2. Caveant omnes a directa vel indirecta suffragiorum procuratione tam pro seipsis quam pro aliis.

§ 3. Postulatio admitti potest solum in casu extraordinario et dummodo in constitutionibus non prohibeatur.

These two canons establish the regulations or laws to be observed in the election of superiors. We may say that can. 506 determines the preliminaries, whilst can. 507 governs the act of election.

§ 1 of can. 506 enjoins all the members of *religious institutes of men,* before they proceed to the election of higher superiors, *to take an oath* by which they promise to elect only such candidates as they think should, before God, be chosen. This oath was prescribed by Clement VIII, and reinforced so strongly by a decision of the S. C. Concilii,[68] that not a few authors regarded it as essential.[69] The Code cannot be construed as enjoining it under penalty of nullity of the election, though it imposes it as a most serious and grievous obligation, as is evident not only from the sacredness of the oath itself, but also from the importance of the business in hand.

The oath may be administered either by the presiding officer or by the notary of the religious institute shortly before the election takes place, and must be taken by " each and every member of the chapter." This term

---

68 " *Nullus omnino,*" July 25, 1599, § 23; S. C. C., Sept. 21, 1624, § 1.

69 Ferraris, *Prompta Bibliotheca,* s. v. " *Electio,*" IV, 7 ff.

would indicate that each has to take the oath singly, yet the electors would no doubt comply with the spirit of the law if all answered in a body, while one pronounced the formula of the oath.[70]   The holding up of three fingers of the right with the left hand on the breast is sufficient, whilst the formula is pronounced.

The Code then defines the *object* of *the oath*. This object is more precisely described in the constitution of Clement VIII, thus: to elect him whom, in conscience, they believe to be more righteous and more fit.   Our Code throughout uses the term "fit" (*idoneus*), not worthy (*dignus*).   Therefore it is left to the conviction of everyone of the electors to give his vote to the one whom he believes more fit to fill the office.   Fitness must be judged according to the qualities required by, and the obligations imposed on, the office under consideration. One quality should, according to St. Benedict's Rule, never be overlooked, *viz., discretion.*[71]

§§ 2 and 3 treat of the election of superiors in communities of *nuns* (*moniales*), that is, sisterhoods with solemn vows.   If they are subject to the Ordinary of the diocese, the latter or his delegate, with two priests as tellers, must be present at the election of the superioress, without, however, entering the enclosure.   If the nuns are subject to a *regular prelate,* he must be present, though also in this latter case the Ordinary of the diocese must be duly informed of the day and hour of the election, and may be present himself or by proxy at the election, together with the regular prelate, who must

---

70 The formula might read: "*Ego N. N., huius capituli membrum, promitto et iuro, me electurum quem secundum Deum eligendum esse existimo. Sic me Deus adiuvet (et haec sancta Dei evangelia)*" — these last words only if the Gospel is used.

71 Rule c. 64.   Piatus M., *l. c.*, I, 494, justly remarks that the physical, mental, and spiritual qualities should be considered conjointly.

cede the presidency to the bishop. The confessors in ordinary of the nuns may not be appointed tellers at such elections.

As already stated, there are only a few convents in this country to which this canon applies. Observe that the Ordinary or his delegate are not allowed to enter the enclosure, which is here intended to be the papal one; but they may watch the procedure at the grate of the church.

Neither the bishop, nor his chancellor, nor his vicar general, nor his delegate are entitled to gather or register the votes.[72] This right belongs to the two tellers, who, according to our Code, must be priests, but not regular confessors of the nuns. The same rule applies to the regular prelate who attends the election.[73] The votes must be deposited in a closed urn or box, which is to be opened by the prelate, bishop, or regular prelate, and the two tellers. The result is to be announced by the prelate. The same process must be repeated if the election was without result.

§ 4 rules that the Ordinary in whose diocese the election of a *superioress general of a woman's congregation* takes place, should assist thereat either himself or by a delegate. If the institute is a diocesan one, the Ordinary may ratify or nullify the election, according to his good pleasure and conscience. A distinction is here made between *papal* and *diocesan congregations of women*. At the election of a superior general of the first class the Ordinary in whose diocese the election is held, acts as delegate of the Holy See, and presides either himself or by proxy.[74] But he has no right to nullify the election

---

[72] S. C. EE. et RR., June 19, 1671; April, 1729 (Bizzarri, *l. c.*, p. 265 f.; p. 323 f.).

[73] *Trid.*, sess. 25, c. 6, de reg.;

Richter, *Trid.*, p. 409; S. C. Rel., Aug. 27, 1910 (*A. Ap. S.*, II, 732).

[74] Leo XIII, "*Conditae*," II, n. 1.

if it has been held according to common law and the constitutions of the order. If the Ordinary is accompanied
by one or two priests, these are not to act as tellers or
to meddle in the election, by insinuation or other means.
They are mere spectators. The election of tellers is the
first act of the chapter meeting. Besides two tellers or
scrutineers, there should also be chosen a secretary.[75]
The duties of the tellers consist, as explained in Vol. II
under can. 171, in collecting the votes, counting them,
and comparing their number with that of the persons
entitled to vote. If the number of votes is equal to
that of the voters, and no invalid ballot is found, the
votes deposited in the urn are opened and read before
the chapter. All these acts must be faithfully recorded
by the secretary, who, like the tellers, is bound by the
obligation of natural and official secrecy. The bishop
and his delegate may be present in the election room,
for the law of enclosure does not debar him.

Over *diocesan institutes* the Ordinary enjoys greater
power. Not only may he preside at the election of the
superioress, but he may nullify the election or reject the
person elected according to the dictates of his conscience.[76] After the third ballot, if no election has taken
place, the bishop may appoint anyone he chooses. This
right belongs to the Ordinary also in elections of papal
congregations.[77] The question may be asked whether
the *delegate* of the bishop may claim the same right as
the bishop himself if he were present. The answer is
affirmative if the Ordinary enjoined his delegate to act
for him without reservation, but negative if he has
reserved to himself the power of ratification or nullifica-
tion or made an exception in regard to a certain person,

75 " *Normae*," n. 226.　　　　77 Cfr. can. 101, § 1.
76 " *Conditae*," I, n. 9.

or posited a condition. For, on the one hand, the Ordinary has full power over diocesan congregations, and, on the other, the delegate acts as a *mandatarius*, who must stick to the terms of his mandate and is not allowed to transgress the limits of his commission. However, in elections performed in papal congregations, the bishop's delegate must, like the bishop himself, observe the regulations laid down in the Constitutions and is therefore not at liberty to ratify or nullify the election unless a substantial mistake was made. Neither are the bishop or his delegate entitled to take exception to any person elected if she enjoys the qualities prescribed by the common law and the constitutions of the institute.

The three paragraphs of can. 507 govern the *act of election*. The first refers to the rules laid down in can. 160–182. Whenever, therefore, a chapter is held for the purpose of an election, the rules referred to must be strictly obeyed, and the regulations in the constitutions of the respective religious congregation or order governing elections may be followed only in so far as they are not against canons 160–182. These, we believe, have been sufficiently explained in our Vol. II.

§ 2 is taken verbally from Clement VIII's "*Nullus omnino,*" which strictly forbids any *soliciting* or procuring of *votes*, either for oneself or for another, directly or indirectly. Direct solicitation consists in campaigning for a candidate by collecting votes or getting promises to the effect of having that person elected in preference to another. Indirect solicitation consists in secretly influencing the electors, by words, in writing, or by promises, insinuations, and favors, on behalf of a candidate. All such machinations are strictly prohibited. If direct, they may approach simony, *i. e.*, giving temporal things for a spiritual thing, such as the office of superior.

Altogether different from soliciting votes is the *tractatus praevius* or preliminary meeting, at which the merits or demerits of the candidates are freely and charitably discussed, in order to facilitate the election. This is not forbidden, and often produces good results, especially in a community of which many members live outside the convent and know but little of the qualities of the candidates and the needs of the congregation at large. But even in such preliminary meetings all pressure and solicitation must be avoided.

§ 3 mentions *postulation* as being admissible in an extraordinary case if the constitutions do not prohibit it. Concerning that point enough has been said under can. 179 ff. But attention must be drawn to the injunction of the Code that one who is not strictly eligible to office by reason of a canonical impediment may be postulated only in an *extraordinary case*. This means that, as a rule, an election should take place, and only if the candidate suffering from a canonical impediment is absolutely necessary for the welfare of the community, may he be postulated. In the petition that has to be sent to the S. Congregation of Religious asking for the privilege of postulation, the fact must be mentioned that the Constitutions prohibit postulation if this is the case. In such a case the suppression of the prohibition mentioned would invalidate the grant of the favor, because the legislator could not be supposed to know of the particular law, *i. e.,* the Constitutions, and therefore might not grant postulation if he knew. Therefore the reasons for postulation forbidden by the Constitutions and against the common law must be stronger than in the case of prohibition only against the common law.

Here again attention may be drawn to the strict definition of *postulation* and the canonical impediments set forth in can. 304. All confirm our view that the abbot of a Benedictine monastery may be elected but not postulated by another monastery of the same congregation. The reason why we restrict the statement to monasteries of the *same congregation* lies in the fact of *stability*, which, though primarily intended for the monastery, was occasionally extended to the congregation. Besides, since each congregation differs from all others in some point of discipline, it would not be advisable to elect an abbot from a different congregation, although the common law (can. 504) only speaks of profession in the same *religio*, and does not therefore exclude other congregations of the same order. The idea that there is a sort of mystic matrimony between the abbot and his monastery we reject absolutely, since it has no prop in the new Code, which rather favors temporary superiors.

RESIDENCE OF SUPERIORS

CAN. 508

In sua quisque domo Superiores commorentur nec ab eadem discedant, nisi ad normam constitutionum.

Religious superiors shall reside in their respective houses, which they are not allowed to leave except as far as the Constitutions permit.

This is the law of *residence* enjoined on superiors, not only of higher, but also of lower rank, because the canon mentions superiors in general. What it says concerning the *respective house* is to be understood of the office itself. Hence the general has to reside in the generalate, or if this is not accessible, in the house which serves as generalate (*casa generalizia,* in Italian). The provincial must reside in the house assigned to him as his habitual dwelling; the local superior, in the house of the local community, and so forth. A stricter rule is laid down, as we shall see presently, concerning enclosure.

The *obligation* of residence, grave as it is in general, varies according to the importance and requirements of the office. If it is true that a bishop's duties demand his personal residence in the diocese, it is perhaps not too much to say that a religious superior must exert his influence and authority within the community assigned to him, because a religious superior, too, is chosen in view of his personal qualities (*de industria personae*). Furthermore, a certain amount of enclosure or separation from the world and its affairs [78] is incumbent also on superiors. Lastly, the vow of stability, for instance, with the Benedictines, forbids frequent absence from the monastery, for one is not released from this vow by becoming a superior. Of course, if business or necessity or evident utility, or Christian charity, or the command of a higher superior call one away, he is justified in absenting himself, not only in the court of conscience but before the legislator as well, provided, of course, the respective Constitutions are properly observed.

DUTY OF INSTRUCTING THEIR SUBJECTS

CAN. 509

§ 1. Omnis Superior debet notitiam et exsecutionem decretorum Sanctae Sedis, quae religiosos respiciunt, suos inter subditos promovere.

§ 2. Curent Superiores locales:

1.° Ut saltem semel in anno, statis diebus, publice legantur propriae constitutiones, itemque decreta quae publice legenda Sancta Sedes praescribet;

---

[78] C. 1, § 5, Clem. III, 10, forbids the frequenting of princely courts, and § 7, *ibid.*, strictly enjoins residence in the place of office, unless for the sake of studies.

2.° Ut saltem bis in mense, firmo praescripto can. 565, § 2, christianae catechesis habeatur instructio pro conversis et familiaribus, audientium conditioni accommodata, et, praesertim in religionibus laicalibus, pia ad omnes de familia exhortatio.

Superiors should see to it that the decrees made by the Holy See for religious are made known to their subjects and carried into practice. For this purpose n. 1 of the following paragraph insists that at least once a year, on stated days, the Constitution be publicly read together with those decrees which the Holy See *shall* prescribe to be read.

This is a timely injunction, in concordance with Malachy 2, 7: " For the lips of the priest shall keep knowledge, and they shall seek the law at his mouth; because he is the angel [messenger] of the Lord of hosts." *Knowledge* presupposes study of the law, and especially of canon law, whilst *putting into effect* supposes knowledge and authority, or at least good will. The decrees referred to as more particularly touching religious, are those of the Holy Office concerning matters of faith,— all of which, as explained under can. 501, § 2, pertain to that Congregation; [79] the decree about the manifestation of conscience; [80] the decree on the *litterae testimoniales* before receiving novices,[81] etc. This rule was made by the S. Congregation of Religious, which enjoined seven decrees to be read publicly.[82] However, since these decrees are at least substantially embodied in the Code we

[79] S. O., May 15, 1901.

[80] " *Quemadmodum*," Dec. 17, 1890.

[81] S. C. super Statu Regul., " *Romani Pontificis*," Jan. 25, 1848.

[82] The S. C. Rel., July 3, 1910, mentions, besides those two: " *Singulari quidem*," March 27, 1896; " *Perpensis*," May 3, 1902; " *Sacra Tridentina*," Dec. 30, 1905; " *Praeter ea*," Sept. 1, 1909; " *Ecclesia Christi*," Sept. 7, 1909; " *Sanctissimum*," Jan. 4, 1910.

believe we are correct in stressing the future tense of n. 1, § 2. Hence, unless the reading of these old decrees is especially prescribed by the Constitutions, they need no longer be read publicly. But any decree which the Holy See shall in future order to be read, must be read publicly. It would, however, be in keeping with the spirit of our canon if the section of the Code dealing with religious would be frequently read in religious communities.

No. 2 of § 2 speaks of *catechetical instruction* to be given at least twice a month, in a manner adapted to their capacity, to the *laybrothers or sisters* and dependents (*familiares*) of every religious community, and in lay institutes a pious exhortation to all members of the family. The novices (see can. 565, § 2) should receive more frequent instruction. Observe that the canon does not insist on such conferences for clerical institutes, the reason evidently being that they are supposed to have been instructed before and trained in the principles of the spiritual life, and to live in a higher atmosphere. Too many conferences may easily become a burden to the *conferencier* as well as to the hearers. The legislator wisely tells the lecturer not to speak above the heads of the hearers. Some practical subjects are mentioned in a decree of the S. C. of Bishops and Regulars, *viz.:* mental prayer, choir service, examination of conscience, frequent confession, silence, chapter of faults, reading at table and from Holy Scripture, pastoral conferences, regular discipline, acquisition of solid virtues, and other spiritual exercises.[88]

88 Aug. 22, 1814 (Bizzarri, *l. c.*, p. 44 f.).

DUTY OF REPORTING TO THE HOLY SEE

Can. 510

Abbas Primas, Superior Congregationis monasticae et cuiusvis religionis iuris pontificii Moderator supremus debet quinto quoque anno vel saepius, si ita ferant constitutiones, relationem de statu religionis ad Sanctam Sedem per documentum mittere, subsignatum a se cum suo Consilio et, si agatur de Congregatione mulierum, etiam ab Ordinario loci in quo suprema Antistita cum suo Consilio residet.

The abbot primate, the superior of every monastic congregation, and the superior general of every pontifical institute must send every five years, or if the Constitution prescribes it, oftener, a written report on the status of his community to the Holy See. This report must be signed by the respective superior and his counsellors; and when the congregation is one of women, also by the Ordinary in whose diocese the general superioress with her counsel resides. This law, in its general form, is new, for the 1906 decree of the Congregation of Bishops and Regulars touched only religious with simple vows.[84] This same decree has appended an " Instruction," which contains ninety-three questions to be answered, somewhat like a questionnaire for exemption claimants. This instruction, however, cannot be simply extended to all religious, and it might be reasonably shortened. It contains a preamble and three parts: on persons, things (especially property), and discipline, on which a report was to be made every three years. Hence the insertion into our Code of the phrase: " or oftener," if the

---

[84] July 16, 1906 (*Annal. Eccl.*, 1906, t. XIV, p. 340 ff.); English text in Appendix to this volume.

Constitutions so determine. The Code says, "*per docu-mentum mittere*," to send a written statement, probably in order to preclude the pretext of taking a trip to the Eternal City. What was formerly demanded only of religious congregations, is now enjoined on all religious without distinction, except diocesan institutes, which are responsible only to the Ordinaries.

VISITATION

CAN. 511

Maiores religionum Superiores quos ad hoc munus constitutiones designant, temporibus in eisdem definitis, omnes domos sibi subiectas visitent per se, vel per alios, si fuerint legitime impediti.

CAN. 512

§ 1. Ordinarius loci per se vel per alium quinto quoque anno visitare debet:

1.° Singula monialium monasteria quae sibi vel Sedi Apostolicae immediate subiecta sunt;

2.° Singulas domos sive virorum sive mulierum Congregationis iuris dioecesani.

§ 2. Visitare quoque eodem tempore debet:

1.° Monasteria monialium, quae regularibus subduntur, circa ea quae ad clausurae legem spectant; imo etiam circa alia omnia, si Superior regularis ea a quinque annis non visitaverit;

2.° Singulas domos Congregationis clericalis iuris pontificii etiam exemptae, in iis quae pertinent ad ecclesiam, sacrarium, oratorium publicum, sedem ad sacramentum poenitentiae;

3.° Singulus domos Congregationis laicalis iuris pontificii non solum in iis, de quibus in superiore

numero, sed etiam in aliis, quae internam disciplinam
spectant, ad normam tamen can. 618, § 2, n. 2.

§ 3. Quod ad bonorum administrationem attinet,
serventur pra▪scripta can. 532–535.

Can. 513

§ 1. Visitator ius et officium habet interrogandi religiosos quos oportere iudicaverit et cognoscendi de iis
quae ad visitationem spectant; omnes autem religiosi
obligatione tenentur respondendi secundum veritatem,
nec Superioribus fas est quoquo modo eos ab hac obligatione avertere aut visitationis scopum aliter impedire.

§ 2. A decretis Visitatoris recursus datur in devo-
lutivo tantum, nisi Visitator ordine iudiciario proces-
serit.

These three canons establish, first and above all, the
duty of the religious superiors as to visitation, secondly,
the part assigned by law to the Ordinary concerning the
same business, and, lastly, the rights and duties implied
by visitation.

The fourth Lateran Council (1215) ordained that at
the general chapters visitors should be appointed, who
should be sent out in the name of the Holy See and correct whatever needed correction.[85] The Council of
Vienne (1311–1313) ruled that visitation should be made
every year by the Ordinaries or others of the monasteries
of nuns and opportune remedies employed against abuses
which seem to have crept in.[86] The Council of Trent
repeated the aforesaid canons and enjoined frequent
visitation upon all superiors, especially the heads of orders, who should also visit the monasteries called *com-*

---

[85] C. 7, X, III, 35.   [86] C. 2, Clem. III, 10.

mendae.[87] All these laws prove the importance of canonical visitation.

Can. 511 provides that the *higher superiors* of religious orders as well as congregations, whom the constitutions entrust with the office of visitors, should, at times stated in the constitutions, visit all the houses subject to them. If they are lawfully prevented from performing that office personally, they may send others in their stead. It is evident that here regular or ordinary visitors are intended, because they perform that task in virtue of their office. Besides these, there may be extraordinary visitors and visitations for certain special causes, which are made known to the visitors, or perhaps to the Apostolic See, which may send a visitor under the circumstances. Hence surprise visitations are possible.[88] As a rule, however, visitations are to be made at *stated times*, the determination of which is left to each institute.

The extent of the visit is indicated by the phrase *all houses,* in as far, namely, as they are subject to the superiors. For it may be that some houses are exempt from visitation, or at least from visitation by a certain superior. All such conditions should be determined by the rule and constitutions.

The Code permits the regularly appointed visitator, in case of a lawful impediment, to send a *substitute,* according to the well-known rule of Canon Law, "What one may do himself, he may do through another." [89] Note, however, that the delegate must follow the instructions of the *delegans,* and should the latter die before the delegate has begun his visitations, the delegation

87 Sess. 25, cc. 1, 8, 20, de reg.
88 The visit of the late Abbot-Primate of the Benedictines to America, in 1910–1911, was not a canonical visitation, nor had he been sent by the Holy See to our country for that purpose.
89 Reg. Iuris in 6°, 68, 72.

would cease unless it was given by the Constitutions. A visitation is supposed to have commenced after the reading of the letter of delegation to those who are to be visited.[90] For the rest, the delegate, unless something is especially excepted, enjoys the same power and has the same duties as the one who delegated him, as shall be seen in can. 513.

Under can. 512, § 1, the *Ordinary of the diocese* must, either himself or by delegate, every five years visit every convent of nuns in his diocese subject either to himself or immediately to the Holy See; also the houses of male and female diocesan congregations. The law gives full sway to the Ordinary over two kinds of institutes: *Nuns with solemn vows,* whose convents are subject either to the Ordinary himself or immediately to the Holy See, and *diocesan congregations* of both sexes. Concerning both no exception is made as to persons, places or things to be visited; and hence, as shall be seen in the following canon, they are subject to visitation in all respects. The only difference between the two kinds of religious, so far as episcopal visitation is concerned, lies in the fact that the convents of nuns with solemn vows are visited by the Ordinary as a delegate — *de iure* — of the Holy See, and the houses of diocesan congregations by the Ordinary in his own capacity. The effect is the same.

According to § 2 the bishop may also visit:

(1) The convents of nuns with solemn vows, which are subject to a regular superior, concerning the *enclosure* and everything else, if the regular superior has not made a canonical visitation for five years; for in this case the Ordinary is called upon to supply the negligence of the superior. As to the enclosure, the Ordinary is entitled to examine the communion-crate and the confes-

---

90 Piatus M., I, 638 (ed. 2).

sional-crate, the inner and outer walls of the enclosure, the interior choir, the dormitories, cells and other rooms under enclosure. The Ordinary should wear his rochette and mantellette, be accompanied by two priests, and proceed without the assistance of any religious. If the Ordinary visits a convent because of the neglect of the regular superior, he is entitled to ask any nun personally, inquire about the observance of the enclosure and the number of religious, alumnae, and servants, and require a statement of the temporal and financial affairs.[91]

(2) He may also visit the houses of *clerical papal congregations,* including those that enjoy exemption, but only in what pertains to the church, sacristy,[92] public oratory, and confessional. There may be doubt concerning the phrase: *sedem ad sacramentum poenitentiae* — the seat for sacramental confession. Is the singular number instead of the plural (*sedes*) purposely made use of? Benedict XIV, in "*Firmandis,*" speaks only of one confessional, namely, that reserved to the parish priest.[93] But this interpretation appears to us too formal. Probably the term "seat" is here to be taken as a synecdoche or metaphor expressing all the confessionals. For the rest we refer to what we have said under canon 344.

(3) The Ordinary should also visit the houses of the *lay institutes* with papal approbation, not only concerning the places mentioned under n. 2, but also concerning other matters which belong to the *internal discipline,* with due regard to can. 618, § 2, n. 2.

As to the administration of *temporal affairs,* especially property, the Ordinary must observe the rules enacted in can. 532–535, which make a distinction between con-

91 S. C. EE. et RR., Sept. 8, 1725 (Bizzarri, *l. c.,* p. 319 f.).

92 The Latin reads *sacrarium;* but is certainly not to be understood of the waste place for sacred things, but of the sacristy proper.

93 Nov. 6, 1744, § 7.

vents of nuns and monasteries of regulars, houses of papal institutes and of diocesan congregations. Note, however, that the bishop or Ordinary has no right to make any change in any point of discipline which is in accord with the constitutions approved by the Holy See, or the approbation of which is pending.

Can. 513 determines the *rights and duties of the canonical visitator,* which, according to § 1, are to ask any religious who he thinks should be asked, and to take cognizance of everything pertaining to a canonical visitation. On the other hand all religious are obliged to answer truthfully, and the superiors are not allowed to prevent them from fulfilling this obligation, or otherwise to impede the visitation. The *questions* which the visitor should chiefly ask, according to approved authors,[94] are the following:

(a) About the *regular discipline,* observance of vows, rules and constitutions, life in common and spiritual exercises in the choir and elsewhere, fast and abstinence, fraternal charity;

(b) Concerning the *duties to be performed by the superiors and officials,* teachers and employers towards their subjects and inferiors, about conferences and chapters of faults, schools and instruction, reading of the decrees prescribed, observance of laws and customary rubrics;

(c) *Regarding temporal affairs,* especially Mass obligations, founded and manual, property and debts, method of bookkeeping, alienation, etc.

The Code furthermore says that the visitator should *take cognizance* of everything pertaining to visitation. Though not explicitly stated in the Code, a distinction lies between visitators endowed with jurisdiction proper,

94 Cfr. Piatus M., I, 639 ff. (ed. 2).

such as Ordinairies and regular prelates, or exempt visitors, and visitators endowed with domestic power (*potestas dominativa*) only. The former may inflict censures, whereas the latter may not, but may deal out such penalties only as the constitutions permit; and these, since they are given for non-exempt religious, cannot include ecclesiastical censures. This distinction becomes important in the way of procedure, which may be either paternal (also called evangelical) [95] and judiciary or canonical, as is evident from § 2.

A visitator should proceed paternally and use the canonical remedies only in extraordinary cases, as, *e. g.,* when a religious has committed a crime that calls for juridical procedure. But procedure supposes a plaintiff and witnesses, or at least a strong opinion against the accused religious, and therefore the beginning of a trial, as shall be explained in the fourth book.

The next question arises as to the *obligation of answering truthfully* the questions of the visitator. This supposes, first and above all, that the visitator has been admitted. If he acts in an official capacity and is lawfully appointed, admission cannot be refused to him by the religious. The members of the community must answer his questions, each according to the dictates of his conscience, with a view to the common welfare. But what if the visitator should demand of a religious that he reveal the secret misdeeds of other religious? Is the one thus asked bound to obey? Our answer is negative, for the office of visitator is limited to the public welfare of the community, and, therefore, as long as transgressions are secret, the transgressor has a right to his good name also before the visitator.[96] Should a crime have been com-

---

95 Math. 18, 15; cf. Suarez, *De Rel.,* tr. X, l. 10, c. 8, n. 9 (Vol. 16, 1101 f.).

96 Suarez, *l. c.,* maintains the affirmative opinion, but this must be called entirely peculiar to the So-

mitted, which is liable to become notorious to the detriment and diffamation of the whole community, the revelation of that crime would be required by the common welfare. But transgressions which have been committed long ago, or have been remedied, or are known only by hearsay, or to the visitator only as an entrusted secret, are not to be manifested, even though the visitator should demand it.

The last clause of § 1 admonishes superiors not to deter their subjects from doing their duty at the time of visitation, and not to impede the latter. The text is plain enough. Superiors should not send religious away at the time of the visitation, or force them by threats to keep silence.

§ 2 of can. 513 says that *no appeal in suspensivo from the decrees of the visitator* is permissible, unless he has proceeded in a judiciary way. Reference is made to the Constitution of Benedict XIV, "*Ad militantis,*" of March 30, 1742, which rules that no inhibition, or what is here called recourse, may be had from decrees concerning divine worship and its due observance according to the sacred liturgy nor from decrees concerning the care of souls, the repair of churches, the administration of the sacraments in churches, the spiritual and temporal government of convents of nuns.[97] Therefore the decrees and corrections enjoined by the visitator must by all means be carried into effect. Should they prove irksome, or, what is worse, should they contradict the Constitutions and lawful customs of the congregation, recourse may be had to the S. C. of Religious. Sisters of papal congregations may appeal from the decrees of the Or-

ciety of Jesus; his quotations from sacred writers are to be taken for what they are worth. The natural law is above individual pious sentiments.

[97] *Bull.*, Prati, 1845, t. I, p. 164, nn. 6, 10, 19, 20.

dinary to the metropolitan or the Apostolic Delegate.

We add that the visitator, unless he foresees judiciary procedure, should not take anyone with him, either as secretary or counsellor, as the paternal way requires secrecy.[98]

PASTORAL DUTIES AND RIGHTS

CAN. 514

§ 1. In omni religione clericali ius et officium Superioribus est per se vel per alium aegrotis professis, novitiis, aliisve in religiosa domo diu noctuque degentibus causa famulatus aut educationis aut hospitii aut infirmae valetudinis, Eucharisticum Viaticum et extremam unctionem ministrandi.

§ 2. In monialium domo idem ius et officium habet ordinarius confessarius vel qui eius vices gerit.

§ 3. In alia religione laicali hoc ius et officium spectat ad parochum loci vel ad cappellanum quem Ordinarius parocho suffecerit ad normam can. 464, § 2.

§ 4. In funeribus servetur praescriptum can. 1221, 1230, § 5.

§ 1 says verbaily — the text is too important to brook paraphrastic translation —: " In every clerical institute the superiors have the right and duty to administer, either themselves or through another, the Eucharistic Viaticum and Extreme Unction to the sick professed members and novices and to others who dwell day and night in the religious house, either by reason of service, or education, or hospitality (*hospitii*) or sickness." This is a reasonable and welcome extension of the privileges granted to some orders [99] in favor of their dependents.

---

[98] Piatus M., I, 643 (ed. 2).
[99] For instance, to the Barna- bites; S. C. EE. et RR., July 21, 1848 (Bizzarri, *l. c.*, p. 563 f.).

(1) *All clerical* institutes (*i. e.*, orders or congregations), no matter whether exempt or non-exempt, whether of papal or diocesan institution, enjoy the right and have the duty of taking spiritual care of their *sick* members. This care devolves first and above all upon the superior, and, in case he is impeded, upon any one commissioned by him. Note that *only clerical institutes* are here intended, that is to say, orders and congregations whose members are mostly priests, or should be mostly priests by virtue of their constitutions, though, perhaps, in consequence of extraordinary conditions, for instance an epidemic, war, etc., the number of lay brothers is greater than that of priests.

(2) The *sick members* enumerated are of a twofold class: religious and others. The term *religious* comprises the novices, concerning whom no difficulty was ever raised. But the term *aliive* was not always understood in the same sense. These *others*, then, must dwell by *day and by night* in the religious house. By " day and by night " may signify habitual or protracted dwelling, or one day of twenty-four hours; however, "*diu*" (from *dies*) generally has the meaning of a protracted stay, *i. e.*, lasting more than one day, although we believe that in case of sickness the principle that " favors should be widely interpreted " may be applied here. The next term, "*religious house*," is doubtless to be taken as the entire premises or precincts which belong to a religious house, for it seems to stand for the well-known canonical expression "*intra septa*[1] *monasterii*," *i. e.*, within the walls or hedges of the monastery. Hence even a number or group of buildings may be understood as constituting " a religious house," so long as religious actually

[1] *Septa* is used by Cicero to designate the inclosure within which the Roman people voted in the assemblies (*comitia*).

possess and inhabit the buildings. Thus a hospital, hostelry, school, house for hired hands, workshops, etc., if they form part and parcel of a religious house, though distinct from it, may truly be said to be religious houses. However, these buildings must be within the precincts of the dwelling of the religious, else they would not fall under the category of religious houses, which are houses inhabited by religious. Therefore a distant farm house or villa, or a college or school entirely separated from the religious house and attended perhaps by only one religious, cannot be said to share the privileges of religious houses.

Religious houses, then, may shelter servants, students, guests or sick people. The first class, *servants — causa famulatus* — are those who work for the religious and live within the precincts of the monastery under the habitual (though not religious) obedience of the superiors.[2] Hence they must have board and lodging in the religious house, or at least in a building on the premises of the religious house, though they may truly be called hired hands. But if they have their lodging outside the religious house they may not be called servants. Another class who falls under the category of *familiares* or dependents is that of *boarding students,* who, together with their education, also receive board and lodging from the clerical institute. But day-scholars are excluded. The next category is that of *guests,* who live in the religious house habitually. Hence if a religious house would keep boarders, say, for instance, young Catholic men or students who work in shops or study at school, these would be living in a religious house.[3] Thus, also, if a pilgrims' house would be attached to a religious house, the

---

[2] S. C. EE. et RR., July 21, 1848 (Bizzarri, *Coll.,* p. 564 ff.).

[3] *Ibid.;* the case is identical with the one in the text.

guests would belong to the latter. We furthermore believe that also single guests who have come to visit some of their religious relatives or friends, and live in the religious house or guests' department (*foresteria*) at least for one full day, may be beneficiaries of our canon. The last class is that of *sick persons* who are cared for by the religious in their own house, no matter whether they are related to the religious or not. Of course, this would be all the more so if the religious should manage a hospital on their own premises. Workingmen employed by the monastery, who would not otherwise enjoy the privilege, if nursed in their sickness in a clerical religious house, would also be included.

(3) The sacraments to be administered are the *Sacred Viaticum* and *Extreme Unction*. These appertain to strictly parochial rights.[4] Confession and communion, the administration of which is not exclusively the pastor's right, needed no mention. This paragraph marks a decided but benevolent change from former restrictions.[5]

Can. 514, § 2 vindicates the same rights and duties to the *confessor of nuns* with solemn vows and his *locum tenens*. Therefore, should any of the foregoing classes of persons live in a monastery of nuns, the confessor or his representative may administer the last sacraments to him. Female servants, alumnae (the socalled *educande* [6] in Italian monasteries), female guests — the male sex is excluded in virtue of the inclosure,— and sick persons would have to be attended by the confessor, not by the parish priest in whose parish the convent is situated.[7]

---

4 Can. 462, 3.

5 Pius IX, "*Apostolicae Sedis*," 1869, II, 14.

6 A number of decisions in the *Regesta S. C. EE. et RR.* treat of these.

7 S. C. EE. et RR., May, 1788 (Bizzarri, *l. c.*, p. 348); two sisters were collecting for nuns but maintained by the same as their quasi-servants.

Note, however, that this is a privilege granted only to nuns with solemn vows.

§ 3 of the same canon says: in every other lay institute the same right and duty is incumbent on the pastor or the chaplain appointed by the Ordinary under can. 464, § 2.

Hence, in all *lay institutes* of religious, male or female,[8] the religious themselves as well as their servants, students, guests, and sick persons in their care, must by right be attended by the *pastor* in whose parish the institute is located. For, unless papal exemption can be proved, the parish priest is the pastor of such non-clerical and non-exempt religious. A difficulty might arise in our country from the fact of linguistic parish divisions. Where English and Italian or German speaking parishes overlap, who is the pastor? This depends, first and above all, upon the will of the founder or foundress, which should, if possible, be respected. Secondly, custom must be consulted, and, lastly, if these two factors are not sufficient to settle the question, the Ordinary should decide, so as to satisfy the needs of the community as well as the claim of the pastor.

However, as stated above, the Ordinary may, for just and weighty reasons, exempt any religious community from the jurisdiction of the pastor and subject it to its *own chaplain.* In that case the spiritual rights and duties mentioned in § 1, *viz.,* concerning the administration of the last sacraments, belong to the chaplain and the pastor may not interfere. Of course, prudence and justice require that the Ordinary notify the pastor of such quasi-exemption, in order to avoid unnecessary trouble.

8 The Salesian sisters employed in education had asked for exemption, but the S. C. EE. et RR., April 19, 1844 (Bizzarri, *l. c.,* p. 497), answered: not expedient.

Notice the beginning of the text: *lay* religious. After mentioning clerical orders and nuns with solemn vows, the legislator proceeds to lay religious, where there are no distinctions made as to exemption. This affects the Christian Brothers as well as the Brothers Hospitallers of St. John of God; for both are lay institutes. However the bishop may — and certainly the institutes named deserve that attention — give them their own chaplain.

§ 4 of canon 514 determines the sepulture of religious, which is fully treated under can. 1221 and can. 1230, § 5, but may here be briefly described as follows: The bodies of professed members and novices are to be carried into the church or chapel of the religious house, unless novices have chosen another church for their funeral; the right of accompanying the corpse to the church of burial belongs to the religious superior. Should any member die outside the religious house and so far away from it that the corpse could not easily be transported to the church of the religious, he shall be buried from the parish church where he died; but novices may choose any church they wish.

Servants, as described above, have the same privileges in regard to sepulture as novices, and may therefore be buried from the chapel of the religious or any other church they may select.

Sisters and novices of sisterhoods who die in the religious house should be carried by the Sisters to the threshold of the enclosure, and thence, if they are exempt from the pastor's jurisdiction, to the church of the religious house, where the chaplain shall perform the funeral rites. If they are not exempt from the pastor's jurisdiction, the pastor must conduct the funeral services from the entrance of the enclosure to the church and chapel, where he shall hold the exequies.

HONORARY TITLES DENIED TO RELIGIOUS

Can. 515

Prohibentur tituli dignitatum vel officiorum mere honorifici; soli, si id permittant constitutiones, tolerantur tituli officiorum maiorum, quibus religiosi in propria religione reapse functi sint.

Ambition is the root of many evils in the Church and a vice more contemptible in a religious than in any other person. Therefore our canon quite naturally forbids religious to accept any honorary titles of dignities and offices. However, if the Constitutions permit, they may retain the title of higher offices which they once held in their own institute. This precludes the assumption of the title of Monsignore by any religious. The privilege of pontificating does not entitle one to bear the name of *titular abbot* if the dignity of *abbot* was never really held by the claimant. As to the Franciscans Pius X decided that only ex-ministers and ex-procurators general are allowed to keep that title in the whole order, and the ex-provincials in their province, together with precedence and active and passive voice at the general or provincial chapter, respectively, but not at the meetings of the "definitores." [9]

COUNSELLORS AND PROCURATORS

Can. 516

§ 1. Supremus religionis aut monasticae Congregationis Moderator, Superior provincialis et localis saltem formatae domus habeant suos consiliarios, quorum

---

[9] " *Quo magis,*" Oct. 23, 1911 (*A. Ap. S.,* III, 560 f., n. VIII); such titles were sought for by hook and crook to share in the chapters and elections; S. C. EE. et RR., Feb. 8, 1718 (Bizzarri, *l. c.,* p. 305 f.).

consensum aut consilium exquirant ad normam constitionum et sacrorum canonum.

§ 2. Sint etiam pro administratione bonorum temporalium oeconomi: generalis qui religionis universae bona administret, provincialis qui provinciae, localis qui singularum domorum; qui omnes suo fungantur munere sub directione Superioris.

§ 3. Oeconomi generalis et provincialis munus gerere Superior ipse non potest; munus vero oeconomi localis, quamvis melius a munere Superioris distinguatur, componi tamen cum eo potest, si necessitas id exigat.

§ 4. Si de modo oeconomos eligendi constitutiones sileant, a Superiore maiore cum consensu sui Consilii eligantur.

§ 1 of can. 516 prescribes that the superior general of religious, and the president of a monastic congregation, the provincial and local superior of a canonically established house (*domus formata*), should have *counsellors*, whose consent or advice they should ask according to their constitutions and the prescriptions of the sacred canons. This was the wise counsel given by St. Benedict to abbots, and later entered as a law into the Decretals.[10]

A decree of 1909 made it imperative for all superiors to have counsellors, especially in financial matters.[11] This decree has partly been embodied in our Code, which, however, is not very explicit about the number or mode of electing the counsellors, although Cardinal Gasparri refers to that decree, which determines the number of counsellors as well as the manner of electing them. The counsellors should be at least four in number in com-

10 Reg. S. Ben., c. 3; lib. III, tit. 10, de his quae fiunt a praelato sine consensu capituli.

11 Cfr. *A. Ap. S.*, I, 696 f.

munities with twelve or more chapter members, and two in such as have a smaller number of capitulars. All of them should be elected by the chapter for three years. They give their vote by secret ballot, whenever a decisive (not a merely consultive) vote is required. Thus, according to the same decree, the local superior would be bound by their vote in making debts or assuming obligations to the amount of less than $200, the provincial in cases amounting to less than $1000. However, since the Code directly mentions the constitutions as a norm for establishing the necessity of obtaining the consent of the counsellors, these must also be looked to for guidance regarding the affairs and amounts for which such consent is required. But one thing is certain: counsellors there must be, and they should be chosen by the chapter, not by the superior alone; otherwise it would be illusory to require the vote of counsellors, who are supposed to represent the chapter, or convent, or province. For if the superior were allowed to choose three, and the chapter one, the superior would be able always to have his own way. And this is neither the intention of the law-giver nor the purpose of counsellors.

The most important affairs which demand the *consent* (not merely advice) of the counsellors, according to our Code, are:

(a) The appointment of an *administrator* or procurator (*oeconomus*) (Can. 516, § 4);

(b) The *alienation* of property (Can. 534, § 1);

(c) *Admission* to the novitiate or simple profession (Can. 575, § 2);

(d) The *dismissal* of a professed member (Can. 547, § 1; Can. 650, § 1).

§ 2 of can. 516 requires an *oeconomus* or administrator of temporal affairs (procurator) — one for the whole institute, one for the province, and one for each single house; all to perform their duties under the direction of the respective superiors.[12]

§ 3 says that the superior himself may not be general or provincial administrator at the same time, but that the offices of local superior and local administrator are compatible, if it is necessary to combine them.

§ 4 says that if the constitutions do not determine the mode of appointing the administrator, the latter must be chosen by the higher superior with the consent of the counsellors. The Council of Trent had ruled that the administration of the property of religious should be in the hands of officials who could be removed at will by the superior. However, if the administrator is chosen with the consent of the counsellors, it is, to say the least, becoming that they should also be consulted about that official's removal. Only a few Benedictine congregations appoint an administrator for the whole congregation, but a local procurator is chosen from among the community, according to the Holy Rule (can. 31), generally by the abbot, without whose command he may do nothing. Hence, though the constitutions be silent about the mode of appointing the procurator, the rule of the O. S. B. vindicates that right to the abbot; but the Code requires the coöperation, i. e., consent of the counsellors, and this ruling must be followed.

THE PROCURATOR GENERAL

CAN. 517

§ 1. Quaevis virorum religio iuris pontificii procuratorem generalem habeat, qui, secundum constitutio-

---

[12] Note that the procurator is not a superior, and hence subject to minor superiors.

nes designatus, negotia propriae religionis apud Sanctam Sedem pertractet.

§ 2. Antequam praescriptum in constitutionibus tempus exspiret, ne amoveatur, inconsulta Sede Apostolica.

Every papal congregation of men must have a procurator general, who is to be designated according to the constitutions, and must transact all business between the congregation and the Holy See.

The procurator general may not be removed from his office without the consent of the Holy See before his term determined in the constitutions has expired.

The S. Congregation of Bishops and Regulars by a decree approved by Pius VII, Aug. 22, 1814, ordained that all religious institutes which were not at all or inadequately represented in the Papal States, should have a procurator general residing in Rome.[13] Most of the older and more centralized orders had such an official for centuries. As to the Benedictines, single congregations, e. g., the Cassinese, the English, and that of Subiaco, maintained relations with Rome by means of a procurator general, and the right of each congregation to have its own procurator in Rome was not taken away when the abbot primate was created.[14]

---

13 " Ubi primum," Bizzarri, l. c., p. 42 f.

14 Leo XIII, " Summum semper," July 12, 1893, I.

CHAPTER II

CONFESSORS OF CLERICAL INSTITUTES

CAN. 518

§ 1. In singulis religionis clericalis domibus deputentur plures pro sodalium numero confessarii legitime approbati, cum potestate, si agatur de religione exempta, absolvendi etiam a casibus in religione reservatis.

§ 2. Superiores religiosi, potestatem audiendi confessiones habentes, possunt, servatis de iure servandis, confessiones audire subditorum, qui ab illis sponte sua ac motu proprio id petant, at sine gravi causa id per modum habitus ne agant.

§ 3. Caveant Superiores ne quem subditum aut ipsi per se aut per alium vi, metu, importunis suasionibus aliave ratione inducant ut peccata apud se confiteatur.

These three paragraphs treat of the appointment of confessors and of the faculties of superiors in houses of religious institutes of clerics.

§ 1 provides that in each house a number of confessors proportionate to the number of inmates should be appointed, duly approved, and endowed with the faculty of absolving from cases reserved in the religious order concerning exempt religious. Here *appointment* means nothing else but the designating of one as confessor. This is generally done after an examination, or at least a verification of the fitness of the person to be appointed. *Approval* signifies the grant of jurisdiction or faculty to hear confessions validly and licitly. This is an act of public jurisdiction (*in foro externo*), for although the faculty of hearing confessions belongs to the court of conscience, yet the granting of that faculty is a result of jurisdiction proper. Therefore approval can be given only by one who enjoys jurisdiction. Concerning *clerical exempt religious orders,* the superiors of the same are empowered to grant delegated jurisdiction or approval, not only to priests of their own order, but also to priests of the secular clergy or of another order. The superior of an *exempt lay congregation* may present a confessor to the Ordinary in whose diocese the house is located in order to obtain from him the necessary jurisdiction.[1] Hence in the former case the religious superior of exempt clerical religious grants, in the name of the Sovereign Pontiff, yet in virtue of his ordinary power, the delegated jurisdiction to those whom he deems fit, whereas in exempt lay congregations the jurisdiction is given by the Ordinary.

The *number of confessors* to be appointed should be in proportion to the number of religious whose confessions are to be heard. Clement VIII speaks of two, or three, or more, according to the number of religious.[2] The opinion of some authors, that to each confessor should be assigned a certain number of religious, so that they would be bound to confess to that one exclusively, is intolerable.[3]

The *members* who may confess to the confessors approved by the superior of clerical exempt religious are

---

[1] Can. 875. [3] Justly rejected by Piatus M.,
[2] "*Sanctissimus,*" May 26, 1593, I, 402 (ed. 2).
[3] 3.

those mentioned under can. 514, § 1, *viz.:* the religious, the novices, the servants, the students, the guests, and sick persons, provided the conditions set forth in said can. 514, § 1 are verified.[4]

The *superiors* who may grant delegated jurisdiction, or the faculty of hearing the confession of these members, are the higher superiors who enjoy jurisdiction *in foro externo;* therefore, the superior general of an exempt order, the provincial, and, in the case of monastic bodies, the abbot of each independent monastery.[5] Concerning conventual priors and guardians some authors doubted their jurisdiction or power of granting faculties, but the majority were on the affirmative side, and justly so; for the Constitution of Pius V, "*Romani Pontificis,*" expressly mentions the conventual priors as endowed with the same faculties as the Ordinaries with regard to absolution and dispensation.

Concerning *female religious* and novices of orders as well as of congregations, no matter whether they be otherwise subject to a regular prelate, the faculty of hearing their confessions is given by the *Ordinary alone* in whose diocese their house is located.[6]

Finally a word about *reserved cases* from which the confessors duly approved either by the religious superior or by the Ordinary may absolve. Clement VIII had permitted religious superiors, with the consent of their counsellors, to reserve certain cases, eleven in number.[7] Our Code[8] grants the same power to the superiors gen-

---

4 See can. 875.

5 The Abbot Primate and Abbots Presidents are not empowered to give faculties either for the order or for their respective congregation; neither may cloistral priors, except by subdelegation, grant such faculties, because this power is from the Pope and may therefore be subdelegated.

6 Can. 876.

7 "*Sanctissimus,*" May 26, 1593, § 3.

8 Can. 896.

eral and abbots with their counsellors' consent, with due regard to certain restrictions, as seen in can. 519. However, after having granted that power, the Code *restricts the number of reserved cases* to four. Therefore it seems evident that the legislator wishes to limit the eleven cases to not more than four, and these of the "most grievous and atrocious crimes of public character."[9] Consequently we hold that the religious superiors are now-a-days no longer entitled to reserve more and other cases than determined by the Code. An obligation of reserving cases has never been enjoined, neither is it stated in the Code, which, moreover, plainly says that any duly approved confessor can absolve from them without being bound to refer the case to the superior.

§ 2 states that religious superiors who have power to hear confessions, may, if asked by them spontaneously and of their own accord, hear the confessions of their *subjects,* but should do so only for grave reasons and not habitually; besides, they must observe the laws and regulations prescribed (*servatis de iure servandis*). But they should beware lest they, either themselves or by means of others, endeavor to induce any of their subjects to confess to them. This law, already insisted upon by Clement VIII,[10] the Code emphasizes anew.

What is meant by "*servatis de iure servandis*"? Nothing else but the observance of the rules laid down in the Code concerning the administration of penance,[11] because the superiors, too, are bound to the seal of confession and may make no use of what they know from confession for the government of their subjects in whatever shape or form.

9 Can. 897.
10 Clem. VIII, "*Sanctissimus,*" § 2; S. O., July 5, 1899.
11 Can. 885 ff.; can. 908 ff.

LIBERTY OF CONSCIENCE

CAN. 519

Firmis constitutionibus quae confessionem statis temporibus praecipiunt vel suadent apud determinatos confessarios peragendam, si religiosus, etiam exemptus, ad suae conscientiae quietem, confessarium adeat ab Ordinario loci approbatum, etsi inter designatos non recensitum, confessio revocato quolibet contrario privilegio, valida et licita est; et confessarius potest religiosum absolvere etiam a peccatis et censuris in religione reservatis.

This canon embodies a decree, first issued for Rome, and then extended to all religious,[12] which aroused the religious zeal or anger of some superiors who endeavored to move Pius X to withdraw it.[18] And yet it stands, and now appears in the Code. It says: "Without detriment to the constitutions which prescribe or advise confession to be made at stated times to appointed confessors, a religious, even an exempt one, may, to quiet his conscience, go to confession to a confessor approved by the Ordinary of the diocese, though this confessor be not one of those appointed for religious, and the confession thus made is valid and licit, every privilege to the contrary being hereby revoked; besides, said confessor (though not of the appointed ones) can absolve such a religious also from all sins and censures reserved in his order." This decree did away with restrictions — of very doubtful efficacy — concerning the obligation of confessing to a traveling companion or that of confess-

---

[12] Aug. 5, 1913; May 3, 1914; S. C. EE. et RR., July 4, 1862 (Bizzarri, l. c., p. 155).

[18] We were in Rome at that time and could give the name of a certain superior who approached the Pope.

ing to appointed confessors only. On the other hand, it leaves the regular discipline about usual confessors and confessions untouched. That part of the constitutions which regulates this point is still in force, unless they run counter to the present canon, in which case they are void. The *number of times* which the religious may choose to go to another than the appointed confessor is not determined. His conduct is conditioned simply and solely by the *state of his conscience*,— a purely subjective matter with which the religious superior has no right to interfere. Hence a religious may choose another confessor whenever and as often as he thinks it wholesome for his conscience. Religious are now treated like other Catholics and this so-called privilege is done away with — to the relief of consciences and to the avoidance of torture and other worse consequences.

But what about the cases reserved in the order or congregation to which the disturbed religious belongs? The Code does not prohibit such reservation,[14] as stated above; but the confessor chosen may absolve from reserved cases without any scruple or obligation to report to the religious superior, which report is always connected with the danger of breaking the seal of confession.

CONFESSORS OF SISTERS

The following canons treat of the confessor-in-ordinary of Sisters, of extraordinary confessors, of provisions in particular cases, of the qualities, appointment, duration of office of confessors and their removal from office. It may be safely said that these canons embody former Apostolic constitutions, and especially that most excellent one of Benedict XIV, " *Pastoralis curae*," of

14 Supposing, however, that their number does not exceed four.

Aug. 5, 1748, and it is to be hoped that these wise laws
will finally be carried into effect by every prelate everywhere.

THE ORDINARY CONFESSOR

CAN. 520

§ 1. Singulis religiosarum domibus unus dumtaxat
detur confessarius ordinarius, qui sacramentales confessiones universae communitatis excipiat, nisi propter
magnum ipsarum numerum vel aliam iustam causam
sit opus altero vel pluribus.

§ 2. Si qua religiosa, ad animi sui quietem, et ad
maiorem in via Dei progressum, aliquem specialem
confessarium vel moderatorem spiritualem postulet,
eum facile Ordinarius concedat; qui tamen invigilet ne
ex hac concessione abusus irrepant; quod si irrepserint,
eos caute et prudenter eliminet, salva conscientiae
libertate.

§ 1 of this canon says that only *one* confessor-in-ordinary should be appointed for each house of nuns (and
Sisters). He shall hear the confessions of the whole
community, unless because of too great a number or for
another just cause it is necessary to employ several confessors. The reason for appointing but one confessor
lies in the unity and uniformity of regular discipline and
spiritual guidance for religious women. It is exactly
the same reason for which only one pastor is appointed
for each parish. However, the number of persons to be
heard, or other reasons may make it advisable to appoint
one or more additional confessors, which the canon
promptly grants. Thus, *e. g.*, the S. Congregation of the
Council permitted the canons regular of Rimini to assign
a vice-confessor in cases of absence or sickness of the

ordinary confessor of nuns.[15] Note here and throughout the following canons, that no distinction is made
between nuns and Sisters; for the approbation depends in
all cases entirely upon the Ordinary.

§ 2. If any Sister, in order to quiet her conscience or
to progress more rapidly on the path of holiness, should
demand a special confessor or spiritual director, the
Ordinary should readily grant the request, but at the
same time see to it that no abuses arise, and if such
should spring up, he shall root them out cautiously and
prudently, duly safeguarding liberty of conscience. The
first clause of this paragraph is almost verbally taken
from the above-quoted Constitution of Benedict XIV,
who justly reproaches some religious superiors for acting
too severely towards Sisters. The Pontiff at the same
time lays down the prudent rule that the qualities of the
Sister as well as those of the confessor demanded should
be carefully examined, and if no reason for suspecting
either is to be discovered, the request may safely be
granted. Abuses would be a disturbance of the regular
discipline, extravagant expenses, a bad example, etc. But
a little inconvenience to the superiors or the portress or
the cook could not be styled an abuse.

CAN. 521

§ 1. Unicuique religiosarum communitati detur confessarius extraordinarius qui quater saltem in anno ad
domum religiosam accedat et cui omnes religiosae se
sistere debent, saltem benedictionem recepturae.

§ 2. Ordinarii locorum, in quibus religiosarum com-
munitates exsistunt, aliquot sacerdotes pro singulis
domibus designent, ad quos pro sacramento poeniten-

---

15 Richter, *Trid.*, sess. 25, c. 10, of course, needed also the appro-
de reg., p. 412 f.; this confessor, bation of the bishop.

tiae in casibus particularibus recurrere eae facile possint, quin necessarium sit ipsum Ordinarium toties
quoties adire.

§ 3. Si qua religiosa aliquem ex iis confessariis ex-
petat, nulli Antistitae liceat nec per se nec per alios,
neque directe neque indirecte, petitionis rationem inquirere, petitioni verbis aut factis refragari, aut quavis
ratione ostendere se id aegre ferre.

This canon grants an *extraordinary confessor* to every
religious community at least four times a year.[16]   To him
all the Sisters must present themselves, at least to receive
his blessing if they do not wish to confess.   This confessor, of course, like the ordinary one, must be approved by the Ordinary of the diocese, although he may
have been presented by the regular superior.   The Sisters
are not obliged to confess to the extraordinary confessor
if they do not wish; but they must present themselves in
order to receive his blessing.   This is also done for a special purpose, *viz.*, that they may not accuse either the
Ordinary or the superior of neglecting their duty with
regard to offering an opportunity for quieting their conscience.

But the lawgiver goes still further in § 2, calling upon
the Ordinary in whose diocese communities of Sisters
exist, to designate for each house several priests on whom
the Sisters may call for confession in particular cases.

The decree of Feb. 3, 1913, from which our text is
taken, says that these confessors should be designated
for each house.[17]   Now it may be asked whether confessors appointed, for instance, for the Sacred Heart
Convent, may validly hear confessions in the Precious

---

16 *Trid.*, sess. 25, c. 10, says *three*   17 *A. Ap. S.*, V, p. 63, 4.
times a year.

Blood Convent. That this question is not quite superfluous appears from a query put to the S. C. Concilii, thus: Whether the regular confessors who had been appointed and approved for hearing confessions of nuns of one monastery or for one time may be considered approved for hearing confessions of all monasteries and forever? The answer [18] was, "*Negative.*" However, we must pay attention to the term *designent* used in our canon. Hence the solution must be: If the Ordinary has granted general faculties [19] for hearing confessions of nuns or Sisters, and has not made a special condition or inserted a restrictive clause, the confessors appointed for the Sacred Heart Convent may validly hear confessions in the Precious Blood Convent, and vice versa. As to *licitness*, the answer depends partly on the will of the Ordinary, and partly on custom.

If a religious, says § 3, demands one of the aforesaid confessors, the superioress is not permitted, either directly or indirectly, either personally or through others, to inquire for the reason of the demand, or to refuse the petition either in word or deed, or to show herself displeased in any way. Neither the counsellors, nor the mistress of novices, nor any other official or third person is entitled to interfere in matters of conscience, either directly by demanding reasons for the petition, or indirectly by asking what the Sister may have done, where she was, who has spoken to her, who was in the parlor, etc., even by way of a joke. Nor may the superiors deny the petition by an evasive or downright refusal, or by sending her on an errand, or giving her work that would prevent the fulfilment of her wish. Neither should they shrug

18 S. C. C., June 7, 1755 (Richter, *Trid.*, p. 413).

19 This should be expressed in terms like these: *etiam ad monialium*, or better: *etiam ad omnium religiosarum confessiones audiendas.*

their shoulders or use uncharitable words, or "make a face" at the petitioner, or let her feel it afterwards, or ridicule or criticise her.

CAN. 522

Si, non obstante praescripto can. 520, 521, aliqua religiosa, ad suae conscientiae tranquillitatem, confessarium adeat ab Ordinario loci pro mulieribus approbatum, confessio in qualibet ecclesia vel oratorio etiam semi-publico peracta, valida et licita est, revocato quolibet contrario privilegio; neque Antistita id prohibere potest aut de ea re inquirere, ne indirecte quidem; et religiosae nihil Antistitae referre tenentur.

If notwithstanding the concessions made in can. 520 and 521, a Sister, to quiet her conscience, goes to a confessor approved by the Ordinary for hearing confessions of women, the confession thus made in any church or public or semi-public oratory is valid and licit, every privilege to the contrary being hereby revoked; neither is the superioress allowed to hinder such a one or make inquiries about the matter, even indirectly, nor are the Sisters obliged to report to the superioress.

The Roman congregations [20] had made allowance for secularized religious and for Sisters who because of their health or for other motives are compelled to confess outside the religious house. Such Sisters could go to confession to any priest who was approved for hearing confessions of both sexes (*pro utroque sexu*), although he had not been specially approved for hearing Sisters' confessions (*pro monialibus*). This decision was received into the decree of Feb. 3, 1913, which adopted the phrase "*pro utroque sexu.*" Our Code has another reading,

[20] S. C. EE. et RR., Aug. 22, 1852 (Bizzarri, *l. c.*, p. 129).

viz., "*pro mulieribus approbatum.*" In some countries, Belgium, France, and our own State of Louisiana, if we are not mistaken, the Ordinaries give special faculties for hearing women's confessions.[21] However, in most of our provinces there is no distinction made as to secular or lay persons concerning sex, but the formula generally reads: "*ad audiendas fidelium confessiones.*" Hence wherever the clause "*pro mulieribus approbatum*" is not in use, any confessor approved for hearing the confessions of the faithful of both sexes has the faculty of hearing the confessions of Sisters who come to a church or public or semi-public oratory.

Attention may be drawn to the term *religiosae,* nuns or Sisters. It stands to reason that a strictly cloistered nun is not allowed to leave the enclosure to go to confession. This is clearly expressed in the decree of 1913, which reads: "If it should happen that any nun or Sister would, for any reason, be outside her own religious house." Therefore a strictly cloistered nun could leave the convent only for such reasons as permit a departure from the conventual "*clausura.*" The admonition to the superioress is plain enough in the light of what has been said in the preceding canon.

CAN. 523

Religiosae omnes, cum graviter aegrotant, licet mortis periculum absit, quemlibet sacerdotem ad mulierum confessiones excipiendas approbatum, etsi non destinatum religiosis, arcessere possunt eique, perdurante gravi infirmitate, quoties voluerint, confiteri, nec Antistita potest eas sive directe sive indirecte prohibere.

21 Cfr. Innoc. XIII, "*Apostolici ministerii,*" May 23, 1723; Ballerini-Palmieri, *Opus Theol. Morale,* 1893, Vol. V, p. 286 f.

Any Sister who is seriously ill, though not in danger of death, may call any priest approved for hearing the confessions of women, though not especially appointed for Sisters, and confess to him as often as she desires during the duration of her illness, and the superioress may not forbid it, either directly or indirectly. This is a concession for all Sisters, whether cloistered or not, and is more extensive even than that granted by Benedict XIV, because he added that the sick Sister must be in danger of death. Concerning the distinction of approbation for women and for Sisters nothing else need be added except that the Ordinary is bound to explain or emphasize that distinction.

QUALITIES OF CONFESSORS

CAN. 524

§ 1. In munus confessarii religiosarum et ordinarii et extraordinarii deputentur sacerdotes, sive e clero saeculari, sive religiosi de Superiorum licentia, morum integritate ac prudentia praestantes; sint insuper annos nati quadraginta, nisi iusta causa, iudicio Ordinarii, aliud exigat, nullam potestatem in easdem religiosas in foro externo habentes.

§ 2. Confessarius ordinarius non potest renuntiari extraordinarius nec, praeter casus in can. 526 recensitos, rursus deputari ordinarius in eadem communitate, nisi post annum ab expleto munere; extraordinarius vero immediate ut ordinarius renuntiari potest.

§ 3. Confessarii religiosarum tum ordinarii tum extraordinarii interno vel externo communitatis regimini nullo modo sese immisceant.

As confessors-in-ordinary and confessors extraordinary the bishop should appoint priests either of the secular or regular clergy (the latter with the permission of their superiors) who are known for probity of life and prudence. They should be forty years of age unless in the Ordinary's judgment a just reason requires a departure from this rule. These confessors have no jurisdiction *in foro externo* over the religious. Benedict XIV required for both ordinary and extraordinary confessors [22] certain qualities which are now modified somewhat. Thus the Code makes no distinction between priests of the secular and the regular clergy. *Mature age* is required, unless circumstances such as a want of priests justify a suspension of that rule, in which case the lack of age must be supplied by good moral standing and prudence, which even age does not always guarantee. These confessors are warned to exercise no power or jurisdiction *in foro externo*, for instance, by censuring the religious or settling affairs or reserving cases which require an ecclesiastical trial.[28] Neither may they dispense in cases in which the pastors are empowered to dispense,[24] for this power, though given by law and belonging to the extra-judiciary court, requires jurisdiction *in foro externo*. This warning is or was opportune in convents of nuns subject to the regulars, who may have thought that their prelate, whom they represented, was endowed with such jurisdiction proper.

The ordinary confessor of a Sisters' community may not be appointed extraordinary confessor except a year after his term as ordinary confessor has expired; nor may the ordinary confessor be re-appointed for the same community until a year has elapsed (exceptions noted in

22 " *Demandatam*," Dec. 24, 1743, ¶ 24; " *Pastoralis curae*," " *Quamvis iusto*," April 30, 1749, ¶ 14.

28 Can. 893, ¶ 1.

24 Can. 1245, ¶ 1: dispensation

from servile work, fast and abstinence; of course the confessors may declare in single cases of single penitents that the law of fast, etc., does not bind.

can. 526) ; but the extraordinary confessor may be immediately installed as confessor-in-ordinary.

The confessors of Sisters, ordinary as well as extraordinary, *shall in no way meddle* in the internal or external government of the community. This canon should deter confessors from playing the " factotum " of the Sisters. The *internal regimen* means religious discipline, authority of the superiors, election of superiors and officials, order of the day and employment of Sisters in the various branches, schools, hospitals, etc. The *external government* comprises the relation of the Sisters to the Ordinary, the visitator, and the parish priest, their congregational business, administration of property, etc. All these things do not concern the confessor, who, however, if asked, is allowed to give advice.

APPOINTMENT OF CONFESSORS

CAN. 525

Si religiosarum domus Sedi Apostolicae immediate subiecta sit vel Ordinario loci, hic eligit sacerdotes a confessionibus tum ordinarios tum extraordinarios; si Superiori regulari, hic confessarios Ordinario praesentat, cuius est eosdem pro audiendis illarum monialium confessionibus approbare et Superioris negligentiam, si opus sit, supplere.

The Ordinary of the diocese appoints confessors-in-ordinary as well as extraordinary for such Sisters' houses as are either immediately subject to the Apostolic See or to the Ordinary himself. If the house is subject to a regular prelate, the latter presents the confessors to the Ordinary of the diocese, who grants the usual approbation (faculties) for hearing the confessions of the nuns, and also, if necessary, supplies the superior's negligence.

It is not necessary to explain this canon, because of nuns subject to a regular prelate there can scarcely be question among us. However, if there should be such houses, the negligence here mentioned must be that of granting an extraordinary confessor or of refusing to comply with can. 520, §2, and can. 521, 522, 523.

Benedict XIV mentions a special case, which, however, falls under the rubric, ": quieting of conscience," *viz.*, if a Sister should have a strong and almost invincible aversion against a regularly appointed confessor. In such cases, he says, the Ordinary may supply a confessor, and even allow the nun to have recourse to the S. Poenitentiaria.[25]

DURATION OF THE CONFESSOR'S OFFICE

CAN. 526

Religiosarum confessarius ordinarius suum munus ne exerceat ultra triennium; Ordinarius tamen eum ad secundum, imo etiam ad tertium triennium confirmare potest, si vel ob sacerdotum ad hoc officium idoneorum penuriam aliter providere nequeat, vel maior religiosarum pars, earum quoque quae in aliis negotiis ius non habent ferendi suffragium, in eiusdem confessarii confirmationem, per secreta suffragia, convenerit; dissentientibus tamen, si velint, aliter providendum est.

The rule is that no confessor of Sisters (nuns) shall hold this office for more than three years. However, the Ordinary may leave him in office for three and even six years longer, if (a) no other priest fit for the place is available, or (b) if the majority of the religious votes, by secret ballot, for the confirmation in office of the confessor; in which scrutiny also such religious may cast a

---

25 "*Pastoralis curae,*" (*Bull.*, II, p. 401 f.).

vote who would otherwise be excluded from voting. However, for those who vote against ratification provision should be made, if they demand it.

The limit, therefore, is nine years, beyond which term the Ordinary has no right to stretch the period of office. The regular term is three years, and only in two instances may this be protracted.

Concerning fitness, can. 524, § 1 must be consulted; it implies maturity of age, probity of life, and prudence.

But what is the Ordinary to do if a pastor is confessor of a religious house located in the country? If he does not wish to change the pastor after nine years, he has to appoint the neighboring priest as confessor, at least for one year, after which, according to can. 524, § 2, the pastor may again become confessor for another nine years.

What is said above concerning the *majority of votes* is to be understood of the absolute majority. Those who are entitled to vote are all the professed Sisters, though perhaps only in temporary vows, who would otherwise be prevented from voting, for instance, in business matters or at the election of a superior.[26]

How to provide for those who are opposed to the reinstatement of the confessor is, of course, a rather delicate matter. They must manifest their desire of having another confessor to the Ordinary, who shall send another priest, for a time at least, until the feeling of animosity has subsided.

REMOVAL OF CONFESSORS

Can. 527

Loci Ordinarius, ad normam can. 880, potest, gravem ob causam, religiosarum confessarium tam

26 Cfr. Bizzarri, *Collectanea*, p. 116; *Normae*, n. 217 ff.

ordinarium quam extraordinarium amovere, etiamsi monasterium regularibus subdatur et ipse sacerdos a confessionibus sit regularis, nec tenetur causam amotionis cuiquam significare, excepta Apostolica Sede, si ab ea requiratur; de amotione autem debet Superiorem regularem monere, si moniales regularibus subdantur.

This canon is modelled upon can. 454, § 5, and must be combined with can. 880. The Ordinary of the diocese may, for weighty reason, remove a Sisters' confessor, ordinary or extraordinary, even though the convent be subject to regulars and the confessor be one of the regulars. The bishop is not bound to state the reason for removal to any one except the Apostolic See, upon demand; but he must inform the regular superior to whom the nuns are subject.

Though the canon, as it sounds, is new law, yet the bishop could formerly remove a confessor of nuns subject to regulars if the latter's superior had been notified and failed to comply with the bishop's demand.[27] Even now the bishop is not entitled to remove a confessor except for grave reasons which touch the office, and, besides, he may not remove all confessors of the same religious house at one time because such a removal would be not only senseless, but injurious to the spiritual welfare of the nuns[28] and to the moral character of the priests involved.

---

[27] Gregory XV, " *Inscrutabili,*" Feb. 5, 1622, § 5, and the decisions of. S. C. C., *ad calcem, ibid.*

[28] Clement X, " *Superna,*" June 21, 1670, § 6; S. C. EE. et RR., Nov. 20, 1615 (Bizzarri, *l. c.,* p. 21: " *ex nova causa eaque ad confessiones ipsas pertinente* ").

CONFESSORS OF LAY INSTITUTES OF MEN

CAN. 528

Etiam in laicalibus virorum religionibus deputetur, ad normam can. 874, § 1, 875, § 2, confessarius ordinarius et extraordinarius; et si religiosus aliquem specialem confessarium expostulet, illum Superior concedat, nullo modo petitionis rationem inquirens neque id aegre se ferre demonstrans.

Also in lay institutes of men an ordinary and an extraordinary confessor must be appointed, according to can. 874, § 1, where the Ordinary is enjoined to give a confessor either from the secular or religious clergy, and the religious must have the permission of his superior for being confessor; and according to can. 875, § 2, where it is said that in exempt lay institutes the superior may propose the confessor to be approved by the Ordinary. If any member wishes to have a special confessor, the superior must grant the petition and is not allowed to ask for a reason or to show displeasure.

CHAPLAINS

CAN. 529

Si agatur de religionibus laicalibus non exemptis, Ordinarii loci est sacerdotem a sacris designare et a concionibus probare; si de exemptis, Superior regularis eosdem sacerdotes designat eiusque negligentiam supplet Ordinarius.

In non-exempt lay institutes the Ordinary of the diocese appoints a priest for saying Mass and preaching; in exempt lay institutes the regular superior designates these priests, or, in case of the superior's negligence, the Ordinary of the diocese.

The *functions* of a chaplain, therefore, consist in holding divine service and preaching;[29] beyond that he is only allowed to perform sacred functions for which the Ordinary grants special powers, or in as far as the religious are exempt from parish organization.

Chaplains, too, should abstain from meddling in the internal and external régime of the communities to which they are assigned.

MANIFESTATION OF CONSCIENCE

CAN. 530

§ 1. Omnes religiosi Superiores districte vetantur personas sibi subditas quoquo modo inducere ad conscientiae manifestationem sibi peragendam.

§ 2. Non tamen prohibentur subditi quominus libere ac ultro aperire animum suum Superioribus valeant; imo expedit ut ipsi filiali cum fiducia Superiores adeant, eis, si sint sacerdotes, dubia quoque et anxietates suae conscientiae exponentes.

All religious superiors are strictly forbidden to induce their subjects by any means whatever to manifest their conscience to them. But the subjects may of their own accord open their mind to their superiors: nay it is even expedient for religious to approach their superiors with confidence, and if they are priests, to reveal to them doubts and anxieties of conscience.

Note that *all superiors,* not only those of nuns,[30] are affected by this general prohibition. Voluntary manifestation of conscience is not forbidden, but rather recommended.

---

29 See can. 1338, § 3.

30 " *Quemadmodum,*" Dec. 17, 1890, was chiefly intended for superiors of Sisters.

CHAPTER III

CAN. 531

Non modo religio, sed etiam provincia et domus sunt capaces acquirendi et possidendi bona temporalia cum reditibus stabilibus seu fundatis, nisi earum capacitas in regulis et constitutionibus excludatur aut coarctetur.

Can. 531 establishes nothing else but the well-known and ancient truth that there are religious who are capable of owning property and others who are not. Not only the institute as such, it says, but each province and house are capable of acquiring and possessing temporal goods together with a stable income or funds, unless their rule or constitutions exclude or restrict this right.

This right of single ecclesiastical corporations to own property is an inherent right not only of the whole Church,[1] but of each society and corporation which forms part and parcel of the Church. Blackstone says [2] the third absolute right inherent in every Englishman is that of property, which consists in the free use, enjoyment and disposal of all his acquisitions, without any control or diminution, save only by the laws of the land.

The origin of private property is probably founded in

---

1 Cfr. can. 1495.
2 Blackstone-Cooley, *Commentaries*, Chicago, 1879, I, 137; II, 8.

nature. By an easy transposition we may say that, since each institute, or province, or community consists of single persons — though they are not all Englishmen — endowed with that inherent right, it follows that the community as such also possesses the same. But it is also true that this right is controlled by the laws of a higher authority, which, so far as religious corporations are concerned, is that of the Apostolic See. We do not mean that the Apostolic See is the real owner of all corporative religious property. This would be incompatible with the true notion of property right.[3] The immediate and proper subject of property is the community itself, whether it be regarded as a legal fiction (*viz.*, the single members as one juridical or artificial person) or simply as a group of physical persons acting under special rules as far as representation is concerned, and governed by special rules as regards succession.[4] For it legally matters but little which theory is adopted either before the ecclesiastical or the civil courts. But essential to any corporation, in general, are two elements: a *group of members* and *corporate rights* vested in them as a corporation, asserted and applied by lawful representatives, be they trustees, managers, or directors. To these a third essential element must be added, as far as positive laws are concerned, namely, the *sanction of legitimate authority*. Though it is perfectly true that corporations were originally created by the mere act and voluntary association of their members,[5] and are therefore natural products of human and ecclesiastical society, yet the Church as well as the State is entitled to interpose its authority. The Church must give its ap-

---

3 Exception, of course, is to be made concerning orders (mendicant) incapable of possessing property.

4 Cfr. *New International Encycl.*, 1904, V, 438.

5 Blackstone-Cooley, *l. c.*, I, 472.

probation. But the State is also concerned, since all temporal property is located within its territory and falls within its sphere. The U. S. does not recognize any ecclesiastical corporations as such, though it does acknowledge them as private civil corporations subject to the laws of each State. Therefore it is important that religious communities, at least those which, according to ecclesiastical law, are capable of holding property, should be *chartered,* because the charter grants them legal existence, fixes their right of making by-laws, and, in a word, endows them with an official character, which the courts must acknowledge.[6]

This last observation gives rise to a question, *viz.,* Is it in accordance with the " public policy " of any of our States to grant or acknowledge a charter to religious societies?

As stated above, the U. S. does not create or acknowledge any ecclesiastical corporation as such. Hence a purely religious society, for instance, for perpetual adoration need hardly apply to the State legislature for a charter. However, if an educational or charitable purpose is involved, the State will readily grant corporate rights. Thus, *e. g.,* a charter was issued by the New Jersey legislature, on March 5, 1868, to St. Mary's Abbey, Newark.[7] Thus also the Shakers and Oneida Communities received a charter from State legislatures. St. Mary's Abbey was acknowledged as " a society of religious men living in a community and devoted to charitable works and the education of youth." [8]

---

6 Cfr. K. Zollmann, *American Civil Church Law,* 1917, p. 81 ff., a splendid contribution to the science of laws as prevailing in our country with regard to ecclesiastical institutions.

7 Cfr. Brief in behalf of Plaintiff in Error, Supreme Court, Oct. term, 1913, n. 267.

8 *Ibid.,* p. 5.

Certainly such an institution cannot be said to be against *public policy*. By public policy is meant that principle of the law which holds that no subject can lawfully do that which has a tendency to be injurious to the public or against the public good, and which may be termed the "policy of law" or "public policy in relation to the administration of law." Whatever is contrary, or alleged to be so, must be determined from the constitution and laws and judicial decisions of each State. No religious society approved by the Church can embody a fact or principle which an honest man has to condemn, but all contain some things which all men ought to approve. All distinctly inculcate the duty of honest industry, contentment with a competency, and charity to the poor and suffering.[9] We may safely apply to any Catholic corporation or religious body what has been said of the Shakers' Community: So long as piety is recognized by common assent, and by the legislature, as a valuable constituent in the character of our citizens, the general law must foster and encourage what tends to promote it. In legal estimation, it must be viewed as what is not only estimable in itself, but as an appurtenance to the character of individual citizens, of great value to society, for its tendency to promote the general weal of the whole community.[10]

However, it is sometimes objected that by the *vow of poverty* one surrenders the inherent and natural right to acquire and hold property in his own name — a surrender to which our Constitution is apparently opposed.[11] We answer: If by surrendering his right to personal property a professed member of a religious community

---

[9] *Ibid.,* p. 45; p. 47; p. 55.
[10] *Ibid.,* p. 55.
[11] This was the plaintiff's plea in the case of St. Mary's Abbey vs. the heirs of Fr. Augustine Wirth, O.S.B.

would also surrender his right to a decent support and existence, it might be granted that there is something immoral in the vow of poverty. However, this is not and has never been the case. The very definition given by cánonists should disperse any misgivings as to absolute surrender. They say that the vows are a bilateral contract between the individual member and the religious community, in virtue of which the former promises to devote his life and work and possessions to the community, in lieu of which the latter has to support him in health and sickness unto death. We might as well call marriage an immoral contract because it involves the surrender of the body.[12] A court in Maine said concerning the community of the Shakers that a contract with another to serve him for ten years, for an acceptable compensation, can not be proved to be illegal. This leads us to another aspect of the question. A religious community consists of various members, some of whom take the vows forever, while others take them only for a determined time, after which they may step out. No absolute surrender can be construed in the case of the last-mentioned class. Even those who have taken perpetual vows may be " secularized " with the cooperation of ecclesiastical authority. It is precisely for this reason that religious corporations have adopted by-laws governing cases of secession, by which they provide for the welfare of the community and its continuance and prevent seceding members from claiming compensation for services performed during their membership.

A last remark may conclude this section. How can a corporation endowed with property rights arise out of members who have given up their rights? Or, if all the members have vowed poverty, how may the community

12 I Cor. 7, 4.

possess property? The apparent paradox disappears if it is remembered that those who enter the religious state, although they surrender the right of possessing personal property, do not waive that of possessing property in common, as members of such or such a community, so far as the higher authority permits. To this authority, *viz.*, the Sovereign Pontiff, it belongs to decide whether or not property rights are attached to an ecclesiastical corporation. As to the vow, it requires no more than that personal claims be given up. Besides, let it again be emphasized, no religious can surrender the claim to decent support, for such an act would amount to suicide. Lastly, there are members, even in religious orders with solemn vows, who retain the right of holding property, for instance, the clerics with simple vows and lay brothers. Nor must it be overlooked that the Church may grant to a society property rights which are denied to the individual members. And this precisely is the distinction, alleged in our canon, between orders capable of property rights and such as are incapable of possessing — at least a certain kind of — property. However, even the so-called *Mendicant Orders* enjoy a certain right to property. The name Mendicant is applied to those religious orders which, by virtue of their original or primitive rule, observe poverty not only individually, but also as communities or convents, and are satisfied with alms humbly begged, or donations freely given, or things acquired by the labor and industry of the members.[13] But with the exception of the brown Franciscans and the Capuchins the Council of Trent decreed that even Mendicant Orders should possess land.[14] Concerning the two orders mentioned it is generally understood that the immovable property in their charge (convents, churches,

13 Reiffenstuel, III, 31, n. 27.   14 Sess. 25, c. 3, de reg.

etc.) is held by the Apostolic See [15] as immediate proprietor, whilst the members and actual occupants have the usufruct of the same. Neither of these two orders is capable of receiving legacies, if the sum itself is to be delivered to them, but they may obtain and use the interest of legacies paid annually by the heirs.[16]

CAN. 532

§ 1. Bona tum religionis, tum provinciae domusque, administrentur ad normam constitutionum.

§ 2. Expensas et actus iuridicos ordinariae administrationis valide, praeter Superiores, faciunt, intra fines sui muneris, officiales quoque, qui in constitutionibus ad hoc designantur.

This canon provides that the property of a religious order or congregation, as well as that of the different provinces and houses, should be administered according to the rules laid down by the respective constitutions, which are supposed to agree with the common law, or, at least, to be approved by the Apostolic See.

§ 2 says that expenses and *juridical acts* of ordinary administration may be validly made or performed by the superiors within the limits of their office, and by the different officials appointed under the constitutions. Civil law requires that the names of the officials of corporate societies be registered at the State treasury. This requirement must be complied with also by ecclesiastical corporations if they are acknowledged as private civil corporations, otherwise their officials may not perform legal or juridical acts. For juridical acts are such as are harmonized with the law for the sake of legal validity.

15 Cfr. can. 582, 2°.
16 S. C. C., May 31, 1721; Oct. 3, 1731 (Richter, *Trid.*, p. 396 f.).

Thus acts of buying and selling are juridical acts if performed in conformity with the law. *Acts of ordinary administration* are such as occur frequently and are performed without special formalities, such as are required, *e. g.,* if expenses are to be incurred that exceed the limits allowed by the Constitutions and the common law.

THE ORDINARY'S RIGHTS

. CAN. 533

§ 1. Pro pecuniae quoque collocatione servetur praescriptum can. 532, § 1; sed praevium consensum Ordinarii loci obtinere tenentur:

1.° Antistita monialium et religionis iuris dioecesani pro cuiusvis pecuniae collocatione; imo, si monialium monasterium sit Superiori regulari subiectum, ipsius quoque consensus est necessarius;

2.° Antistita in Congregatione religiosa iuris pontificii, si pecunia dotem professarum constituat ad normam can. 549;

3.° Superior vel Antistita domus Congregationis religiosae, si qui fundi domui tributi legative sint ad Dei cultum beneficentiamve eo ipso loco impendendam;

4.° Religiosus quilibet, etsi Ordinis regularis alumnus, si pecunia data sit paroeciae vel missioni, aut religiosis intuitu paroeciae vel missionis.

§ 2. Haec item servanda sunt pro qualibet collocationis mutatione.

§ 1 refers, first and above all, to the *investment of money,* which must be made according to the constitutions with the *previous consent* of the *Ordinary,*

(1) As often as, and in whatever amount, the superioress of nuns (*monialium*), or of a diocesan institute, wishes to invest money. If the nuns are subject

to a regular prelate, the superioress must also ask the consent of the prelate;

(2) The superioress of a papal congregation of religious must obtain the consent of the Ordinary in case she wishes to fix the dowry of a professed member in money, according to the rule laid down in can. 549;

(3) The superiors and superioresses of religious congregations need the consent of the Ordinary in case they wish to use for the house or school funds that were given or bequeathed for divine worship or benevolent purposes;

(4) Religious, including members of the regular orders, need the consent of the Ordinary for investing money which was given to the parish or mission, or to the religious himself for a parochial or missionary purpose.

The same rules must be observed if any change of investment is made.

This canon *does not touch* communities of men with solemn vows, but it embraces, in one way or the other, all other religious, even women with solemn vows, and individual regulars as far as they are connected with parish work. The reason for this difference lies in exemption. It may seem strange that the superiors of female congregations approved by the Holy See are not subject to the same regulation as superioresses of nuns of diocesan congregations regarding investment of money. Can. 510 solves the riddle, for it requires that the quinquennial report to be sent to the Holy See must first be submitted to the Ordinary in whose diocese the mother-house is, and who is therefore entitled to examine the financial state of such congregations in order to persuade himself as to the truthfulness of superiors, etc.

(1) First among the matters subject to the consent of

the Ordinary we note *investment of money (pro pecuniae collocatione)*. To *invest* [17] is to spend money in the purchase of property, especially for permanent use, or to put capital into other forms of property, for instance, government or other bonds, shares in stock companies, etc. But we do not call it investing when we put money into a bank, even though with the intention of obtaining interest; for money is generally put into banks in order to facilitate trading by checks and drafts, which is the common way in our country, though not yet so universal in Italy and elsewhere. Therefore the consent of the Ordinary is not required for banking money; the opposite opinion would lead to absurdities. [18] But any investment properly so-called, as defined above, needs consent. The amount is stated in the text, which simply says: for *any* money (*cuiusvis pecuniae*), little or much. The *consent* of the Ordinary need not be asked each time, but may be given for a certain sum, to be invested in various ways, or even for a certain time, nor is written consent prescribed, oral being sufficient.

(2) Episcopal consent is required if the superioress of any papal institute wishes to *fix the dowry* in money or cash. The reason for this ruling is to be sought in can. 549, which demands that the dowry be established "in safe, licit, and fruitbearing titles." Hence, if the dowry is to be demanded in cash, rather than in secure titles, the consent of the Ordinary must be asked.

(3) The superiors of religious congregations, whether of men or women, must obtain the consent of the Ordinary if they wish to use *funds donated or bequeathed for purposes different from those for which they were*

[17] Cicero uses the expression, "*collocare pecuniam in fundo*," to invest money in landed property.

[18] Neither is the daily buying and selling of cattle, products, implements, etc., properly called an investment.

given. Thus, for instance, a pious lady may have given or bequeathed a certain sum for the chapel or church of a religious community, or another may have left a donation or legacy for an orphanage or home for the aged. Now although these religious may own the chapel or be in charge of the charitable work, the use of such funds for other purposes is not allowed except with the consent of the Ordinary, he being the guardian of all charitable institutes and places of worship.[19] However, if the funds are given to a religious congregation because of the charitable works it does, they may be freely administered and used by the superior without asking the bishop, who must only see to it that the money is used properly and according to the intentions of the donor.[20] Canonical visitation is the proper occasion for investigating, as also the examination of the quinquennial report.

(4) Any religious, even though a member of a regular order, must have the consent of the Ordinary if he wishes to invest *church or mission money, viz.,* money received from pew-rent, receipts from seats, church collections, collections taken up at lectures in favor of the church, house collections and subscriptions. In this category also belongs money given to a religious for his mission or church, but not personal donations, or such donations as are given to a religious because he is a religious or a member of a certain community. Hence any investment of church money needs the consent of the Ordinary of the diocese in which the church or mission is located, not of the Ordinary in whose diocese the investment is to be made.

§ 2 prescribes that the Ordinary's consent must also be obtained — not only asked for — for a *change of in-*

---

[19] Cf. can. 1493, 1513-1515; Leo XIII, " *Conditae,*" II, 9.

[20] Cf. Bastien-Lanslots, *l. c.,* p. 146 f.

vestment. Thus if the money was invested in real estate and is to be re-invested in stocks or bonds, or conversely, episcopal consent must be obtained. If the money was loaned on interest, and is now to be invested in real estate, the consent is also required.

ALIENATION

CAN. 534

§ 1. Firmo praescripto can. 1531, si agatur de alienandis rebus pretiosis aliisve bonis quorum valor superet summam triginta millium francorum seu libellarum, vel de contrahendis debitis et obligationibus ultra indicatam summam, contractus vi caret, nisi beneplacitum apostolicum antecesserit; secus, requiritur et sufficit licentia, in scriptis data, Superioris ad normam constitutionum cum consensu sui Capituli seu Consilii per secreta suffragia manifestato; sed si agatur de monialibus aut sororibus iuris dioecesani, accedat necesse est consensus, in scriptis praestitus, Ordinarii loci, necnon Superioris regularis, si monialium monasterium eidem subiectum sit.

§ 2. In precibus pro obtinendo consensu ad contrahenda debita vel obligationes, exprimi debent alia debita vel obligationes, quibus ipsa persona moralis, religio vel provincia vel domus, ad eum diem gravatur; secus obtenta venia invalida est.

The first paragraph contains two main clauses, divided by the sum of alienation, and the second clause finds its demarcation line in the kind of religious. The whole paragraph treats of alienation of church or religious property. *Alienation* means any act by which property is either diminished or deteriorated, transferred or exchanged, as by sale, gift, renting, mortgaging of a specified piece of property (*hypotheca specialis*), contract, lease or other transmission by mutual consent of the parties concerned.[21]

The reason for setting up laws against alienation is the conservative spirit of the Church, who naturally wishes to have property destined for religious purposes to remain in the possession of the ecclesiastical owner. A thousand years before Paul II issued the famous decretal "*Ambitiosae*" (1468), popes and synods enacted rules against unlawful and detrimental alienation. Leo I told the bishops that they were dispensers, not proprietors of church property, and therefore not allowed to donate, change or sell it, and that if anything was to be sold or exchanged, it must be done with the consent of the clergy.[22] The seventh general synod (II Nic., 787) forbade bishops and abbots to grant any church property to worldly princes or to persons under penalty of deposition.[23] This legislation continued until Paul II made the rather strict law against alienation,[24] which, however, was seldom carried out "beyond the mountains." Pius IX ("*Apostolicae Sedis*," 1869) renewed the laws against alienation and wished them to be enforced everywhere.[25] Our Code adopts these laws in a modified shape, so that they are now written and general laws, and ignorance can no longer be pretended.

In can. 534 the Code rules, first, that can. 1531 must be observed. That canon provides:

§ 1. No property may be alienated for less than it is appraised.

§ 2. Unless circumstances advise otherwise, alienation

21 Engel, III, 13, n. 13; Black-stone-Cooley, *l. c.*, II, 287.
22 C. 52, C. 12, q. 2.
23 C. 19, *ibid.*
24 Cfr. tit. 13, X, III; tit. 9, 6°.

III; tit. 4, Clem. III; c. un. *Ambitiosae*, Extrav. Comm., III, 4.
25 "*Apostolicae Sedis*," Oct. 12, 1869, IV, 3

must be made by public bidding, or at least by advertisement, and to the highest bidder.

§ 3. The money received by alienation must be invested cautiously, securely, and usefully for the benefit of the Church.

The quintessence of this canon is: business methods and safety. Auction or bidding are prescribed, as we learn from innumerable decisions, in order to prevent squandering of property or undue personal favoritism, or, what is worse, nepotism. But auctioning is not always advisable, especially if profane eyes and ears are to be kept away.

The Code goes on to say:

(1) An Apostolic indult is required for the alienation of precious things or other goods exceeding 30,000 francs or lire in value, as also for making debts over and above that sum. Any contract made before the Apostolic indult has been obtained is ecclesiastically invalid.

The Apostolic indult is a permission granted by the Congregation of Religious, to which application must be made.

(2) The *matter* alienated may be either precious things or property. By the name *precious things* are understood church vessels, vestments, treasures and books which have a special value, either by reason of antiquity or of artistic excellence.[26] "Other goods" (*aliisve bonis*) comprise especially immovable property, such as buildings and landed estates, but also [27] certain rights and revenues, e. g., a lease on coal-fields or mines, liabilities to certain burdens or duties, the right of fishing or hunting, rights of way, etc. Revenue would be State pensions, bonds, stocks, etc. If the value exceeds the

---

[26] Engel, III, 13, n. 5; Reiffenstuel, III, 13, n. 12.

[27] C. 1, Clem. III, 4; Reiffenstuel, III, 13, n. 10.

sum of 30,000 francs or lire, the transaction requires an Apostolic indult. Selling of stocks and produce is no alienation.

(3) How much is *30,000 francs or lire in our money?* In normal times, such as the Code doubtless has in view, it would be about 6,000 dollars. " And for that small sum we have to ask Rome? " This question was put to us more than once, and those who put it asserted that a lira or franc is practically equal to a dollar of our money, and hence the Code means $30,000. However, this reasoning is wrong. We know from experience that a dollar does not equal a franc, but that the average proportion would be about $1:2\frac{1}{2}$, that is to say, one dollar would buy as much as two lire and a half in Italy or two francs and a half in France. Furthermore, it is well known that the bishops needed special faculties to alienate property exceeding $5,000.[28] Gradually, because of the decline in the value of money, the Holy See raised the sum from 10,000 francs to 30,000 francs, which it considers almost excessive. To fully convince the reader that the legislator intended the market value of Italian or French currency as the standard of valuation (*i. e.,* about $6,000 in our money), we will state this case: A rescript arrives from Rome, which costs 8 lire, or about $1.60. Will the prelate remit $ 8 instead of $1.60? We believe, however, that now-a-days about $10,000 or $12,000 would correspond to the intention of the Code, because land as well as building material have risen so much in value that $6,000 are really but a small sum for religious institutes worthy of that name. On the other hand, it is a lamentable fact that religious houses often run into debt simply in order to outshine one

---

[28] *Conc. Balt., III,* n. 20; Bachofen, *Compendium Iuris Reg.,* p. 305.

another. The Roman Court, as we know, could tell tales to that effect.

(4) The Code then applies the requisite of an Apostolic indult to the *contracting of debts* to the same amount. Here observe the difference between the new legislation as set forth in our Code and that of the S. Congregation of Religious, July 30, 1909, which required an Apostolic indult for any sum exceeding 10,000 lire, whilst our Code raises the sum to 30,000 lire or francs — the two being almost equal in market value before the war.

The next clause of can. 534, § 1, rules that if the sum does not exceed 30,000 lire or francs, the *written permission of the superior*, according to the respective constitutions, is *required and sufficient*, provided the consent or counsel (given by secret ballot) of the chapter was obtained. Cardinal Gasparri, in his notes, refers to the above-quoted instruction of the S. Congregation of Religious of 1909, which, therefore, may be said to be the will of the legislator, at least as a directive norm. No. I of the instruction referred to requires the *consent* of the chapter or counsel of either the religious house, or the province, or the congregation or order, according as the matter touches these entities respectively. But our Code leaves it to the constitutions, which must therefore be consulted. No. V of the instruction insists that every superior have counsellors elected by the free choice of the community; their number to be four if the community has more than twelve members, and two, if there are less than twelve. No. VI rules that the votes are to be given secretly and are decisive, and the permission granted by the superior in accordance with the decisive votes given by the counsellors, or the chapter, must always be given in writing. No. VII gravely enjoins religious superiors not to hide any income, debts, obligations, or donations of value from their counsellors. The sum below 30,000 lire, for which the consent of the counsellors or chapter is required, is not stated in the Code, except in so far as it refers to the Constitutions. But one thing is certain, namely, that under the new Code *consent* is required, not only *advice,* and therefore any transaction performed by the superior without the consent required by the Constitutions would be not only illicit, but invalid.[20]

The second part of the second clause treats of *nuns and Sisters of a diocesan congregation* who wish to alienate or contract debts below the sum of 30,000 francs. These, says the Code, must obtain the written consent of the Ordinary of the diocese, and if they are subject to a regular prelate, also the written consent of the latter. Hence these nuns and Sisters must first and above all obtain the consent of the chapter or counsellors, given by secret vote; secondly, the written consent of their ecclesiastical superiors, either of the Ordinary alone, if they are a diocesan institute, or of both the Ordinary and the regular prelate, if they are nuns with solemn vows. Why are the Sisters of a papal institute not obliged to obtain the consent of the Ordinary? Because their constitutions, which must necessarily contain a chapter on temporal administration, are approved by the Pope, who regulates that matter according to common law and the constitutions.

The *petition* submitted to obtain the papal consent for contracting debts or obligations must state all the debts and obligations of the corporation, institute, province or house up to the day of the petition. If no mention thereof is made, the rescript is invalid. What *debts* are

[20] Cfr. can. 105.

is evident.   As to *obligations,* the term includes all financial or economical titles, bonds or deeds whereby the
maker obliges himself, his heirs, executors, and administrators, to pay a certain sum of money on an appointed
day.[30]   This may be done legally or informally, by a
mortgage or note, by giving security or bail, conditionally
or absolutely.   Mass-obligations are not included because
they are not financial obligations.

The Code requires that mention be made of all debts
or obligations, no matter how large or small the sum —
because no amount is specified — in the application for
a papal indult, if required according to can. 534, § 1,
that is to say, if the institute wishes to contract new debts
or obligations exceeding the sum of 30,000 francs or lire. .
The statement must be truthful, because subreptitious
mention might invalidate the rescript,[31] especially if a
considerable sum were concealed.

To complete the law on alienation we may add that the
Code has also fixed penalties [32] which increase with the
sum unjustly alienated, the greatest of which is excommunication, not reserved to any one.   A religious superior may be deprived of his office and rank if he alien-
ates without the necessary consent a sum less than 30,000
francs.   Furthermore any religious may appeal to the
S. Congregation of Religious, or to the Ordinary, if his
or her superior violates the laws laid down in canon 534,
as the Decretals,[33] which are not corrected or repealed in
our Code, clearly state.

It is, however, evident that papal consent is not required in cases of urgent need, as, for instance, to satisfy
creditors demanding immediate payment through a court,

---

30 Blackstone-Cooley, II, 340; S.
C. Rel., July 30, 1909 (*A. Ap. S.,*
I, 696).

31 Can. 42, § 1, cannot be applied
here.

32 Can. 2347.

33 C. 6, X, III, 13; c. 2, 6°, III, 9.

or in case of absolute necessity or charity admitting of
no delay, or in case of evident utility where postponement
would entail a serious loss.[84]   But the law requiring the
chapter's consent can never be set aside, for cases of such
urgency are hardly imaginable.

RENDERING OF ACCOUNTS

CAN. 535

§ 1. In quolibet monialium monasterio etiam exempto:

1.° Administrationis ratio, gratis exigenda, reddatur
semel in anno, aut etiam saepius si id in constitutionibus praescribatur, ab Antistita Ordinario loci, itemque
Superiori regulari, si monasterium sit eidem subiectum;

2.° Si ratio administrationis Ordinario non probetur, ipse potest opportuna remedia adhibere, etiam
removendo, si res postulet, oeconomam aliosque administratores; quod si monasterium sit Superiori
regulari subiectum, eum Ordinarius, uti prospiciat,
moneat; quod si ille neglexerit, ipse per se consulat.

§ 2. In aliis mulierum religionibus, ratio administrationis bonorum quae dotes constituunt, Ordinario
loci reddatur occasione visitationis et etiam saepius,
si Ordinarius id necessarium duxerit.

§ 3. Loci Ordinario ius insuper esto cognoscendi:

1.° De rationibus oeconomicis domus religiosae
iuris dioecesani;

2.° De administratione fundorum legatorumque de
quibus in can. 533, § 1, nn. 3, 4.

§ 1. For every monastery of nuns, even those who are
exempt,

---

84 Bastien-Lanslots, l. c., p. 229.

1.° The superioress must furnish gratuitously once a year, or oftener if the constitutions so prescribe, an account of her administration to the Ordinary of the diocese, and to the regular superior if the monastery be subject to regulars.

2.° If the Ordinary does not approve of the account of the administration furnished him, he may apply the necessary remedies, including even the removal from office of the procuratrix and other administrators; but if the monastery is subject to a regular superior, the Ordinary shall request him to see to it; and if the regular superior fail to do so, the Ordinary himself must deal with the case.

§ 2. In other institutes of women, the account of the administration of the property constituted by the dowries must be furnished to the local Ordinary at the time of the canonical visitation, and even oftener if the Ordinary deems it necessary.

§ 3. The Ordinary of the diocese has also the right of enquiring into:

1.° The economic status of every religious house with diocesan approval;

2.° The administration of the funds and bequests made for divine worship or charitable work, as well as of all property belonging to the church or mission, although administered by regulars.

To this canon we will only add that it would be advisable for the bishop to appoint as *auditor* for that purpose a priest whose practical knowledge he could make use of at visitations.

RESPONSIBILITY AND DONATIONS

Can. 536

§ 1. Si persona moralis (sive religio, sive provincia, sive domus) debita et obligationes contraxerit etiam cum Superiorum licentia, ipsa tenetur de eisdem respondere.

§ 2. Si contraxerit regularis cum licentia Superiorum, respondere debet persona moralis, cuius Superior licentiam dedit; si religiosus votorum simplicium, ipse respondere debet, nisi de Superioris licentia negotium religionis gesserit.

§ 3. Si contraxerit religiosus sine ulla Superiorum licentia, ipsemet respondere debet, non autem religio vel provincia vel domus.

§ 4. Firmum tamen semper esto, contra eum, in cuius rem aliquid ex inito contractu versum est, semper posse actionem institui.

§ 5. Caveant Superiores religiosi ne debita contrahenda permittant, nisi certo constet ex consuetis reditibus posse debiti foenus solvi et intra tempus non nimis longum per legitimam *amortizationem* reddi summam capitalem.

Can. 537

Largitiones ex bonis domus, provinciae, religionis non permittuntur, nisi ratione eleemosynae vel alia iusta de causa, de venia Superioris et ad normam constitutionum.

§ 1. If a corporation (whether an institute, a province, or a house) contracts debts and obligations, even with the permission of superiors, it is personally responsible for them.

§ 2. When a regular, with the permission of his superiors, contracts debts and obligations, the corporation whose superior gave the permission, bears the responsibility; if it is a religious with simple vows, he himself is responsible, unless he acted with the permission of the superior, and on behalf of the institute.

§ 3. If a religious contracts debts and obligations without any permission of superiors, he himself is responsible, but not the institute, the province or the house.

§ 4. In every case, it is a rule that an action can always be brought against him for whom the contract has been a source of profit.

§ 5. Superiors must beware not to allow the contracting of debts unless it be certain that the interest on them may be met from current revenue, and that within a reasonable time the capital may be paid off by means of a lawful sinking-fund.

This canon is intended to protect religious institutes and to warn outsiders against unguarded dealing with religious who have not the proper authorization. It is evident that a corporation acting in its own name is responsible for its action, although the superior alone may have sanctioned it, for the quality of a juridical person is inherent in the corporation as such, not in the superior. A regular superior with solemn vows cannot form a corporation sole, unless he has obtained a special papal indult. Hence legal action must be instituted against the corporation as such.

§ 2 speaks of *individual religious* contracting debts. Here a distinction is made. A *regular*, or member of an order with solemn vows, is incapable of transacting business and therefore the corporation as such is liable for his acts. A *religious with simple vows* retains the right to acquire and own property, and consequently must be held personally responsible for all business transacted by him, unless he is the authorized representative of the community. This is also true of a religious with simple vows who, though belonging to an order with solemn vows (for instance, a lay brother or a cleric in temporary profession) contracts debts or obligations without being commissioned thereto by his superior.

§ 3 is taken from the Decretals,[35] where there is a canon of the IVth Lateran Council which says that a convent should not be held responsible if a religious went security for another or borrowed money without the consent of chapter or superior, unless the transaction was favorable to the community. Lay persons may sometimes be deceived by a religious who pretends to act in the name of his community, but careful business men will always assure themselves of the official character of any religious they may have to deal with.

Notice that in this paragraph (3) no distinction is made between regulars and religious with simple vows; hence the text covers all.

Though the ancient ecclesiastical law seemingly excludes *legal action* against a religious institute, the Code says in § 4 that such action may be instituted for unfair dealing. Therefore a business man may sue a religious institute to recover money or goods acquired by a member who acted without authority. But the first subject to be dealt with would be the offending religious himself, and then only the community. The latter could be condemned to restitution or compensation if the enrichment was illegal. Attention must be drawn to can. 120 (*privilegium fori*), which requires the Ordinary's permission for citing religious before a civil court.

§ 5 warns religious against making debts which would

[35] C. 4, X, III, 22.

weigh too heavily on the community. What the Code says of *amortization* or reduction and extinction of debts by means of a sinking-fund is certainly good advice. On the other hand, however, it is a well-founded saw that debts are a good thing for religious communities because they stimulate the members to untiring labor and prevent religious houses from becoming too rich.

Can. 537 prohibits the making of presents out of the goods of a religious house, province, or institute, unless by way of almsgiving or for other just reasons and with the consent of the superior and in conformity with the constitutions. The reason for this prohibition lies in the vow of poverty as well as in the desire of cutting off opportunities for feasts and banquets, as we read in a circular letter of the S. Congregation of Bishops and Regulars, of July 28, 1708.[86] The Code has taken as its standard the Constitution of Urban VIII, "*Nuper*," of Oct. 16, 1640, which mitigated the severe Constitution of Clement VIII, "*Religiosae congregationes*," of June 19, 1594. The latter had prohibited any gifts or donations by religious and obliged the receiver to make restitution. Urban VIII permitted presents in token of gratitude or for other religious motives, which turn to the benefit of the house, excluding, however, donations of any considerable amount by superiors as well as officials and individual religious in their own name, enjoining that all be done in the name of the monastery.[87] Urban VIII did not revoke that part of Clement VIII's Constitution which obliged to restitution the recipients of presents illegitimately made by religious.

Here it may not be amiss briefly to state the moral obligations of donors and recipients in case they have acted

86 Bizzarri, *l. c.*, p. 398.
87 S. C. EE. et RR., Feb, 1791 (Bizzarri, *ibid.*).

against canons 536 f. Supposing the sum alienated or donated (*e. g.*, to relations or friends) is over $10, which, according to Innocent XII ("*Romanus Pontifex*") was considered enough to reserve the case to the S. Penitentiary,[38] we may say:

a) A *religious with solemn vows*, being unable to own property, cannot make restitution in the proper sense. But he is obliged to tell the recipients that they must restore the value of the present, unless they are poor or unwilling to make restitution. If they are in good faith and it is not likely that an admonition would avail, the donor may omit this admonition and leave them in good faith. If the recipient is poor and needy, nothing is to be done.

b) A *religious with simple vows*, who retains the right of holding property, is obliged to make restitution out of his own means, supposing that he or she has property or may expect such in the future; and this obligation never ceases. Of course, if he can prevail upon the recipient to restore the goods given out of the religious property, this would be the simplest way out of the difficulty. It may be added that tips to waiters or porters, small gifts as tokens of gratitude, etc., do not oblige to restitution, and if made for a good reason, are not against poverty. Religious articles, such as medals, pictures, etc., may be given without fear of violating poverty. A religious when travelling is allowed to act like a gentleman towards those whose help or assistance or good will he needs. Finally, can. 537 allows donations to be made as alms or for any just reason, provided the superior consents.

---

38 There is, of course, no longer any reservation, because common law makes no mention thereof. The religious (exempt) superior might reserve the case if there were an urgent reason for doing so. Besides, 10 *scudi* would now-a-days barely amount to $50.

This consent may be presumed in cases of urgency or necessity. Too rigid an insistence upon poverty when charity calls is against the very groundwork of religion. Religious are not to be stingy, but the saying of the Apostle was also intended for them: " It is a more blessed thing to give rather than to receive " (Acts 20, 35). Besides, every religious community has a social position to fill and a social duty to live up to. The ancient monasteries were fully aware of this great and noble task.

ADMISSION TO RELIGIOUS INSTITUTES

CAN. 538

In religionem admitti potest quilibet catholicus qui nullo legitimo detineatur impedimento rectaque intentione moveatur, et ad religionis onera ferenda sit idoneus.

Every Catholic who is not prevented by any legitimate impediment, and is inspired by a right intention, and fit to bear the burdens of the religious life, can be admitted to the same.

Four general conditions are here set up for entering the religious life:

(1) The aspirant must be a *Catholic*, for the Code does not legislate, at least not directly, for non-Catholics. Besides, since no religious institute can legally exist without the approval of the Church, and the Church in concrete terms is the Catholic Church, it is evident that the religious state is open only to such as acknowledge the legitimate authority of that Church. Finally, as a matter of experience, the religious state appears to prosper only within the pale of the Catholic Church.[39]

(2) The person who wishes to enter a religious institute *must not suffer from any legitimate impediment* (see

---

[39] It is a well-known fact that some Anglicans endeavored to imitate the example of the Catholic Church, not at all to the detriment of the latter, as some communities returned corporatively to the Mother Church.

can. 542). The natural law precludes the assumption of the religious habit by a person who is mentally unsound.[40] As to bodily defects, it may be well to follow the instruction of Clement VIII (1603), which demands that the postulant be examined to ascertain whether he suffers from a considerable deformity, or shows sign of great bodily debility or stupidity (*fatuitas*). For such defects, though not disgraceful to the individual, may draw ridicule upon a religious community and the religious state in general.[41]

(3) A *right intention* is required because the end of the religious life is holy,—namely, Christian perfection, which demands full attention and a determined effort. A right intention is the glory of God and one's own salvation. Any other would be either sinful or dangerous. A wrong intention would be material interest, provision for life, honor and dignities.[42] It is not without reason, therefore, that canonists require a special vocation as a condition of admission to the religious state. On the other hand, St. Thomas is satisfied with a general call, which may also satisfy us. This general call, he says, consists in the invitation of Christ to follow the evangelical counsels.[43] An ambiguous use of terms seems, however, to have caused some divergency of opinion.[44] The invitation to the higher life is extended to all, but the actual choice of the religious state seems to proceed from either efficacious or sufficient grace, no matter how we look at the working of that mysterious divine impulse. The word of our Lord: "He that can take it, let him take it," (Matt. 19, 12) is a strong argument in favor of a special vocation, unless we choose to deny the

---

40 Cf. c. 15, X, III, 31.
41 Bizzarri, *l. c.*, p. 848, 5.
42 C. 20, C. 16, q. 7.

43 S. Th., II-II, q. 189, a. 10.
44 Cf. Piatus M., I, 32 ff.

suave workings of divine providence. Only we must guard against a too specialized drawing to the religious state. The safest means to arrive at a practical result for each one is to pray and to consult with others.

(4) The last general requisite is *fitness* for bearing the burdens of the religious life. This fitness may be either *general* or *special*. *General fitness* must be considered from the view-point of the three religious vows, particularly that of chastity, because celibacy is not to everyone's taste. Obedience, too, may deter some from embracing a state which requires self-denial and subordination. *Special* fitness turns upon the nature of each religious order or congregation. Some are of a contemplative trend — of these there are but few in our country — whereas others have an active tendency; some spend much time and labor on choir service and schools, while others devote themselves to missionary and charitable work. Each requires a peculiar mental and physical [45] aptitude in the aspirant.

[45] An important defect of the body would be the lack of a limb endowed with special functions, for instance, hand, leg, nose, ear, eye (Bizzarri, *Coll.*, p. 848); perhaps after the war a more lenient practice will be admitted.

CHAPTER I

DURATION

CAN. 539

§ 1. In religionibus a votis perpetuis mulieres omnes et, si agatur de religione virorum, conversi, antequam ad novitiatum admittantur, postulatum ad sex saltem integros menses peragant; in religionibus vero a votis temporariis, ad necessitatem et tempus postulatus quod attinet, standum constitutionibus.

§ 2. Superior maior praescriptum postulatus tempus potest prorogare, non tamen ultra aliud semestre.

§ 1 distinguishes between various orders of men and women, such with perpetual and such with temporary vows. In religious institutes of *women* with *perpetual vows* the period of postulancy must last at least six whole months. The same rule applies to the *lay brothers* of male orders with perpetual vows. In institutes with temporary vows the duration of the postulancy is regulated by the respective constitutions.

§ 2. The higher superior can prolong the time prescribed for the postulancy, but not beyond another term of six months.

PLACE, DRESS, ENCLOSURE

CAN. 540

§ 1. Postulatus peragi debet vel in domo novitiatus vel in alia religionis domo in qua disciplina secundum constitutiones accurate servetur sub speciali cura probati religiosi.

§ 2. Postulantes vestem induant modestam ac diversam a veste novitiorum.

§ 3. In monasteriis monialium adspirantes, dum postulatum peragunt, lege clausurae tenentur.

The postulancy must be made either in the novitiate house or in another house of the institute, where the discipline prescribed by the constitutions is faithfully observed under the special care of an experienced religious.

The postulants should wear a humble dress, different from that of the novices.

In the monasteries of nuns (with solemn vows) the aspirants, during their postulancy, are bound by the law of enclosure.

CAN. 541

Postulantes, antequam novitiatum incipiant, exercitiis spiritualibus vacent per octo saltem integros dies; et, iuxta prudens confessarii iudicium, praemittant generalem anteactae vitae confessionem.

Before beginning their novitiate, postulants should make a spiritual retreat of at least eight full days, and according to the discretion of the confessor, a general confession of their past life.

To these three canons we will only add that they do not affect the validity of the novitiate or profession; that in clerical religious houses only the lay brothers, not the

clerics, have to make the six months' postulancy; that
the institutes with perpetual vows cannot force the members to a postulancy lasting more than a year, even though
the constitutions prescribe a longer term, as the latter
in this point are devoid of legal force.

CHAPTER II

THE NOVITIATE

A certain period of probation for aspirants has always been customary in religious institutes. Thus Pachomius in his rule [1] prescribes a term of probation, and Cassian in his " Institutions " speaks of it also.[2] This term of probation must have been a hard time for novices and candidates. The *term of a year* has been hallowed by a long-standing tradition; almost all the ancient rules prescribe it.[3] The *place* of the novitiate was separate from the rest of the monastery. At St. Gall in Switzerland, for example, the novices had their own enclosure, dining-room, kitchen, dormitory, infirmary, and laundry, as we see from the plan of that famous abbey built by Gotzbert in the beginning of the ninth century. Later, among the Cluniacenses, if the number of novices was small, they were allowed to mix with the professed members.[4] Probation chiefly turned upon obedience and capability of bearing the burdens of the religious life.[5]

1 Reg., c. 49 (Migne, 23, 70).

2 *Inst.*, l. IV, cc. 3 ff. (Migne, 49, 154 ff.).

3 Migne, 66, 816.

4 Migne, 66, 812; concerning the change of dress, custom was different in different monasteries; *ibid.*, Col. 836.

5 The devices employed sometimes bordered on the ridiculous and are not to be imitated now-a-days.

ARTICLE I

THE CONDITIONS REQUIRED FOR ADMISSION TO THE NOVITIATE

CAN. 542

Firmo praescripto can. 539–541, aliisque in propriis cuiusque religionis constitutionibus,

1.° Invalide ad novitiatum admittuntur:

Qui sectae acatholicae adhaeserunt;

Qui aetatem ad novitiatum requisitam non habent;

Qui religionem ingrediuntur vi, metu gravi aut dolo inducti, vel quos Superior eodem modo inductus recipit;

Coniux, durante matrimonio;

Qui obstringuntur vel obstricti fuerunt vinculo professionis religiosae;

Hi quibus imminet poena ob grave delictum commissum de quo accusati sunt vel accusari possunt;

Episcopus sive residentialis sive titularis, licet a Romano Pontifice sit tantum designatus;

Clerici qui ex instituto Sanctae Sedis iureiurando tenentur operam suam navare in bonum suae dioecesis vel missionum, pro eo tempore quo iurisiurandi obligatio perdurat.

2.° Illicite, sed valide admittuntur:

Clerici in sacris constituti, inconsulto loci Ordinario aut eodem contradicente ex eo quod eorum discessus in grave animarum detrimentum cedat, quod aliter vitari minime possit;

Aere alieno gravati qui solvendo pares non sint;

Reddendae rationi obnoxii aut aliis saecularibus negotiis implicati, ex quibus lites et molestias religio timere possit;

Filii qui parentibus, idest patri vel matri, avo vel aviae, in gravi necessitate constitutis, opitulari debent, et parentes quorum opera sit ad liberos alendos vel educandos necessaria;

Ad sacerdotium in religione destinati, a quo tamen removeantur irregularitate aliove canonico impedimento;

Orientales in latinis religionibus sine venia scripto data Sacrae Congregationis pro Ecclesia Orientali.

Without prejudice to the rules laid down in can. 539–541, and to others contained in the constitutions proper to each institute,

1.° The following are *invalidly* admitted to the noviti-ate:

Those who have belonged to a non-Catholic sect. The term "*adhaerere*" certainly means a wilful act on the part of the candidate, or, in other words, a formal heretic or schismatic, as may be seen from can. 1325, § 2, where the definitions of heretic and schismatic are given. In both a wilful, stubborn act is required. Hence a boy or girl educated by non-Catholic parents or relatives would not fall under the prohibition, as long as he or she had merely materially and unknowingly followed a non-Catholic sect, and never pertinaciously denied an article of the Catholic faith. On the other hand, a *sect* is an organization based on contradiction to the Catholic faith and the unity of the Church. Hence it matters nothing whether one is a formal adherent of a Protestant sect or of a schismatical body. For in neither case can he be validly admitted to the novitiate. Besides, a sect is generally understood as a body that proclaims some kind of Christian profession, as is evident from the Constitution of Pius IX, "*Apostolicae Sedis*," Oct. 12, 1869.[6] Hence apostates from the Catholic faith, and members of a non-Christian denomination (Buddhists, Mohammedans, Jews) are not comprised in this prohibition. However, as the Code uses the term *acatholicae*, non-Catholic, it would seem to include all sects opposed to the Catholic faith, but not individual apostates, as long as they are not members of an organized sect. This latter interpretation seems very probable, because the underlying reason of the prohibition is not only horror of heresy, but weakness of faith, as there is even now an impediment against receiving orders for neophytes,[7] and formerly was an irregularity from "defect of confirmed faith."

Those who have not reached the age required for the novitiate, which, according to can. 555, is fifteen years.

Those who enter religion under the influence of violence, or grave fear, or are induced thereto by fraud; also those whom the superior receives under pressure of the same influences. Compulsion (*vis*) destroys the voluntariness of an act; grave fear diminishes it; fraud, if deliberate and inspired by the intention of coaxing one into the religious state, affects the consent of the contracting party.

Physical compulsion is no longer as common as formerly, when parents brought their young children to the monastery. A notable case is that of Gottschalk, who was an oblate at Fulda under Rhabanus Maurus.[8] The Decretals mitigated this practice, which to us seems appalling, and ruled that a boy was free to embrace the

---

[6] I, 1: "*Omnes a christiana fide apostatas et omnes ac singulos haereticos quocumque nomine censeantur et cuiuscumque sectae existant.*"

[7] Can. 987.

[8] He wrote a work on the "Oblation of Boys," in which he defends the prevailing custom (Migne, 125, 419 ff.).

religious state after fourteen years, and a girl could repudiate her parents' decision after she had reached the age of twelve.[9] Of *grave fear* that prompted one to enter religion an instance is mentioned in the Decree of Gratian.[10] Landulph of Corsica through fear of death and the remembrance of his sins left his wife and became a monk. Alexander III declared the step null and void and allowed Landulph to return to his wife. Grave fear may be inflicted by foolish parents or relatives, who sometimes use means of persuasion of a very doubtful character, such as threats, to induce their children to enter the religious state. All such measures render the step invalid.

A more knotty question is that of *deceit,* because it cannot be easily proved.[11] However, circumstances sometimes uncover a fraud. Thus, for instance, if parents, desirous of keeping their property together, induce their younger sons or daughters to enter religion, there is palpable fraud. Deceit may also be practiced by the religious, for instance, by holding out a good and pleasant position, honors and dignities, or, as the saying is, a good time, or by hiding the truth and the real conditions of the community. However, not every kind of deceit necessarily makes admission to the novitiate invalid, but it must be a fraudulent device either on the part of those who have influence over the candidate or on the side of the institute which he joins, and it must be *decisive* in causing him to enter.[12] A person who is of age and of sound mind is not easily deceived.

The Code says, furthermore, that if the superior has been induced to receive a candidate by compulsion, fear or deceit, the act would be invalid. This may happen

9 Cc. 8, 12, X, III, 31.　　　　　11 Reiffenstuel, III, 16, 32 ff.
10 C. 2, C. 33, q. 5.　　　　　　12 Reiffenstuel, II, 14, n. 8 f.

by threats against the superior himself, or against the religious house (defamation), or financial reverses, etc. It would be deceit if the candidate pretended to be intelligent, healthy or rich, whilst in reality he is the opposite. But mere lack of riches or brain — unless the candidate were too dull for any occupation — would not be sufficient to make the admission invalid. Feigned health would be sufficient, but a physician's verdict may save an institute from deceit of this kind. The moral character is more liable to be made an object of deception. However, the testimonials required and a sincere statement of the candidate's past life would give some clue to a wise action on both sides. If the candidate should nevertheless have succeeded in deceiving the order or congregation, the latter would be justified in dismissing him even after profession. The same must be said concerning health,[13] if a serious defect was concealed, as well as of debts, which must be revealed to the religious superior.

A married person as long as the marriage bond lasts. Since *divorce* is not acknowledged by the Church, a divorced husband or wife cannot enter religion. But if the ecclesiastical authority (episcopal or Roman court) decides against the existence of a marriage, the parties are free. As to the sentence of the episcopal court it must be understood of the final sentence not appealed. *Separation,* granted either perpetually or for a time by the ecclesiastical court, does not dissolve the marriage tie, and therefore parties thus severed cannot be admitted to a religious institute. Neither can mutual consent or permission solve the marriage bond, wherefore the old practice on this head must be discarded.[14] The text is

13 Cfr. can. 637.
14 Cf. X, III, 32. With the con-

sent of his wife a man could enter religion on condition that the wife, brief, but clear and pointed, and we believe our notes on it to be correct.[15]

Those who are or have been bound by the bonds of religious profession. This law excludes all who are or were members of any other religious community by profession. Of course, the profession must have been *valid,* otherwise he was not bound (*obstrictus*). Hence if a profession is for any reason declared null and void, the one who made it may be validly admitted to the novitiate. Note that *any* valid profession, whether temporary or perpetual, simple or solemn, has the effect of binding one to the religious institute in which it is made. For the text simply says, without distinction: religious profession.

Those who are menaced with punishment for a serious crime, of which they have been or can be accused. A crime is a public transgression in a matter that touches the public welfare, and in civil law has a penal sanction attached to it. Under this heading falls the threefold category of crimes, *viz.,* treason, felony, and misdemeanor, although the latter might perhaps be excluded here, because the text says: *gravis* (serious) crime. Note that the Code does not limit the term to ecclesiastical crimes, but simply says a serious crime of which one has been or can be accused. The reason is evident, *viz.,* to protect the decorum and reputation of the religious life, which should not be a shelter and refuge for criminals. The wording, "who are amenable to punishment" (*quibus imminet poena*), supposes that the penalty is probable. Hence if one should be declared

---

if under fifty years, would also enter a religious order, or, if beyond that age, would take the vow of chastity.

15 Papi, H., *Religious Profession,* 1918, p. 14: " A married person, while his or her partner is alive "— does not render the text adequately.

" not guilty," although he may have committed the crime, he may be validly received, though not while the trial is pending.

Every bishop, whether residential or titular, even though only nominated by the Roman Pontiff. The reason for this prohibition lies in the mystic marriage between the bishop and his diocese, which also forbids a transfer from one diocese to another, except by special permission from the Pope.[16] *"Designatus"* (nominated or appointed) means promulgated by the Pope in public consistory. Consequently a bishop-elect, or one merely postulated or presented for the episcopate, but whose election is not yet ratified, postulation not admitted, or presentation not effected by investiture, may freely be admitted to the religious state. Consecration is not required to make the prohibition effective.

Clerics who, by a disposition of the Holy See, are bound by oath to consecrate themselves to the service of their diocese or mission, for the period during which their oath binds them. This is the impediment that arises from the title of the *service of the Church* for which one is ordained. The oath is taken before one is ordained subdeacon [17] and contains a special clause prohibiting entrance into religion.

The North American College in Rome is now under the superintendence of the S. C. Consistorialis, which watches over the taking of this oath, and grants dispensations from the same.[18] If the title of *servitium Ecclesiae* is changed into another, *e. g.,* that of patrimony or pension, which may be done by the bishop with the

16 C. 2, X, I, 7; c. 18, X, III, 31, which latter text justly says that if a weighty or solid reason is advanced, the petition shall easily be granted.

17 Cfr. the Instruction of the S. C. Prop. Fidei, April 27, 1871 (*Collectanea S. C. P. F.*, II, n. 1369).

18 S. C. Consist., Jan. 7, 1909 (*A. Ap. S.*, I, 148 ff.).

permission of said sacred Congregation, the obligation ceases. If one is ordained on any other ecclesiastical title, for instance, that of patrimony, the oath must not be taken, and the clergyman is, on that score, free to enter religion.

Can. 542 then continues as follows:

2.° The following are *illicitly* but validly admitted [to the novitiate] :

Clerics in sacred orders, without the consent of the local Ordinary or against his will, if his objection is based on the serious loss to souls that their withdrawal would entail, when that loss cannot by any means be otherwise avoided. This is the old practice followed by the Roman Court, as several constitutions, especially that of Benedict XIV, " *Ex quo,*" Jan. 14, 1747, prove. The welfare of souls being the supreme law, it is but natural that private desires and aspirations must make way for it. Ordinary politeness, if nothing else, would dictate that a clergyman who wishes to join a religious order should manifest his desire to the Ordinary. In case the latter is persuaded of the necessity of retaining such a priest in the service of the diocese, he may claim him even after he has made his profession.[19] But a bishop is not entitled to keep a priest from entering the religious state on the plea that he is indebted to the diocese for his seminary expenses, because a clergyman is not bound to repay these.[20]

Those who are burdened with debts which they are unable to discharge. These were dealt with severely by Sixtus V, but more leniently by Clement VIII. Our Code makes their admission merely illicit.[21] Note that

---

19 Benedict XIV, " *Ex quo.*"
20 Nilles, *Disputationes Selectae,* p. 55; Piatus M., *l. c.,* I, 74.
21 Sixtus V, " *Cum de omnibus,*"
Dec. 1, 1587; Clement VIII, " *In suprema,*" Jan. 2, 1602; " *Cum ad regularem,*" March 19, 1603.

no one who is heavily indebted is to be admitted to the religious state, even though the order or congregation he wishes to enter is willing to pay his debts. Such an offer would imply alienation, which is not permitted. Minor debts may be assumed by a religious community. *Heavy* debts is a relative term, depending on one's fortune. One is heavily indebted if compelled to declare himself insolvent, or to sell all his property to satisfy his creditors.

Those who are liable to furnish accounts or are implicated in other secular negotiations from which the institute may have reason to fear lawsuits and annoyances. Hence all public officials liable to render accounts, guardians and tutors, trustees and treasurers, administrators and procurators must first acquit themselves of their accounts before they can be received. This was the meaning of the Constitution of Sixtus V, " *Cum de omnibus,*" Dec. 1, 1587.

Persons whose parents, that is, father or mother, grand-father or grand-mother, are in great necessity and need their assistance, and parents whose help is necessary for the support and education of their children. The Code is explicit as to the degrees of relationship within which persons are bound to succor their relatives. Parents or grand-parents would be in " great necessity " if they depended for support solely on the child or grandchild who wishes to enter the religious state. *A parent's* first duty is to support and educate his or her children. However, if these can be cared for equally well by others, the parent would be permitted to join a religious order, as the text speaks conditionally.

Those who in religion would be destined for the priesthood, from which, however, they are debarred by an irregularity or other canonical impediment. On these impediments consult can. 984 to 991. *Illegitimate* children may be licitly received into a religious order or congregation with solemn vows, because the Code [22] reasserts the old law [23] that solemn profession removes irregularity and admits one to holy orders, the priesthood included, but not to higher orders or dignities. Note that these impediments affect only members of a clerical institute who are destined for the priesthood. Hence lay religious and women's congregations and orders are not touched by the prohibition at all.

Orientals may not be received into institutes of the Latin rite without the written permission of the S. Congregation for the Eastern Church. This applies to all Orientals who belong to the Oriental Rite. For those who have, with the Holy See's permission, changed to the Latin rite, there is no impediment as to being received into a Latin institute.[24] This canon is a logical corollary of can. 98, which prohibits indiscriminate mingling of the Oriental and the Latin rites.

THE RIGHT OF ADMITTING NOVICES, ETC.

CAN. 543

Ius admittendi ad novitiatum et subsequentem professionem religiosam tam temporariam quam perpetuam pertinet ad Superiores maiores cum suffragio Consilii seu Capituli, secundum peculiares cuiusque religionis constitutiones.

The right of admitting to the novitiate and to the subsequent profession, whether temporary or perpetual, be-

---

[22] Can. 984, 1°.

[23] Cfr. X, I, 17; 6°, I, 11; c. 14, X, V, 34; Reg. Iuris 87, in 6°.

[24] On the Aventine Hill in Rome in the Xth century there was a monastery, S. Alessio, in which Latin and Greek monks lived under one abbot, the former following the rule of St. Benedict, the latter that of St. Basil.

longs to the higher superiors, who, however, depend on the vote of the council or chapter, according to the requirements of the constitutions of each particular institute.

The reception of novices is a matter of great importance for the upkeep of discipline, and concerns not only the individual postulant, but the whole community, and therefore it is but proper that the whole community should have a share in it. The Code instructs superiors and convents to coöperate in the matter. In congregations with a chapter, properly so-called, like the Benedictines, the whole chapter must vote on each case, and this vote is not only consultive, but decisive. Where *counsellors* take the place of the chapter, they must be consulted and their vote obeyed. In each case the majority decides, and only when there is a tie, is the superior's vote decisive. For the rest, the constitutions must determine the manner of receiving novices.

We may add that the Ordinary of the diocese has no right to admit candidates to the novitiate of papal institutes, but under the Constitution " *Conditae* " of Leo XIII he is entitled to be informed about the candidates who wish to be received, and those who are to be admitted to vows; he may also examine them, according to the customary rules, and if no objection is found, admit them.[25] This, however, does not mean that the Ordinary may arbitrarily reject some and command others to be received.

TESTIMONIALS

Can. 544

§ 1. In quavis religione omnes adspirantes, antequam admittantur, exhibere debent testimonium recepti baptismatis et confirmationis.

[25] I, n. 7; cf. can. 552.

§ 2. Adspirantes viri debent praeterea testimoniales litteras exhibere Ordinarii originis ac cuiusque loci in quo, post expletum decimum quartum aetatis annum, morati sint ultra annum moraliter continuum, sublato quolibet contrario privilegio.

§ 3. Si agatur de admittendis illis qui in Seminario, collegio vel alius religionis postulatu aut novitiatu fuerunt, requiruntur praeterea litterae testimoniales, datae pro diversis casibus a rectore Seminarii vel collegii, audito Ordinario loci, aut a maiore religionis Superiore.

§ 4. Pro clericis admittendis, praeter testimonium ordinationis, sufficiunt litterae testimoniales Ordinariorum in quorum dioecesibus post ordinationem ultra annum moraliter continuum sint commorati, salvo praescripto § 3.

§ 5. Religioso professo, ad aliam religionem ex apostolico indulto transeunti, satis est testimonium Superioris maioris prioris religionis.

§ 6. Praeter haec testimonia a iure requisita, possunt Superiores quibus ius est adspirantes in religionem cooptandi, alia quoque exigere, quae ipsis ad hunc finem necessaria aut opportuna videantur.

§ 7. Mulieres denique ne recipiantur nisi praemissis accuratis investigationibus circa earum indolem et mores, firmo praescripto § 3.

§ 1. In every institute, all the aspirants, before being admitted, must present a *certificate of their baptism and confirmation*. The certificate of baptism may be issued by the pastor or his assistant, but it must be signed in the name of the pastor and sealed with the parish seal. The certificate of confirmation may be issued by the diocesan chancellor but must bear the diocesan seal.

Until he has presented his certificate of baptism and confirmation an aspirant cannot receive the religious habit.[26]

§ 2. The *male aspirants* must, besides, furnish *testimonial letters from the Ordinary* of the place of birth, and from the Ordinary of whatever other place in which, after completing their fourteenth year, they have lived for more than a year, morally continuous, notwithstanding any privilege to the contrary. This rule was inculcated by the decree "*Romanos Pontifices,*" of Jan. 25, 1848, which need no longer be read at table, the promulgation of the Code being sufficient.[27] The Code fixes fourteen years instead of fifteen, as did the decree. The Ordinary of the place of birth is the one in whose diocese the father of the candidate lived when the candidate was born. Persons of illegitimate parentage follow the domicile of the mother. Besides the testimonials of the bishop of the place of birth, the candidate must have letters from the Ordinaries of all other dioceses in which he has dwelt for more than one morally continuous year. The phrase *morally continuous* indicates habitual residence. A few weeks' absence from a diocese would not impair this moral continuity of residence. Much depends on the intention, but if a man comes and goes, but always returns to the same place, he is morally present in the diocese in which that place is situated.

§ 3. When there is question of admitting aspirants who have been in a *seminary,* a *college,* or in a postulancy or novitiate of *another institute,* testimonial letters, given,

---

26 S. C. EE. et RR., May 29, 1857, n. 2 (Bizzarri, *l. c.,* p. 850). Of course, these rules are to be urged only in normal times; in times like ours it is often impossible to obtain the necessary information. In every such case the S. C. Rel. should be informed of the facts, and if no answer comes, the novitiate may be begun licitly,— its validity not being in question.

27 Cfr. can. 509, § 2, 1, which says those decrees shall be read which the Holy See will in future prescribe (*prescribet*).

according to the circumstances, by the rector of the seminary or college, after consulting the local Ordinary, or by the higher superior of the institute, are also necessary. This paragraph enumerates three hypotheses: (a) the aspirant may have been a student of a seminary or (b) of a college, or (c) a postulant or novice of a different religious order. But in neither case is § 2 invalidated, wherefore the Code says, *praeterea,* besides, *viz.,* besides the testimonials demanded in § 2, supposing, of course, that the aspirant belongs to the male sex.

Seminary means a theological (grand) seminary, but does not exclude a preparatory (petit) seminary. The term *college* includes academies for young ladies, because § 7 includes female religious. Now if a candidate has been an alumnus of such a seminary or college or academy, no matter how long, he must present testimonial letters from the respective rector or president or superioress. Before they issue such testimonial letters, these officials must consult the Ordinary of the diocese and obtain his approval. Testimonial letters thus approved and signed by the Ordinary, or his vicar-general or chancellor, may serve at the same time as episcopal testimonials as to residence in the diocese, where such are required. A nine months' stay in a seminary or college or academy would in itself not make it necessary for an aspirant to obtain testimonial letters from the Ordinary of the diocese in which the seminary or college or academy is situated.[28] Sometimes it happens that students spend the whole year in such an institution. Observe that no seminary or college, even though conducted by exempt religious, is free from the obligation in question. The last clause provides that aspirants who have

[28] A three months' vacation would certainly interrupt the "morally continuous" year supposed to require such a testimonial.

been *postulants or novices* of some other institute must
also present testimonial letters from the higher superiors
(those mentioned in can. 488, n. 8). Note, first, that
the Ordinary need not be consulted before issuing such
testimonial letters. Secondly, that the term *alius religionis* may be insisted upon. For *religio* means an organization different from others. Consequently a change
from one province to another, or from one monastic
congregation to another of the same order would not
require testimonial letters from the religious superior
who had dismissed the postulant or novice. The decree
of the S. C. Rel., Sept. 7, 1909, mentions only dismissal
from " orders and religious congregations," [29] although
in another decree (April 5, 1910) the same congregation
speaks of a " religious family." [30] But the latter decree
is only an interpretation of the former, and therefore,
until an authentic interpretation is given to the contrary,
we cling to the strict wording of the Code.

§ 4. For the admission of *clerics*, it suffices, besides
the certificate of ordination, to have testimonial letters
from the Ordinaries of the dioceses in which the clerics
have lived for more than one morally continuous year
after ordination, without prejudice to the prescription
of § 3. *Ordination* is the conferring of higher and
minor orders, and includes the first tonsure,[31] by which
one formally enters the ranks of the clergy. Clerical aspirants to the religious life, therefore, need: (a) a *certificate of ordination*, (b) *testimonial* letters from the *Ordinaries*, as stated in this paragraph and in § 2, *if* they have
lived in their dioceses for one morally continuous year;
(c) testimonial letters from the superior of a seminary,
college or religious institute, *if* they had been received

29 *A. Ap. S.*, I, 701.   31 Can. 950.
30 *Ibid.*, II, 231.

as seminarians, students, postulants or novices.[32] The reason why they do not need testimonial letters from the bishop of their place of birth lies in the fact of their ordination, which presumes the necessary documents.

§ 5. For a *professed religious* passing, by virtue of an apostolic indult, to another institute, the testimony of the higher superior of the institute which he leaves suffices. One who, having made temporary or perpetual, simple or solemn profession in one order or congregation, wishes to be transferred to another, and has obtained a papal indult permitting him to make the change, needs only the testimony of the superior of the order he desires to leave. This superior is the general or provincial, or, if the order or congregation is distributed into provinces, the local superior. Should the aspirant have changed previously, only the superior of the institute to which he last belonged must give his testimonial letters. But before granting them, the superior should carefully investigate the character of the applicant.[33]

§ 6. Besides these testimonials required by law, the superiors, who have the right of admitting aspirants to the institute, can exact *others* also, if it seems to them necessary or opportune. This rule was no doubt made in order to provide surer guaranties for the moral and physical fitness of candidates.

§ 7. *Women* are not to be received until careful investigation has been made regarding their character and conduct, with due regard to § 3.

We will add a decision of the Roman Court [34] concerning the necessity of testimonial letters: for they are necessary only to make the profession licit, but not to make it

---

[32] S. C. EE. et RR., Nov. 5, 1852 (Bizzarri, *l. c.*, p. 849).

[33] S. C. EE. et RR., Nov. 5, 1852,

ad 2; May 29, 1857, ad 3 (Bizzarri, *l. c.*, p. 849 f.).

[34] S. C. super Statu Regul., May 1, 1851 (Bizzarri, *l. c.*, p. 841, n. 9).

valid. The same view is taken by our Code, which no-where, neither in can. 555 nor in can. 572, makes testi-monial letters a condition for the validity of the novitiate or profession. But superiors are gravely obliged in con-science to see that such letters are furnished when re-quired by law.[35]

<h3 style="text-align:center">TESTIMONIALS — CONTINUED</h3>

<h3 style="text-align:center">CAN. 545</h3>

§ 1. Qui litteras testimoniales ex praescripto iuris dare debent, eas non ipsis adspirantibus, sed Superiori-bus religiosis dent gratuito intra trimestre spatium ab arum requisitione, sigillo clausas et, si agatur de illis qui in Seminario, collegio vel alius religionis po-stulatu aut novitiatu fuerint, a Superiore iuramento firmatas.

§ 2. Si ob graves rationes iudicaverint se eis respon-dere non posse, causas Apostolicae Sedi intra idem tempus exponant.

§ 3. Si reposuerint adspirantem satis non esse sibi cognitum, per aliam accuratam investigationem ac fide dignam relationem Superior religiosus suppleat; si vero nil reposuerint, Superior requirens de non recepta responsione Sanctam Sedem certiorem reddat.

§ 4. In suis litteris testimonialibus, postquam dili-gentem investigationem, etiam per secretas notitias, in-stituerint, referre debent, graviter eorum conscientia onerata super veritate expositorum, de adspirantis natalibus, moribus, ingenio, vita, fama, conditione, sci-entia; sitne inquisitus, aliqua censura, irregularitate aut alio canonico impedimento irretitus, num propria

---

[35] " Gravissime onerata conscien-tia eorum "; cfr. can. 2411, which states that careless superiors may be deprived of their office.

familia eius auxilio indigeat, et tandem, si agatur de
illis qui in Seminario, collegio, aut alius religionis po-
stulatu aut novitiatu fuerint, quanam de causa dimissi
sint vel sponte discesserint.

§ 1. Those who must, according to the law, give testimonial letters, should not consign them to the aspirants,
but to the religious superiors, and this gratuitously within
three months from the date of request, closed and sealed,
and if the aspirants are persons who have been in a seminary, a college, postulancy or novitiate of another institute, the testimonial letters must be signed under oath by
the superior.

As to the testimonial letters, they may be private, without official character, but they must be sealed. Concerning the superior's oath, it must be given in writing, for
instance: " In witness whereof I invoke the name of
Almighty God and hereto set my hand " (and seal, if the
writer has an official seal).

According to § 2 and § 3, if they who are to give
testimonial letters feel that they cannot comply with the
request for them, they must make known the reasons
to the Holy See (S. C. Rel.) within the time stated, i. e.,
three months. If they reply that the aspirant is not sufficiently known to them, the religious superior shall supply the deficiency by making careful inquiries of sources
worthy of credence; but if they give no reply, the superior who made the request must inform the Holy See
that he has received no response. Of course, this legislation is intended for normal times, when mail travels
safely. Other reports may be made by those who knew
the aspirants,— parents, relatives, pastors, teachers,
friends, schoolmates, etc. The decree from which our
text is chiefly taken admonishes the superior to keep the

candidate in the convent for at least three months and test him carefully.[86]

§ 4. In their testimonial letters, the Ordinaries and superiors, after having made careful investigation, even by secret enquiries, must give information, the accuracy of which they are under grave obligation in conscience to control, on the birth, conduct, character, life, reputation, condition (social status), and learning of the aspirant; whether he be suspect, or under any censure, irregularity, or any other canonical impediment; whether his family needs his help; and, finally, when there is question of persons who have been in a seminary, a college, or in a postulancy or novitiate of another institute, the reasons for their dismissal or spontaneous departure. This moral passport needs no further explanation. The term "*inquisitus*" may mean, "demanded in court," either civil or ecclesiastical. This seems to be confirmed by can. 542, § 1, but the official English translation renders it by "suspect," as given above.

CAN. 546

Omnes qui praedictas informationes receperint, stricta obligatione tenentur secreti servandi circa notitias habitas et personas quae illas tradiderunt.

All those who have received the aforesaid information are strictly obliged to keep secret not only the information itself, but also the names of the persons who supplied it.

[86] S. C. super Statu Regul., May 1, 1851 (Bizzarri, *l. c.*, p. 840).

Can. 547

§ 1. In monasteriis monialium postulans afferat dotem in constitutionibus statutam aut legitima consuetudine determinatam.

§ 2. Haec dos ante susceptionem habitus monasterio tradatur aut saltem eius traditio tuta reddatur forma iure civili valida.

§ 3. In religionibus votorum simplicium, quod ad religiosarum dotem pertinet, standum constitutionibus.

§ 4. Dos praescripta condonari ex toto vel ex parte nequit sine indulto Sanctae Sedis, si agatur de religione iuris pontificii; sine venia Ordinarii loci, si de religione iuris dioecesani.

In monasteries of nuns, the postulant shall provide the dowry fixed by the constitutions or determined by lawful custom. This dowry must be given to the monastery before the reception of the habit, or at least its payment guaranteed in a manner recognized by the civil law.

In institutes with simple vows, the constitutions must be obeyed with regard to the dowries of religious women. The prescribed dowry cannot be condoned either totally or partially, without a papal indult in the case of institutes approved by the Holy See, in pontifical, or without the consent of the local Ordinary in the case of diocesan institutes.

Dowry means a security in money or its equivalent for the purpose of maintaining a religious institute. Hence it is not a donation, nor an offering to gain entrance,[37] which would be simony, but a permissible and irreprehensible mode of guaranteeing the necessary support.

---

[37] This was the opinion of the Febronian canonist Van Eybel; cfr. Bachofen, *Compendium Iuris Reg.*, p. 109.

Neither must it be confounded with legacies, bequests, hereditary acquisition, patrimony, or pension. If a monastery of Sisters has no special law or rule concerning dowries — which should not be less than $100 — the following canons do not concern it. The amount of the dowry should be established in the constitutions, and any condonation, either total or partial, requires the consent of the legitimate authority (§ 4). The amount fixed by the constitutions may not be raised without the permission of the Holy See.[88] The dowry must be secured in a form that is valid according to the laws of the State. A notary public and witnesses are therefore required. Any secure source of income, either money or title-deeds, government or State bonds, bank deposits, shares in sound stock companies, are admissible. But the dowry itself or guarantee thereof must be delivered before the candidate receives the habit.

CAN. 548

Dos monasterio seu religioni irrevocabiliter acquiritur per obitum religiosae, licet haec nonnisi vota temporaria nuncupaverit.

The dowry is irrevocably acquired by the monastery or the institute on the death of the religious, even though she had made profession of only temporary vows. For as long as a Sister lives, the monastery is the sole trustee or administrator of her dowry.

CAN. 549

Post primam religiosae professionem dos in tutis, licitis ac fructiferis nominibus collocetur ab Antistita

---

[88] The reason is that it would be alienation, which is prohibited, and derogate from the authority of the Holy See, which had approved the constitutions.

cum suo Consilio, de consensu Ordinarii loci et Superioris regularis, si domus ab hoc dependeat; ŏmnino autem prohibetur eam quoquo modo ante religiosae obitum impendi, ne ad aedificandam quidem domum aut ad aes alienum exstinguendum.

After the first profession of the religious, the superioress with her council, and with the consent of the local Ordinary and the regular superior, if the house be dependent on regulars, must place the dowry in a safe, lawful and productive investment; but it is strictly forbidden that, before the death of the religious, the dowry be expended for any purpose, even for the building of a religious house or the payment of debts.

For any alienation of the dowry an apostolic indult is required. However, the interest accruing from the dowry may be used for any purpose.

Can. 550

§ 1. Dotes caute et integre administrentur apud monasterium vel domum habitualis residentiae supremae Moderatricis aut Antistitae provincialis.

§ 2. Ordinarii locorum conservandis religiosarum dotibus sedulo invigilent; et praesertim in sacra visitatione de eisdem rationem exigant.

The dowries must be carefully and integrally administered at the monastery or house of habitual residence of the Mother General or Mother Provincial.

The local Ordinaries must diligently see that the dowries of the religious are conserved; and they must demand an exact account thereof, especially at the canonical visitation.

CAN. 551

§ 1. Dos religiosae professae sive votorum sollemnium sive votorum simplicium quavis de causa discedenti integra restituenda est sine fructibus iam maturis.

§ 2. Si vero religiosa professa ad aliam religionem ex apostolico indulto transeat, durante novitiatu, fructus, salvo praescripto can. 570, § 1; emissa vero nova professione, dos ipsa huic religioni debentur; si ad aliud eiusdem Ordinis monasterium, huic debetur ipsa dos a die transitus.

If, from whatever cause, a professed religious with either solemn or simple vows leaves the institute, her dowry must be returned to her intact, but not the interest already derived therefrom.

But if, by virtue of an apostolic indult, the professed religious joins another institute, the interest on the dowry, during her new novitiate, without prejudice to the prescription of can. 570, § 1, and, after the new profession, the dowry itself must be given to the latter institute; if the religious passes to another monastery of the same order, the dowry belongs to it from the day the change takes place.

This canon refers to can. 570, § 1, concerning a Sister changing from one religious institute to another, which allows a certain alimony for the postulancy and novitiate.

EXPLORATIO VOLUNTATIS, OR EXAMINATION

CAN. 552

§ 1. Religiosarum etiam exemptarum Antistita debet Ordinarium loci, duobus saltem mensibus ante, certiorem facere de proxima admissione ad novitiatum et ad professionem tum temporariam tum perpetuam sive sollemnem sive simplicem.

§ 2. Ordinarius loci vel, eo absente aut impedito, sacerdos ab eodem deputatus, adspirantis voluntatem, saltem triginta diebus ante novitiatum et ante profes-sionem, ut supra, diligenter et gratuito exploret, non tamen clausuram ingrediens, num ea coacta seductave sit, an sciat quid agat; et, si de pia eius ac libera vo-luntate plane constiterit, tunc adspirans poterit ad novitiatum vel novitia ad professionem admitti.

The superioress even of exempt religious must inform the local Ordinary, at least two months in advance, of the approaching admission to the novitiate and to the profession both of temporary and perpetual or of solemn or simple vows. Hence the bishop must be informed three times, viz., before the novitiate, before temporary profession, and before perpetual profession.

The local Ordinary, or, if he is absent or otherwise impeded, a priest delegated by him, must, at least thirty days before the admission to the novitiate and to pro-fession, carefully examine the disposition of the aspirant, and this gratuitously, without, however, entering the en-closure. He must inform himself as to whether she has been forced or beguiled, and if she understands the im-port of what she is doing, the step she is about to take; and if he is fully satisfied regarding her pious intention and freedom of action, then the aspirant may be ad-mitted to the novitiate, or if already a novice, to pro-fession. The examination must be made free of charge, and outside the enclosure, at least if the convent has papal enclosure. This is the safeguard against physical or moral compulsion erected by the Council of Trent [89] and the Roman Congregations.

[89] Sess. 25, c. 17, de reg.

ARTICLE II

THE TRAINING OF NOVICES

CAN. 553

Novitiatus incipit susceptione habitus, vel alio modo in constitutionibus praescripto.

The novitiate begins with the reception of the habit, or in any other manner prescribed by the constitutions. It was not always customary to doff the secular dress and don a special religious habit when one became " converted." At least St. Benedict's Rule (c. 58) would seem to teach us differently. A synod of Aix-la-Chapelle (816–817) enjoined that the secular dress should not be changed until one had promised obedience. However, Benedict of Aniane (482) assumed the monastic habit as a novice and the Clunians tonsured their novices and clothed them with the monk's habit, except the cowl (*cuculla*) ; and ever since the IXth and Xth centuries the custom of investing novices with a religious habit became almost universal.[40] Yet exceptions were and are made, and hence the Code refers to the constitutions of each institute. What is necessary is that the novice as well as the community know the exact date of the beginning of the novitiate.

ERECTION OF THE NOVITIATE

CAN. 554

§ 1. **Erigatur domus novitiatus ad normam constitutionum; si vero agatur de religione iuris pontificii, ad**

---

40 Cfr. Migne, 66, 837.

eam erigendam necessaria est licentia Sedis Apostolicae.

§ 2. Plures in eadem provincia novitiatus domus, si
religio in provincias divisa sit, designari nequeunt, nisi
gravi de causa et cum speciali apostolico indulto.

§ 3. Superiores in novitiatus ac studiorum domo ne
collocent, nisi religiosos qui sint ad exemplum regularis
observantiae studio.

The novitiate house shall be erected in accordance with
the prescriptions of the constitutions; but in case of institutes approved by the Apostolic See the permission
of the latter is necessary for the erection. If the institute is divided into provinces, more than one novitiate
must not be erected in the same province without a
grave reason and a special apostolic indult. Superiors
shall have in the novitiate houses and houses of study
only religious who are exemplary in their zeal for regular observance. A novitiate may be erected by diocesan
institutes with the permission of the bishop, according to
their own constitutions. But any order or congregation
which has received the decree of recognition (*decretum
laudis*), or has been formally approved by Rome, must
have permission from the S. C. of Religious. Note that
permission for founding a religious house does not include permission to erect a novitiate, unless express mention was made of it in the petition.

§ 2 emphasizes a law which was first given and observed in Italy, but is now general, at least in a certain
measure. Clement VIII had ruled that only one novitiate, designated for each province by the Apostolic See,
could receive novices validly.[41] The Code is not so strict.

41 "*Regularis disciplinae,*" March 12, 1596; "*Sanctissimus,*" June 20,
1599, § 1.

It merely enjoins that each province should have but one novitiate. This rule binds only those religious institutes which are divided into provinces. The term *province* must be interpreted strictly. It does not mean a congregation, but a local or national organization. One novitiate for each province will, as a rule, accommodate and be adequate to the training of all novices (cfr. can. 501, § 3). If, however, the number is too large, or linguistic or other difficulties render it advisable to have more than one novitiate, a special indult is required — *special*, because not implied in the one given according to § 1 of this canon by the Apostolic See.

REQUISITES FOR THE VALIDITY OF THE NOVITIATE

CAN. 555

§ 1. Praeter alia quae in can. 542 ad novitiatus validitatem enumerantur, novitiatus ut valeat, peragi debet:

1.° Post completum decimum quintum saltem aetatis annum;

2.° Per annum integrum et continuum;

3.° In domo novitiatus.

§ 2. Si longius tempus in constitutionibus pro novitiatu praescribatur, illud ad validitatem professionis non requiritur, nisi in eisdem constitutionibus aliud expresse dicatur.

§ 1. Besides the other conditions enumerated in can. 542 for the validity of the novitiate it is further required that the novitiate be made:

1.° After the aspirant has completed at least the fifteenth year;

2.° For an entire and uninterrupted year;

3.° In the novitiate house.

§ 2. If the constitutions prescribe more than one year for the novitiate, the extra time is not required for the validity of the profession, unless the constitutions expressly declare otherwise.

The conditions enumerated under can. 542, § 1, have been dealt with. The other three conditions are plain enough. We need only add that the age is the same for both *sexes, viz.,* the fifteenth year, fully completed. A *full year* comprises 365 days, even though the novitiate be begun or finished in a leap-year. But the severity of some older canonists, who insisted upon moments, is out of place under the new Code. Thus if one commences his novitiate on the morning of June 21st, 1919, he may make his profession on June 21st, 1920, at any time of the day. But if he commenced the novitiate at noon or in the evening of June 21st, he could not validly make his profession until June 22, 1920 (cfr. can. 34). The term *continuum* here means physically and morally uninterrupted, of which more shall be said in the following canon. The *novitiate house* is the special building or space reserved for novices. Where only a certain space or room or department is set aside for the novitiate, the whole house is a quasi-novitiate. Novitiate here simply means the house or place approved by the Apostolic See for the training of novices, though it is evident that the Holy See wishes to see a special novitiate house erected for every province and congregation. Thus the English Benedictine Congregation has a novitiate house, and Leo XIII fully approved its rule.[42] Proper training and uniformity of discipline can be achieved only where there is *one* novitiate.

§ 2 allows religious institutes to insert in their constitutions a clause decreeing a longer novitiate, but they

42 " *Diu quidem,*" June 29, 1899.

must explicitly state whether this clause touches the validity of the novitiate. If they merely say, " the novitiate lasts two years " without making it a condition of validity, one year is sufficient.

INTERRUPTION OF THE NOVITIATE

Can. 556

§ 1. Novitiatus interrumpitur, ita ut denuo incipiendus ac perficiendus sit, si novitius, a Superiore dimissus, e domo exierit, aut domum sine illius licentia non reversurus deseruerit, aut extra domum, etsi reversurus, ultra triginta dies sive continuos sive non continuos permanserit quacunque ex causa, etiam de Superiorum licentia.

§ 2. Si novitius ultra quindecim, sed non ultra triginta dies etiam non continuos, de Superiorum licentia vel vi coactus extra domus septa permanserit sub Superioris obedientia, ad validitatem novitiatus necesse et satis est dies hoc modo transactos supplere; si non ultra quindecim dies, supplementum potest a Superioribus praescribi, sed non est ad validitatem necessarium.

§ 3. Superiores licentiam manendi extra septa novitiatus, nisi iusta et gravi de causa, ne impertiant.

§ 4. Si novitius a Superioribus in aliam novitiatus domum eiusdem religionis transferatur, novitiatus non interrumpitur.

The novitiate is interrupted, and must be recommenced and completed: (a) if the novice is sent away by the superior and leaves the house, or (b) if, without the permission of the superior, he leaves the house with the intention of not returning, or (c) if, even with the superior's permission from whatever motive, he has re-

mained for more than thirty days, whether continuously
or not, outside the house, although he may return to it.

Here are three distinct cases. The first is *dismissal*
by the superior, followed by the departure of the novice.
If the dismissal would be revoked before the novice had
left the house or premises, there would be no interruption.[43] But there is interruption as soon as the dismissed
novice has left the house, even though the dismissal is
made upon false accusations, and the novice be reinstated.
For our text cannot be otherwise construed, although
some authors[44] deny interruption in that case. A somewhat different aspect is offered by this case: A novice
is dismissed and leaves the house after having spent a
full and continuous year in the novitiate, and later is re-
admitted; what then? We believe with solid writers that
there is no interruption of the novitiate in this case, because the novitiate had already ended.

The case mentioned under (b) supposes *two conditions:* leave without permission and the intention of not
returning. Whenever these two conditions are present,
there is an interruption, no matter whether the novice
leaves with or without the habit, or for a long or a short
time. Neither is the nature of the action to be considered, as Suarez says;[45] for such a novice is looked upon
as a deserter (*deseruerit*), and desertion requires no
specified length of time, if the will is there.

The last (c) case supposes only one condition, *viz.:
absence protracted for more than thirty days,* even though
with the permission of the superior and for a just reason.
Hence if a novice would live on a farm or in a summer
resort ten days in one month, ten days in another month,

43 Piatus M., *l. c.*, I, 99.   45 *De Rel.*, tract. VII, l. V, c. 15,
44 Ferrari, *De Statu Religioso,*   n. 6 (ed. Paris, Vol. 15, p. 368 f.).
1906, p. 78.

and ten days, say, with a specialist (physician), the novitiate would be interrupted and would have to be recommenced. The same holds true if a novice would spend three days each month in a physician's office, away from the novitiate. But if he would spend fifty-nine half-days away from the novitiate house, he would not interrupt his novitiate, because the law by *day* understands a space of twenty-four hours.[46]

Note the phrase: *in the novitiate house.* If a person would spend, say, thirty-one days in a religious house which is not designated as the novitiate house, his novitiate would be interrupted. Living on a farm away from the house where the novitiate is established, for more than thirty days, would also involve an interruption.

§ 2. If a novice, with the permission of superiors or constrained by force, has passed more than *fifteen but not more than thirty days, even interruptedly,* outside the precincts (*septa*) of the house, under obedience of the superior, it is necessary and sufficient for the validity of the novitiate that he supply the number of days so passed outside; if for a period not exceeding fifteen days, the supplementing for this period can be prescribed by the superiors [46] but it is not necessary for validity. This text is a repetition of two decrees of the S. C. Relig., May 3, 1914, the latter of which (Paris.) also explains what is meant by "*vi coactus.*" It is military service which one had to render.[47] The decision is remarkable as it concerns a novice who was forced to serve as a soldier in the barracks of a city, we suppose Paris, where the religious have a novitiate. The soldier spent all the time he could spare from military service in the novitiate house and obeyed the orders of the religious superior. But the S. Congregation justly held that the time thus

46 Can. 32, § 1.   47 *A. Ap. S.,* VI, 229 f.

divided between military service and the duties of the novitiate should not be reckoned as fulfilling the requirements for the novitiate. Compelled by force may also refer to a contagious disease, for instance, smallpox, cholera, etc., which require a quarantine in a house especially destined for such purposes.[48] Therefore if this separation would not last more than thirty days, the novitiate would not be interrupted.

§ 3. Superiors must not grant novices permission to remain outside the precincts of the novitiate except for a just and grave reason. No superior can grant such a permission for more than thirty days without involving an interruption of the novitiate.

§ 4. If the novice be transferred by the superiors to another novitiate of the same institute, the novitiate is not interrupted.

CAN. 557

Integer novitiatus peragatur in habitu quem constitutiones pro novitiis praescribunt, nisi speciales locorum circumstantiae aliud exigant.

The full year of the novitiate must be spent *in the habit* prescribed *for novices* by the constitution, unless special local circumstances determine otherwise. Nonobservance of this law does not invalidate the novitiate. Local custom, especially in missionary countries, may justify not wearing the habit, at least in public. In the U. S. novices do not usually appear in public in their religious habit. This custom, the Code says, may be respected.

---

[48] The same would have to be said of mental aberration lasting more than thirty days, although occasional lucid intervals might be in evidence. Yellow fever, they say, is not really contagious, but carried chiefly by mosquitos, against which a bar might be needed.

Can. 558

In religionibus in quibus duae sunt sodalium classes, novitiatus pro altera classe peractus, pro altera
non valet.

In institutes whose members are divided into two
classes, the novitiate made in one class does not avail
for the other. Thus the novitiate made by lay Brothers
or Sisters is not valid for clerical members or choir nuns
if the latter constitute a class for themselves.

THE MASTER OF NOVICES AND HIS ASSISTANT

Can. 559

§ 1. Novitiorum institutioni praeficiendus est Magister, qui sit annos natus quinque saltem ac triginta,
decem saltem ab annis a prima professione professus,
prudentia, caritate, pietate, religionis observantia con-
spicuus et, si de clericali religione agatur, in sacerdotio
constitutus.

§ 2. Si ob novitiorum numerum vel aliam iustam
causam expedire visum fuerit, Magistro novitiorum
adiungatur socius, eidem immediate subiectus in iis
quae ad novitiatus regimen spectant, annos natus saltem triginta, quinque saltem ab annis a prima professione professus, cum ceteris dotibus necesariis et opportunis.

§ 3. Uterque ab omnibus officiis oneribusque vacare
debet, quae novitiorum curam et regimen impedire
valeant.

§ 1. The training of the novices must be entrusted to
a master who shall be at least thirty-five years of age,
and professed for at least ten years from the date of his
first profession, and be distinguished for prudence, char-

ity, piety, and fidelity to regular observance, and if the institute be clerical, he must be a priest.

§ 2. A companion or assistant should be given to him, if the number of novices or other reasons require it. This assistant shall be immediately subject to the master in all matters pertaining to the government of the novitiate, and must be at least thirty years of age, and professed five years from the date of his first profession and have the other necessary and suitable qualities.

§ 3. Both (master and assistant) should be free from all other occupations which could hinder them in the care and government of the novices.

CAN. 560

Magister novitiorum eiusque socius eligantur ad normam constitutionum, et si quod in his tempus ad durationem muneris praescriptum sit, eo durante, ne removeantur sine iusta gravique causa; sed iidem rursus eligi possunt.

The master of novices and his assistant shall be selected according to the direction of the constitutions, and, if these prescribe a fixed term of office, they must not within that time be removed from their charge without a just and grave cause; besides, they may be reappointed.

CAN. 561

§ 1. Uni Magistro ius est et officium consulendi novitiorum institutioni, ad ipsumque unum novitiatus regimen spectat, ita ut nemini liceat hisce se, quovis colore, immiscere, exceptis Superioribus quibus id a constitutionibus permittitur ac Visitatoribus; ad disciplinam vero universae domus quod attinet, Magister, perinde ac novitii, Superiori est obnoxius.

§ 2. Novitius potestati Magistri ac Superiorum religionis subest eisque obedire tenetur.

The master of novices alone has the right and the duty of providing for the proper training of the novices, he alone is charged with the direction of the novitiate, so that none, under whatever pretext, may interfere in these matters, except the superiors, who are permitted to do so by the constitutions, and the visitators; as to the general discipline of the house, the master, together with the novices, is subject to the superior.

CAN. 562

Gravi obligatione tenetur Magister novitiorum omnem adhibendi diligentiam ut sui alumni in religiosa disciplina, secundum constitutiones, sedulo exerceantur, ad normam can. 565.

The master is under grave obligation to employ all diligence in assiduously forming his novices in the discipline of the religious life, conformably to the constitutions and to the terms of can. 565.

CAN. 563

Intra annum novitiatus Magister, ad normam constitutionum, de agendi ratione singulorum alumnorum relationem Capitulo vel Superiori maiori exhibeat.

During the course of the year of novitiate, the master of novices, conformably to the constitutions, must present to the chapter or the higher superior a report concerning the conduct of each of the novices.

CAN. 564

§ 1. Novitiatus ab ea parte domus, in qua degunt professi, sit, quantum fieri potest, segregatus ita ut,

sine speciali causa ac Superioris vel Magistri licentia,
novitii nullam habeant communicationem cum professis, neque hi cum novitiis.

§ 2. Conversis autem novitiis locus separatus adsi-
gnetur.

The novitiate shall be, as far as possible, separated
from that part of the house inhabited by the professed
religious, so that, without a special cause and the permission of the superior or of the master, the novices may
not have communication with the professed religious, nor
these latter with the novices. For the lay-brother novices
a special place must be set apart. Futile reasons are
sometimes advanced to abolish this pedagogically sound
law.

CAN. 565

§ 1. Annus novitiatus debet sub disciplina Magistri
hoc habere propositum, ut informetur alumni animus
studio regulae et constitutionum, piis meditationibus
assiduaque prece, iis perdiscendis quae ad vota et ad
virtutes pertinent, exercitationibus opportunis ad vi-
tiorum semina radicitus exstirpanda, ad compescendos
animi motus, ad virtutes acquirendas.

§ 2. Conversi praeterea diligenter in christiana doctrina instituantur, speciali collatione ad eos habita
semel saltem in hebdomada.

§ 3. Anno novitiatus ne destinentur novitii concionibus habendis aut audiendis confessionibus aut exte-
rioribus religionis muniis, neve dedita opera studiis
vacent litterarum, scientiarum aut artium; conversi
autem in ipsa religiosa domo eatenus tantum fungi
possunt officiis fratrum conversorum (non tamen uti
primarii officiales), quatenus ab exercitiis novitiatus
pro ipsis constitutis non praepediantur.

§ 1. The year of novitiate under the direction of the master must have for its object the forming of the mind of the novice by means of the study of the rule and constitutions, by pious meditation and assiduous prayer, by instruction on those matters which pertain to the vows and virtues, by suitable exercises in rooting out the germs of vice, in regulating the motions of the soul, in acquiring virtues.

§ 2. The lay-brother novices should be carefully instructed in Christian doctrine, for which purpose a special conference should be given to them at least once a week.

§ 3. During the year of novitiate, the novices must not be employed in preaching or hearing confessions, or in the external charges of the institute, or even in the study of letters, the sciences or arts; the lay-brother novices, however, may perform within the religious house itself all the duties of lay brothers (but in a subordinate capacity), in so far only as such duties do not prevent them from taking part in the exercises prescribed for them in the novitiate. Work may be prayer, indeed; but manual labor, if it takes the place of the prayer and religious exercises prescribed for novices, is not a substitute for holy practices, nor an incentive to religious fervor.

Can. 566

§ 1. Circa sacerdotem a confessionibus in mulierum novitiatibus serventur praescripta can. 520–527.

§ 2. In religionibus virorum, salvo praescripto can. 519:

1.° Pro novitiorum numero unus vel plures habeantur ordinarii confessarii, salvo praescripto can. 891;

2.° Confessarii ordinarii, si agatur de religione clericali, in ipsa novitiatus domo commorentur; si de laicali, saltem frequenter ad domum novitiatus accedant, novitiorum confessiones audituri;

3.° Praeter confessarios ordinarios, designentur aliqui confessarii, quos novitii in casibus particularibus adire libere possint, nec Magister aegre id se ferre demonstret;

4.° Quater saltem in anno detur novitiis confessarius extraordinarius, ad quem omnes accedant saltem benedictionem recepturi.

§ 1. As regards the *confessor for the novitiates of women,* the prescriptions of can. 520–527 must be ob-observed.

§ 2. For the *institutes of men,* without prejudice to can. 519:

1.° There shall be, according to the number of novices, one or more ordinary confessors; but the religious superior and the master of novices are allowed to hear the confessions of the novices for a grave reason in special cases, if the novices ask them to do so of their own accord (can. 891).

2.° In clerical institutes the ordinary confessors for the novitiate shall live in the novitiate house itself; while in lay institutes they shall at least frequently visit the novitiate house to hear the confessions of the novices.

3.° Besides the ordinary confessors other confessors must be designated, to whom in particular cases the novices may freely go; nor may the master of novices manifest any displeasure at this.

4.° At least four times a year the novices are to be given an extraordinary confessor, to whom all are to present themselves at least to receive his blessing.

Can. 567

§ 1. Novitii privilegiis omnibus ac spiritualibus gratiis religioni concessis gaudent; et si morte praeveniantur, ad eadem suffragia ius habent, quae pro professis praescripta sunt.

§ 2. Ad ordines, durante novitiatu, ne promoveantur.

§ 1. The novices enjoy all the privileges and spiritual favors granted to the institute; and if they die during the novitiate, they have a right to the same suffrages as are prescribed for the professed members.

§ 2. They must not be promoted to orders during the novitiate.

Concerning the *privileges* of novices, it has always been maintained that they share all of them, as far as they are capable, because they go by the name of religious as to favors. Therefore theirs are the privileges of the *forum* and *canonis*, and immunities, the privilege of exemption if their institute is exempt, the privileges of dispensation, commutation of vows, and absolution. As to *spiritual favors* they can gain all the indulgences granted to their institute, as far as they are capable, and no restriction is made in favor of professed members. Another spiritual right they enjoy is that to have offered for them, if they die, the prayers for the repose of the soul which, the Code says, must be offered for novices as well as professed members. We confess that this clause appeared new to us, and no quotation is given in support of it in Cardinal Gasparri's notes. But it is a logical interpretation of the general rule that novices partake of the favors of religious proper. However, the distinction between persons in sacred orders and in minor orders, between lay-brothers and clerical members, is certainly to be retained. Hence if a definite number of masses and communions are prescribed for each class, the novices are entitled to the same according to the class to which they belong.

A privilege not especially mentioned here, but certainly still in force, which therefore may safely be made use of, is that granted to the Dominicans by Pius V, and six years ago extended *to all novices*. This privilege permits novices to make profession in *case of sickness* which according to the judgment of the physician may be considered *danger of death*. Now this privilege may be made use of, provided (1) the novitiate was duly commenced and the novice admitted by the actual superior of the novitiate; (2) that the vows be pronounced according to the usual formula and without addition as to the length of time or character of the vows, whether temporary or perpetual.

The *effects* of that profession are merely to gain the plenary indulgence in the form of a jubilee indulgence, but no other juridical effects follow. Hence the religious institute obtains no material right as to said novice's property or other rights; and the novice may afterwards freely leave the institute or be dismissed therefrom, and must renew the profession after the time of the novitiate has expired.[49a]

RENUNCIATION OF PROPERTY

CAN. 568

In novitiatus decursu, si suis beneficiis vel bonis quovis modo novitius renuntiaverit eademve obligaverit, renuntiatio vel obligatio non solum illicita, sed ipso iure irrita est.

[49] Clem. VIII "*Cum ad regularem*" March 19, 1603.

[49a] S. C. Rel., Sept. 10, 1912 (*A. Ap., S.*, V., 589 f.).

The Council of Trent[50] strictly forbade the giving away of property by novices under pain of nullity. The reason for this enactment is to guarantee the freedom of the novice, so that no obstacle may detain him if he wishes to return to the world. Our Code formulates this rule as follows: If, during the novitiate, the novice in any way whatever renounces his benefices or his property, or encumbers them, such a renunciation or encumbrance is not only illicit but null and void.

Hence (1) no *ecclesiastical benefice,* as defined under can. 1409, may be renounced by the novice, no matter what its value or importance may be. Hence no parish, no chaplaincy, no canonicate, no prebend, if they are canonical benefices, may be given up. But what about *our parishes?*[51] Although they perhaps lack an essential feature of benefices, *viz.,* objective perpetuity, we believe that the mind of the legislator regards them as benefices.[52] For, as we have said, the end of the law is to safeguard liberty, which may be just as seriously impaired by the resignation of a parish as of a strict benefice. (2) The novice may not renounce his property — *bona.* To this category belong all donations of considerable amount, title-deeds or other claims to property, shares, bonds, interest, contracts which are more favorable than injurious to the novice,[53] legacies and bequests already received or to be received during the novitiate; but *not* small donations or alms given to the poor or to the monastery, nor legacies or inheritances to be expected after the death of relatives or friends.[54] (3) *Renunciation* may be made in favor of friends, relatives or other persons, also in favor of the institute one wishes to enter, or of another

50 *Trid.,* sess. 25, c. 16 de reg.
51 Can. 584.
52 This law, although seemingly restrictive, yet is favorable to the novice, and therefore open to a broad interpretation.
53 Cfr. Piatus M., I, 124.
54 Reiffenstuel, III, 31, n. 136.

institute. It means to disclaim any right to such goods. *Obligation* is here understood not only in the legal sense of bond or bail, but in a wider sense, comprising vows, oaths, promises, and the moral duty which binds one to do or omit something. For any such act is a restriction of liberty. Now all such acts are declared *null and void,* and therefore would not bind the novice nor convey a legal title to the recipient. Hence even though the civil court would uphold the legality of such an act, in conscience those benefited by it could not accept the property.

CAN. 569

§ 1. Ante professionem votorum simplicium sive temporariorum sive perpetuorum novitius debet, ad totum tempus quo simplicibus votis adstringetur, bonorum suorum administrationem cedere cui maluerit et, nisi constitutiones aliud ferant, de eorundem usu et usufructu libere disponere.

§ 2. Ea cessio ac dispositio, si praetermissa fuerit ob defectum bonorum et haec postea supervenerint, aut si facta fuerit et postea alia bona quovis titulo obvenerint, fiat aut iteretur secundum normas § 1 statutas, non obstante simplici professione emissa.

§ 3. Novitius in Congregatione religiosa ante professionem votorum temporariorum testamentum de bonis praesentibus vel forte obventuris libere condat.

§ 1. Before the profession of simple vows, whether temporary or perpetual, the novice must cede, for the whole period during which he will be bound by simple vows, the administration of his property to whomsoever he chooses and dispose freely of its use and usufruct except the constitutions determine otherwise.

§ 2. If the novice, because he possessed no property,

omitted to make this cession, and if subsequently property should come into his possession, or if, after making provision, he becomes under whatever title the possessor of other property, he must make provision, according to § 1, for the newly acquired property, even if he has already made simple profession.

§ 3. In every religious congregation the novice, before making profession of temporary vows, shall freely dispose by will of all the property he actually possesses or may subsequently possess.

The enactment of this canon would at first sight appear contrary to can. 568, which forbids any renunciation or encumbrance of property. Here certain acts are permitted which seemingly violate that prohibition. However, the contradiction is but apparent. For can. 568 speaks of the time during the novitiate (*in novitiatus decursu*), whereas can. 569 refers to the period immediately preceding profession. The Tridentine Council[55] permitted a disposal of property to be made within two months before profession. Besides, in can. 569 the question turns on ceding the administration and disposal of the use and usufruct, whilst can. 568 speaks of the property itself. *Administration* means the management of affairs pertaining to property or estates of any kind, also incorporeal rights, such as copyrights and patent rights. Now this function must be given to another, who may be a layman, or the religious order or congregation itself.[56] Of course, this must be done in a legal form, in other words, in court, unless the religious community is acknowledged by law as a civil corporation, in which latter case the by-laws should provide for such eventualities.

The next act which a novice should freely perform is

---

55 *Trid.*, sess. 25, c. 16, de reg.
56 S. C. super statu Reg., June

12, 1858, n. 9 (Bizzarri, *l. c.*, p. 856: " *ac etiam suo ordini.*")

to *dispose of the use and usufruct of his property*. There is a little difficulty as to the term *use*. If it involved the consumption of the whole property it would impair the freedom of the owner and run counter to can. 581, which says that professed religious of simple vows cannot validly renounce their property, except within the sixty days immediately preceding the taking of solemn vows. Hence use must here be taken as an application to a good and useful purpose of the *income* from the capital or property. This is more clearly expressed in a declaration of June 12, 1858, where we read of "expending and using the income or revenues (*redditus*)."[57] *Usufruct* is the temporary use of a thing, or profit and advantage derived therefrom without destroying or wasting its substance, for instance, of a house or farm.

The cession of the administration and disposal of such property must be made before simple profession and remains in force for the whole period during which the subject is bound by simple vows.

§ 2 applies this ruling to two cases: (a) when a novice had no property, the administration of which he would have to cede, or of which he could freely dispose, but comes into the possession of property subsequently; (b) when he foresees an increase of his property after simple profession. In both cases, says the Code, the simple profession does not prevent the novice from ceding the administration and disposing of the property newly acquired.

§ 3 mentions the testament or *last will*, by which a novice, before making profession of temporary vows, shall dispose of the property he actually possesses or may subsequently possess. This, of course, only for the

57 *Ibid.*, cfr. *Normae*, n. 115.

case of death.   The Code restricts the making of a last will to novices of *religious congregations*, excluding the orders, which, however, may be benefited by an act of the novice *inter vivos*, or a donation, properly so-called.

Can. 570

§ 1. Nisi pro alimentis et habitu religioso in constitutionibus vel expressa conventione aliquid in postulatu vel novitiatu ineundo solvendum caveatur, nihil pro impensis postulatus vel novitiatus exigi potest.

§ 2. Quae adspirans attulerit et usu consumpta non fuerint, si e religione, non emissa professione, egrediatur, ei restituantur.

Except the constitutions or a formal agreement require the payment of a certain sum for food and clothing during the postulancy or novitiate, nothing may be exacted to defray the expenses of the postulancy or novitiate.

All that the aspirant brought with him and has not consumed, shall be returned to him if he leaves without making profession.

The ancient monastic rules were not in favor of demanding anything, in whatever shape or form, from those who knocked at the door of the monastery.[58]   Councils forbade the exaction of fees for admission to the religious state, justly comparing such money to simoniacal extortion.[59]   The same rule, although in a somewhat mitigated form, was followed by the S. Congregation of Bishops and Regulars.

The mitigation consisted in permitting a moderate tuition fee to be charged for the time of probation, an oblation for the sacred functions and for a banquet, but not

---

[58] Cfr. Migne, 66, 831 ff.

[59] Cfr. cc. 2, 3, C. 1, q. 2; c. 5, C. 20, q. 3; c. 2, X, 35; cc. 19, 25, 30, 40, X, V, 3; *Trid.*, sess. 25, c. 16, de reg.

too sumptuous.   But no stipulation as to these latter offerings was allowed, and the custom of receiving or demanding any admission fee reprimanded.[60]   Our Code con-
firms this practice, but adds that the expenses must be
either mentioned in the Constitutions or determined by
special agreement.

ENDING THE NOVITIATE

CAN. 571

§ 1. **Novitius potest religionem libere deserere, aut
a Superioribus vel a Capitulo, secundum constitutiones,
quavis iusta de causa dimitti, quin Superior vel Capitulum teneantur dimissionis causam dimisso pate-
facere.**

§ 2. **Exacto novitiatu, si iudicetur idoneus, novitius
ad professionem admittatur, secus dimittatur; si
dubium supersit sitne idoneus, potest a Superioribus
maioribus probationis tempus, non tamen ultra sex
menses, prorogari.**

§ 3. **Votis nuncupandis spiritualia exercitia novitius
praemittat per octo saltem solidos dies.**

The first paragraph of this canon provides

(1) That a novice may freely leave the institute.

(2) That he may be for any just cause dismissed by
the superiors or chapter, who are not bound to make
known to him the reasons for his dismissal.

(3) That the dismissal must be according to the terms
of the constitutions.

As to the last point note that the Code insists upon the
constitutions of the institute.   If these prescribe that the
chapter has the right to dismiss novices, the chapter must
decide each case by secret ballot.   If the constitutions

---

[60] S. C. EE. et RR., Dec. 11, 1789 (Bizzarri, *l. c.*, p. 396).

are silent on this point, the superior may dismiss the novice. But neither superior nor chapter are obliged to make known to the novice the reason for his dismissal; for, as the novice is free to leave, so the institute is free to dismiss one whom it deems unfit. However, justice requires that no one be dismissed without a just cause, because arbitrary proceeding might destroy or injure the good name of the novice. Therefore a Decretal of Gregory IX ruled that if the novice absolutely insisted on remaining to serve God, he should be allowed to do so.[61] Of course this meant that he must be willing to observe the rule and fit himself for membership, for no religious institute or society can be compelled to retain an unfit member.

§ 2. After the completion of the novitiate, the novice, if deemed fit, shall be admitted to profession; otherwise he shall be dismissed; but if there arises a doubt regarding his fitness, the higher superiors can prolong the novitiate, but not beyond six months. Some misgivings might arise as to religious institutes which prescribe a two years' novitiate; have their superiors, too, the right to prolong the novitiate for six months? Our answer is, yes, because, on the one hand, the Code (can 555, § 2) admits a two years' novitiate, and, on the other, it only says, *exacto novitiatu*, after the novitiate is completed. If the text would say, after the year's novitiate (*exacto novitiatus anno*) the answer would be negative; this, however, is not the wording of the text.

The last paragraph of can. 571 prescribes a spiritual retreat of at least eight whole days before profession. "Eight whole days" means that the retreat must commence in the morning and end in the evening of the eighth day, so that profession takes place on the morning of the ninth, or on the evening of the eighth day.

61 C. 23, X, III, 31.

CHAPTER III

RELIGIOUS PROFESSION

The term profession, from *profiteri*, denotes an external act of conviction. Thus we speak of the profession of faith, and St. Paul says: "With the heart we believe unto justice; but with the mouth confession is made unto salvation."[1]

Religious profession, therefore, is an external act of the mind by which one embraces the religious state, or the external testimony of one who aspires to be a servant of God. It is well known that the ancient ascetics had a predilection for the word profession and defined it as a "covenant with God."[2] This flows from the very essence of the religious state, which involves service or worship of God.

As the Sacraments have their visible signs, so, too, religious profession is clothed in outward ceremonies. As the "second baptism"[3] (thus it was styled), profession was ever surrounded by more or less elaborate *rites*. We know from St. Benedict's Rule (c. 58) that the act of profession was performed in the oratory in the presence of the abbot and the community; that the novice made a promise the contents of which were formulated according to the rule and written in the document, which is signed by the novice and placed upon the altar. This was followed by the investiture. Thenceforth the

---

[1] Rom. X, 9.
[2] St. Basil, *Reg. Iusior*, tr. 14 (Migne, *P. G.*, 31, 950); Herwegen, *Beiträge zur Gesch. des alten Mönchtums*, 1912, III, I, p. 6.
[3] Migne, *P. L.*, 66, 827.

novice was a member of the community, with all the obligations and rights of membership. A document was drawn up containing his petition to be received, as well as the promise to live perpetually in the community under the obedience of the abbot, for the purpose of striving after perfection.   Note, however, that after the act was performed, the newly professed was considered to be a member of the congregation endowed with rights.   According to the ideas of the olden time, the obedience promised was looked upon as a sort of personal vassalage to the abbot.   It would hardly be possible now-a-days to conceive of such absolute subjection, and the spirit of our time is opposed to any such relation.   Yet the spirit of obedience, being essential to the religious state, can never be sacrificed to the idol of a falsely so-called democracy.

Concerning the *sacred virgins*, we know from St. Ambrose that the bishops " consecrated " them, usually on the feast of the Resurrection, on which, as he says, Baptism is conferred in the whole world.[4] The bishop blessed the veil and put it on the head of the virgin.[5] This veil seems to have covered the head and upper part of the body like a helmet or breast-plate. Its color was sombre, in opposition to the yellow bridal veil,[6] because it signified holy sorrow.[7] The ceremony was accompanied by appropriate prayers and the people answered: " Amen." [8] It is evident that the sacred veil signified the mystic espousal with Christ, to whom these virgins dedicated themselves.

Having said this much concerning the rite and significance of profession, which is nothing else but public en-

4 Migne, P. L., 16, 331, 348.
5 Opp. Nicetae, Migne, P. L., 52, 1099 f.
6 Ramsay-Lanciani,. Roman Antiquities, 1901, p. 478.
7 Migne, P. L., 52, 1000.
8 Migne, P. L., 16, 372.

trance upon the exclusive service of God, according to a determined rule or constitution, we may now hear what the Code says concerning profession. The classification of profession into temporary, perpetual, simple, and solemn is to some extent new. For, as said before, to the middle of the XVIth century only one profession, the solemn, was acknowledged, which was supposed to take place after the novitiate. With the exception of the Jesuits this practice was followed by all religious institutes until 1858, when the S. C. super Statu Regularium issued the decree, "*Neminem latet.*" This decree enacted that after the novitiate the members of male religious institutes should take simple vows, which were to be continued for three years from the date of the simple profession, or longer, according to the prudent judgment of the superiors, but not beyond twenty-five years. Leo XIII ("*Perpensis,*" May 3, 1902) extended this decree to nuns with solemn vows. Yet it has always been the opinion of authors and the practice of the Roman congregations up to a few years ago to consider these simple vows as perpetual on the part of the religious. But lately the Roman Court commenced to regard them as temporary or triennial, and this view has been embodied in the Code.

REQUISITES OF VALIDITY

CAN. 572

§ 1. Ad validitatem cuiusvis religiosae professionis requiritur ut:

1.° Qui eam emissurus est, legitimam aetatem habeat ad normam can. 573;

2.° Eum ad professionem admittat legitimus Superior secundum constitutiones;

3.° Novitiatus validus ad normam can. 555 prae-
cesserit;

4.° Professio sine vi aut metu gravi aut dolo emittatur;

5.° Sit expressa;

6.° A legitimo Superiore secundum constitutiones
per se vel per alium recipiatur.

§ 2. Ad validitatem vero professionis perpetuae sive
sollemnis sive simplicis, requiritur insuper ut praeces-
serit professio simplex temporaria ad normam can. 574.

1. For the validity of any religious profession whatever it is required that he who makes it be of the legitimate *age, viz.*, for the first temporary profession he must
have completed his sixteenth year; for *perpetual* profession, whether simple or solemn, the twenty-first, according to

Can. 573

Quilibet professionem religiosam emissurus oportet
ut decimum sextum aetatis annum expleverit, si de
temporaria professione agatur; vicesimum primum, si
de perpetua sive sollemni, sive simplici.

The Code determines the minimum age, but leaves the
question as to a more advanced age undetermined. The
Normae[9] rule that in institutes with simple vows the
candidate should not be more than thirty years, and although these are not law, yet if the constitutions contain a prescription to that effect, it would not be against
the law. But they may not go below the minimum as
fixed by can. 573.

2. The novice must be *admitted* by the lawful *superior*

---

[9] N. 61. Those who had passed the 30th year, in female congregations,
needed a papal indult.

according to the constitutions. Who that superior is, must be determined by the rule and the constitutions (cfr. can. 543).

3. The profession must be preceded by a *valid novitiate* according to the terms of can. 555, which have been explained *supra*.

4. The profession must be *free from compulsion, fear, and fraud*. These three conditions may be reduced to one: *freedom of profession*. For further explanations see under can. 542, 1.° *Deceit (dolus)* would be present if the one professing subscribed the formula of profession either in a faulty way or with the wrong name.

5. The profession *must be expressed in formal terms*. This means that it must be made either in writing, or if orally, in such a way that no reasonable doubt is left as to the consent of the one who makes it. A deaf and dumb person would, therefore, have to express his consent in writing to eliminate all doubt. *Tacit profession* is no longer [10] admitted. It used to be assumed [11] if the novice was admitted to capitular acts (voting) permitted only to professed members, or allowed to wear the religious habit after a year's novitiate. Now profession, to be valid, must be made in words or signs which formally express the intention.

6. The profession *must be received by the lawful superior* or his *representative* (as mentioned in can. 543). Note the distinction between No. 2 and No. 6. There admission to profession was the subject of the enactment, here the question turns about the superior, in whose presence the profession must be made. The constitutions determine who is the legitimate superior authorized

---

10 S. C. EE. et RR., June 12, 1858; Leo XIII, "*Perpensis*" May 3, 1902.

11 Cf. cc. 22, 23, X, III, 31; cc. 1, 3, 4, 6°, III, 14.

to receive professions. In diocesan congregations the bishop of the diocese is entitled to this privilege, whilst in papal institutes it depends entirely on the constitutions.

The *delegate* of the lawful superior [12] should be a priest if the ceremony takes place during Mass and the delegate personally receives the profession. Wherefore in the formula of profession both the superior's name and that of the delegate must be mentioned. However, if profession is made into the hands of the superioress, or her delegate (who may be any professed sister) the formula of profession must contain the name of the diocesan Ordinary, in whose hands the profession is made, and also the name of the delegate of the Ordinary, if the latter is not personally present at the ceremony. For the rest we refer to can. 576.

For the validity of perpetual profession, whether solemn or simple, the following requirements are laid down:

TEMPORARY PROFESSION

CAN. 574

§ 1. In quolibet Ordine tam virorum quam mulierum et in qualibet Congregatione quae vota perpetua habeat, novitius post expletum novitiatum, in ipsa novitiatus domo debet votis perpetuis, sive sollemnibus sive simplicibus, praemittere, salvo praescripto can. 634, votorum simplicium professionem ad triennium valituram, vel ad longius tempus, si aetas ad perpetuam professionem requisita longius distet, nisi constitutiones exigant annuales professiones.

§ 2. Hoc tempus legitimus Superior potest, renovata a religioso temporaria professione, prorogare, non tamen ultra aliud triennium.

12 *Regula Iuris*, 68, in 6°.

§ 1. In every order, both of men and of women, and in every congregation with perpetual vows (except the case of transfer according to can. 634) the novice must, after completing the novitiate, and in the novitiate house itself, make profession of simple vows; this profession, which must precede perpetual vows, whether solemn or simple, is valid for three years, or for a longer period if the age required for perpetual profession has not been reached, unless the constitutions prescribe annual professions.

§ 2. The legitimate superior can prolong this period, but not beyond three years, the religious meanwhile renewing the temporary profession.

Here we have the new legislation, no longer a wavering practice. In every religious institute, therefore, whether of men or of women, exempt or not exempt, papal or diocesan, a *temporary profession*, lasting as a rule, for three years, must precede perpetual profession.

Profession in general, we said, is the public entrance upon the religious state according to a determined rule or constitution. In this are included the three essential elements of the religious state: poverty, chastity, and obedience. Only the last element might be more elaborate; for obedience supposes acceptance. Hence, more fully defined, profession is *a bilateral contract by which one consecrates himself to God through the three vows, and to the service of a community approved by ecclesiastical authority, the religious superior accepting the vows in the name of the Church and admitting the person to share in the rights and privileges of the community.*[13]

13 Thus Schmier, *Iurisprudentia Canonico-Civilis*, l. III, li, 1, c. 3, n. 168; Schmalzgrueber, III, 31, 187 f.; Wernz, *Jus Decret.*, III, n. 640.

It would be useless, and we might say dangerous, to attempt [14] to deny that religious profession partakes of the nature of a contract: useless, because the essential elements of a contract are present, *viz.*: two parties, mutual consent, and obligation.   It would be dangerous, because who would enter the religious state if his spiritual welfare were not safeguarded and his support guaranteed? We may look at the consecration of oneself to God from the highest view-point of mysticism and absolutism, a man endowed with reason and free will cannot, from the viewpoint of natural law, abstract from the idea of receiving rights for assuming duties, nor from the right to an honest living.   The Rule of St. Benedict is not opposed to this view.[15]   For promise and petition must be rewarded, and they are recompensed, because henceforth the *professus* is to be considered a member of the congregation,[16] and membership without rights would be a mere phantasm.

Applying the definition set forth above, it is evident that a distinction must be made between temporary and perpetual, simple and solemn profession.   *Temporary profession* does not involve such an absolute and lasting contract as *perpetual profession*.   In regard to the latter the difference between simple and solemn vows is most important.   *Simple perpetual profession* implies no absolute and irrevocable covenant, whilst *solemn perpetual profession,* by its very nature, spells irrevocable consecration to God and acceptance of the same on the part of the religious superior in the name of the Church.   The difference will become more palpable when the conse-

14 Molitor, *Religiosi Iuris Capita Selecta,* 1909, p. 69 ff., who " selected " for his aim the aggrandizement of abbatial power.
15 Reg., c. 58.

16 A *pactum* or covenant was contained in the formula of profession prescribed by S. Fructuosus of Braga (VIIth century).

quences and obligations are considered (can. 579 and title XIII, ch. I).

Temporary profession may be made after the *age* of sixteen has been completed; *perpetual profession* after the 21st year. Hence if one makes profession at the age of sixteen, he has to remain in simple profession for five full years. The term may even be protracted for three years more, if the superior finds it necessary. A difficulty may arise concerning the date from which the superior may prolong the temporary profession: is it from the lapse of the third year of profession or from the age of twenty-one years, completed? If the end of the third year of temporary profession coincides with the twenty-first year completed there is no difficulty. For instance, a Sister would have to make profession on Nov. 21, 1918, having completed her twenty-first year of age as well as the third year of temporary profession. She wavers in her decision; — may the superioress prolong her time for one, two, or three years? Yes. And in the meanwhile she may renew the profession every year on Nov. 21. But what, if the Sister should be twenty-four years of age when she would have to make perpetual vows? Is the superioress in that case allowed to prolong her profession — to the limit of three years? Yes, because (as we believe) the dividing line is not so much the twenty-first year completed, this being only the minimum, than the date of temporary profession. This is especially convenient for institutes which prescribe five years' annual profession — a custom that may certainly be followed, since the text itself admits annual profession. But at the same time the triennial term must be kept and the prorogation should only be applied in really doubtful cases, and until the Code can be fully applied. Note that the Code makes the temporary profession imperative only for institutes in which perpetual vows are taken. But it includes all these institutes. Hence also *lay brothers* of religious orders, who would take solemn or simple perpetual vows, must now make, first the temporary profession, and after three (respectively five years, if the candidate was only 16 at the time of the first profession) perpetual vows.

The Code excepts *cases of transfer* (see can. 634).

The *legitimate superior* who may prolong the period of temporary profession is the one who admits to profession, not the one who assists at the act; therefore the higher superior.

Can. 575

§ 1. Exacto professionis temporariae tempore, religiosus, ad normam can. 637, vel emittat perpetuam professionem, sollemnem vel simplicem secundum constitutiones, vel ad saeculum redeat; sed etiam, durante tempore professionis temporariae, potest, si dignus non habeatur qui vota perpetua nuncupet, dimitti a legitimo Superiore ad normam can. 647.

§ 2. Suffragium Consilii seu Capituli pro prima professione temporaria est deliberativum; pro subsequente professione perpetua, sollemni vel simplici, est consultivum tantum.

When the period of temporary profession has expired, the religious, according to can. 637, must either make perpetual profession, whether solemn or simple, according to the constitutions, or return to secular life; but even during the period of temporary profession he can, if not judged worthy to pronounce perpetual vows, be dismissed by the legitimate superior in accordance with can. 647.

The vote of the council or chapter for the first temporary profession is deliberative; for the subsequent perpetual profession, solemn or simple, it is advisory only.

This canon clearly shows that the temporary profession is a sort of protracted novitiate. At the age of twenty-one, if the temporary profession or three years' term expires at the same time, or after the three years' profession, but not before the twenty-first year of age, the religious may freely return to the world, if he does not wish to assume the responsibility of perpetual vows, or have the temporary profession prolonged according to can. 574, § 2. Besides, he may be dismissed if he lacks the necessary qualities. In the latter case it must be observed: (a) That *sickness* contracted after the first profession during the temporary profession is no cause for dismissal; only if it had been deceitfully concealed or simulated at the time of the first profession would it be a sufficient reason for dismissing one (can. 637); (b) that the terms of can. 647 must be observed, as shall be explained later.

What is prescribed in § 2 concerning the *nature of the vote or ballot* is now law, and has been since 1862, when the S. C. Regularium decreed that the *chapter, i. e.,* the whole electoral college, or the *counsellors, i. e.,* a chosen number of religious, must *decide* by secret ballot whether or not one is to be admitted. But at that time the simple profession was considered perpetual in religious orders. Hence, logically, the admission to solemn profession had not necessarily to be submitted to the decisive vote again, the advisory vote being sufficient. However, since the new legislation changes the nature of the first profession into a merely temporary affair, it would have been but logical to change the advisory vote for perpetual profession into a decisive vote.

Can. 576

§ 1. In emittenda professione religiosa servetur praescriptus in constitutionibus ritus.

§ 2. Documentum emissae professionis, ab ipso professo et saltem ab eo coram quo professio emissa est, subscriptum, servetur in tabulario religionis; et insuper, si agatur de professione sollemni, Superior eam excipiens debet profitentis parochum baptismi de eadem certiorem reddere, ad normam can. 470, § 2.

§ 1. In making the religious profession, *the rite prescribed by the constitutions must be observed. Rite* means the sum total of the formalities or ceremonies which surround the religious act. Hence, it is essentially distinct from the consent of the religious, by which he dedicates himself to the service of God, and which the lawful superior accepts in the name of the Church, and the rite *does not affect the validity of the act,* unless the constitutions rule otherwise. Rite, therefore, indicates the place, time, and ceremonies prescribed by the 'constitutions and the decree of the Congregation of Rites, Aug. 27, 1894.

(a) As to the *place,* can. 574 says that the temporary profession should be made in the *novitiate house itself.* For other professions, whether annual or perpetual, simple or solemn, the Code prescribes no definite house, but leaves the matter to custom and the constitutions. But it may be safely assumed that the *oratory* or chapter room is the proper place for making profession.

(b) Concerning the *time,* as far as the period or term is not considered, nothing special is required or prescribed that would affect validity. Any day, therefore, and any time of the day may be called suitable for profession.

(c) The *ceremonies,* if the constitutions do not prescribe otherwise, are those contained in the above-mentioned decree of the Sacred Congregation of Rites.[17] They are briefly as follows: If profession takes place *during Mass*, the celebrant, who is to receive the profession, after having taken the Precious Blood, and after the recital of the *Confiteor, Misereatur,* and *Indulgentiam,* turns towards the candidates, holding in his hand the Sacred Host. Each candidate reads with a loud voice the formula of profession and thereupon receives the Blessed Sacrament.

At the *renewal* of vows, the celebrant turns towards the altar and waits until all have read the formula of renewal. This is read aloud by one and repeated by the others. After this recital all receive Holy Communion in the order of precedence established by the date of profession. However, adds the decree, this method of making profession must not be appended in the respective constitutions. Besides, it is chiefly intended for Sisters' and lay institutes. We may also cite a decision — not a general decree — of the same Congregation, given in reply to a query of a former arch-abbot of the Beuronese Congregation. He had asked whether at the solemn profession made during Mass other prayers may be added from authentic sources of the Roman Rite. The S. Congregation answered: "It is not expedient." [18]

The nuns with solemn vows receive the veil, ring and crown (wreath) at the simple profession; but the formula of solemn profession, which may, at the request of the superioress or community, be made publicly, must expressly contain the words: solemn profession.[19]

§ 2. A *written declaration of the profession*, signed by

---

[17] *Decreta Authentica,* n. 3836, which is not a particular decision, but a general decree, specially approved by Leo XIII.

[18] *Decreta Authentica,* n. 3736.

[19] S. C. EE. et RR., Jan. 15. 1903 (*Annal. Eccl.,* XI, p. 415).

the person professed and at least by him in whose presence the profession was made, must be kept in the archives of the institute. Besides, the superior who has received solemn profession must notify the pastor in whose parish the professed religious was baptized, according to can. 470, § 2.

This paragraph contains two different clauses; the first concerns a written declaration of the profession, the second registration in the baptismal record.

The "*Normae*" (n. 99) prescribed — and this rule still holds good — that the *formula of profession* must be substantially inserted in the constitutions. It must be clear and simple, expressing that the religious consecrates himself to God by the three vows, according to the constitution of the institute, either temporarily or perpetually. The formula actually used in the ceremony of profession may be more elaborate, but should not contain any essential additions.

As St. Benedict (c. 58) had already provided, this formula must be *written* or signed by the person who makes the profession. If he is unable to write, he may make the sign of the cross on the paper and then place it on the altar. St. Benedict says nothing, however, of the superior signing the formula. Perhaps the abbot signed the document, because it was considered a sort of legal contract; promise and petition and the whole apparatus of ancient documents seem to point to that,[20] and hence it is not surprising that the legislator demands that the one in whose presence the profession was made should also subscribe to the formula. Notice the wording *coram quo*, "in whose presence,"— an evident allusion to St. Benedict's Rule (c. 58), which says, "in the presence of all" (*coram omnibus*). There might be a

[20] Herwegen, *l. c.*, p. 4.

doubt whom the legislator means. Is it the superior into whose hands the profession is supposed to be made, or the superior who acts as his representative? In diocesan congregations there is little difficulty. For the one in whose presence the profession is made is the Ordinary or his delegate, who therefore has to sign the document or formula of profession. In papal institutes, especially of women, there is the superioress and the priest who assists at the rite of the profession. Which of them must sign the formula? We believe we are justified in saying (according to can. 572, § 1, 6) that the superioress or her delegate assisting at the profession has to sign the formula of profession together with the religious.

The document thus signed — if other bystanders wish to sign the Code does not forbid it — must be preserved in the archives of the institute. By institute (*religio*) the law implies that every order, or congregation, or convent, or monastery has its archives. It matters little in which of these archives the document is preserved.[21]

The second clause provides that the fact of *solemn profession be registered in the baptismal record* of the parish where the solemnly professed religious was baptized. Therefore the baptismal records ought to have a special column for such entries.

The reason for this ruling is not far to seek. For can. 1073 makes solemn profession, and simple profession by special apostolic indult,[22] an impediment to marriage.

---

21 This is also in accordance with St. Benedict's Rule (c. 58): "*in monasterio reservetur.*"

22 This is the case of the Society of Jesus.

RENEWAL OF VOWS

CAN. 577

§ 1. Elapso tempore ad quod vota sunt nuncupata, renovationi votorum nulla est interponenda mora.

§ 2. Superioribus tamen facultas est ex iusta causa permittendi ut renovatio votorum temporariorum per aliquod tempus, non tamen ultra mensem, anticipetur.

When the period for which the vows have been taken has expired, they must be immediately renewed. Superiors, however, are empowered, for a just cause, to anticipate the renewal of vows, but not beyond one month.

It is evident that the *renewal* of vows here is meant not as an act of mere devotion, but as producing juridical obligations. Therefore at the moment when the period, say one year, has elapsed, the renewal must take place after the 365th day, or on the first day after the year is completed. A sufficient reason for *anticipating* the renewal of vows would be sickness, departure for a study house, or a certain task. Of course, it is supposed that the religious freely consents to the anticipation. A *month*, canonically, is a period of thirty days.[28]

RIGHTS AND OBLIGATIONS OF PROFESSED PERSONS

CAN. 578

Professi a votis temporariis, ed quibus ni can. 574:

1.° Fruuntur iisdem indulgentiis, privilegiis et spiritualibus gratiis, quibus gaudent professi a votis sollemnibus aut professi a votis simplicibus perpetuis; et si morte praeveniantur, ad eadem suffragia ius habent;

---

28 Cfr. can. 32, § 2.

2.° Eadem obligatione tenentur observandi regulas et constitutiones, sed, ubi viget chori obligatio, divini officii privatim recitandi lege non obstringuntur, nisi sint in sacris constituti aut aliud constitutiones expresse praescribant;

3.° Voce activa et passiva carent, nisi aliud in constitutionibus expresse caveatur; tempus autem praescriptum ad fruendum voce activa et passiva, silentibus constitutionibus, computetur a prima professione.

Those who have made profession of temporary vows treated of in can. 574:

1.° Enjoy the same indulgences, privileges, and spiritual favors as the professed of solemn vows or of simple perpetual vows; and in case of death they are entitled to the same suffrages.

2.° They are equally obliged to the observance of the rule and constitutions, but where choir service is obligatory, they are not bound by law to the private recitation of the divine office, except they are in holy orders or the constitutions expressly impose it.

3.° They have neither active nor passive vote, except the constitutions expressly declare otherwise; but the time requisite for the enjoyment of an active and passive voice, when the constitutions are silent on the matter, is to be reckoned from the date of the first profession.

The first number puts all members of a religious community, order or congregation on an equal footing concerning *spiritual rights and privileges*. The Code mentions indulgences, spiritual favors, and *privileges*. What the last-mentioned term means has been sufficiently explained in the first book, title V.

Of *indulgences* the Code speaks in the third book, can. 911 ff. A *spiritual favor* is of a somewhat mixed nature.

It may be called a privilege, since every privilege is a favor,[24] yet it is restricted to the court of conscience. Such a favor is absolution from censures or reserved cases, change of private vows, dispensation from fast and abstinence, etc. Privileges one enjoys as far as he is capable of making use of them. Privileges granted to clerical orders as such are not intended for orders or congregations of women; privileges given to priests cannot be used by clerics who have only minor orders, etc. Among spiritual favors are also the *prayers for the dead*. These, the Code says, are enjoyed by those who have made profession of temporary vows in the same measure as by those who have taken perpetual vows; but we suppose, with the distinction noted under can. 567.

The second number of our canon enjoins the *same obligations* on all, with one exception. All professed religious are bound by the vow of obedience to observe the rule and constitutions of the community to which they belong. The exception noted concerns the recitation of the *Breviary*. Most of the religious orders prescribe the public recitation of the divine office in choir, at which all have to attend who are not legitimately excused. The divine office, according to common agreement, forms part and parcel of the religious state, and therefore all the members of every religious community are bound in conscience to take part in it in the spirit of the Church and according to their respective constitutions. Now the Church says that in religious communities which demand attendance in choir, also those members who have made profession of temporary vows, should be present at the divine office.[26] On the other

---

24 Suarez, *De Legibus*, VII, 2, 7.

25 Piatus M., *l. c.*, I, 96 f.

26 Cf. can. 589, § 2, where allowance is made for those engaged in studies.

hand, the Church does not oblige these to private recitation, unless, in accordance with can. 135, they are in higher orders, *i. e.*, at least subdeacons, or unless the constitutions prescribe private recitation. The Code does not mention custom. Therefore mere custom would not oblige them to private recitation, and this should be taught in the novitiate in order not to create an erroneous conscience.

No. 3 determines the *right to vote*. This is either *active, i. e.*, the right of partaking in capitular acts by casting one's vote; or *passive, i. e.*, the right to being appointed or elected to an office or prelacy. Both these rights are given radically by temporary profession, but are suspended — until when? Here the Code stops short, whilst Cardinal Gasparri refers the reader to certain decisions. We know them, but they do not settle the controverted point. The quintessence of all these declarations is that the date from which the right of active and passive voice is to be reckoned is that of the first profession. Thus, for instance, to be elected superior, ten years of profession, according to can. 504, are required; the date from which this period must be reckoned is the first or temporary profession. However, the constitutions may fix another date. But when does the right of *active* voice start? A declaration of the S. C. super Statu Regularium, June 12, 1858, would seem to insinuate that this right commences on the date of solemn profession.[27] Where only simple perpetual profession is made, it would naturally follow that this right starts from the date of the perpetual profession. No law text, however, prescribes the requisite of minor orders for enjoying the active voice, although particular constitutions may make higher or sacred orders a condi-

27 Bizzarri, *l. c.*, p. 858 f.

tion for the exercise of the ballot.[28] In *female congregations* the active, not passive, voice is now granted only to such who have made perpetual vows. Yet, if the constitutions say that those with temporary vows may partake in the election of a delegate for the chapter, this right must be respected, as it was formerly granted according to the "*Normae*" (n. 217), and the Code upholds these constitutions. Therefore a superioress would not be entitled to exclude a Sister with temporary vows from exercising that right on the strength of can. 578. Only if the constitutions are not explicit on this point, the Sisters with temporary vows may be excluded. But in that case *all* must be treated equally, because no superior has a right to limit the number of votes except for reasons expressed in common law [29] or the constitutions. The same holds good of all religious orders and congregations, the reason being evident. Arbitrary proceedings and injustice would result from the contrary practice.

EFFECTS OF RELIGIOUS PROFESSION

CAN. 579

Simplex professio, temporaria sit vel perpetua, actus votis contrarios reddit illicitos, sed non invalidos, nisi aliud expresse cautum fuerit; professio autem sollemnis, si sint irritabiles, etiam invalidos.

This and the following canons determine what are called the effects or consequences of religious profession. Can. 579 establishes these in general. Note that there is but one distinction made, *viz.:* between simple

---

28 The decretals and the Council of Trent demanded higher orders only for cathedral and collegiate churches, in order to stimulate the members to receive these orders.

29 Cfr. c. 14, X, I, 6; c. 32, 6°, I, 6; this is called the limitation of votes (*coarctatio votorum*).

and solemn profession. *Simple profession,* whether temporary or perpetual, renders acts contrary to the vows illicit but not invalid, unless it be otherwise formally expressed; while *solemn profession* renders such acts also invalid, if they can be nullified.

1. *Simple profession,* being a species of bilateral contract between the religious institute or community and the professed member, necessarily produces certain effects. Some of these have been mentioned in can. 578, *viz.:* the rights and obligations in general. The present canon speaks of certain *"acts contrary to the vows."* *Contrary* means opposed to another person or thing, so as to destroy it, or at least incompatibility. Thus we say truth is contrary to falsehood, coldness to warmth, in the same subject, at the same time, and under the same conditions. The *vows* referred to are the three religious vows of poverty, chastity, and obedience, not excluding special vows. The acts contrary to these vows are declared to be either illicit or invalid. They are *illicit,* in as far as they are simply forbidden by the vows themselves, or, let us rather say, they are prohibited because contrary to the vows, without any penal sanction or nullifying consequence being attached to the prohibition. *Invalid* are acts which are contrary to the vows and have an ecclesiastical sanction attached to them by which they are rendered destitute of any juridical value. Acts are illicit, therefore, because they are immoral, invalid because, besides being immoral, they are juridically or legally null and void. It is evident that the Church alone has the right to make the distinction between simple and solemn profession. In matter of fact the State pays little attention to the effects of religious profession. Hence it is, especially in matters of property rights, all-important that religious communities should

make by-laws determining the position of their members as to business transactions and compensation due them in case they choose to leave.

Acts contrary to the vow of *poverty*, induced by *simple profession*, are the free and independent disposal and administration of property after this has been ceded to the community. Hence a religious with simple vows may not dispose of his own property or that of the community. If he would dispose of his personal property, freely and without permission of the superior, he would commit a sin against the vow of poverty. But if he would dispose of community property, he would also commit a sin against justice, and be obliged to restitution, as far as he is capable, and as far as a serious damage would have been done to the community, unless the latter would be in a condition and ready to condone the damage. Restitution, however, is required only if the amount of property disposed of illegitimately would involve a grievous sin. This depends not only on the customs of the respective institute, but also on the size and welfare of the community, the value of money, and the extent of the damage done, as well as on personal persuasion and ability. We cannot name fixed sums,—five, ten or more dollars. It looks ridiculous to us to weigh a grievous sin by dollars and cents, as if to set an admission fee to purgatory or hell. We leave that to the moralists. Such acts contrary to the vow of poverty are illicit, but valid, *i. e.*, an illicit disposal of property would be legally valid and the contracting parties would be held responsible. However, the terms of can. 536 must be taken into consideration here, especially § 3 and § 4, as explained above.

The *vow of chastity* imposed by simple profession covers the whole matter of the *virtue of chastity*, but no more. The distinction between simple and solemn profession becomes very palpable in reference to marriage. For simple profession renders a *marriage* of a religious with a lay person or another religious of simple profession merely *illicit*, but not invalid, provided, of course, the ecclesiastical formalities have been duly observed. A pastor, or rather the Ordinary, would certainly have to stay such a marriage until the religious would have been dispensed or dismissed. An exception to this rule is the simple vow of chastity taken by the scholastics of the *Society of Jesus*, which renders a subsequent marriage not merely illicit but also invalid.[30] This so-called privilege is nothing but an application of the old theory[31] that every vow taken in a religious order is a solemn vow and therefore entails this invalidating impediment.

The vow of *obedience* excludes all contrary acts in as far as the rule and the constitutions are concerned. Authors generally enumerate under this heading *private vows* and *paternal authority*. *Private vows* are vows made by a religious before entering the religious state, for instance, a pledge in the form of a vow or promise to recite the Little Office of the Blessed Virgin. Simple profession extinguishes all previous vows as long as one remains in simple profession. But a vow made forever revives if the subject leaves the religious state.[32] A vow made in favor of a third person, for instance, to recite certain prayers or keep a fast for another's benefit, supposing that the promise was accepted by the other, would not be extinguished by simple profession, because made to a third person and not contrary to the religious state, as we presume. A pilgrimage promised in favor

---

[30] Gregory XIII, "*Quanto fructuosius*," Feb. 1, 1583; "*Ascendente Domino*," May 25, 1584; Papi, *l. c.,* p. 39.

[31] Cfr. c. 10, X, III, 32; cc. 3, 7, X, IV, 6; c. m. 6°, III, 15.

[32] Cfr. can. 1312 f.

of a third person, however, could be changed into some other good work, either by the religious superior or by a confessor empowered by the proper authority.[32]

Paternal authority is excluded, because obedience and piety are transferred to the religious superiors, *i. e.*, ultimately, God. Therefore parents who claim their sons and daughters after profession sin against the will of God and should be properly instructed, either in the confessional or outside the sacred tribunal.[34]

2. *Solemn profession* is one taken in an order with solemn vows, acknowledged as such by the Church. It has the following effects:

The *vow of poverty* excludes the right of owning property and disposing of anything without the permission of the lawful superior. The Code does not insert the clause, "unless special provision has been made." Hence a last will, or a gift *inter vivos* made by a solemnly professed religious, in favor of a convent or other pious cause would be invalid.[35] But the Holy See (S. C. Rel.) may grant the faculty of disposing or possessing, as was done in favor of nuns in France and Belgium,[36] where extraordinary conditions seemed to demand an exception. If these same nuns would establish a foundation in this country, they could not claim the privilege here, and would make only simple profession, according to

---

[32] Cfr. c. 4, X, III, 34: "He does not violate the vow who changes a temporary service into the perpetual observance of religion." *S. Th.*, II–II, q. 88, art. 12, ad 1; q. 189, art. 3, ad 3; confessors taken from orders have that power.

[34] Bouix, *De Iur. Reg.*, I, 617.

[35] S. C. EE. et RR., March 11, 1853 (Bizzarri, *l. c.*, p. 620 f.). A religious had been forced by the government to remain outside the convent and obtained an indult from the S. Poenitentiaria to use money for himself and for pious purposes; he made a will in favor of a pious cause before a notary public, which was declared invalid, because the indult was only for the court of conscience, and besides he was ordered to return to his convent.

[36] Bouix, *l. c.*, I, 493 ff.; Piatus M., I, 10 ff.

the decree of the S. C. of Bishops and Regulars, Sept. 30, 1864,[37] unless the S. C. of Religious would make special rules for them.

With regard to the *vow of chastity,* solemn profession, according to our Code (can. 1073), entails an invalidating impediment to matrimony, and hence an attempted marriage between a solemnly professed and a lay person, or another religious, would be null and void before the Church. Only if there were danger of death could the Ordinary or pastor rectify such an unlawful marriage, provided, however, neither of the contracting parties were a priest.[38]

As to the *vow of obedience,* we must repeat what we have said concerning simple profession, *viz.,* that solemn profession extinguishes all private vows and paternal authority.

As to vows note that, though one may be secularized or dispensed afterwards, these vows do not revive, because solemn profession is supposed to produce this effect irrevocably.

Such, then, is the relation of certain acts which are contrary to the vows. The Code proceeds to the further determination of acts which specifically touch the vow of poverty.

PROPERTY AND RIGHT OF ADMINISTRATION

CAN. 580

§ 1. Quilibet professus a votis simplicibus, sive perpetuis sive temporariis, nisi aliud in constitutionibus cautum sit, conservat proprietatem bonorum suorum et capacitatem alia bona acquirendi, salvis quae in can. 569 praescripta sunt.

---

[37] Bizzarri, *l. c.,* p. 723 f.   [38] Cfr. can. 1043 f.

§ 2. Quidquid autem industria sua vel intuitu religionis acquirit, religioni acquirit.

§ 3. Cessionem vel dispositionem de qua in can. 569, § 2, professus mutare potest non quidem proprio arbitrio, nisi constitutiones id sinant, sed de supremi Moderatoris licentia, aut, si de monialibus agatur, de licentia Ordinarii loci et, si monasterium regularibus obnoxium sit, Superioris regularis, dummodo mutatio, saltem de notabili bonorum parte, non fiat in favorem religionis; per discessum autem a religione eiusmodi cessio ac dispositio habere vim desinit.

§ 1 states that those who have made profession of simple vows, temporary or perpetual, retain the *proprietorship of their property* and the capacity to acquire other property, unless the constitutions declare otherwise; with due regard to can. 569.

In order to fully understand this paragraph we must examine what *dominium* or ownership involves.[39] It is generally defined as the right to have, hold, and dispose freely of a corporeal thing, unless it be prohibited by law. Thus one possesses a house or a farm. This right is clearly distinguished from the so-called usufruct or useful dominion. Thus a renter has the usufruct of a house or farm, but he cannot be styled the owner.

A *radical dominion* must necessarily retain the essential elements of the definition of ownership or dominion, but it has a somewhat restricted meaning. And this we find in the limitation appended by law. Wherefore one may have and hold and even dispose of corporeal things, but the disposal is limited by law, or, let us say, suspended, whilst having and holding are not limited. A

---

39 Cfr. Barbosa, *Tractatus Varii, s. v. "Dominum," "Proprietas"* (p. 188, p. 287); also the commentaries on the Decretals, bk. II, tit. 12; Hill, *Ethics*, ed. 8, p. 229; Blackstone-Cooley, *l. c.*, II, 1 ff.

similar way of limiting the disposal of property is found in minors, in whose name their guardians and tutors act, because the law, out of due consideration for younger people who sometimes act rashly, has restricted their freedom of action. How far the Code wishes to apply this restriction will be seen in § 3.

The text of § 1 says that they retain "the capacity to acquire other property" (*alia bona*). This text is taken from "*Perpensis*," 1902, where we read: "If during the period of simple vows other property accrues to them by any lawful means, they retain the radical dominion thereof, etc." The meaning evidently is, if a fortune comes to them which they did not acquire by financial operations, or by increasing the capital through interest, but as it were unexpectedly (*obvenire*) or at least without coöperation. Because "ordaining that their revenues must go to increase their capital," [40] is an act of administration, which is only allowed with the permission of the superior, as the S. C. of Bishops and Regulars, Nov. 21, 1902, in accordance with "*Perpensis*," decided.[41] What has been stated under can. 569 need not be repeated here; we will only say that for such an acquisition no permission of the superior is mentioned, hence not required.

§ 2. Whatever a simple professed religious acquires by personal *labor or in respect of his institute, belongs to the institute*. An ancient principle is here renewed with the addition: "in respect of the institute." The reason for this clause is the dualistic status of a religious who may act as such and as an official person. Thus a reli-

---

[40] Thus Papi, *l. c.*, p. 51, who thinks that for such an act no permission of the superiors is required; but he seems to be wrong.

[41] *Analecta Eccl.* 1904, XII, p. 248.

gious may be pastor of a parish, a Sister may be employed as nurse in a railroad or State hospital, or as a school teacher. Here a distinction must be made according to can. 533, § 1, 4. What he acquires for his mission or parish or school does not belong to the religious house, but mass stipends, fees or offerings for special lectures, if they are not intended to benefit his church, the salary — subtracting, of course, necessary household expenses — the profit from selling books, literary or art products — all this belongs to the institute of which he is a member. Thus also the earnings of a religious who practices a profession or performs manual labor belong to the order. A Sister acting as nurse or as teacher must surrender her salary to the religious community to which she belongs. If she receives donations, she must ascertain the intentions of the donors. A donation given to her personally, for instance, for good nursing or teaching, belongs to the religious house of which she is a member; if the present is made for the hospital or school, it belongs to the latter.[42]

§ 3 refers to can. 569, which governs the cession or disposition of property to a trustworthy person. Now both these acts, the appointment of an administrator and the disposal of the revenues, should not be arbitrarily modified during the period of simple profession, but only with the permission of the superior general, unless the constitutions permit a free change. Nuns may make a change with the permission of their Ordinary and their regular prelate, if they are subject to one; however, such change, even with proper permission, may never be made in favor of the religious institute, at least no notable part of the property; and all provisions made for the appoint-

42 Clement VIII, May 20, 1601 (Bizzarri, l. c., p. 521).

ment of an administrator and the disposal of property become null and void after one has left the religious institute.

a) The *permission* required is not qualified, but it would seem that an express or explicit permission is meant, since a habitual one might involve arbitrary changes. A case in point was decided June 2, 1905. A Sister had made a disposal of her fortune or property, half of which she willed to her institute, and the other half to her brother. In course of time her brother needed a larger subsidy. Was the sister allowed to change her will? The S. Congregation answered: Yes, with the permission of the superioress.[48] From this we may also deduce what a notable part of a property would be, *viz.*, a little over half of the total income or revenues.

b) *Nuns* must have the permission of the Ordinary, and in case of their being subject to a regular prelate, also that of the latter.

c) *After one has left a religious* institute, all provisions as to cession of administration and disposal of revenues cease automatically. The reason for this enactment is evident. Retaining the proprietorship during the period of simple profession after leaving the institute — we suppose legitimately — the religious becomes a lay person with all personal rights restored. The canon, however, does not state whether the institute would have to reimburse only the capital made over to the institute, or also the interest. Here again constitutions and by-laws ought to safeguard the rights of both, individual religious and institute. The intention of the lawgiver may be guessed from can. 531, § 1, where the dowry is mentioned. This, said canon says, must, when a religious leaves the institute, be restored to her entirely, but with-

48 S. C. EE. et RR. (*Anal. Eccl.*, 1906, XIV, p. 250).

out the interest due. Hence an enactment might be made in the by-laws to the effect that the entire capital deeded over to the institute must be restored without the interest accruing thereto in the course of time.

RENUNCIATION OF PROPERTY BEFORE SOLEMN PROFESSION

CAN. 581

§ 1. Professus a votis simplicibus antea nequit valide, sed intra sexaginta dies ante professionem sollemnem, salvis peculiaribus indultis a Sancta Sede concessis, debet omnibus bonis quae actu habet, cui maluerit, sub conditione secuturae professionis, renuntiare.

§ 2. Secuta professione, ea omnia statim fiant, quae necessaria sunt ut renuntiatio etiam iure civili effectum consequatur.

Aside from special indults granted by the Holy See, a professed religious of simple vows cannot validly renounce his property except within sixty days preceding solemn profession, but within this time he must renounce in favor of whomsoever he pleases, all the property which he actually possesses, on condition of his profession subsequently taking place.

This renunciation should, after profession has been made, be followed by the necessary civil formalities to make it effective also according to the civil law.

The Code applies the rule laid down by the Tridentine Council [44] concerning *renunciation* of all property which a religious actually, *hic et nunc*, possesses. This rule concerns only orders in which *solemn* vows are taken, and only such property as the members *actually possess before* solemn profession.

[44] Sess. 25, c. 16, de reg.

Hence any property they may receive *after* solemn profession must be disposed of according to can. 582. Renunciation means abdicating ownership as well as disposal. Of course a last will, being made *mortis causa,* is not a renunciation proper, because revocable. Donations or bequests would seem to be the proper way of renouncing property. The *time* runs sixty days, counting forward to the prospective day of solemn profession. Hence, if for one reason or another, solemn profession would have to be postponed, the abdication would still hold good. The *beneficiary* of a renunciation may be any person capable of possessing, including the religious institute. But the *legal form* (notary public and witnesses) is to be applied only after profession has taken place, for neither binds by ecclesiastical law before the solemn vows are taken.

PROPERTY RECEIVED AFTER SOLEMN PROFESSION

Can. 582

Post sollemnem professionem, salvis pariter peculiaribus Apostolicae Sedis indultis, omnia bona quovis modo obveniunt regulari:

1.° In Ordine capaci possidendi, cedunt Odini vel provinciae vel domui secundum constitutiones;

2.° In Ordine incapaci, acquiruntur Sanctae Sedi in proprietatem.

After solemn profession, likewise without prejudice to special indults of the Apostolic See, all the property which comes in whatever way to a solemnly professed religious belongs to the order, or province, or house, according to the constitutions, if the order is capable of ownership; if the order is incapable of ownership, the Holy See becomes the owner of such property.

This canon distinguishes between *mendicant* and non-mendicant orders.[45] The former are those whose primitive rule forbids ownership in common, not only in the individual members. Such are the brown Franciscans, the Capuchins, the Carmelites, etc. The Society of Jesus has a peculiar constitution, which forbids professed houses to possess real estate in common, whilst houses of probation and colleges enjoy real ownership.[46] *Non-mendicant* orders are the shoed Augustinians, the Benedictines, the Cistercians, the Dominicans, the Praemonstratensians, etc. Note that the Code says: "*without prejudice to special indults.*" Such may be granted to single institutes and cannot be discussed here. In the non-mendicant orders, or such as have obtained special indults from the Holy See, the solemnly professed member, after solemn profession, acquires everything for his institute.[47] This may be the order itself, if it be centralized, or the province, if endowed with the qualities of a corporation, or the local house, which is chiefly the case with the Benedictines and similar monastic orders and congregations. It all depends on the respective constitutions. Nothing is exempt from the capability of possessing property enjoyed by such orders, or provinces, or houses. Hence movable and immovable property, revenues and salaries, pensions and bequests, legacies and wills, may be conveyed to such institutes, as well as literary and patent rights, etc., so far as the law does not interfere.

The second clause may cause some little trouble, inasmuch as the Holy See is not recognized by our government as a corporation, except in the Philippines and

---

45 The Code is absolutely silent about mendicant congregations.

46 Pius V, "*Cum indefessae,*" July 7, 1571; Wernz, *Ius Decret.,* III, n. 592 (1 ed.).

47 Cfr. c. 11, C. 12, q. 1; c. 6, X, III, 35; c. 1; Clem. V, II; cc. 3. 5. Extrav. Ioan. XXII, tit. 14; Bizzarri, *l. c.,* p. 520 ff.

Porto Rico, and the territory included in the treaty of Paris after the Spanish-American War.[48] Therefore houses incapable of owning property, or at least real estate, should obtain from the Holy See a special indult or else incorporate their property as diocesan property, as a corporation sole or aggregate. The civil government, of course, acknowledges no mendicants, and from that point of view there is little difficulty. "As a sovereign power, a political and ecclesiastical State, the Catholic Church can acquire property in the various States only by treaty with the government at Washington."[49] This is simply a logical consequence of the separation of State and Church existing in this country.

SIMPLY PROFESSED MEMBERS OF RELIGIOUS CONGREGATIONS

CAN. 583

Professis a votis simplicibus in Congregationibus religiosis non licet:

1.° Per actum inter vivos dominium bonorum suorum, titulo gratioso abdicare;

2.° Testamentum conditum ad normam can. 569, § 3, mutare sine licentia Sanctae Sedis, vel, si res urgeat nec tempus suppetat ad eam recurrendi, sine licentia Superioris maioris aut, si nec ille adiri possit, localis.

Those who have made profession of simple vows in any religious congregation:

1.° May not abdicate gratuitously the dominion over their property by a voluntary deed of conveyance;

2.° May not alter a will made according to can. 569,

---

48 Zollmann, *l. c.*, p. 47 f.

49 K. Zollmann, *ibid.* This does not, of course, imply that the Catholic Church is incapable of possessing property; as a matter of fact ecclesiastical institutions own property, but as private civil corporations.

§ 3, without the permission of the Holy See, or, if the case be urgent and time does not admit of recourse to the Apostolic See, without the permission of the higher superior, or, if recourse cannot be had to him either, without the permission of the local superior.

The first number treats of *donations*. A donation is a free gift of something not due to the receiver, or, as our text says, *titulo gratuito*. A donation made to show gratitude or to recompense merits is not a donation in the proper sense.[50] Nor is a bilateral contract, *e. g.*, a loan or sale, a donation. For the text itself requires that an abdication of ownership must follow the act made in favor of another. But ownership is not lost by contract, loan or sale, which involve only a change. Furthermore, notice the phrase, *bonorum suorum*,— of their property. This would imply one's whole fortune or property, or at least the bulk thereof. Hence small donations which would not entail a great loss, and donations made out of gratitude or in acknowledgment of services rendered are not forbidden.

No. 2 speaks of a *last will*, which takes effect only after the death of the testator, and must, of course, be vested with the necessary formalities. In can. 569, § 3, the novice is admonished — it cannot be called a strict law, as is apparent from the milder form of the subjunctive (*condat*) — to make a will. After he has made one, it may be changed only with the *permission of the Holy See*. The reason for this ruling lies in the sacredness of the last will, as well as in the fact of religious being bound to the supreme authority more closely than laymen. Besides, a religious being looked upon as a minor needs to be protected in his freedom.

This permission may in *urgent cases*, which do not ad-

50 Reiffenstuel, III, 24, n. 5.

mit of the delay involved in recourse to the Apostolic See,
be given by the superior general, or by the provincial,
or the local superior, if the higher superior cannot be
reached.   An urgent case would be a sudden departure
from the religious congregation caused by an unforeseen
call to arms, sickness, etc.   The canon affects all religious
with simple vows, whether temporary or perpetual, even
of exempt congregations.   For the Code makes no distinction.   On the other hand it does *not affect* the professed members with simple vows of religious *orders,*
and hence lay brothers and clerics with simple vows belonging to such orders are not included.

VACANCY OF BENEFICES

CAN. 584

**Post annum ab emissa qualibet professione religiosa,
vacant beneficia paroecialia; post triennium cetera.**

Parochial benefices become vacant after one year from
the date of any religious profession; other benefices three
years after profession.

We suppose that the term *benefice* must not be pressed
too rigorously, so as to exclude parochial offices.   The
canon would seem to include our country, where benefices
in the strict sense (as understood before the Code) do
not exist.   A pastor who wishes to enter a religious order
cannot resign his office during the period of his novitiate,
according to can. 568.   Under the Decretals [51] a vacancy
was created *ipso iure* by any valid profession made after
the novitiate.   However, since the triennial profession
came into vogue, the vacancy was held to take place only
after solemn profession.[52]   This was inconvenient, since

---

[51] C. 4, 6°, III, 14.
[52] Bened. XIV, "*Ex quo,*" Jan.

14, 1747. The S. C. EE. et RR.,
Aug. 25, 1903, ruled (for the mis-

a parish would then be vacant at least four years, which is against the spirit of the Church. Hence the aspirant was allowed to anticipate his solemn profession. Now the Code rules that the vacancy is to be reckoned one year after profession, no matter whether the latter be temporary or perpetual, simple or solemn. Hence, counting the year's novitiate and one year after the profession, the vacancy of a parish may at most last two years. During that time the bishop has to provide the parish with a vicar, to be paid out of the benefice, if there be such, or out of the usual revenues which furnish the pastor's salary. The pastor, however, may retain or receive what is left over and above the decent support paid to the vicar or substitute. Of course, in special cases, which demand the appointment of a regular pastor, the bishop may have recourse to the Holy See (S. C. Concilii or S. C. Rel.). A canon who is bound to attend choir service in his church loses his share of the daily distributions during his stay in the novitiate and for the three years of profession, but he would not be deprived of the benefice until three years after profession, because a canonicate is not a parochial benefice.[53] Neither are chaplaincies or the offices of assistants and rectors parochial benefices. Hence such would not become vacant until four years had elapsed.

---

sionaries of the S. Heart of Mary) that all residential, hence all parochial, benefices became vacaut at the moment of perpetual profession (*Anal. Eccl.*, 1903, XI, p. 448).

53 Bened. XIV, *l. c.;* Suarez, *De Rel.*, tr. VII, l. V, c. 16, n. 12

(t. 15, p. 375, ed. Paris). The Jesuits are bound to resign after two years' probation. However our canon does not refer to any special constitution or indults or provisions — hence *videant ipsi.*

LOSS OF INCARDINATION

CAN. 585

Professus a votis perpetuis sive sollemnibus sive simplicibus amittit ipso iure propriam quam in saeculo habebat dioecesim.

By perpetual profession, whether solemn or simple, a person ceases to belong to the diocese which he had as a secular.

This canon, as also can. 115, only mentions excardination, and, judging from the lack of any quotations in Card. Gasparri's edition, is entirely new. It refers to the diocese to which one belonged before entering religion. Hence the bishop no longer has a claim on a layman or clergyman who has made his profession as a religious, and the latter's connection with the diocese is severed. This is true even if the institute entered by a cleric is situated within the diocese to which he belonged. The reason is because, as can. 111 says, by embracing the religious life, one ceases to be a vagabond cleric, and his service is transferred to the institute he embraces by perpetual profession.

INVALID PROFESSION

CAN. 586

§ 1. **Professio religiosa irrita ob impedimentum externum non convalescit per subsequentes actus, sed opus est ut a Sede Apostolica sanetur, vel denuo, cognita nullitate et impedimento sublato, legitime emittatur.**

§ 2. **Si autem irrita fuerit ob consensus defectum mere internum, hoc praestito, convalescit, dummodo ex parte religionis consensus non fuerit revocatus.**

§ 3. Si contra validitatem professionis religiosae gravia sint argumenta et religiosus renuat ad cautelam sive professionem renovare sive eiusdem sanationem petere, res ad Sedem Apostolicam deferatur.

§ 1. The religious profession which is invalid by reason of an *external impediment,* is not convalidated by subsequent acts, but must either be healed by the Apostolic See, or a new profession made after the nullity has been discovered and the impediment removed.

This paragraph supposes that the profession, whether temporary or perpetual, simple or solemn, was null and void on account of an *external impediment,* such as one of the conditions mentioned in can. 572, § 1, which are all more or less external, with the exception perhaps of grave fear. What is to be done if an invalid profession must be convalidated? Here is an actual case. A pseudo-provincial admitted several novices to profession. As he had been illegally elected, all his acts were invalid, therefore also the professions. The religious thus invalidly professed renewed their profession annually with the usual words: " If we had not yet obliged ourselves to your Majesty, we would now bind ourselves, and therefore renew our vows." The S. C. of Bishops and Regulars decided (Dec. 10, 1841) that these professions required to be " healed in the root," and the Holy See did so, convalidating them all.[54] Hence the quoted formula of renewal in case of an external impediment is juridically valueless.

Another mode of convalidation is that mentioned in the second clause, *i. e., renewal of consent.* This requires

54 Bizzarri, *l. c.,* p. 476 f.; notice the date 1841, that is to say, before tacit profession had been declared invalid by the " *Neminem latet,*" and declarations of the same Congregation 1858 and ff. years, and by the *"Perpensis,"* 1902.

two conditions: knowledge of the impediment and removal of the same. Hence if the profession was invalid because of lack of age, the professed person must know the fact and wait until the required age is reached. In case the superior holds his office unlawfully, the profession must be renewed in the presence of the lawful superior after the mistake is discovered. The renewal would be more difficult if the time or place of the novitiate affected the validity. For in that case the novitiate would have to be repeated, unless the Holy See granted a dispensation. The similarity between marriage and religious profession in this point is obvious.

§ 2. If the profession be invalid on account of a purely *internal defect of consent*, it suffices for convalidation that the consent be given, provided that consent on the part of the institute has not been revoked. The difference between § 1 and § 2 consists in the fact that the latter concerns the private, not the public welfare, because the formalities were observed, and the vow is a personal one, while the contractual or external matter was supposedly complied with. Here grave fear or momentary mental aberration [55] might enter. Therefore, if one, after the fear has subsided and the mind has returned to its normal condition, would renew his profession, for instance, together with others at the annual renewal, it would be valid, because this is a mere matter of conscience; always provided that the institute has not in some palpable way withdrawn its consent.

§ 3. If there be serious arguments against the validity of a religious profession, and the religious refuses, as a measure of precaution (*ad cautelam*), either to renew the profession or to ask for its convalidation, the matter shall be referred to the Holy See.

[55] Cfr. c. 1, X, I, 40; c. 15, X, III, 31.

The Code says "serious arguments," because futile and imaginary reasons [56] should not be proposed, especially after the time for putting in the claim has elapsed. The S. Congregation to which matters of this kind must be referred, is, of course, that of Religious.

[56] Such arise sometimes from scrupulosity, which must be treated according to the rules given by moralists on scrupulous conscience; sometimes they arise from subsequent dissatisfaction or a critical trend of mind, which must be disposed of, if possible, by resistance to unreasonable claims or pretensions. A weighty reason would be deceit on the part of the institute, or physical weakness on the side of the religious, or a serious doubt as to the correct observance of the required formalities.

TITLE XII

Can. 587

§ 1. Quaelibet clericalis religio habeat studiorum sedes a Capitulo generali vel a Superioribus approbatas, firmo praescripto can. 554, § 3.

§ 2. In studiorum domo vigeat perfecta vita communis; secus studentes ad ordines promoveri nequeunt.

§ 3. Si religio aut provincia studiorum domos rite instructas habere nequeat, aut si quas habet, adire, Superiorum iudicio, difficile sit, religiosi alumni mittantur vel ad recte ordinatam studiorum sedem alius provinciae aut religionis, vel ad scholas Seminarii episcopalis, vel ad publicum catholicum athenaeum.

§ 4. Religiosis, qui studiorum causa longe a propria domo mittuntur, non licet in privatis domibus habitare, sed opus est ut in aliquam suae religionis domum se recipiant, vel, si id fieri non possit, apud religiosum aliquod institutum virorum, vel Seminarium aliamve piam domum, cui sacri ordinis viri praesint, quaeque ab ecclesiastica auctoritate approbata sit.

We need not enlarge upon the text of this title, which forms a glorious page of our Code. *Every clerical institute* must have a house of studies. None is exempt from this rule, except those that are unable to have their own building, and these should send their students either to the study house of another province, or of another institute, or to the diocesan seminary, or to a Catholic university. It is known that Pius X, *f. m.*, endeavored to abolish the small seminaries in Italy because of incompetency of the professors and lack of good example to the students. Of course, if a monastery maintains a theological seminary, this is sufficient. Can. 554, § 3, requires that only religious who lead an exemplary life should be placed in the houses of study, which does not, however, imply that they must be religious " cranks."

CAN. 588

§ 1. Toto studiorum curriculo religiosi committantur speciali curae Praefecti seu Magistri spiritus qui eorum animos ad vitam religiosam informet opportunis monitis, instructionibus atque exhortationibus.

§ 2. Praefectus vel Magister spiritus iis qualitatibus praeditus sit oportet, quae in Magistro novitiorum requiruntur ad normam can. 559, §§ 2, 3.

§ 3. Superiores vero sedulo invigilent ut ea quae can. 595 pro omnibus religiosis praescribuntur, in studiorum domo perfectissime observentur.

The Prefect of Studies must be endowed with the same qualities as the master of novices; if no such person is available, the age limit of thirty-five need not be strictly enforced; but lack of age may be supplied by learning, piety, and prudence.

CAN. 589

§ 1. Religiosi in inferioribus disciplinis rite instructi, in philosophiae studia saltem per biennium et sacrae theologiae saltem per quadriennium, doctrinae D. Thomae inhaerentes ad normam can. 1366, § 2, diligenter incumbant, secundum instructiones Apostolicae Sedis.

§ 2. Studiorum tempore magistris et alumnis officia ne imponantur quae a studio eos avocent vel scholam quoquo modo impediant; supremus autem Moderator et in casibus particularibus alii quoque Superiores possunt pro sua prudentia eos a nonnullis communitatis actibus, etiam a choro, praesertim nocturnis horis, eximere, quoties id studiis excolendis necessarium videatur.

§ 1 requires that religious, before taking up philosophical studies, should be duly instructed in the lower branches. This enactment is less severe than the decree of the S. C. of Religious, of Sept. 7, 1909.[1] Our Code does not determine how many years the academic and how many the collegiate course must comprise. It merely requires (can. 1364, 3.°) that in the smaller seminaries (colleges) the course of studies pursued must be adapted to the general education and the clerical state of the province or region in which the students are to exercise the sacred ministry. Neither does the Code exclude private study of the *humaniora,* because only the theological course must be made in a school properly socalled (can. 976, § 3). Therefore, based upon the rules of sound interpretation, we believe that the necessary knowledge may be supplied by private study, as far as the college training is concerned. The *philosophical course* must last at least two years. The method, doctrine and principles should be taken from St. Thomas Aquinas. But as the Angelic Doctor has not left us a manual of philosophy proper, other manuals may be used that are based on the " *principia Divi Thomae,*" no mat-

1 *A. Ap. S.,* I, 701 ff.

ter whether they be Molinistic or Thomistic in tendency.

The *theological course* must comprise four years, that is, strictly four years, not three with shortened vacations. Each of these four study years should last nine months, neither more nor less.[2]

In theology, too, the "*ratio, doctrina et principia*" of St. Thomas must be followed, and it is the intention of the Holy See that the "*Summa Theologica*" should, if possible, be used as text-book. However, speaking from passive and active experience, we humbly submit that it is almost impossible to comply with this praiseworthy intention. The bulky commentaries needed to elucidate the "*Summa*" would require ten years of study, not to mention other branches which are equally necessary now-a-days. We may also be permitted to say, as a canonist, that the study of Canon Law, now that the new Code is in force, requires more time than was formerly given to it. If the moralists will strictly stick to their subject and abstain from grappling with topics properly belonging to Canon Law, we believe the Code could be mastered in a three years' course, with four hours a week. Moral Theology, if limited to its proper sphere — *i. e.*, the fundamental principles, the Commandments, including the treatise *de iustitia et iure*, and the virtues, could be taught in a three years' course, with three hours a week. This is *our* opinion, for which we claim no authority, but which the legislator, we believe, would not reprimand.

The next paragraph (§ 2) of can. 589 is to be recommended to religious superiors for their pious and efficacious consideration. Overburdening professors and students is somewhat similar to overtaxing the stomach.

---

2 S. C. Rel., Sept. 7, 1909, III (*A. Ap. S.*, I, 702); this rule still holds, May 31, 1910 (*A. Ap. S.*, II, 449 f.) and is referred to by Cardinal Gasparri.

Proficiency and progress can result only from quietly conducted and duly limited courses of study. *Non multa, sed multum!*

YEARLY EXAMINATIONS

CAN. 590

Religiosi sacerdotes, iis tantum exceptis qui a Superioribus maioribus gravem ob causam fuerint exempti, aut qui vel sacram theologiam, vel ius canonicum vel philosophiam scholasticam doceant, post absolutum studiorum curriculum, quotannis, saltem per quinquennium, a doctis gravibusque patribus examinentur in variis doctrinae sacrae disciplinis antea opportune designatis.

This canon provides that all religious who are priests must pass an *annual examination for a period of five years after completing their theological course.* This examination is to cover all the various branches of sacred theology,— the specific matter to be pointed out beforehand — and must be held in the presence of learned and grave fathers. The law exempts from these examinations those who are engaged in teaching dogmatic or moral theology, canon law, and Scholastic philosophy. The higher superiors may exempt others for weighty reasons. This latter clause practically upsets the intention of the legislator. For weighty reasons may always be found, especially in a busy country like ours.

MONTHLY CONFERENCES

CAN. 591

In qualibet saltem formata domo, minimum semel in mense, habeatur solutio casus moralis et liturgici, cui, si Superior opportunum existimaverit, addi potest

sermo de re dogmatica coniunctisve doctrinis; et omnes clerici professi qui studio sacrae theologiae operam navant aut illud expleverunt et in domo degunt, assistere tenentur, nisi aliud in constitutionibus caveatur.

In every house in which there are at least six members, *theological conferences* must be held regularly *once a month*. We reasonably suppose that the legislator does not object to omitting these conferences in the summer vacation time, when many are usually absent, while others are ailing or exhausted, and still others suffering from the heat. At these conferences moral or liturgical cases are to be solved and a discourse delivered on dogmatical or kindred subjects. These meetings must be *attended* by all the professed clerical students of theology and by those clerics present in the house who have already finished their course,[3] unless the constitutions prescribe otherwise. The holding of conferences is a strict duty and has always been inculcated. Attention must be paid also to can. 131.

[3] This rule includes those who have been ordained. We believe that the conferences prescribed in can. 131 may licitly and reasonably be combined with these. Therefore all priests who have obtained faculties for hearing confessions must be present. Besides, if we interpret the term *clerici professi* strictly, all priests or professed clerical members (not lay-brothers) must attend these conferences.

TITLE XIII

CHAPTER I

THE OBLIGATIONS

Can. 592

Obligationibus communibus clericorum, de quibus in can. 124–142, etiam religiosi omnes tenentur, nisi ex contextu sermonis vel ex rei natura aliud constet.

The common obligations of clerics, as laid down in can. 124–142, also bind all religious, unless it appears otherwise from the context of the law or from the nature of the case.

These obligations have, we trust, been sufficiently explained in Vol. II. Note that some of them bind only the clergy, for instance, can. 126 concerning retreats, 120 concerning promptness in accepting the sacred ministry, can. 129–131 regarding study, annual examinations, and conferences, can. 135 respecting the recitation of the Breviary, 143 f. governing residence and incardination. These do not apply to female religious. Some of them do not even concern male religious as such, e. g., can. 128, which is not intended for clerical religious who have made perpetual vows, because can. 585 excardinates them, and unless in case of strict necessity the bishop is not entitled to compel exempt religious to assume the ministry. Other obligations, for instance, as to wearing the clerical dress (can. 126), if this is not distinct from the religious habit, abstaining from worldly and prohibited occupations and amusements (can. 137, 138, 139, 140, 141, 142) oblige all religious of both sexes.[1] Can. 133, concerning housekeepers, obliges religious who are parish priests or act as such.

CAN. 593

Omnes et singuli religiosi, Superiores aeque ac subditi, debent, non solum quae nuncuparunt vota fideliter integreque servare, sed etiam secundum regulas et constitutiones propriae religionis vitam componere atque ita ad perfectionem sui status contendere.

All religious, superiors as well as subjects, are bound not only to observe faithfully and entirely the vows they have taken, but also to order their lives according to the rules and constitutions of the institute to which they belong, and thus tend to the perfection of their state.

The legislator exhorts all religious to live the life required by their state. *Superiors* are not exempt from the observance of the vows, although with them the vow of obedience is seemingly in abeyance. Yet they too are bound by the rule and the constitutions, from which they are not allowed to deviate except in so far as their office or dignity requires, and in so far as they could exempt their own subjects. Besides the lower superiors owe obedience to the higher, and the higher to the Pope and his lawful representatives. The Code binds them all to the fullest extent, unless privileges, sound interpretation, or approved constitutions grant them the right of dispensing or changing in certain cases.

1 Benedict XIV, *Apostolicum ministerium*, May 30, 1753, § 18 (applying chiefly to England).

a) As to the *power of dispensation*, a distinction must be made between exempt and non-exempt institutes. The superiors of an *exempt* religious institute enjoy this power to the same extent as diocesan Ordinaries and, like these, are bound by the regulations laid down in can. 81. Can. 1245 also has a place here because it refers directly to exempt clerical religious. Hence regular superiors of exempt institutes may dispense not only single members but the whole community from the law of fast and abstinence. Over non-exempt religious, the Ordinary or bishop in whose diocese the house is located, exercises this power. As to the dispensations required for ordination, religious superiors have no power, because whatever touches that subject belongs to the bishop.[2]

Religious superiors, whether exempt or not, may *dispense single members*, but not the whole community as such, at least as a rule, from the observance of the precepts contained in the rule or constitutions. However, they may, at times, because the constitutions themselves grant them that right, dispense the whole community from silence, or from a fast prescribed by the constitutions only and not by common law, and from similar obligations.

As to dispensation from *penalties* inflicted by the law (see Book V) and from *irregularities*, the superiors of exempt religious enjoy no more power than diocesan Ordinaries, apart from certain privileges granted to regulars concerning irregularities. With regard to penalties inflicted by the rule and constitutions, the superior general,[3] but not the inferior prelate, may relax them, without prejudice to the constitutions.

---

2 This is evident from the canons on ordination; whether the religious superior may declare one free from irregularity matters little if the Ordinary is not satisfied with his statement.

3 Or the abbot of every autonomous monastery.

Concerning the dispensation from *vows*, note that the religious vows cannot, *per se*, be dispensed from by any superior. But the superior of a clerical exempt institute may dispense from vows that go beyond the three substantial vows, whilst the Ordinary has the same power with regard to non-exempt religious and vows not reserved.[4]

b) As to the *changing* or commutation of vows, or promises made in the form of vows, the Code says that a change into a lesser or less perfect work may be made by the one who has the power of dispensing, provided, of course, the vow be not one of those reserved.[5]

In cases in which the superiors are entitled to dispense their subjects, they may also dispense themselves,[6] although it is wisely added by canonists that they should not do so except through their confessors.[7]

Finally, the superiors of a religious institute may not change the rule or constitutions which are approved by the Holy See. Hence any substantial change of the same must be submitted to the supreme authority. However, this does not exclude the admission of usages which do not affect the substance of the rule and the constitutions. On the other hand it is also certain that a mitigation introduced by custom and approved by the Holy See cannot be abolished except by the Holy See, although a general chapter could adopt a stricter reformation. Should the Holy See formally impose the abolition of such a mitigation, the religious would be obliged to obey, though in that case members who made profession under the mitigated rule or constitutions could scarcely be obliged to accept the reformation, at least if new austerities were

---

[4] Cfr. can. 1313.
[5] Can. 1314.
[6] Can. 201, § 3.
[7] Cfr. Piatus M., I, p. 571 (ed.

2). Concerning the *power of absolution* we refer to Book III (Confession) and Book V (Censures).

imposed,[8] for they had no intention to take upon themselves such "extras."

This leads to the consideration of the question *what the vow of obedience means for all religious.*

(1) The vow of obedience is a promise made to God, by which one obliges himself to obey the religious institute one enters and its lawful superiors.

(2) The *extent* of this vow is commensurate with the rule and the constitutions, but goes no further. However, not only what is explicitly stated in the rule and constitutions falls under the vow of obedience, but also all acts which are necessary for the preservation of the institute itself and for the observance of the rule or constitutions. Thus mutual charity and fraternal obligations, charges and offices of the institute, just penalties and appropriate and moderate exercises, though not expressly stated, oblige by reason of obedience. To read more into the rules and constitutions is absurd, because the religious must have an objective norm. Besides no religious is bound to obey, by reason of the vow, if his superior commands something foolish, indifferent or impossible, or something which would cause serious damage or danger to the religious. On the other hand religious should obey their superior when he commands a reasonable internal act, for instance, the application of a Holy Mass [9] for a certain purpose.

There is a *limit to religious obedience* set by the common law of the Church. As those inferior to the Ro-

---

8 V. Bachofen, *Compendium Iuris Regul.*, p. 129 f.; p. 224.

9 Piatus M., I, p. 288. However it is evident that the internal act must in some way be connected either with the vows or the regular discipline and the rule or constitutions, which all tend to external observance; thus a superior might prohibit saying the office privately during a conventual *missa cantata*, if the singing in common or ceremonies would suffer thereby; otherwise there would be neither a moral nor a juridical reason for such a prohibition.

man Pontiff have no power, in general at least, against
the common law, so neither is a religious bound to obey
a superior commanding anything opposed to that law.
Neither is a religious obliged to obey a superior who is
notoriously deprived of his office,[10] excommunicated or
suspended.[11]

LIFE IN COMMON AND POVERTY

CAN. 594

§ 1. In quavis religione vita communis accurate ab
omnibus servetur etiam in iis quae ad victum, ad ve-
stitum et ad supellectilem pertinent.

§ 2. Quidquid a religiosis, etiam a Superioribus,
acquiritur ad normam can. 580, § 2, et can. 582, n. 1,
bonis domus, provinciae vel religionis admisceatur, et
pecunia quaelibet omnesque tituli in capsa communi
deponantur.

§ 3. Religiosorum supellex paupertati conveniat
quam professi sunt.

§ 1. In every religious institute all must carefully observe the common life even in matters of food, clothing,
and furniture.

§ 2. Whatever is acquired by the religious, including
the superiors, according to can. 580, § 2, and can. 582,
n. 1, must be incorporated in the goods of the house, or
of the province, or of the institute; and all money and
titles shall be deposited in the common safe.

§ 3. The furniture of the religious must be in accordance with the poverty of which they make profession.

St. Benedict in his Rule (c. 1) mentions four kinds of
monks, two of whom were a pretty bad lot, *sara-
bites* and the *gyrovagi*, loafers or ramblers going about

---

10 Piatus M., II, 639.   11 Cfr. can. 2264, etc.

in the garb of religious. In the twelfth century Innocent II tried to do away with all kinds of religious who would not lead a *common life*. What he meant by that phrase is explained by the words: " in the church, in the refectory, and in the dormitory." [12] These three localities indicate almost perfectly the conditions of community life, and no doubt the Code has these three places in view. The church or chapel unites the religious in the praise of God, the dining-room in fraternal charity, and the dormitory in peaceful rest. Of course, recreation, which is but another sort of rest, is also included. Hence an ostentatious avoidance of the recreation-room would show a lack of community spirit.

The Code mentions three things in particular which pertain to a life in common: food, dress, and furniture. Of course this is intended only for healthy members of the community, because reason dictates that the sick and delicate require special care, and the Decretals provided for emergencies.[13] A decree of the S. C. EE. et RR. also mentions uniformity in the employment of medicine and in traveling.[14] However, as to medicine we must reckon with modern methods and leave particulars to the physicians. Only extravagance must be avoided. Travelling, too, is to be judged in the light of modern conveniences (automobiles, etc.), and according to the custom of the country, which, with us, permits the use of a sleeping car for a night's rest.

§ 2 says that whatever is acquired by the religious, including the superiors, either by personal effort or in the form of presents given for the benefit of the house, or of

---

[12] C. 25, C. 18, q. 2. The S. C. EE. et RR., April 22, 1851, forbade superiors, who had not professed a life in common, to reside in a house where the common life is observed (Bizzari, *l. c.*, p. 852).

[13] C. 6, X, III, 35; cfr. *Reg. S. Bened.*, c. 37.

[14] Cfr. Bizzarri, *l. c.*, p. 44.

the province, or of the institute (can. 580) belongs to the community. Money or property may also come by inheritance or donations *inter vivos* (can. 580, 1°). All such acquisitions go into the common treasury.

Is a religious entitled to refuse a donation? A free donation to which the religious is in nowise entitled, he may refuse, because it depends on mere acceptance, which is not an act of dominion. He would, however, offend against charity by refusing a donation if the house or institute to which he belongs were needy. A religious would commit a sin against the vow of poverty if he would refuse a bequest or legacy coming to him by inheritance, or to which he was otherwise entitled, because he would refuse what belonged by right to his institute,[15] supposing the institute to be capable of possessing property.

Another question arises, on account of a decision of the S. C. Rel., July 13, 1913. It was asked, whether a religious of either solemn or simple vows, who had written a book during the time of his profession, was allowed to donate or alienate the manuscript *quocumque titulo?* The answer was "*Negative.*"[16] In order to understand this decision,— which caused some surprise,— it must be remembered that an author, whether he be professed with simple or solemn vows, has full proprietorship over his manuscripts as long as they remain in his hands, so that no superior can compel him to have them published or otherwise make use of them. A manuscript is intellectual property to which the author has a natural right. This right is not denied by that decision. But if the author would donate said manuscript to another, an outsider not a member of his institute, or sell it for any consideration, his ownership would cease, because donation

---

[15] Piatus M., I, p. 244.　　　　[16] A. Ap. S., V, 366.

or alienation are acts of dominion. However, this decision is not in keeping with some papal constitutions, especially that of Clement VIII, "*Religiosae congregationes*," which permits religious to donate manuscripts one to another, and that of Benedict XIII ("*Postulat*") which allows religious who are promoted to the episcopate to take their manuscripts with them.[17] These constitutions are certainly as weighty as any particular decision of a Roman Congregation. We believe the reason for that decision was to ward off the danger of avoiding the necessary *imprimatur*, which is required especially for religious.

No doubt may be raised as to the right of a religious community to the royalties and copyrights belonging to its members under the laws of the country.

With regard to *paintings and sculptures*, canonists[18] draw a distinction: if the material was furnished by the community, the product belongs to the latter, not to the individual artist; but if an outsider has furnished the materials (paint, canvas, brushes, marble, stone, silver, gold, etc.), the work belongs to him.

The next clause touches the *common treasury*, and indirectly the *peculium*. Where the common life is observed as it should be, this rule is safe. But niggardly and miserly treatment of religious is the quickest road to private property (*peculium*). There is no one thing for which the founders of the early religious orders and the laws of the Church had greater horror than this.[19] And,

<hr/>

17 Piatus M., I, p. 243. As long as no other decisions are forthcoming, we cling to the old *sententia communissima*, based as it is on papal constitutions, which allowed full possession of manuscripts to the author; the natural law cannot be overthrown by one particular decision.

18 Piatus M., I, p. 243; what we say in the text is to be taken in the sense that the material would be of considerable value.

19 *Reg. S. Bened.*, c. 55; cfr. c.

indeed, a *peculium* of which the superior knows nothing and over which he has no control, is incompatible with the vow of poverty, supposing, of course, that the religious are treated fairly. On the other hand, the practice of having a *peculium* in common, with the permission of the superior, such as exists here and there in Europe, where it was brought about by the civil government, cannot be rejected as unlawful or against the Code, though, strictly speaking, it is not in conformity with the spirit of poverty.

Can. 595

§ 1. Curent Superiores ut omnes religiosi:

1.° Quotannis spiritualibus exercitiis vacent;

2.° Legitime non impediti quotidie Sacro intersint, orationi mentali vacent, et in alia pietatis officia, quae a regulis et constitutionibus praescripta sint, sedulo incumbant;

3.° Ad poenitentiae sacramentum semel saltem in hebdomada accedant.

§ 2. Superiores suos inter subditos promoveant frequentem, etiam quotidianam, sanctissimi Corporis Christi receptionem; frequens autem, imo etiam quotidianus accessus ad sanctissimam Eucharistiam religiosis rite dispositis libere pateat.

§ 3. Si autem post ultimam sacramentalem confessionem religiosus communitati gravi scandalo fuerit aut gravem et externam culpam patraverit, donec ad poenitentiae sacramentum denuo accesserit, Superior potest eum, ne ad sacram communionem accedat, prohibere.

§ 4. Si quae sint religiones votorum sive sollemnium

11, C. 12, q. 1 (St. Aug.); c. 25, C. 18, q. 2; cc. 2, 4, 6, X, III, 35. The religious who after death was found to have had property, was to be buried in non-consecrated ground, or his body, if possible, to be exhumed.

sive simplicium, quarum in regulis aut constitutionibus vel etiam calendariis communiones aliquibus diebus affixae aut iussae reperiantur, hae normae vim dumtaxat directivam habent.

This canon draws the attention of superiors to some special obligations of piety. They should take care:

§ 1. That all the religious make an annual spiritual retreat; that those not lawfully excused daily assist at Mass and faithfully perform the other exercises prescribed by the rule and constitutions; and that they go to confession at least once a week.[20]

§ 2. Superiors should promote amongst their subjects *frequent, even daily reception of Holy Communion;* and liberty must be given to every properly disposed religious to approach frequently, even daily, the Most Holy Eucharist. Of this exhortation enough was said and written — though not always with due regard to historical facts — when the decree of Pius X, "*Sacra Tridentina Synodus,*" was promulgated, Dec. 20, 1905. We may note that this decree need no longer be read at table, as its substance is embodied in the Code.[21]

§ 3. If a religious has, since his last confession, given grave scandal to the community, or committed a serious external fault, the superior can forbid him to receive Holy Communion until he shall have again approached the Sacrament of Penance. Note the two different clauses: *grave scandal* and *serious external fault.* The two are not necessarily connected. To stay away from the common exercises without excuse or reason may give scandal and yet not involve a serious fault. To strike a superior or co-religious might be grievously sinful and

---

20 We believe that the custom of going to confession every other week in large communities may be tolerated, if the members are allowed to go oftener.

21 Cfr. can. 509, § 2.

yet, if done quietly, not cause grave scandal. Still, in both cases the superior would be entitled to forbid the religious to approach the Sacred Table. This is a ruling taken from the decree " *Quemadmodem*," Dec. 17, 1890, which, by the way, has now lost its penal sanction.

§ 4. If in any institute, whether of solemn or simple vows, the rules or the constitutions or even the calendars assign or prescribe certain fixed days for the reception of Holy Communion, such regulations are to be regarded as merely directive.

This paragraph is taken from the decree on frequent communion, " *Sacra Tridentina*," and means that no real obligation can be derived from said regulations, and hence the superiors must not urge their observance in virtue of the vow of obedience.

THE RELIGIOUS HABIT

CAN. 596

Religiosi omnes proprium suae religionis habitum deferant tum intra tum extra domum, nisi gravis causa excuset, iudicio Superioris maioris aut, urgente necessitate, etiam localis.

All religious should wear the habit of their institute both inside and outside the house, unless a weighty reason excuses them, according to the judgment of the higher, or, in urgent cases, of the local superior. This rule is taken from the Decretals and the Council of Trent.[22] It has, as is well known, been modified for our country,[23] and missionary countries generally. On days when the mercury occasionally shows more than 100 degrees, the contrary custom may be adopted without misgiving.

[22] C. 2; 6°, III, 24; c. 2, *Clem.* III, 1; *Trid.*, sess. 25, c. 19, de reg.

[23] *Conc. Balt. III.*, n. 17; cfr. can. 136.

ENCLOSURE

The nature of coenobitism requires a solitary or retired mode of life. Hence the saying, " As a fish cannot live outside the water, so neither can a monk live outside the monastery." [24] St. Benedict wished to see the monasteries built in such a way that the monks would have no excuse to go outside. [25] St. Gregory the Great expressed to a certain Abbot (Valentine) his surprise that women entered his monastery indiscriminately and called upon the monks to be god-fathers of their children. He forbids the continuation of this lax practice absolutely. [26] The decree of Gratian as well as the well known chapter " Periculoso " of Boniface VIII insist upon enclosure, especially of convents of nuns, and the Tridentine Council enforced these laws vigorously. [27] Later papal constitutions insisted upon them and admitted a mitigation only in favor of founders and ruling princes and princesses. [28] (Cfr. Pius IX, " Apostolicae Sedis," Oct. 12, 1869.) Yet in spite of the endeavor of Pius V to put all female congregations under the same strict laws, practice and theory soon began to distinguish between papal and episcopal enclosure. The former, or strict, enclosure is imposed only on regulars, or, more precisely, those institutes whose members take solemn vows, especially the female orders. The episcopal enclosure is less strict and open to a wider interpretation. The penalties inflicted by law for a violation of the papal may not be applied to the episcopal enclosure. This premised, the Code first treats of

---

[24] C. 8, C. 16, q. 1, which must, however, be taken with a grain of salt.

[25] Reg., c. 66.

[26] Regist. Greg. M., I, 40 (ed. Hartmann-Ewald).

[27] Cfr. c. 1, C. 16, q. 1; c. un. 6°, III, 16; Trid., sess. 25, c. 5, de reg.

[28] See the quotations in Card. Gasparri's edition of the Code.

Can. 597

§ 1. In domibus regularium sive virorum sive mulierum canonice constitutis, etiam non formatis, servetur
clausura papalis.

§ 2. Lege clausurae papalis afficitur tota domus
quam communitas regularis inhabitat, cum hortis et
viridariis accessui religiosorum reservatis; excluso,
praeter publicum templum cum continente sacrario,
etiam hospitio pro advenis, si adsit, et collocutorio,
quod, quantum fieri potest, prope ianuam domus constitui debet.

§ 3. Partes clausurae legi obnoxiae patenter indi-
centur; Superioris vero maioris vel Capituli generalis
secundum constitutiones, aut, si agatur de monasterio
monialium, Episcopi erit clausurae fines accurate
praescribere aut legitimis de causis mutare.

§ 1. In canonically erected houses of regulars, even
though they are not *formatae,* of men as well as women,
the papal enclosure must be observed. *When* a house is
canonically erected, must be deduced from the approval
or permission of the Holy See and of the Ordinary. It
is evident that before the regulars move in, there is no
enclosure. The text says that even in houses which are
not *formatae, i. e.,* have less than six members, the enclosure must be observed. This must, of course, be understood only of a canonically erected house. A so-called
priory or *expositura* or *grangia* (farm house or summer
resort, villa, *villeggiatura*) is not a canonically erected
house, even though inhabited by more than six members
at a time.

§ 2. The law of papal enclosure affects the *whole house*

inhabited by the regular community, including the orchards and gardens reserved to the religious, but not the public church with its sacristy, the guest-house, if there be one, and the parlor, which latter should, where possible, be placed near the entrance to the house. Note carefully the wording of the text, because it mitigates the opinion of some authors.[29] The sacristy is exempt from enclosure, even if it has two doors, of which one leads to the enclosure, provided it immediately adjoins the church. Should another room separate it from the church, the enclosure would have to be applied. As to the *gardens* and *viridaria*, the text does not require that a wall or hedge should separate them from the enclosure proper; it suffices that they be so reserved to the regulars that no one else is allowed access. *Viridaria*, properly speaking, are places set with trees and plants, hence orchards, parks, etc., also places for games. Whether these fall under the law of enclosure must be determined by § 3.

§ 3. The *parts of the house subject to the law of enclosure must be clearly indicated;* it pertains to the higher superior or to the general chapter according to the constitutions, or, in the case of a monastery of nuns, to the Bishop, to determine exactly the limits of the enclosure or to modify them for lawful reasons. This paragraph gives a wide scope to the superiors. However, it is evident that no superior may change the boundaries of the enclosure *ad hoc, i. e.,* for a case of emergency, for instance, to introduce a party into certain rooms, in order to evade the canonical penalty.

Once fixed, the boundaries must remain, unless cogent reasons make a change lawful. Besides, the boundaries

---

[29] Cfr. Ferraris, *Prompta Bibliotheca, s. v. Conventus,* art. III, n. 9 ff.

must be clearly indicated, not only to the regulars themselves, but also to outsiders, for instance, by a sign inscribed, "Private Entrance" or "Positively No Admittance." The superiors and officials should carefully see
to it that no freedom of way or servitude arises from allowing strangers to walk over the private property of
the community. This might cause trouble and unnecessary lawsuits.

ENCLOSURE OF MALE RELIGIOUS

Can. 598

§ 1. **Intra regularium virorum clausuram ne admittantur mulieres cuiusvis aetatis, generis aut conditionis sub quovis praetextu.**

§ 2. **Eximuntur ab hac lege uxores eorum qui supremum actu tenent populorum principatum, cum
comitatu.**

§ 1. Into the enclosure of male regulars women of
whatever age, class, or condition may not under any pretext be admitted.

§ 2. From this law are exempt the wives of actual
rulers of states with their retinue.

The text excludes *all members of the female sex,* including children, which latter it had been customary to
admit. What *genus,* which the authorized translation
renders by "class," means, ·is not so easy to determine.
It may signify birth, family, but also kin, and thus have
the meaning of descent or blood relationship. Thus interpreted, even the female relatives of regulars are excluded. If it is taken to mean birth it would refer to
nobility; but this seems to be included in *conditio.*
Conditio may signify social status or position, rank, pro-

fession, office. No matter how " blue-blooded " a person may be, if a woman,[30] she is excluded.[31]

§ 2 makes *one exception, viz.*, in favor of the wives of actual rulers. There is little danger that any community of regulars in this country will receive such a visit. The President's wife, and the governor's wife, we are sorry to say, are not included in this privilege, because their husbands are not actual rulers in the commonly accepted sense of the word. If the wife of a European monarch should visit a monastery in our country, the law would admit her, because the text does not limit the privilege to their own country.

COLLEGE OR SCHOOL ENCLOSURE

CAN. 599

§ 1. Si domus regularium virorum adnexum habeat convictum pro alumnis internis vel alia opera religionis propria, separata saltem aedis pars, si fieri possit, religiosorum habitationi reservetur, clausurae legi subiecta.

§ 2. Etiam in loca extra clausuram alumnis externis aut internis vel operibus religionis propriis reservata, personae alterius sexus, nisi aequa de causa et de Superioris licentia, ne admittantur.

§ 1. When a house of male regulars has annexed to it a college for boarding pupils, or for other works proper to the institute, a separate part at least of the house should, if possible, be reserved for the habitation of the religious, and subject to the law of enclosure.

§ 2. Even to places outside the enclosure reserved for extern or intern pupils or for works proper to the insti-

---

[30] Hermaphrodites of the male sex prevailingly, might be admitted.
[31] Pius V, *Regularium*, Oct. 24, 1566; Benedict XIV, *Regularis disciplinae*, Jan. 3, 1742.

tute, persons of the other sex should not be admitted except for a just reason and with the permission of the superior.

This enactment sounds more like a guiding norm —" if possible "— than a strict law, and hence it would be uncanonical to apply the full vigor of papal enclosure to these institutes.

PAPAL ENCLOSURE OF NUNS; ADMISSION OF OUTSIDERS

CAN. 600

Intra monialium clausuram nemo, cuiusvis generis, conditionis, sexus, aetatis admittatur sine Sanctae Sedis licentia, exceptis personis quae sequuntur:

1.° Ordinario loci aut Superiori regulari, monasterium monialium visitantibus vel aliis Visitatoribus ab ipsis delegatis licet clausuram ingredi dumtaxat inspectionis causa, cautoque ut unus saltem clericus vel religiosus vir maturae aetatis eos comitetur;

2.° Confessarius vel qui eius vices gerit potest, cum debitis cautelis, ingredi clausuram ad ministranda Sacramenta infirmis aut ad assistendum morientibus;

3.° Possunt clausuram ingredi qui supremum actu tenent populorum principatum eorumque uxores cum comitatu; itemque S. R. E. Cardinales;

4.° Antistitae est, adhibitis debitis cautelis, ingressum permittere medicis, chirurgis, aliisque quorum opera sit necessaria, impetrata prius saltem habituali approbatione ab Ordinario loci; si vero necessitas urgeat nec tempus suppetat approbationem petendi, haec iure praesumitur.

No one, of whatever class, condition, sex or age, may, without papal permission, be permitted within the enclosure of nuns, except the following persons:

1.° The canonical visitator or his delegate, who must be accompanied by a clergyman or religious;

2.° The confessor or his substitute, to administer the sacraments to the sick or to assist the dying;

3.° Rulers of states with their wives and suite, and also cardinals;

4.° After taking due precautions, the superioress may permit the physician, the surgeon, and others whose work is necessary, to enter the enclosure, having previously obtained at least the habitual approval of the local Ordinary, which permission may be presumed in cases which suffer no delay.

Note the difference between the papal enclosure of regulars and that of nuns. The latter admits not even women. The so-called *educande* (pupils) were admitted under a papal permission granted to that effect.

The "*debitae cautelae*" or precautions concerning confessors provide that a religious must be accompanied by another religious, whereas a secular priest needs no companion, but must wear stole and surplice. As to laymen, they must be of good moral character, and should not tarry within the enclosure before sunrise or after sunset.[32] This rule, of course, is not always applicable to physicians and surgeons.

DUTY OF NUNS TO KEEP WITHIN THEIR ENCLOSURE

Can. 601

§ 1. Nemini monialium liceat post professionem exire e monasterio, etiam ad breve tempus, quovis praetextu, sine speciali Sanctae Sedis indulto, excepto

---

[32] Cfr. Greg. XIII, "*Deo Sacris*," Dec. 30, 1572; Alexander VII, "*Felici*," Oct. 20, 1664; Bachofen, *Compendium Iuris Reg.*, p. 163 ff.

casu imminentis periculi mortis vel alius gravissimi
mali.

§ 2. Hoc periculum, si tempus suppetat, scripto
recognoscendum est loci Ordinario.

No nun, after profession, may, under whatever pretext, leave the monastery even for a short time, without
a special papal indult, except in the case of imminent
danger of death or other very serious evil; and this danger, if time permits, must be recognized as such by the
local Ordinary in writing.

The Code almost verbally rehearses former laws,[33]
which seem somewhat rigorous to modern students, but
were most reasonable. Danger of death would be a fire
or threatening collapse of the building, a flood, devasta-
tion brought about by war, danger of defloration, etc. A
Sister suffering from a contagious disease may leave the
convent; and, we believe, also one compelled to undergo
an operation which could not be safely performed in the
convent. The judgment of the sufficiency of the reason
lies with the Ordinary, and in urgent cases with the superioress.[34]

CAN. 602

Clausura monasterii monialium ita circumsepta esse
debet ut, quoad fieri potest, nullus sit in eam vel ab ea
prospectus externarum personarum.

The enclosure of every monastery of nuns should be
protected on every side in such a manner as to prevent, as

---

[33] Cfr. Pius V, "*Decori*," Feb.
1, 1570.

[34] The *Regesta S. C. EE. et RR.*
contain a great number of permissions granted to nuns, especially of
Portugal, who wished to go to
health resorts; they were to travel
in a closed carriage with the cur-
tains down, accompanied by two
other Sisters, and without a prolonged stop.

far as possible, those within from being seen by, or seeing, persons outside. Of course, if the ecclesiastical authorities could always enforce their laws,— as they formerly did in the Papal States,[25]— this canon might also be insisted upon. But a little more light and air would not hurt the nuns.

CAN. 603

§ 1. Clausura monialium, etsi regularibus subiectarum, sub vigilantia est Ordinarii loci, qui potest delinquentes, regularibus viris non exceptis, poenis quoque ac censuris corrigere et coercere.

§ 2. Etiam Superiori regulari custodia clausurae monialium sibi subiectarum commissa est, qui moniales aut alios suos subditos, si quid hac in re deliquerint, poenis quoque punire potest.

The Ordinary of the diocese must diligently watch over the observance of the enclosure of nuns, even those subject to regulars; he must also punish offenders, not excepting male regulars, even with penalties and censures. The regular superiors must do the same and duly punish nuns or other subjects who violate the enclosure.

ENCLOSURE OF RELIGIOUS CONGREGATIONS

CAN. 604

§ 1. In domibus etiam Congregationum religiosarum sive pontificii sive dioecesani iuris clausura servetur, in quam nemo alterius sexus admittatur, nisi ii de quibus in can. 598, § 2 et can. 600, aliique quos ex iustis ac rationabilibus causis Superiores admitti posse censuerint.

---

[25] A proprietor who had raised his house too high and built too many windows, which permitted a view into a convent, had to change it. (Bizzarri, *l. c.*, p. 81.)

§ 2. Praescriptum can. 599 etiam domibus Congregationum religiosarum sive virorum sive mulierum ap-
plicetur.

§ 3. Episcopus in adiunctis peculiaribus, gravibusque intercedentibus causis, potest hanc clausuram,
nisi agatur de religione clericali exempta, censuris
munire; semper autem curet ut eadem rite servetur et
quidquid in eam irrepat vitii corrigatur.

Here we meet the so-called *episcopal enclosure*, which
must be observed in the houses of religious congregations,
whether approved by the Holy See or the diocesan Ordinary. Into their enclosure, says § 1, no one of the other
sex is to be admitted, except actual rulers and the persons mentioned in can. 600; but the superiors (both
higher and local, because the Code does not determine
which), may admit other persons of either sex for just
and reasonable motives. Such a motive would be, *e. g.*,
a visit of relatives, good friends or benefactors, parents
of pupils, etc.

§ 2 applies can. 599 to these congregations, whether
of men or women.

§ 3 says that the bishop may, in particular circumstances and for grave reasons, safeguard the enclosure by
censures, except in the case of an exempt clerical institute. Always, however, he should see to it that the episcopal enclosure is duly observed, and correct any abuses
that may arise. Such an abuse would be a case of episcopal reservation, reserved to the bishop himself, but not
by law. However, as censures in general, and especially
reserved ones, should be few and inflicted only for grave
reasons, it is evident that these reasons would have to
be very particular; for instance, if scandal should have
occurred, or if the community would do only housework

which would exclude communication with the outer world. Yet, at any rate, the enclosure would always be episcopal, not papal.

VISITS

CAN. 605

Omnes quibus est clausurae custodia, sedulo advigilent ne, alienis invisentibus, inutili collocutione disciplina perturbetur et spiritus religiosus detrimentum patiatur.

All those who have the custody of the enclosure shall carefully see lest, from intercourse with outsiders, the discipline be relaxed and the religious spirit weakened by useless conversation. This rule is intended not only for the superiors, but for the master or mistress of guests as well as for the doorkeeper and those who receive visitors.

As Cardinal Gasparri's edition draws our attention to the point, a word may here be added concerning the *access of regulars and laymen to convents of nuns.* A strict prohibition was always maintained concerning regulars,[36] and the S. C. of Bishops and Regulars added very severe regulations with regard to their visits. Lay persons were more easily admitted, but not during Lent, Advent, on vigils or feast-days. Our Code mentions nothing respecting these visits. Hence the former strict regulations, unless they are inculcated in the respective constitutions, may be considered as abrogated.

---

[36] C. un. 6°, III, 16; S. C. EE. et RR., Dec. 6, 1838 (Bizzarri, *l. c.*, p. 437 f.). Such visits were, of course, allowed only at the grates.

CAN. 606

§ 1. Curent Superiores religiosi ut accurate observentur quae sive circa egressum subditorum e clau-
stris, sive circa excipiendos vel adeundos extraneos, in
propriis constitutionibus praescripta sunt.

§ 2. Superioribus fas non est, salvis praescriptis in
can. 621–624, permittere ut subditi extra domum propriae religionis degant, nisi gravi et iusta de causa
atque ad tempus quo fieri potest brevius secundum
constitutiones; pro absentia vero quae sex menses ex-
cedat, nisi causa studiorum intercedat, semper Apostolicae Sedis venia requiritur.

§ 1. Religious superiors must take care that the rules
laid down in their constitutions be faithfully observed
regarding the egress of subjects from the cloister, or their
receiving visits from, or paying visits to, outsiders.

§ 2. Religious superiors may not allow their subjects
to stay outside the house of their own institute except for
a just and grave cause and for as short a time as possible.
But for an absence of more than six months, unless for
study, the permission of the Holy See is always required.

To keep religious from wandering about, Ordinaries
were formerly commissioned to send them back each to
his own house.[87] Alexander III (A. D. 1180) forbade religious to leave their monasteries in order to frequent
lectures on civil law and physical science.[88] We have
read many grants of the S. C. of Bishops and Regulars
touching upon the study of civil law. Now our Code
grants them that permission in general, saving the disposition of can. 587, § 4. The lawgiver makes no distinc-

---

[87] C. 7, X, I, 31.   [88] C. 3, X, III, 50.

tion as to branches of study or private studies, in a library, for instance, or archives.

CAN. 607

Antistitae et Ordinarii locorum serio advigilent ne religiosae, citra casum necessitatis, singulae extra domum pergant.

The superioresses and local Ordinaries shall carefully watch that Sisters do not leave the house singly, without a companion, except in case of necessity.

ASSISTANCE IN THE SACRED MINISTRY

CAN. 608

§ 1. **Curent Superiores ut religiosi subditi, a se designati, praesertim in dioecesi in qua degunt, cum a locorum Ordinariis vel parochis eorum ministerium requiritur ad consulendum populi necessitati, tum intra tum extra proprias ecclesias aut oratoria publica, illud, salva religiosa disciplina, libenter praestent.**

§ 2. **Vicissim locorum Ordinarii ac parochi libenter utantur opera religiosorum, praesertim in dioecesi degentium, in sacro ministerio et maxime in administrando sacramento poenitentiae.**

The religious superiors should always be ready to lend a helping hand, especially if their own Ordinary or a pastor of their diocese calls for assistance in attending to the needs of the people; and this help should be granted willingly not only to the churches and public oratories subject to religious, but also to others, as far as compatible with religious discipline. On the other hand it is but meet that the local Ordinary and parish priests should employ religious, especially those living in the diocese, for the sacred ministry, and particularly for the administration of the Sacrament of Penance. The text is sufficiently clear. But a question connected with the subject may be mooted: Are religious obliged to go on such errands in virtue of obedience? We answer, if the religious character of the community excludes outside work in the sacred ministry, in other words, if the order is exclusively monastic, the members are not obliged to obey. If, however, the order or community is of a clerical nature and aims at procuring the spiritual welfare of others, the religious are not at liberty to refuse the command of the superior.[39] In our country, as far as we are aware, the first-mentioned hypothesis would be verified only in the case of the Trappists, to some extent at least. Benedictines, Cistercians, and the congregations affiliated with them are no longer merely monastic. We may extend the case of obedience to the circumstances of an epidemic or contagious disease; because in that case obedience would demand that religious assist the secular clergy, provided the latter were doing their full duty.

PARISH CHURCHES IN CHARGE OF RELIGIOUS

Can. 609

§ 1. Si ecclesia, apud quam residet communitas religiosa, sit simul paroecialis, servetur, congrua congruis referendo, praescriptum can. 415.

§ 2. In ecclesia religiosarum a votis sive sollemnibus sive simplicibus paroecia erigi nequit.

§ 3. Advigilent Superiores ne divinorum officiorum in propriis ecclesiis celebratio catecheticae instructioni aut Evangelii explanationi in ecclesia paroeciali tra-

---

[39] Suarez, *De Rel.*, tr. VIII, l. II, c. 8, n. 19 (ed. Paris., t. 16, 144); Piatus M., I, p. 288.

dendae nocumentum afferat; iudicium autem utrum nocumentum afferat, necne, ad loci Ordinarium pertinet.

§ 1. If the church attached to the residence of a religious community is at the same time a parish church, the prescriptions of can. 415 are, in due proportion, to be observed. These regulations should be carried out faithfully, because the government of the parish is in the hands of the religious who acts as pastor. To him, therefore, belong the duties of preaching, teaching catechism, applying the *missa pro populo,* etc. Not the religious superior but the pastor is entitled to assist at marriages or to perform funeral services or to baptize children. But, as he enjoys the rights, so he also has the obligations, as the natural law dictates.

§ 2. The churches of nuns or Sisters, whether with solemn or simple vows, cannot be parochial.

§ 3. This last paragraph, taken from the Constitution of Benedict XIV, " *Etsi minime,*" Feb. 7, 1742, shows the care which the Church wishes to see bestowed on parochial work. The religious superiors are commanded to see that the divine office in their own churches does not interfere with the catechetical instruction or the explanation of the Gospel given in the parochial church; it pertains to the local Ordinary to judge whether or not this hindrance exists. Benedict XIV says that the Pontiff would assist the bishop in carrying out his regulations. The welfare of souls is the first and supreme law.

CHOIR SERVICE AND MASS

CAN. 610

§ 1. In religionibus sive virorum sive mulierum, quibus est chori obligatio, in singulis domibus ubi quatuor saltem sint religiosi choro obligati et actu legitime non impediti, et etiam pauciores, si ita ferant constitutiones, debet ad normam constitutionum quotidie divinum officium communiter persolvi.

§ 2. Missa quoque officio diei respondens secundum rubricas quotidie celebrari debet in religionibus virorum et etiam, quoad fieri possit, in religionibus mulierum.

§ 3. In eisdem religionibus sive virorum sive mulierum, sollemniter professi qui a choro abfuerunt, debent, exceptis conversis, horas canonicas privatim recitare.

It is a custom, nay, we might say, a customary law, that religious should chant or recite the divine office. Clement V insisted upon this service, not only in cathedral churches, but in all churches of religious, and exhorted them to recite the office with proper attention and devotion.[40] That St. Benedict devoted eleven chapters of his rule to this matter shows his intention of keeping the sacred fire burning. Hence it is not surprising that the Church imposed this duty on all religious whose constitutions prescribe the recitation of the divine office. Therefore, says § 1, all religious, whether male or female, who are obliged to choir service, are bound to perform it daily in every house in which there are at least four members who are not lawfully prevented, and even fewer if the constitutions so prescribe.

This *obligation* is a *grievous one* for all institutes whose constitutions prescribe choir service, and the superior is not allowed to dispense from it, except in case there be not sufficient members present to perform it. The Code rules that at least four members obliged to

---

40 C. 1, *Clem.* III, 14. Sometimes birds and dogs were brought into church!

choir service must be present in a house for which the choral obligation exists.[41] If the constitutions oblige the members to choir service even when less than four are present, they must be obeyed, even if four, or three, or two novices only were present who could perform the duty.[42] The community, as such, is under strict obligation to chant or recite the divine office, and a superior who would neglect his duty in this respect would be guilty of mortal sin.

On the other hand, *single members,* as such, are not obliged to choir service, at least not *sub gravi,* unless the rule or constitutions or the laws of foundation oblige them, or if the office could not be performed for lack of a sufficient number, or one would by his absence cause scandal to others.[43] Clement VIII, although very severe in inculcating the obligation, allowed superiors to grant a dispensation to choir members who are too much occupied with some special charge or office, *e. g.,* procurators, *oeconomi,* prefects; also teachers and preachers on the days on which they preach and teach; finally those who are sickly or engaged 'in studies.[44]

Of *nuns* with solemn vows, only those are obliged to choir service whose rule or constitutions, approved by the Holy See, impose this obligation. This was decided by the S. C. of Bishops and Regulars, April 19, 1844.[45] The decision added that if a legitimate custom involved this obligation, the nuns would be bound to follow it. As to Sisters with *simple* vows, the same decision says that they are, as a rule, not obliged to choir service. Now the Code must be consulted, and therefore, should the

41 Innocent X, " *Ut in parvis,*" Feb. 10, 1654. § 2.
42 Piatus M., I, 313.
43 Piatus M., I, 311 f.
44 " *Nullus ommino,*" July 25, 1599. § 1. The latter class embraces those who publish and print books for the good of the Church; Piatus M., *l. c.,* I, 314.
45 Cfr. Bizzarri, *l. c.,* p. 495 ff.

constitutions approved by the Holy See oblige a community to choir service, the obligation must be complied with. Hence Dominican, Franciscan and Capuchin Tertiaries, regardless of the primitive rule of these orders, are obliged to choir service only if their constitutions expressly prescribe it. The same applies to Benedictine Sisters with simple vows; unless their approved constitutions oblige them to choir service they are not bound to render it, for the above-quoted decision clearly states: "*ubi vero vota simplicia sint, non teneri.*"

As to the *Breviary*, the Constitution of Pius V, "*Quod a nobis*," July 9, 1568, says that those orders which have had their own Breviary for two hundred years prior to the date of said constitution, may retain it, whereas all others must adopt the Roman Breviary. The orders which had their own Breviary were allowed to adopt the Roman if the superior general and the chapter general favored the change.[46] The modern congregations must all follow the Roman Breviary.

With regard to *nuns* with solemn vows, what has just been said about regulars applies also to them, especially to those who are subject to regulars. *Sisters* with simple vows, if obliged for one reason or another to choir service, generally recite the Little Office of the Blessed Virgin, unless, by a strange mixture of ancient custom and modern legislation, they follow the rule of an order in reciting the full office.[47]

Concerning the *calendar*, this depends upon special indults granted by the Holy See (S. Rit. C.). Those religious who have the privilege of using their own calen-

[46] Hence the Benedictines would be allowed, even now, to adopt the Breviary prescribed by Pius X's Constitution "*Divino afflatu*," Nov. 1, 1911; nor would St. Benedict's Rule (c. 18) be opposed to the change.

[47] This is the case with some Benedictine Sisters of our country.

dar must follow it or adopt the diocesan calendar. *Nuns* subject to regular orders follow the calendar of these orders; others must follow the diocesan calendar, unless special indults grant them the use of their own calendar. *Sisters* with simple vows, with the sole exception of the Franciscans, must adopt the diocesan calendar, to which also their chaplain, even if he has his own ordo, must conform.[48] The Franciscan Sisters aggregated to any of the three branches (Brown Franciscans, Conventuals, Capuchins), although they recite only the Little Office of the B. M. V., are entitled to follow the calendar, Missal and Martyrology of their respective order.[49] Furthermore all regulars who govern a parish not incorporated, or entrusted to them only for a time, must use the diocesan calendar to which the people are accustomed.[50]

§ 2 of can. 610 says: the *Mass* corresponding to the office of the day according to the rubrics must be celebrated daily in the institutes of men and even, where possible, in the institutes of women. *Regulars* who are bound to choir service are certainly obliged to have one conventual Mass sung or read.[51] The same obligation is imposed on *nuns* who are obliged to choir service.[52] (The Code is not opposed to that statement, because the Mass is the principal part of the divine office.) But those who are not obliged to choir service are not bound by a strict obligation to have a conventual Mass, except "where possible." The possibility depends on many circumstances, for instance, whether they have a chaplain, or the means of supporting one, the locality, occupation,

---

[48] S. Rit. C., July 17, 1896; July 9, 1895 (*Decreta Auth.*, n. 3927, n. 3862).

[49] S. Rit. C., Jan. 22, 1906 (*Anal. Eccl.*, t. XIV, p. 106).

[50] S. Rit. C., Feb. 4, 1908 (*Decreta Auth.*, n. 3779).

[51] But they are not obliged to two conventual masses; S. Rit. C., Dec. 2, 1891 (*Decreta Auth.*, n. 3757).

[52] Piatus M., I, p. 327.

and so forth. The same is true, *a fortiori*, of Sisters with simple vows. As to the locality, can. 1192 must be consulted with regard to *semi-public oratories*, which may only be erected with the permission of the Ordinary, who must inform himself as to proper construction.[53] In these semi-public oratories the number of masses is not limited (can. 1193).

As to *rubrics*, the mass must correspond to the office of the day. Where the office of the day is not recited, the calendar or ordo must be followed. The chaplain is supposed to know the rubrics. We will only add that Mass is generally said after the Tierce (or Sext, or None, as the rubrics prescribe) and the color of the feast must be used, unless a votive Mass or *missa de requie* is permitted.

§ 3 says that religious men or women with solemn vows are obliged to the *private recitation* of the divine office if they have been absent from choir. Lay brothers are excepted. This rule, of course, applies only to such religious as are obliged to choir service. Can. 135 obliges all clergymen *in sacris* to the recitation of the divine office, from which they are excused only by physical or moral impossibility. If some particular constitutions oblige *lay brothers* to the recitation of the Little Office of the B. M. V. this obligation does not entail a strict duty,[54] though the prayers prescribed must, of course, be said.

[53] The chapel must not be a mere hallway, nor may a bedroom be placed immediately above the sanctuary, it must be decently furnished and neatly kept.

[54] S. C. EE. et RR., Jan. 29, 1906 (*Anal. Eccl.*, XIV, p. 209 f.; *Congreg. Bavarica O. S. B.*); April 19, 1844 (Bizzarri, p. 495 ff.).

CAN. 611

Omnes religiosi sive viri sive mulieres, libere possunt mittere litteras, nulli obnoxias inspectioni, ad
Sanctam Sedem eiusque in natione Legatum, ad Car-
dinalem Protectorem, ad proprios Superiores maiores,
ad Superiorem domus forte absentem, ad Ordinarium
loci cui subiecti sint et, si agatur de monialibus quae
sub regularium iurisdictione sunt, etiam ad Superiores
maiores Ordinis; et ab istis omnibus praedicti religiosi, viri aut mulieres, litteras item nemini inspicien-
das recipere.

All religious, whether men or women, can freely send
letters, exempt from all control, to the Holy See and its
legate in the country, to their Cardinal Protector, to their
own higher superiors, to the superior of their house when
absent, to the local Ordinary to whom they are subject,
and, in the case of nuns subject to regulars, to the higher
superiors of the order; and from all these persons the
religious, men or women, can also receive letters which
nobody has the right to open.

We add only one thought, which has often struck our
inquiring mind. Authors, especially moralists, base the
right of inspecting letters *sent to religious* on the necessity of maintaining the religious discipline. But they
never mention the natural right which those outside the
house have to privacy and secrecy of correspondence.
It is acknowledged by all that letters should never be
opened or read by persons not concerned. Is a religious
superior by virtue of his office entitled to know the secrets
of the family of a religious? Has he any right to make
use of that knowledge? This is privileged knowledge,

and we fail to see how it can be conducive to the right government of his subjects. Besides the manifestation of conscience not being to be extorted, we fail to see into the claim of knowing the conscience of others.

CAN. 612

Praeter praescriptum can. 1345, si loci Ordinarius ob causam publicam sonitum campanarum, preces aliquas vel sacra sollemnia indicat, religiosi omnes, etiam exempti, obedire debent, salvis constitutionibus et privilegiis suae cuiusque religionis.

Besides the prescription of can. 1345, if the local Ordinary from a motive of public utility prescribes the ringing of the bells, certain prayers or sacred solemnities, all religious, even those exempt, must obey, without prejudice to the constitutions and privileges of each institute.

Can. 1345 rules that the Ordinary is entitled to command religious, even those exempt, to impart a brief instruction in their own churches on feast-days if the people assist at the service. As to the ringing of bells, the recitation of prayers, and solemn services, the Ordinary may command them only for a public cause. Such a one would be war, a public calamity, the election of a pope or the bishop's taking possession of the diocese. Regulars must also insert the *imperata* commanded by the Ordinary, and are not allowed to quit saying it at will.[55] From this injunction of the Ordinary no appeal is permissible,[56] although the privileges of the orders are not thereby touched or revoked. Thus, according to Pius V's Constitution, " *Etsi mendicantium*," May 16, 1567, Ordi-

---

[55] S. Rit. C., April 3, 1821 (*Decreta Auth.*, n. 2613 ad 1 et 2).

[56] Bened. XIV, " *Ad militantis*," March 30, 1743.

naries are not allowed to prohibit regulars from ringing the bells or celebrating the office whenever they please.[57]

[57] S. C. EE. et RR., March 11, 1892 (*A. S. S.*, XXIV, 558).

CHAPTER II

CAN. 613

§ 1. Quaelibet religio iis tantum privilegiis gaudet, quae vel hoc in Codice continentur, vel a Sede Apostolica directe eidem concessa fuerint, exclusa in posterum qualibet communicatione.

§ 2. Privilegia quibus gaudet Ordo regularis, competunt quoque monialibus eiusdem Ordinis, quatenus eorum sint capaces.

§ 1. Each institute enjoys only those privileges which are contained in this Code, or may have been directly granted to it by the Apostolic See; every communication of privileges is henceforth excluded.

§ 2. The privileges which a regular order enjoys belong also to the nuns of the same order, in so far as they are capable of enjoying them.

On privileges in general the reader may consult Vol. I of this Commentary, where mention is also made of the communication of privileges.[1] There are only two sources of privileges: the law and a direct grant by the Holy See. All intercommunication of privileges is forbidden for the future. However, this law, as we stated before, is not retroactive, and hence the orders may retain what they possess, except where the Code rules differently. In order to ascertain what privileges each insti-

---

1 Vol. I, pp. 155 ff.

tute possesses, the superiors of regulars have been called upon, in a circular of the S. C. of Religious, to meet after the war and prepare a list of privileges granted and communicated to their respective orders. Since the different orders enjoy many different privileges, it cannot be our task to collect them. It seems certain that any privilege which concerns the outward activity of the regulars, not merely their internal government and discipline, must now be looked upon as abolished if it contradicts the explicit wording of any part of the Code. Thus, for instance, the hearing of confessions, the celebration of Mass, preaching, and funerals must be judged according to our Code. The privileges concerning ordination *extra tempora* and without the necessary intervals are no longer in effect. We confess that uniformity of law and discipline seems to us a greater benefit than a shadowy so-called privilege, sometimes ostentatiously vindicated. There can be no greater glory than to belong to the Church universal, as long as religious are left free to pursue their vocation and are not unnecessarily molested.

The second section of our canon states that *nuns* with solemn vows partake of all the privileges enjoyed by the regular order whose rule they follow. Note that the text does not say that they must be subject to the prelate of the respective order. Hence though, for instance, Dominican nuns be subject to the Ordinary of the diocese, yet they enjoy all the privileges of the male order. *" In so far as they are capable of enjoying them "* means that female religious cannot partake of the privileges granted to male religious who are employed in the sacred ministry or in the exercise of jurisdiction *in foro externo* and *interno*. But they enjoy dispensations, commutations, and spiritual favors. Thus, for instance, a plenary indulgence granted to the Franciscan Order on the feast of St. Francis may be gained by the nuns of the same order (all three branches), and the brethren O. F. M. may gain a similar indulgence granted for the feast of St. Clare of Assisi (Aug. 12). As to *Sisters*, our Code is silent. Yet it is certain that the Tertiaries of St. Francis who live a common life, though they pronounce only simple vows, if duly aggregated to any of the three branches, partake of all the indulgences granted to the first and second orders, and that their churches and (public or semi-public) oratories are endowed with the same indulgences as those of the first and second orders.[2] Other sisterhoods enjoy only such privileges as are granted by the Code or the Holy See.

CLERICAL PRIVILEGES

CAN. 614

Religiosi, etiam laici ac novitii, fruuntur clericorum privilegiis de quibus in can. 119-123.

Religious, even lay brothers and sisters, and novices, enjoy the privileges of clerics mentioned in can. 119-123. Hence they are inviolable by reason of the *privilegium canonis*, they are not to be dragged before the civil court, are free from military service and public offices, and cannot be stripped of all their possessions in case of insolvency.[3]

They are not allowed to waive these privileges because they are attached not to the person, but to the religious state.

---

[2] S. C. EE. et RR., Nov. 18, 1905 (*Annal. Eccl.*, XIV, 20); S. C. Indulg., Aug. 28, 1903 (*Annal. Eccl.*, XI, 489); S. O., June 7, 1916 (*A. Ap. S.*, VIII, 263 ad 1; but V is now to be suppressed); S. C. EE. et RR., Sept. 1840 (Bizzarri, *l. c.*, p. 450 ff.).

[3] Cfr. Vol. II of this Commentary.

Can. 615

Regulares, novitiis non exclusis, sive viri sive mulieres, cum eorum domibus et ecclesiis, exceptis iis monialibus quae Superioribus regularibus non subsunt, ab Ordinarii loci iurisdictione exempti sunt, praeterquam in casibus a iure expressis.

Regulars, both men and women, including the novices, except those nuns who are not subject to regular superiors, are exempt with their houses and churches from the jurisdiction of the local Ordinary, except in the cases provided for by law.

As to the history of exemption, enough has been said *supra*.[4] Here the Code determines what exemption implies and what persons are exempt, as well as the exceptions to the rule.

1. Exemption means *freedom from the jurisdictional power of the Ordinary* in whose diocese a house is located in all matters except ordination. Exemption is called *passive* in regard to persons, and only by reason of personal exemption do houses and churches share the privilege. Hence, properly speaking, as Benedict XIV says,[5] the houses and churches of regulars are not severed from the diocesan organism; they do not form a separate territory *nullius*. The Code simply says: "*cum eorum domibus*," not *et eorum domus*.

2. Exemption is now granted to *all regulars, i. e.*, to all religious orders with solemn vows, even though the

---

4 Pages 24 sqq.

5 *De Synod. Dioec.*, II, 11, 2; Id., "*Apostolicae servitutis*," March 14, 1743. The statement in the text is of practical value in case of hearing confessions of secular priests, because a regular may hear such confessions in the monastery-enclosure, not only in the church, as at least one moralist claims.

members are not all solemnly professed. Thus also the
novices and lay brothers and clerics with simple vows
enjoy exemption. But we dare not extend the privilege
to the *familiares*,[6] or dependents, as the text does not
mention these, though it expressly includes novices; but
the *familiares* partake of certain other favors granted to
regulars. *Nuns* with solemn vows are withdrawn from
the jurisdiction of the Ordinary only if they are subject
to the power of a regular prelate. All these regulars are
now no *longer obliged to prove* that they enjoy exemption, because, being regulars, they are exempt by law.
Any religious order which conforms to can. 488 of the
Code is entitled to exemption.

Religious congregations, on the other hand, must prove
their claim to exemption by a papal brief, because without such an indult no congregation now enjoys the privilege. Thus the Passionists can produce the privilege
granted them by Clement XIV, Sept. 21, 1771, and the
Redemptorists may point to the Constitution of Pius VI,
" *Sacrosanctum*," of Aug. 21, 1789. Sisterhoods are
not easily granted exemption.[7]

3. Exemption, meaning freedom from episcopal jurisdiction, implies that the episcopal court cannot summon
religious to appear before it; that the exempt religious
need not heed ecclesiastical censures inflicted by the Ordinary; that they may bring their case directly before
the S. Congregation of Religious; that diocesan rules or
statutes do not touch them, except, of course, as far as
the sacred ministry is concerned; that episcopal interference in their domestic affairs and government is entirely excluded; that their property and its administra-

---

6 Cfr. can. 514.

7 The Sisters of the Holy Cross,
of Ingenbohl, Switzerland, among
whom the author spent many a
happy vacation day and whom he
remembers with deep gratitude, enjoy exemption to a certain extent.

tion are in their own hands. This, in general, is the extent of exemption. Should a doubt arise, the Roman *Curia* will decide it if the bishop is not satisfied with the interpretation given by the exempt religious.[8] However, there are exceptions, as the Code says: " *nisi in casibus a iure expressis,*" *i. e.,* in cases expressly mentioned in the Code the exemption ceases and the jurisdictional power of the Ordinary is restored. These cases are generally comprised by the phrase: *etiam exempti.*[9]

REGULARS OUTSIDE THEIR HOUSES

CAN. 616

§ 1. **Regulares extra domum illegitime degentes, etiam sub praetextu accedendi ad Superiores, exemptionis privilegio non gaudent.**

§ 2. **Si extra domum delictum commiserint nec a proprio Superiore praemonito puniantur, a loci Ordinario puniri possunt, etsi e domo legitime exierint et domum reversi fuerint.**

§ 1. Regulars unlawfully absent from their houses, even under the pretext of having recourse to their superiors, do not enjoy the privilege of exemption.

§ 2. Regulars who have committed a crime outside their house and are not punished by their superior, though the latter was warned of the fact, can be punished by the local Ordinary, even though they may have lawfully left their house and have returned to it.

§ 1 is taken from the Council of Trent,[10] where the

---

8 C. 13, X, IV, 17; c. 31, X, III, 39; S. C. C. April 16, 1648; Piatus M., II, p. 7.

9 The most important exceptions are stated in separate canons: 131, 344, 612, 614, 616, 804, 831, 874, 919, 1279, 1293, 1338, 1382, 1385 mostly taken from the Council of Trent.

10 Sess. 6, c. 3 de ref.; sess. 25, c. 4 de reg.

term *unlawfully* is explained. A religious is unlawfully absent from his house if he leaves it without being sent or called by the superior. Hence a religious who would depart from the monastery without the permission of his superior, in order to go to the higher superior, or to Rome, to seek redress from grievances, would be unlawfully absent. However, it is generally understood that if the superior has been duly asked for leave and denied the same, a religious is allowed to go straightway (*recto tramite*) to the superior next in rank. In the latter case, therefore, he would not be deprived of the privilege of exemption. This interpretation appears legitimate because the Code says, " under pretext," which indicates a pretended or feigned reason. One who has asked his superior for leave of departure and has been denied permission, cannot be said to act " under pretext." Besides religious are not denied the right of seeking redress and defending themselves against injustice. The Code says " *extra domum*," which, according to the Council of Trent, means monastery or convent. A monastery or convent is the habitual domicile of a religious, even though he may be absent from it frequently for the purpose of giving missions, lecturing, preaching, etc. Nay even our *expositi* are not unlawfully absent from the religious house, although they may not be said to have their domicile in the convent. Another case was solved by Benedict XIV concerning missionaries in England.[11] He says that if they had to live in private homes, these would be considered as their religious houses, and if they illegally absented themselves from them, they could be punished. But if religious are cast out of their houses by force — as was lately done in France — and cannot come together elsewhere to lead a common life, their tempo-

11 " *Apostolicum ministerium*," May 30, 1753, § 15.

rary lodgment would not be looked upon as a convent.[12]

How long illegitimate absence must last before a religious forfeits the privilege of exemption, is not stated in the Code. A decretal of Martin IV, which is referred to in a note of Cardinal Gasparri's edition, seems to fix fifteen days as the length of a presumed illegitimate absence.[13]

§ 2 mentions another case[14] in which regulars are liable to be punished by the Ordinary, *viz.*, if they commit a *crime outside their house*. The *crime* must be a real crime, that is, a public or scandalous transgression of the law made notorious by the fact of being witnessed by others. It is also generally presumed that it must be committed in daylight, and outside the religious house; if committed in church, or anywhere outside the monastic enclosure, the offender is liable to punishment. Note well that in this paragraph the legislator supposes that the absence is legitimate. Hence whether one is an *expositus*, or absent on a lawful errand, is immaterial in case of crime, as described above.

But the Ordinary may proceed only after the *superior* of the delinquent religious has been warned and failed to proceed within fifteen days from the date of warning. The superior must notify the Ordinary of the punishment inflicted.[15] All this must be observed, even if the religious has returned to his house or convent.

Can. 617

§ 1. Si in regularium aliorumve religiosorum exemptorum domibus eorumve ecclesiis abusus irrep-

12 S. C. C., Sept. 4, 1875; S. Poenit., Sept. 12, 1872; Piatus M., I, 3091.

13 C. 1, Extrav. Comm., III, 8.

14 *Trid.*, sess. 6, c. 3, de ref.; sess. 7, c. 14 de ref.; sess. 25, c. 14, de reg.

15 Cfr. Piatus M., II, p. 74 f.

serint, et Superior monitus prospicere neglexerit, Ordinarius loci obligatione tenetur rem ad Sedem Apostolicam statim deferendi.

§ 2. Domus autem non formata manet sub peculiari vigilantia Ordinarii loci, qui, si abusus irrepserint et fidelibus scandalo fuerint, ipse per se potest interim providere.

1. If abuses have crept into the houses or churches of regulars or of other exempt religious, and the superior, having been warned of the fact, neglects to provide a remedy, the local Ordinary is bound to refer the matter immediately to the Apostolic See.

§ 2. Every house in which there are less than six members, remains under the special vigilance of the local Ordinary, who, if abuses arise and become a source of scandal, can himself provisionally deal with them.

The first paragraph of this canon is entirely new, and we daresay, not exactly in keeping with the privilege of exemption, because the Ordinary is set up as a sort of policeman over exempt monasteries.   The second section recalls the regulations which emanated under Urban VIII, decree June 21, 1625, and Innocent X, "*Instaurandae*," Oct. 15, 1652, "*Ut in parvis*," Feb. 10, 1654.   But the Code cannot be supposed to wish to contradict the constitution of Leo XIII, "*Romanos Pontifices*," May 5, 1881, which grants exemption even to smaller houses of regulars.

RELIGIOUS CONGREGATIONS

CAN. 618

§ 1. Religiones votorum simplicium exemptionis privilegio non gaudent, nisi specialiter eisdem fuerit concessum.

§ 2. In religionibus tamen iuris pontificii Ordinario loci non licet:

1.° Constitutiones ullatenus immutare aut de re oeconomica cognoscere, salvo praescripto can. 533-535;

2.° Sese ingerere in regimen internum ac disciplinam, exceptis casibus in iure expressis; nihilominus in religionibus laicalibus ipse potest ac debet inquirere num disciplina ad constitutionum normam vigeat, num quid sana doctrina morumve probitas detrimenti ceperit, num contra clausuram peccatum sit, num Sacramenta aequa stataque frequentia suscipiantur; et, si Superiores de gravibus forte abusibus admoniti opportune non providerint, ipse per se consulat; si qua tamen maioris momenti occurrant, quae moram non patiantur, decernat statim; decretum vero ad Sanctam Sedem deferat.

§ 1. Institutes with simple vows *do not enjoy the privilege of exemption*, unless it has been specially granted to them, as was done in the case of the Passionists, Redemptorists, and some others.

§ 2. As regards institutes approved by the Holy See, the local *Ordinary* may not:

1.° Make any change in the constitutions or enquire into the temporal administration, saving the dispositions of canons 533-535;

2.° Interfere in the internal government and discipline, except in the cases expressed by law; nevertheless, in regard to *lay religious*, he can and must enquire:

a) Whether the discipline is maintained according to the constitutions;

b) Whether sound doctrine and good morals have suffered in any way (through Modernism or other heretical tendencies);

c) Whether there have been breaches of the law of enclosure;

d) Whether the Sacraments are duly and regularly frequented;

e) If superiors having been warned of the existence of grave abuses, have failed duly to remedy them, the Ordinary himself shall *provide;* if, however, something of greater importance, which will suffer no delay occur, he shall *decide* at once, and report his decision to the Holy See.

The " *Conditae* " of Leo XIII, from which these rules are taken, furthermore says that the Ordinary is not allowed to limit or modify the authority granted to religious superiors by their constitutions; that the appointment to offices and charges belongs to the chapter and council of each house, but that the Ordinary himself or his delegate may preside at the chapters which make such appointments. The enclosure, called episcopal, is under the supervision of the bishop. As to the Sacraments, the Ordinary must see to it that they are administered according to the laws of the Church. These congregations are also subject to the Ordinary in whatever regards censures, reserved cases, dispensations from vows not reserved to the Pope, dispensations from general laws, as far as the Ordinary can dispense therefrom, and also with respect to public prayers (cf. can. 612). Abuses may creep into the management of schools, hospitals, asylums, especially concerning debts and buildings, the treatment of inmates, pronounced favoritism, indiscriminate communication with persons of the other sex, etc. If the abuse be a serious one, the Ordinary ought to gather written information, if possible supported by affidavits, and then draw the attention of the superior to the matter and give him time to correct the evil. If after some time no result appears, the Ordinary may summon the superior and threaten ecclesiastical punishment, including censures. All matters of greater importance must subsequently be reported to Rome. This report must embody the testimony of reliable witnesses who are ready to make oath to the facts they assert. Of course, in case of grave scandal, the Ordinary can punish the delinquent immediately, even by removal, if necessary. Note the terms *provide* and *decide;* the former is paternal and non-judiciary, whilst the latter spells judicial or at least summary trial and sentence.

PUNISHMENTS

CAN. 619

In omnibus in quibus religiosi subsunt Ordinario loci, possunt ab eodem etiam poenis coerceri.

In all cases in which religious are subject to the local Ordinary, he may coerce them even by penalties.

There can no longer [10] be any dispute as to the power of the Ordinary to proceed according to the penal Code against all religious in cases in which they are subject to him. In order to render that power efficacious, various papal [17] constitutions had already decided that it included the infliction of censures. Exemption is not absolute, but relative, *i. e.,* it reaches only so far as the law grants it. The Ordinary's power of correction may be wielded not only at the time of the canonical visitation, but whenever religious make themselves guilty of transgressions which the law has expressly placed under the power of the Ordi-

---

10 Cfr. Piatus M., II, p. 8 ff.

17 Greg. XV, " *Inscrutabili,*" Feb. 5, 16, § 4, § 6; Innocent X, " *Cum sicut,*" May 14, 1648, § 4. No privilege can now be claimed against the common law, unless it be granted since the promulgation of the Code.

nary. The latter, however, is not allowed to stretch the law.

CAN. 620

Per indultum ab Ordinario loci legitime concessum, obligatio legis communis cessat quoque pro religiosis omnibus in dioecesi commorantibus, salvis votis et constitutionibus propriis cuiusvis religionis.

Every indult lawfully granted by the local Ordinary dispensing from the obligation of the common law, avails likewise for all religious living in the diocese, without prejudice to the vows and particular constitutions of their own institute.

With regard to this enactment consult can. 1245, which empowers Ordinaries to dispense from fast and abstinence in particular cases. This indult may be applied also to religious communities, as has been decided by the Holy Office, Dec. 20, 1871. There is but one restriction,— that of the *vow*. Thus the Minimi have a special vow of fasting, from which the superiors cannot dispense. Our Code adds: without prejudice to the *constitutions*, which might be interpreted as if the superiors could not use the episcopal indult whenever the constitutions prescribed a day of fast or abstinence. However, since the Ordinaries and superiors of exempt orders are by common law entitled to dispense in said cases (can. 1245, § 3), we believe that they may legally apply the power granted if the whole diocese is exempt from a restriction. Besides, the S. C. of Bishops and Regulars has declared that superiors of religious congregations may dispense in particular cases from the constitutions.[18]

18 March 2, 1894; Bachofen, *Comp. Iuris Reg.*, p. 383. Too rigorous an application of the constitutions when the whole diocese is

Therefore, they too may apply the indult granted by the Ordinary in a particular case, especially since the dispensation is granted and all that is needed is to apply it. If there should be any scruple, especially in female communities, the Ordinary may be asked to dispense in their behalf, provided, of course, no special vow stands in the way.

BEGGING

CAN. 621

§ 1. Regulares, qui ex instituto mendicantes vocantur et sunt, eleemosynas in dioecesi, ubi religiosa domus est constituta, quaerere valent de sola Superiorum suorum licentia; extra dioecesim vero indigent praeterea licentia scripto data ab Ordinario loci in quo eleemosynas colligere cupiunt.

§ 2. Hanc licentiam Ordinarii locorum, praecipue dioecesium finitimarum, nisi gravibus et urgentibus de causis, ne denegent neve revocent, si religiosa domus ex mendicatione in sola dioecesi, in qua est constituta, vivere nullo modo possit.

The Council of Trent [19] did not favor begging, and doubtless it had good reasons for its sweeping prohibition. Yet subsequent papal constitutions [20] mitigated this somewhat harsh measure, or rather furnished an authentic, but extensive, interpretation of the Tridentine law. This interpretation safeguarded the right of *regulars who by their rule belong to the class of mendicant orders* to beg alms in the diocese in which their house is situated. All that is needed is the oral or written per-

---

dispensed and the supreme lawgiver allows the use of a dispensation, does not foster the spirit of willingness nor respect for the law.

[19] Sess. 21, c. 7, de ref.
[20] Pius V, " *Etsi mendicantium.*" May 16, 1567; Clement XI, " *Exponi nobis,*" July 8, 1717.

mission of their superior, either local or higher. This is the law laid down in the first paragraph of our canon. However, if they wish to beg outside their own diocese, regulars must obtain the written leave of the Ordinary in whose diocese they wish to beg.

§ 2 admonishes the Ordinaries, especially of adjoining dioceses, not to refuse or withdraw the license allowing mendicant regulars to beg, except for weighty and urgent reasons, if the religious house cannot possibly subsist on the alms gathered in the diocese in which it is situated.

It is certain that, according to the rule of St. Francis and certain authentic declarations of the Holy See,[21] the begging must be done by the regulars themselves. The text would also seem to exclude begging by letter or other indirect means. This is borne out by our Code, which recalls the fact that the mendicants need only the permission of their superiors to beg. The Apostolic grant, which is a privilege granted to mendicants only, must be interpreted according to the old law (cf. can. 623).

NON-MENDICANT ORDERS AND CONGREGATIONS

Can. 622

§ 1. Alii omnes religiosi Congregationum iuris pontificii, sine peculiari Sanctae Sedis privilegio, stipem petere prohibentur; quibus, si hoc privilegium impetraverint, opus erit praeterea licentia scripto data ab Ordinario loci, nisi aliter in ipso privilegio cautum fuerit.

§ 2. Religiosi Congregationum iuris dioecesani stipem quaeritare nequaquam possunt sine licentia scripto data tum ab Ordinario loci in quo sita est

21 *Const. cit.*

eorum domus, tum ab Ordinario loci in quo stipem
quaerere cupiunt.

§ 3. Religiosis, de quibus in §§ 1 et 2 huius canonis,
Ordinarii locorum licentiam quaeritandae stipis ne
concedant, praesertim ubi sunt conventus regularium
nomine et re mendicantium, nisi sibi constet de vera
domus vel pii operis necessitate, cui alio mòdo occurri
nequeat; quod si necessitati provideri possit stipe
quaerenda intra locum seu districtum vel dioecesim in
qua iidem commorantur, ampliorem licentiam ne lar-
giantur.

§ 4. Sine authentico et recenti rescripto Sacrae Congregationis pro Ecclesia Orientali, Ordinarii latini nec
sinant orientalem ullum cuiusvis ordinis et dignitatis
in proprio territorio pecuniam colligere, nec suum
subditum in orientales dioeceses ad eundem finem
mittant.

§ 1. The Code now passes to institutes which do *not
belong to the class of mendicant orders, and to papal congregations.*   These, it says, need a special indult from the
Holy See in order to be allowed to collect alms.   A special indult is one not included in the approval of the con-
situations, or at least not specifically mentioned in that approval.[22]   Besides this papal indult, these institutes need
the written permission of the local Ordinary, unless this
is not required by reason of a special provision made in
the papal indult.   Hence the Ordinary in whose diocese
they wish to beg, must be asked for his permission, and
the granting of it as to time and place and persons depends entirely on his judgment.

§ 2. *Diocesan institutes* need the written permission of

---

[22] In Latin the papal indult would   *non obstante iure ordinarii de
contain the clause: nulla requisita   petenda licentia*, etc.
vel obtenta Ordinarii licentia, or,

the Ordinary of the diocese in which their house is located, as well as of that of the Ordinary in whose diocese they wish to beg.[23]

§ 3. Both kinds of religious mentioned (§§ 1 and 2) should not be permitted by the Ordinary to beg, unless the latter is convinced of the absolute neediness of the religious house and the necessity of their work. If the necessary means can be provided within their own place, or district, or diocese, no permission to go begging elsewhere is to be granted. The restriction made in this paragraph applies especially to dioceses in which there are convents of regulars who are in name and reality mendicants. This last clause is very just and based upon the old rules prohibiting a convent from being erected within about three hundred feet from a convent of mendicants.[24]

§ 4. Latin Ordinaries may never allow an *Oriental* of any order or dignity (patriarch, metropolitan, bishop, priest, religious of either sex) to collect alms in their dioceses without an authentic and recently issued rescript of the S. Congregation for the Oriental Church; nor should Latin Ordinaries send any collectors into Oriental dioceses. Authenticity is proved by the seal and signature of the S. C. for the Oriental Church; "recently issued" means not more than six months old. If a priest cannot show such a document, he should not be allowed to say Mass and should be publicly denounced.[25]

23 S. C. EE. et RR., *Singulari quidem*, March 27, 1896.
24 Cfr. Piatus M., II, p. 284.
25 Alexander VIII, *Alias ema-*navit, Oct. 21, 1690; Clement XII, *Dudum*, March 26, 1736; S. C. Prop. Fide, June 1, 1912 (*A. Ap. S.*, IV, 532 ff.)

Can. 623

Non licet Superioribus stipem colligendam committere, nisi professis aetate animoque maturis, maxime si de mulieribus agatur, nunquam autem iis qui in studia adhuc incumbunt.

Superiors must not entrust the collection of alms to others than professed subjects of mature age and character, especially in the case of women, and never may students be so employed.[26]

Can. 624

Quod vero attinet ad modum in quaeritanda stipe servandum et ad disciplinam a quaestuantibus custodiendam, religiosi utriusque sexus stare debent instructionibus a Sede Apostolica hac de re datis.

As to what concerns the method to be followed in seeking alms and the discipline to be observed by those who seek them, religious of both sexes must conform to the instructions given by the Holy See on this subject.

These instructions are:

(1) That there should always be two sent out seeking alms; only in case of strict necessity is it permitted to send one, and he or she must be of approved moral character.

(2) When begging outside the place where their convent is located, religious should lodge with the clergy or pious benefactors.

(3) They should not remain outside their convent longer than one month, if begging in their own diocese; and not longer than two months if in a strange diocese.

(4) When begging in the place where their convent is

[26] S. C. Rel., Nov. 21, 1908 (*A. Ap. S.*, I, 153 ff.)

situated they are not allowed to remain out over night.

(5) They must conduct themselves humbly, modestly, and be clean in appearance, avoid places not suitable to their religious profession, and comply with their religious duties.

(6) Superiors are under strict obligation to make these instructions known to their subjects.

(7) If religious seeking alms do not conduct themselves properly, but give scandal, the Ordinary of the diocese may proceed against them according to law (cf. can. 616, § 2).

(8) Religious who go begging must carry with them the necessary permit, either from their superiors (cf. 621), or from both superior and Ordinary (if required according to can. 622) and be ready to show the same to the pastors and Ordinaries upon demand. The permission of the Ordinary is supposed to be valid until expressly revoked.[27]

PONTIFICAL RIGHTS OF ABBOTS

Can. 625

Abbates regulares de regimine, legitime electi, debent intra tres menses ab electione benedictionem accipere ab Episcopo dioecesis in qua monasterium situm est; postquam vero benedictionem receperint, praeterquam potestate conferendi ordines ad normam can. 964, n. 1, fruuntur privilegiis de quibus in can. 325, excepto pileolo violaceo.

Lawfully elected abbots who actually govern a community must be blessed by the bishop in whose diocese the monastery is located, within three months from the

27 S. C. Rel., Nov. 21, 1908 (A. Ap. S., I, 154 f.).

date of election. After they have been blessed, they
enjoy the power of conferring the tonsure and minor
orders on those subject to them by virtue of the religious
(at least simple) profession, and also, according to can.
325, the privilege of using pontificals, except the purple
skullcap.

Concerning the right of pontificals some historical notes
have been given in the section dealing with exemption.
We add that formerly abbots had to ask the bishop three
times for the blessing, and if he refused, they enjoyed
their rights without the blessing.[28] Now the Code makes
it imperative on all, even temporary abbots, who formerly
(e. g., in the Cassinese Congregation) did not receive it,
to obtain the blessing. It follows that the bishop is
obliged to impart it when requested. Should he demur,
recourse may be had to the S. C. of Religious.

After an abbot has been duly blessed, he enjoys two
rights in particular: he may *confer first tonsure and
minor orders* and he may *pontificate.*

The first is plainly stated in can. 964, 1.° Three conditions are required for licit and valid ordination. The
abbot must be blessed, he must be a priest, and the *ordi-
nandus* must be his own subject. (a) He must be
blessed, whether by the diocesan or another bishop is immaterial as to the validity of the orders to be conferred.
No privilege shall any longer be granted in this matter.[29]
(b) The abbot must himself be a *priest,* which is not only
appropriate, but absolutely required. (c) The one who
is to be tonsured [30] or promoted to minor orders must be
the *abbot's own subject* by virtue of at least simple pro-

---

28 C. 1, X, I, 10.

29 Formerly an abbot, even though
not blessed, could by an apostolic
privilege, confer these orders; S.

C. C., May 11, 1624; March 16,
1647 (Richter, *Trid.*, p. 199).

30 C. 3, 6°, V, 7 mentions tonsure
only.

fession. The once mooted question [81] whether ordination performed on one who is not subject to the abbot was only illicit, but not invalid, is now settled; it is invalid. A religious becomes subject by profession to that abbot in whose hands and name he makes profession, or rather for whose community he pronounces the vows. Therefore an Abbot President or the Abbot Primate can no longer confer minor orders on the members of the congregation or of the order, unless their faculties are renewed, or unless these were understood as privileges. But even in that latter sense, it would not seem safe to act on them.[82]

The second abbatial *privilege* is that of *pontificating*, *i. e.*, performing pontifical functions with throne and baldachino. Abbots may also wear a pectoral cross and a ring set with a precious stone, wherever they go. But the purple skullcap is not allowed them, except by indult. The Code does not limit the right of pontificating to a certain number of times, and hence the decree of Alexander VII, Sept. 27, 1659, is obsolete. However, as prelates *nullius* are allowed to pontificate only in their own territory (can. 325), the privilege of using pontificals seems to be restricted to their own churches, *viz.*, such as are fully incorporated with the order. Neither would it be in accordance with the Code if abbots would pontificate outside the diocese without the consent of the Ordinary of the other diocese, since can. 337 requires this even for bishops. Nor does the Code (see can. 625, as compared with can. 325) grant to abbots the right of consecrating churches and altars, otherwise it would not enumerate that power specifically under can. 325, § 2.[83]

---

81 Cfr. Bachofen, *Comp. Iuris Reg.*, p. 255 f.

82 Card. Gasparri refers to no decree of the S. C. EE. et RR., which had granted that faculty to the Abbot Primate and Abbots Presidents; but unless profession is explicitly made for the monastic congregation — not for the monastery — the text is against that privilege or faculty.

83 Cfr. can. 1147, § 1.

CHAPTER III

OBLIGATIONS AND PRIVILEGES OF RELIGIOUS PROMOTED TO ECCLESIASTICAL DIGNITIES OR ADMINISTERING PARISHES

The laws laid down in the following chapter are partly new and partly taken from Leo XIII, "*Romanos Pontifices*," May 8, 1881. History, as said elsewhere, testifies that monks were not found incapable of ruling a diocese or parish or even the whole church. Concerning parishes, the Decretals made it obligatory that a companion should be given to the pastor if possible.[1] But on account of the scarcity of fit members this rule was often neglected, and, in fact, by contrary custom, abolished. The Apostolic See thereupon set up the law (called "recent" by Benedict XIV) that regulars should not be appointed to pastoral charges without an apostolic dispensation.[2] However, it was always and is still understood that if a parish is *pleno iure* incorporated with a monastery, the latter can, without an indult, appoint one of its members to govern it, because such a parish has become a regular benefice.[3]

CAN. 626

§ 1. Religiosus nequit, sine Sedis Apostolicae auctoritate, ad dignitates, officia aut beneficia promoveri, quae cum statu religioso componi non possint.

---

[1] C. 5, X, III, 35 says that ancient canons allowed the monks to be pastors.

[2] "*Cum nuper*," Nov. 8, 1751.

[3] The principle stated above touched only secular benefices, *i. e.*, such offices as by original right were held by the secular clergy.

§ 2. Legitime ab aliquo collegio electus, nequit electioni assentiri sine licentia Superioris.

§ 3. Si voto teneatur non acceptandi dignitates, specialis Romani Pontificis dispensatio est necessaria.

§ 1. No religious may, without the authority of the Apostolic See, be promoted to any dignity, office, or benefice which is incompatible with the religious state. To a *dignity* in the proper sense, *i. e.*, an ecclesiastical office which implies precedence, rank, and jurisdiction, if it be a secular office, a religious cannot be promoted without a dispensation. But the supreme pontificate and the episcopacy has never been, by law, barred to religious. Hence the dignities here intended must refer to cathedral chapters. The *vicar-generalship* may also be included, as this dignity, according to can. 367, is to be conferred on secular priests only, unless the government of the diocese is entrusted to a religious family. *Office* would comprise all the minor offices, such as canonicates, pastorships, or chaplaincies held by secular priests, and also benefices, though, as stated before, if a parish belongs to a religious family by decree of the S. C. of Religious, a religious may be appointed to it.[4] Besides, as seen from the chapter on pastors and assistants, religious may be appointed temporary pastors or substitutes. Whether religious may be appointed *diocesan consultors* seems doubtful, because can. 425 requires consultors to reside in or near the episcopal city. But religious are not excluded from the office of *synodal examiners*, provided, of course, they have the permission of the superior or are themselves superiors. Neither does the Code forbid religious who are pastors to be rural deans. The main reason for excluding them from these offices is the in-

4 Cfr. can. 432, 456.

compatibility of the latter with the religious profession. Now where the Code does not explicitly state that the religious clergy is excluded, as is the case with the vicar-generalship, religious are capable of assuming offices which do not interfere with their profession. Hence a religious who is lawfully appointed pastor may also assume offices which are generally conferred on pastors.

§ 2. *One who is legally elected by an electoral college may consent to his election only with the permission of his superior,* as the Decretals [5] already stated. Hence a religious who would be elected superior for another monastery than his own, would need the special permission of his own superior. A general license to that effect is insufficient,[6] though if the electors had asked the superior before election to permit the choice of one of his subjects, this would suffice. An abbot who is elected bishop needs the consent of the Holy See for leaving his monastery.[7] Of course, here in this country this is of little practical value, since the Apostolic See, by freely appointing bishops is supposed to give its consent. For the rest, such cases are not frequent.

§ 3. If religious are bound by a vow not to accept ecclesiastical dignities (not mere offices), a special dispensation is required from the Roman Pontiff. This vow may be a religious vow, as the last class of the Jesuits pronounce, or a private conditional one. The Code makes no distinction.[8]

---

5 C. 27, 6°, I, 6. Neither is the superior obliged to ask the advice of his chapter or counsellors; *ibid.*, § 1.

6 Engel, I, 6 n. 44.

7 C. 36, 6°, I, 2.

8 Urban VIII, "*Honorum*," Feb. 24, 1643, § 2. A vow is conditional if made dependently on the will of the superior; if made before profession, the superior may annul it afterwards; can. 1312, § 1.

CAN. 627

§ 1. Religiosus, renuntiatus Cardinalis aut Episcopus sive residentialis sive titularis, manet religiosus, particeps privilegiorum suae religionis, votis ceterisque suae professionis obligationibus adstrictus, exceptis iis quas cum sua dignitate ipse prudenter iudicet componi non posse, salvo praescripto can. 628.

§ 2. Eximitur tamen a potestate Superiorum et, vi voti obedientiae, uni Romano Pontifici manet obnoxius.

A religious who is created cardinal or appointed bishop, either residential or titular, remains a religious with all the rights and obligations proper to his profession, but may exempt himself from such obligations as he deems incompatible with his dignity, without prejudice, however, to the rule laid down in can. 628.

He is also exempt from the jurisdiction of his superiors and by virtue of the vow of obedience becomes subject to the Roman Pontiff. Hence a religious thus promoted enjoys all the privileges and spiritual favors which his institute enjoys, and remains bound by the *obligations* proper to his state. He must observe the rule and the constitutions, as far as they do not conflict with his new dignity. This entails the observance of the fast and abstinence and the penances prescribed by the rule and constitutions. Whether these prescriptions are compatible with his dignity, the religious dignitary himself is allowed to judge.[9] As to the *Breviary* he must follow that of his diocese, and if another religious recites with him, he also may follow the bishop's breviary.[10] A Cistercian, we presume, would be obliged to add the Office of the

9 Benedict XIII, "*Custodes*," May 6, 1864 (Bizzarri, *l. c.*, p. March 7, 1726; S. C. EE. et RR., 712 ff.).
10 S. Rit. C., June 11, 1605.

Blessed Virgin, unless important occupations excused him. With regard to the *habit,* a religious dignitary has to wear the same as his religious brethren, as far as form and color are concerned,[11] but may have it trimmed with purple buttons. Canons regular and such as are especially privileged, may dress like secular bishops.

CAN. 628

Religiosus ad dignitatim episcopalem vel aliam extra propriam religionem evectus:

1.° Si per professionem dominium bonorum amiserit, bonorum, quae ipsi obveniunt, habet usum, usumfructum et administrationem; proprietatem vero Episcopus residentialis, Vicarius Apostolicus, Praefectus Apostolicus, acquirit dioecesi, vicariatui, praefecturae; ceteri, Ordini vel Sanctae Sedi, ad normam can. 582, salvo praescripto can. 239, § 1, n. 19;

2.° Si per professionem dominium bonorum non amiserit, bonorum quae habebat, recuperat usum, usumfructum et administrationem; quae postea ipsi obveniant, sibi plene acquirit;

3.° In utroque autem casu de bonis, quae ipsi obveniunt non intuitu personae, debet disponere secundum offerentium voluntatem.

A religious promoted to the episcopal or any other dignity outside of his institute must observe the *vow of poverty* as follows:

1. If he has lost the right of possessing property,— as is the case with solemnly professed religious — he retains the use, usufruct, and administration of all property that comes to him during his actual exercise of the dig-

---

11 Benedict XIII, " *Custodes* "; however, the Apostolic See may grant and has granted dispensation to wear the regular episcopal dress.

nity, but the property itself belongs to the diocese, vicariate, or prefecture apostolic, if the religious is a residential bishop, vicar, or prefect apostolic. If he is none of these, the property belongs either to the order, if the latter is capable of possessing property, or to the Holy See, if it is a mendicant order. A titular bishop is therefore obliged to his monastery, or province or order, which may claim all his belongings after his death. However, Cardinals may bequeath their appurtenances to a church, or pious place, or religious community; otherwise they go to the pontifical sacristy, with the sole exception of the ring, pectoral cross, and reliquaries.[12]

2. A religious who has not lost the right of owning property by his profession, by promotion to a dignity regains the use, usufruct, and administration of all the property he possessed at the time of his profession; and what comes to him after his promotion, belongs to him as owner. In other words, he does not differ in this respect from a secular bishop.

3. However, a religious with solemn or simple vows, if promoted to a dignity, must use all donations that he receives according to the intention of the donor, unless they are intended for his own person.

ABDICATION

Can. 629

§ 1. Dimisso cardinalatu vel episcopatu vel expleto munere extra religionem sibi a Sede Apostolica commisso, religiosus ad religionem redire tenetur.

§ 2. Potest tamen Cardinalis et Episcopus religiosus quamlibet suae religionis domum eligere in qua degat; sed caret voce activa et passiva.

12 Can. 239, § 1, 19; can. 1298, § 1.

When a religious cardinal or bishop resigns or goes out of office, because his mission is discharged, for instance, as a legate or special envoy of the Holy See, he must return to his institute. If he has held the dignity of cardinal or bishop, he may choose any religious house for his home, but is not entitled to either an active or a passive voice. And this prohibition holds not only for the respective house, but for the whole institute.[18] Of course, if the religious dignitary is bound to return *ad penates*, his institute is bound to support him.[14]

RELIGIOUS AS PASTORS

CAN. 630

§ 1. Religiosus, qui paroeciam regit sive titulo parochi sive titulo vicarii, manet adstrictus ad observationem votorum et constitutionum, quatenus haec observatio potest cum muneris sui officiis consistere.

§ 2. Quare, in iis quae ad religiosam disciplinam attinent, subest Superiori, cuius proinde est, et quidem privative respectu Ordinarii loci, in eius agendi rationem circa haec omnia inquirere eumque, si casus ferat, corrigere.

§ 3. Bona quae ipsi obveniunt intuitu paroeciae cui praeficitur, ipsi paroeciae acquirit; cetera acquirit ad instar aliorum religiosorum.

§ 4. Non obstante voto paupertatis, eidem licet eleemosynas in bonum paroecianorum, vel pro scholis catholicis aut locis piis paroeciae coniunctis, quovis modo oblatas accipere aut colligere, et acceptas sive collectas administrare, itemque, servata offerentium voluntate, pro prudenti suo arbitrio, erogare, salva semper vigilantia sui Superioris; sed eleemosynas pro

18 Paul IV, " *In sacra*," July 19,   14 S. C. C., Sept. 25, 1858.
1559, § 2.

ecclesia paroeciali aedificanda, conservanda, instaur-
anda, exornanda accipere, apud se retinere, colligere
aut administrare pertinet ad Superiores, si ecclesia sit
communitatis religiosae; secus ad loci Ordinarium.

§ 1. A religious who governs a parish, either as pastor
or as vicar, remains bound by the vows and the constitutions in so far as compatible with his office.

§ 2. Therefore, as to religious discipline, he is responsible, not to the Ordinary, but to his superior, who may
inquire into his conduct and correct him, if necessary.

§ 3. Property intended for the parish belongs to the
parish; all else is acquired for his religious brethren.

§ 4. Notwithstanding the vow of poverty, he may collect and receive alms for the benefit of his parishioners,
of Catholic schools and pious institutions connected with
the parish, and administer and distribute such alms according to his own judgment and the intention of the
giver, under the supervision, however, of the superior.
But to receive, retain, collect, and administer alms intended for the building, maintenance, restoration, and
ornamentation of the parochial church appertains to the
religious superiors if the church belongs to the religious
community; otherwise to the Ordinary.

This last clause of § 4 seems impractical, and, in many
cases, we fear, will prove unfeasible. Besides, it would
throw an unbearable burden on religious superiors who
have many parochial churches. Furthermore it may
cause troubles with regard to trustees and parishioners,
who are entitled to know how the money is spent.
Lastly, can. 533, § 1, n. 4, requires a separate account
for parish money and religious money. All this would
seem to demand a host of officials in the convent itself.

It is an entirely new regulation which has yet to stand the test of experience.

CAN. 631

§ 1. Idem parochus vel vicarius religiosus, licet ministerium exerceat in domo seu loco ubi maiores Superiores religiosi ordinariam sedem habent, subest immediate omnimodae iurisdictioni, visitationi et correctioni Ordinarii loci, non secus ac parochi saeculares, regulari observantia unice excepta.

§ 2. Ordinarius loci, ubi eum suo muneri defecisse compererit, opportuna decreta condere ac meritas in eum poenas statuere potest; in quo nihilominus Ordinarii facultates minime privativae sunt, sed Superior ius cumulativum cum ipso habet, ita tamen ut, si aliter a Superiore, aliter ab Ordinario decerni contingat, decretum Ordinarii praevalere debeat.

§ 3. Quod attinet ad parochi vel vicarii religiosi remotionem e paroecia, servetur praescriptum can. 454, § 5; et quod ad bona temporalia, praescriptum can. 533, § 1, n. 4, et can. 535, § 3, n. 2.

§ 1. Religious pastors or assistants, although exercising the sacred ministry in the house or place where the higher superiors of the institute have their habitual residence, are immediately subject, in all matters concerning their pastoral charge, to the jurisdiction, visitation, and correction of the Ordinary of the diocese, just like secular pastors, with the sole exception of the regular discipline.

§ 2. If a religious pastor or vicar neglects his duties, the Ordinary of the diocese may issue opportune orders and inflict merited penalties. However, he may not proceed by himself alone, but must proceed in union with the religious superior; if the decisions of the latter conflict with those of the Ordinary, the latter's decree must prevail.

§ 3. Concerning the removal of a religious pastor or assistant, can. 454, § 5, must be observed, and as to the temporalities, can. 533, § 1, n. 4, and can. 535, § 3, n. 2.

CAN. 632

**Religiosus nequit ad aliam religionem, etiam stric-
tiorem, vel e monasterio sui iuris ad aliud transire sine
auctoritate Apostolicae Sedis.**

No religious can, without authorization from the Holy
See, pass to another institute, even stricter, or from one
independent monastery to another.

This is now the general rule, based partly on the old
law. For the rest, this whole Title is entirely new, as the
lack of quotations in Card. Gasparri's edition plainly indicates. Hence the commentator, according to can. 6, must
interpret the law according to the wording of the text
itself, and only where a doubt arises, may he resort to
the old law.

The Council of Trent[1] forbade the passing of religious
from a stricter to a laxer order. A laxer order or congregation was one which prescribed fewer external austerities (fasting, abstinence, vigils, silence, labor). The
Carthusians were and are looked upon as the strictest.
A transition to a stricter order, if done from zeal to lead
a more perfect life, and with the permission of the superior, could formerly be effected without the interposition
of the Apostolic See.[2] Now, however, no change is al-

1 Sess. 25, c. 19 de reg.   2 C. 5, X, III, 31.

lowed without papal permission. Note the term *religio*, which means a society of religious distinct from others, whether an order or a religious congregation. Thus no one is allowed to pass from the Benedictine to the Franciscan order, or from the Sacred Heart Sisters to those of St. Joseph, or from one *autonomous monastery* to another of the same institute. Autonomous monasteries are complete juridical entities, and religious generally make the profession for the monastery, not for the order or congregation. The vow of stability is clearly emphasized. A Jesuit may therefore transfer himself from one province to another, but a Benedictine or Cistercian may not even change his monastery without papal permission. Of course transfer is here understood as implying transfer of the vows made for one monastery to another independent monastery. A temporary though protracted transfer for reason of studies (can. 606), or help, or removing occasions of sin (can. 661, § 2), needs no Apostolic indult. Here again we must add that the faculties formerly granted to the Abbot Primate and abbot presidents are no longer valid. Furthermore, it must be noted that the text, by using the term *religio*, includes diocesan institutes.

Can. 633

§ 1. Transiens ad aliam religionem novitiatum peragere debet; quo durante, manentibus votis, iura et obligationes particulares, quas in religione derelicta habuit, suspensa manent, et ipse obligatione tenetur Superioribus novae religionis et ipsi novitiorum Magistro parendi etiam ratione voti obedientiae.

§ 2. Si in religione ad quam transiit, professionem non edat, ad pristinam religionem redire debet, nisi interim votorum tempus exspiraverit.

§ 3. Transiens ad aliud monasterium eiusdem Ordinis nec novitiatum peragit nec novam emittit professionem.

§ 1. He who passes to *another institute*, must make a novitiate, during which the vows remain intact, while the rights and particular obligations which he had in the former institute are suspended, and he is bound to obey the superior of his new institute and the master of novices even by virtue of the vow of obedience. This is the substance of § 1; but what, for instance, if a member of the Minimi, with his vow of perpetual abstinence and fast, enters a less strict order? The text says that " the vows remain intact." We believe, however, that, since the *transiens* has obtained permission from the Holy See, the latter included a dispensation from, or rather suspension of, the obligation of the particular vow, until the novice has made profession. The vows mentioned are chiefly the three principal vows of the religious state. Vows privately made in the former institute may be declared invalid or not binding by the lawful superior of the new institute.[3]

§ 2. If he does not make profession in the new institute, he must return to his old one, unless the term of his vows expire in the interval. The latter clause, of course, holds only in the case of temporary profession; hence, in orders with triennial vows before the solemn vows, and in religious congregations where annual vows are made for a certain term before the perpetual vows are taken. Should the time of temporary profession not have elapsed when he would have to return, he must go back to the former institute, or ask for a rescript of exclaustration until his time expires.

3 Can. 1312 f.

§ 3. He who passes to another monastery of the same
order makes neither a new novitiate nor a new profession. Note the term *order*, because the text evidently
refers to such monasteries as are autonomous (*sui iuris*),
and to monastic congregations of the same order. Generally, a retreat of some days is prescribed before incor-
poration in the new monastery or congregation. Therefore a change from one monastic congregation to another
only requires a papal indult, but no new novitiate or new
profession is necessary, no matter how different the discipline may be.

CAN. 634

Sollemniter professus aut professus a votis simplicibus perpetuis, si transierit ad aliam religionem cum
votis sollemnibus vel simplicibus perpetuis, post novitiatum, praetermissa professione temporaria, de qua
in can. 574, vel admittatur ad professionem sollemnem
aut simplicem perpetuam, vel ad pristinam redeat religionem; ius tamen est Superiori eum probandi diu-
tius, sed non ultra annum ab expleto novitiatu.

If a person who has made profession of solemn or of
simple perpetual vows joins another institute with solemn
vows or with simple perpetual vows, he must, after the
novitiate, omit the temporary profession spoken of in
can. 574, and make profession of solemn vows or of
simple perpetual vows, according to the institute, or he
must return to the former institute. The Superior, however, has the right to prolong the period of probation,
but not beyond one year after the completion of the
novitiate.

Can. 635

Transeuntes ad aliud monasterium eiusdem religionis a die transitus, ad aliam vero religionem ab edita nova professione:

1.° Amittunt omnia iura et obligationes prioris religionis vel monasterii et alterius iura et officia suscipiunt;

2.° Religio vel monasterium a quo bona servat, quae ipsius religiosi ratione iam ei quaesita fuerunt; quod spectat ad dotem eiusve fructus et alia bona personalia, si qua habeat religiosus, servandum praescriptum, can. 551, § 2; demum nova religio ius habet pro novitiatus tempore ad iustam retributionem, si eidem locus sit ad normam can. 570, § 1.

Those who pass to another monastery of the same institute, from the day of transition, but if to another institute, from the day of their new profession:

1.° Lose all the rights and obligations of their former institute or monastery and assume all the rights and duties of their new institute or monastery;

2.° Abdicate, in favor of the monastery or institute which they leave, the *property* that they may have acquired as religious; thus all books, chattels, donations or legacies already received and appropriated by the former institute or monastery belong to it. As to the *dowry* and its interest and other personal property of the religious, if he had such, only the interest of the dowry due during the novitiate goes to the new institute during the term of the novitiate, whereas the dowry itself passes to the new institute only after profession. If a Sister passes from one convent of the same institute to another, her entire dowry passes to the latter on the day of her transfer. Besides, if the constitutions or mutual agreement permit compensation for board and habit, the same must be made for the time of the novitiate.

Personal belongings are manuscripts, works of art, devotional articles, clothing. These go with the person. Besides, any fortune or inheritance falling to the religious after the day of his passing from one monastery to another of the same order, or from the day of profession in a new institute, belongs to the latter. Hence title deeds, notes, etc., not cashed or used, must be handed over by the former institute or house to the latter.

As to the *dowry*, a distinction was formerly made. If the monastery or institute from which a transfer was made, was the cause of the religious taking leave, it was bound to restore the full dowry; but if no cause or fault could be charged, it was only bound to a certain amount of pro rata support.[4]

As to § 1 it may not be amiss to observe the following: since the Code simply states that the rights and duties of the new monastery are assumed, it is evident that no restriction as to these rights can be validly made as a quasi-condition of admittance, if for instance active and passive voice should be surrendered. Besides the Code makes no reference to rule or constitutions, and therefore should these permit such restrictions, they are simply out of force.

Can. 636

Sollemnitas votorum in eo qui legitime secundum superiores canones vota simplicia in Congregatione religiosa nuncupat, eo ipso exstinguitur, nisi aliud in apostolico indulto expresse caveatur.

The solemnity of the vows of one who, according to the foregoing canons, lawfully makes profession of sim-

---

[4] S. C. EE. et RR., May 30, 1856 (Bizzarri, p. 645 ff.).

ple vows in a religious congregation, is by that fact abolished, except an apostolic indult expressly determines otherwise. In the light of this canon we believe the interpretation given above of can. 633, § 1, is completely justified.

TITLE XV

By leaving the religious state is meant either a lawful
or an illicit breaking of the juridical bond by which one
is connected with a religious institute, which one entered
by profession. Profession, as we have seen, may be
either temporary or perpetual, and its effects vary, especially if perpetual profession is at the same time solemn.
One may leave the religious state in a perfectly lawful
way, or he may forsake it unlawfully. Of all these
points our Code treats, beginning with the most lawful
one, *i. e.*, by the cessation of the obligation incurred by
temporary profession.

CAN. 637

**Professus a votis temporariis, expleto votorum tem-
pore, libere potest religionem deserere; pariter religio
ob iustas ac rationabiles causas eundem potest a reno-
vandis votis temporariis vel ab emittenda professione
perpetua excludere, non tamen ratione infirmitatis,
nisi certo probetur eam ante professionem fuisse dolose reticitam aut dissimulatam.**

One who has made profession of temporary vows may,
when the term of the vows has expired, freely leave the
institute; likewise, the institute, for just and reasonable
motives, can exclude a religious from renewing the temporary vows or from making profession of perpetual
vows; not, however, because of ill-health, except it be

clearly proved that the religious had fraudulently hidden or dissimulated the illness before profession.

From this text it again appears that temporary profession, whether triennial or annual, may truly be called a protracted novitiate; otherwise a religious could not leave the institute after his term has expired. Formerly, *i. e.*, up to a few years ago, such a conception of the simple profession never occurred to anyone. What is said in the second clause concerning the *institute* itself, that it may refuse to admit a religious to solemn or perpetual vows, is based on the same idea. Non-admittance is only a milder form of telling a religious to break off his relations. But as the vow is not yet solved, the legislator requires *reasons*. Such would be palpable signs of the lack of a religious vocation, mental debility, protracted absence from the services of the community, etc. *Infirmity* or ill-health is not considered a lawful reason. A decision of the S. C. of Bishops and Regulars [1] says that if a sickly disposition should have existed prior to profession, this would be no reason for exclusion; but if the religious himself concealed the state of his health by fraudulent testimonies of a physician, or by his own assertions, this would be a sufficient ground for not admitting him to solemn or perpetual profession. A physician's testimony, accompanied by an affidavit to the effect that the religious had deceived the institution by his assertions, would be legal proof, as would also be the testimony of two witnesses in whose presence the religious before his first profession asserted that he was in good health if it can be proved by a physician's sworn certificate that the illness existed before he entered; for in such a case deceit or fraud is evident. To conceal the true condition of one's health is a merely negative act,

[1] May 13, 1904, O. S. B. (*A. S. S.*, XXXVII, 445).

whilst to dissimulate it means to use positive means to hide the truth. Both have the same effect, *viz.*, to deceive.

A question may here be asked: A cleric had made profession, Aug. 15, 1915, therefore previously to May 19, 1918, and his vows were considered perpetual on his part. On Aug. 15, 1918, his simple vows would expire. May he apply our canon in his case and leave the religious state? We believe the affirmative answer would be upheld by the Roman Court. For not only did it look upon these simple vows as strictly triennial for at least a few years prior to the Code, which we know from personal experience, but the authentic answers given to several questions lead to that assumption. Thus the answer to the question concerning *sponsalia* and other impediments contracted before the new Code went into force was that betrothal and other impediments already contracted and to be contracted were to be treated according to the existing law.

SECULARIZATION

Can. 638

Indultum manendi extra claustra, sive temporarium, idest indultum *exclaustrationis*, sive perpetuum, idest indultum *saecularizationis*, sola Sedes Apostolica in religionibus iuris pontificii dare potest; in religionibus iuris dioecesani etiam loci Ordinarius.

The Apostolic See alone can grant an indult, either for temporary absence or perpetual secularization, to members of papal institutes; whilst the Ordinary of the diocese may grant such an indult to members of diocesan institutes.

Temporary absence is called *exclaustratio,* or sometimes *sæcularisatio ad tempus, i. e.,* permission to stay outside the monastery for one or three years, after the expiration of which the religious could apply for perpetual secularization. Now he may get the latter at once, but he must clearly state in his petition what he wishes. If he is a priest or cleric in higher orders, he must send in the documents of his superior with another from an Ordinary who is willing to receive him into his diocese. Both must be sent to the S. C. of Religious. The reasons for the request (ill-health, necessary support of parents, mental depression, unjust treatment, etc.) must be stated in the petition.

Can. 639

Qui indultum exclaustrationis ab Apostolica Sede impetravit, votis ceterisque suae professionis obligationibus, quae cum suo statu componi possunt, manet obstrictus; exteriorem tamen debet habitus religiosi formam deponere; perdurante tempore indulti caret voce activa et passiva, sed gaudet privilegiis mere spiritualibus suae religionis, et Ordinario territorii ubi commoratur, loco Superiorum propriae religionis, subditui etiam ratione voti obedientiae.

Whoever has obtained from the Holy See the indult of *exclaustration,* remains bound by his vows and the other obligations of his profession compatible with his state. There is no dispensation granted from the observance of the vows, whereas other obligations imposed by the rule or constitutions, for instance, concerning fast and abstinence, discipline or scourging, and other penances, may be dispensed with. As to the habit, the text says that it must not be worn exteriorly, hence an interior sign of it, as, for instance, a small-sized scapular or girdle, is

not forbidden. As long as the indult lasts the religious
has no right to either an active or a passive voice in the
institute, and hence could not be lawfully elected to an
office without a dispensation. But he enjoys the spiritual favors granted to his institute, especially the indulgences to be gained on certain feast days. Lastly, instead
of to the superior, he is subject to the Ordinary of the
diocese in which he lives, by virtue of the vow of obedience. Concerning poverty it may be added that he is
allowed as much as he needs for his support, but whatever he acquires belongs to the institute. If he wishes
to return, the institute must receive him without a new
novitiate.

SECULARIZATION PROPER

CAN. 640

§ 1. Qui, impetrato saecularizationis indulto, religionem relinquit:

1.° A sua religione separatur, habitus eiusdem exteriorem formam debet deponere, et in Missa et horis
canonicis, in usu et dispensatione Sacramentorum
saecularibus assimilatur;

2.° A votis liberatus manet, firmis oneribus ordini
maiori adnexis, si in sacris fuerit; non tenetur obligatione horas canonicas vi professionis recitandi nec aliis
regulis et constitutionibus adstringitur.

§ 2. Si ex apostolico indulto in religionem rursus
recipiatur, novitiatum ac professionem instaurat et
locum inter professos obtinet a die novae professionis.

§ 1. When a professed religious, having obtained an
indult of secularization, leaves his institute:

1.° He is cut off from his institute and must lay aside
the religious habit and, as to Mass and canonical hours,
is likened to seculars;

2.° He is freed from his vows, without prejudice to the obligations attaching to major orders, if he has received them; he is not obliged to the recitation of the canonical hours by virtue of his profession, nor is he bound by other rules and constitutions.

§ 2. If, by virtue of an apostolic indult, he is received again into the institute, he must make a new novitiate and profession, and his place amongst the professed members must be reckoned from the day of his new profession.

All this is new legislation and applies to religious of both sexes. Since a complete separation takes place by secularization, the mutual obligations between the institute and the individual religious cease, as do also the rights. Therefore new by-laws to that effect should be set up in conformity with the Code, especially concerning property and claims to compensation. What the text says concerning the Missal touches especially the Dominicans, who follow a somewhat different way in saying Mass. The rule concerning canonical hours affects all who have a Breviary different from that used by the secular clergy. The vows are now — this is an innovation — completely dissolved for all secularized religious not in higher orders. There is no longer an obligation to observe celibacy or to recite the Breviary, except, of course, when the discharged member is in higher orders.

INCARDINATION VS. SECULARIZATION

CAN. 641

§ 1. Si religiosus in sacris constitutus propriam dioecesim ad normam can. 585 non amiserit, debet, non renovatis votis, vel obtento saecularizationis indulco, ad propriam redire dioecesim et a proprio Ordinario recipi; si amiserit, nequit extra religionem sacros ordines exercere, donec Episcopum benevolum receptorem invenerit, aut Sedes Apostolica aliter providerit.

§ 2. Episcopus religiosum recipere potest sive pure et simpliciter, sive pro experimento ad triennium: in priore casu religiosus eo ipso est dioecesi incardinatus; in altero, Episcopus potest probationis tempus prorogare, non ultra tamen aliud triennium; quo etiam transacto, religiosus, nisi antea dimissus fuerit, ipso facto dioecesi incardinatus manet.

§ 1. A religious in higher orders, who, having made only temporary vows, has not been excardinated from his own diocese, must return to that diocese and be received by his Ordinary, in case he has not renewed his temporary vows or obtained an indult of secularization. If, having made perpetual vows, he has been excardinated, he may not exercise the sacred orders outside his institute until a benevolent Ordinary receives him into his diocese or the Apostolic See otherwise provides for him.

The last sentence is taken from "*Auctis Admodum,*" Nov. 4, 1892, which also threatens the penalty of suspension for those who leave the monastery before having been received into a diocese or otherwise provided with a sufficient patrimony. However, this penalty is not mentioned in the Code and therefore abolished. But the condition of having first found a bishop remains, unless the Apostolic See makes different provision in its indult, as it sometimes does when the secularized religious has a sufficient patrimony and therefore need not resort to means unbecoming to his state.

§ 2. The bishop may receive a secularized religious

either unconditionally or on trial. If unconditionally, the religious is by that fact incardinated in the diocese; if on trial for three years, the trial may be protracted for three years more, hence the whole term of trial may last six years, but no longer; at the expiration of that term the religious becomes *ipso facto* incardinated, unless he was dismissed before.

This law is very opportune and does away with the uncertainties apt to befall secularized religious. However, it is a new law which went into effect May 19, 1918, and is not retroactive. A bishop may now give a secularized religious a three or six years' trial and after that the religious is *ipso facto* incardinated, unless the bishop previously dismisses him from the diocese.

SECULARIZED RELIGIOUS PROHIBITED FROM HOLDING CERTAIN OFFICES

CAN. 642

§ 1. Quilibet professus, ad saeculum regressus, licet valeat, ad normam can. 641, sacros ordines exercere, prohibetur tamen sine novo et speciali Sanctae Sedis indulto:

1.° Quolibet beneficio in basilicis maioribus vel minoribus, et in ecclesiis cathedralibus;

2.° Quolibet magisterio et officio in Seminariis maioribus et minoribus seu collegiis, in quibus clerici educantur, itemque in Universitatibus et Institutis, quae privilegio apostolico gaudent conferendi gradus academicos;

3.° Quocunque officio vel munere in Curiis episcopalibus et in religiosis domibus sive virorum sive mulierum, etiamsi agatur de Congregationibus dioecesanis.

§ 2. Haec valent quoque de iis qui vota temporaria, vel iuramentum perseverantiae, vel peculiares quasdam promissiones ad normam suarum constitutionum ediderunt et ab eisdem dispensati fuerunt, si per sex integros annos eisdem ligati fuerint.

§ 1. A professed who leaves his institute may exercise the sacred orders in accordance with can. 641, but unless he receives a new and special indult to that effect from the Holy See:

1.° He may not hold any ecclesiastical benefice in a major or minor basilica or cathedral. This means that no canonicate or prebend of any kind can be given to him. If benefice is taken as synonymous with *office*, a secularized religious is also debarred from the offices of pastor or assistant at a cathedral church. However, *salvo meliori iudicio*, since penalties are odious, we believe that *benefice* must be taken in the strict sense, and excludes our cathedral churches, though it must be confessed that the intention of the law would also affect cathedral churches of our country.

2.° He is not allowed to accept the office of teacher or official in clerical seminaries, higher or lower (petit seminaries) in which clergymen are educated or in Catholic universities or institutions endowed with the right of conferring academic degrees (*e. g.*, the Catholic University of America, St. Vincent's Seminary, Beatty, Pa.).

3.° Neither may he hold any office or charge in an episcopal court (chancellor, examiner, etc.), or in religious houses of men or women (as confessor or chaplain), although these may be diocesan institutions.

§ 2. These regulations apply also to those who pronounced only temporary vows, or took the oath of perseverance, or made other promises according to their constitutions, if they are dispensed from them, provided, however, that they have lived under these obligations for a period of at least six years. From this it follows that a novice who left his institute before making his profession, or after his temporary profession expired, does not fall under these rather severe restrictions.[2] For the latter was not dispensed, but free to leave (can. 637), whilst a novice needed no dispensation, had taken no vows and made no promises. Wherefore the beginning of § 1, "*Quilibet professus, ad saeculum regressus,*" although somewhat general, must be interpreted according to § 2.

COMPENSATION

CAN. 643

§ 1. Qui e religione, expleto votorum temporariorum tempore aut obtento saecularizationis indulto, egrediantur vel ex eadem fuerint dimissi, nihil possunt repetere ob quamlibet operam religioni praestitam.

§ 2. Si tamen religiosa sine dote recepta fuerit nec ex propriis bonis sibimet providere valeat, religio ex caritate eidem dare debet ea quae requiruntur ut modo tuto ac convenienti domum redeat, ac providere ut, naturali aequitate servata, per aliquod tempus, mutuo consensu vel in casu dissensus ab Ordinario loci determinandum, honeste vivere possit.

§ 1. Whoever leaves his institute, whether at the expiration of the term of temporary vows or by virtue of an indult of secularization, or whoever has been dismissed, cannot seek compensation for the services rendered by him to the institute.

§ 2. In the case of a female religious who has been re-

---

[2] The S. C. Rel. (June 15, 1909) made these regulations to protect the religious state.

ceived without a dowry and cannot provide for herself out of her own resources, the institute should, in charity give her what is necessary for her to return safely and becomingly to her home, and provide her for a certain period with the means, to be determined by mutual agreement or, in case of disagreement, by the local Ordinary, of an honest livelihood in accordance with natural equity. Natural equity must take into consideration the usefulness of the member as well as the material condition in which she finds herself at the moment of leaving. Note the phrase, "*ex caritate*," as an act of charity, not justice. Hence a member will appeal in vain to the civil court if this canon is properly incorporated in the by-laws.[3]

APOSTATES AND FUGITIVES

Can. 644

§ 1. Apostata a religione dicitur professus a votis perpetuis sive sollemnibus sive simplicibus qui e domo religiosa illegitime egreditur cum animo non redeundi, vel qui, etsi legitime egressus, non redit eo animo ut religiosae obedientiae sese subtrahat.

§ 2. Malitiosus animus, de quo in § 1, iure praesumitur, si religiosus intra mensem nec reversus fuerit nec Superiori animum redeundi manifestaverit.

§ 3. Fugitivus est qui, sine Superiorum licentia, domum religiosam deserit cum animo ad religionem redeundi.

§ 1. An apostate from religion is one who, having made profession of perpetual vows, whether solemn or simple, unlawfully leaves the religious house with the

---

3 Cfr. Zollmann, *American Civil Church Law*, p. 80 ff.

intention of not returning or who, with the intention of withdrawing himself from religious obedience, though he has lawfully left the house, does not return to it.

§ 2. The perverse intention mentioned in § 1, is legally presumed when the religious has not returned within a month nor manifested to his superior his intention of returning.

It is *illegal* for a religious to leave the monastery without the permission of the superior, whether he lays aside his habit or not, provided he is determined not to return. This intention is not present if he leaves the monastery with the purpose of seeking a higher superior to demand redress for supposedly unjust treatment by his own superior.[4] If, however, he transfers himself to another religious institute without a papal indult, he is considered an apostate, because he wishes to withdraw himself from the obedience due to the superior into whose hands or for whose house he has made profession.[5]

The Code most reasonably gives *one month* for deliberation. After the lapse of that term the religious who refuses to return is presumed to be an apostate. But this *presumption* is only *de iure* and may be shattered by ordinary proofs. Thus, for instance, if the religious could prove by one trustworthy eye-witness that he wrote to the superior and the letter was lost, the presumption would cease; or if the superior misplaced or neglected to open the letter, and would find or open it later, presumption would be null, and the religious could not be called an apostate. Thus, also, if the religious was prevented by some accident from writing or returning home, he would not be an apostate.

4 This is common teaching; cfr.   Oct. 21, 1588; "*Ad Romanam,*"
Piatus M., I, 196.   Oct. 21, 1589.
5 Sixtus V, "*Cum de omnibus,*"

§ 3. A *fugitive* is one who, without the permission of his superiors, deserts a religious house with the intention of returning to the institute. Here, too, a perverse intention must be supposed, consisting in the will and desire of getting rid of the obligation of religious obedience. To go away for fun or in a roaming spirit would be merely a stealthy withdrawal.[6] Neither must he be considered a fugitive who dwells with persons who know him well and have no suspicion of his irregular leave.[7] The Code does not say how long a time must elapse until a religious is to be regarded as a fugitive. This point may be determined by the constitutions or by custom. In houses where the religious may be absent for several days without suspicion or attention, it would be unreasonable to be hasty in branding one as a fugitive. Here again it must be stated that every religious has the right to seek a higher superior to obtain relief from injustice.[8]

OBLIGATIONS OF APOSTATES AND FUGITIVES

CAN. 645

§ 1. Apostata et fugitivus ab obligatione regulae et votorum minime solvuntur et debent sine mora ad religionem redire.

§ 2. Superiores debent eos sollicite requirere, et ipsos, si vera poenitentia acti redeant, suscipere; reditum vero monialis apostatae vel fugitivae caute curet loci Ordinarius, et, si agatur de monasterio exempto, etiam Superior regularis.

§ 1. Neither an apostate nor a fugitive is freed from the obligation of his rule and vows, and must without delay return to his institute.

---

6 Piatus M., I, p. 205.
7 Sixtus V, "*Cum de omnibus,*"
§ 20.

8 Santi-Leitner, III, 31, n. 45
(Vol. III, p. 313).

§ 2. The superiors must seek them with solicitude, and receive them, if they return repentent; but as to apostate or fugitive nuns, the local Ordinary shall prudently see to their return, and the regular superior also, in the case of an exempt monastery. ·

A decree of the S. C. of Bishops and Regulars [9] says that apostates and fugitives who repair to a convent of other regulars or religious, must be returned by the superiors of that convent, and that deserters must return under the penalties threatened for apostates. The penalties against apostates and fugitives are stated in can. 2385 f., *infra*.

Apostates in the strict sense of the word are subject to excommunication, reserved to the higher superior if the institute is exempt, or to the Ordinary of the diocese in which they live. However, in the former case any priest with ordinary faculties may absolve them (can. 519). If they are reserved to the Ordinary, the confessor must have faculties from the same, which are also granted to the canon penitentiary (can. 401).

Fugitives are deprived of any office they may hold and suspended if they are clerics in higher orders. This suspension is reserved to the higher superiors.

Should an apostate religious die outside his monastery — concerning confession note that all reservations cease *in articulo mortis* — his so-called property formerly was held to belong to the *Camera Apostolica*.[10] Now-a-days the civil courts would probably decide in favor of the religious institute or of the heirs, if the latter would claim the property.

9 Aug. 11, 1758 (Bizzarri, *l. c.*, p. 330). This decision proves the correctness of our interpretation as to the unlawfulness of an arbitrary transfer to another institute; cfr. also cc. 7, 24, X, III, 31.

10 Piatus M., I, 204.

TITLE XVI

After mentioning legal and illegal egress from a religious institute, the Code draws attention to the part which the institute itself may take in dismissing members who are no longer regarded as desirable. Every society must have ways and means for expelling unfit members. The Code begins by mentioning three facts which entail *ipso facto* dismissal.

CAN. 646

§ 1. Ipso facto habendi sunt tanquam legitime dimissi religiosi:

1.° Publici apostatae a fide catholica;

2.° Religiosus, qui fugam arripuerit cum muliere; aut religiosa quae cum viro;

3.° Attentantes aut contrahentes matrimonium aut etiam vinculum, ut aiunt, civile.

§ 2. In his casibus sufficit ut Superior maior cum suo Capitulo vel Consilio ad normam constitutionum emittat declarationem facti; curet autem probationes facti collectas in domus regestis asservare.

§ 1. The following religious are *ipso facto* regarded as lawfully dismissed:

1.° Religious who have publicly apostatized from the Catholic faith;

2.° A religious who has run away with a person of the opposite sex;

3.° Religious who attempt or contract marriage, even civil marriage.

Apostates from the Catholic faith are those who renounce Catholic doctrine or morality. Hence if a religious would openly deny even one article of faith, he would be an apostate, the same if he became a Mohammedan, or Buddhist, or Brahman, etc., or joined a heretical sect, or became a " free-thinker," for it hardly seems possible that any one could combine this state of mind with the *obsequium fidei* — due submission to the faith.[1] But, as stated, the defection must be public, *i. e.,* either by public profession, or by evidence obtained from official sources.

Regarding n. 2, note that the intention of marrying each other is not required. *Marriage* is considered in n. 3. Those are said to *attempt matrimony* who cannot contract a valid (even though " purely civil ") marriage under the law of the Church.[2]

In all such cases the higher superior, with his chapter or council, according as the constitutions prescribe, should make a declaration of the fact and preserve the documentary proofs thereof in the archives of the house. They are often needed later, especially if the apostate religious should attempt a trial. The higher superior is the one who, according to the constitutions, has the right to dismiss. The constitutions must also determine whether the superior must call the whole chapter, or the counsellors only.

[1] Avanzini, *Comment. in " Apostolicae Sedis,"* 1883, p. 4 ff.

[2] A civil marriage is one contracted before the officials of the state.

CHAPTER I

CAN. 647

§ 1. Professum a votis temporariis sive in Ordinibus sive in Congregationibus iuris pontificii dimittere potest supremus religionis Moderator vel Abbas monasterii sui iuris cum consensu sui Consilii per secreta suffragia manifestato, vel, si agatur de monialibus, Ordinarius loci et, si monasterium sit regularibus obnoxium, Superior regularis, postquam monasterii Antistita cum suo Consilio fidem de causis scripto fecerit; in Congregationibus vero iuris dioecesani, Ordinarius loci in quo religiosa domus sita est, qui tamen iure suo ne utatur Moderatoribus insciis vel dissentientibus.

§ 2. Ii omnes, graviter eorum onerata conscientia, religiosum dimittere nequeunt, nisi servatis quae sequuntur:

1.° Causae dimissionis debent esse graves;

2.° Possunt se habere sive ex parte religionis sive ex parte religosi. Defectus spiritus religiosi qui aliis scandalo sit, est sufficiens dimissionis causa, si repetita monitio una cum salutari poenitentia incassum cesserit, non vero infirma valetudo, nisi certo constet eam ante professionem fuisse dolose reticitam aut dissimulatam;

3.° Licet Superiori dimittenti certo innotescere debeant, non est tamen necesse ut formali iudicio com-

probentur. At religioso semper manifestari debent,
data eidem plena respondendi licentia; eiusque responsiones Superiori dimittenti fideliter subiiciantur;

4.° Contra dimissionis decretum est religioso facultas recurrendi ad Sedem Apostolicam; et pendente
recursu, dimissio nullum habet iuridicum effectum;

5.° Si de mulieribus agatur, servari debet praescriptum can. 643, § 2.

§ 1 determines who are the superiors who may dismiss religious with temporary vows.

(1) In *orders and congregations with papal approval*
this right belongs to the *superior general,* in autonomous monasteries, to the *abbot;* but the general as well
as the abbot can only proceed with the *consent of the
counsellors,* which must be given by secret ballot. Note
the term " consent," which binds the superior under pain
of acting invalidly.

(2) If a *nun* is to be dismissed, the *Ordinary* may dismiss her after the superioress with her counsellors has
given a written attestation of the motives for the dismissal; if the convent is subject to regulars, the *regular
prelate* may also dismiss her. The declaration of 1858
permits the general to subdelegate the business of dismissal to at least three prudent and honest religious for
distant provinces.[1] This may still be admitted, according to Regula Juris, n. 68: " What one is permitted to
do himself, he may do through others." The Code does
not exclude this assumption, but rather favors it (see
can. 668).

(3) In *diocesan congregations* the right of dismissing
a Sister belongs to the *Ordinary* in whose diocese the

---

[1] S. C. super Statu Regul., June 12, 1858, n. IV (Bizzarri, *l. c.,*
p. 856).

house is located. However, he should not act without the knowledge of the superioress or against her just opposition. Such an arbitrary procedure would tend to relax discipline and undermine the authority of the superioress.

§ 2. These superiors and Ordinaries can dismiss a religious only on the following conditions, the observance of which constitutes for them a grave obligation in conscience:

1.° The *motives* for the dismissal must be *grave;*

2.° These motives may be either on the side of the institute or on the part of the religious. Thus a scandalous lack of the religious spirit would be a sufficient reason. A religious who, though often admonished, and even punished, refuses to mend his ways, may be dismissed. But ill-health, unless fraudulently concealed or dissimulated before profession, would not be a sufficient motive for dismissal.

3.° Although the superior who is entitled to dismiss a religious must be aware and certain of the motives, it is *not* necessary that they be proved by a *judicial* process, *i. e.,* no witnesses, summonses, judge, plaintiff, and sentence are required; not even written documents. However, says the Code, the motives must be made known to the religious, and full liberty to reply given him; and his replies must be faithfully submitted to the superior effecting the dismissal.

4.° The religious has the right to appeal against the decree of dismissal to the Holy See, *i. e.,* the S. Congregation of Religious; and pending the appeal, which should, of course, be notified to the superior, the dismissal has no juridical effect. This is a recourse or appeal *in suspensivo.*

5.° In the case of religious women, can. 643, § 2, concerning provision, must be observed.

EFFECTS OF DISMISSAL

CAN. 648

Religiosus dimissus ad normam can. 647 ipso facto solvitur ab omnibus votis religiosis, salvis oneribus ordini maiori adnexis, si sit in sacris, et firmo praescripto can. 641, § 1, 642; clericus autem in minoribus ordinibus constitutus eo ipso redactus est in statum laicalem.

A religious (with temporary vows) dismissed according to can. 647 is *ipso facto* freed from all his religious vows, without prejudice to the obligations attaching to major orders (celibacy and the Breviary) if he has received them. A religious in higher orders who is dismissed by his superiors must return to his own diocese and obey the prescriptions of can. 642. A cleric in minor orders simply returns to the lay state.

Here a doubt occurs because of the wording of can. 642, § 2, where those who have made profession of temporary vows are laid under said restrictions only in case they have been professed for six years. Are they obliged to the rule of said canon if dismissed before six years have elapsed? We believe they are, because it is not a mere voluntary dispensation, but a forced dispensation by reason of dismissal, which the legislator wishes to punish more severely. But we state this opinion with all due reserve.

CHAPTER II

CAN. 649

In virorum religionibus clericalibus non exemptis et laicalibus, ut professus a votis perpetuis dimitti possit, praecedant necesse est tria delicta cum duplici monitione ac defectu emendationis ad normam can. 656–662.

The dismissal of a member who has made profession of perpetual vows in a non-exempt clerical or in a lay institute is effected in pretty much the same way as in an exempt clerical institute. The member to be dismissed must have been convicted of at least three offences; he must have been admonished twice and proved incorrigible. These points are further developed in can. 656–662.

CAN. 650

§ 1. Haec si constiterint, supremus religionis Moderator cum suo Consilio, perpensis omnibus facti adiunctis, deliberet num locus sit dimissioni.

§ 2. Si maior suffragiorum numerus pro dimissione steterit;

1.° In religione iuris dioecesani res tota deferatur ad Ordinarium loci in quo religiosa professi domus sita est, cuius est dimissionem pro suo prudenti arbitrio decernere ad normam can. 647;

2.° In religione iuris pontificii ipse supremus religionis Moderator dimissionis decretum ferat; quod tamen ut suum sortiatur effectum, debet a Sede Apostolica confirmari.

§ 3. Religioso ius est suas rationes libere exponendi; eiusque responsiones in actis fideliter referendae sunt.

When these facts (*i. e.*, the three offences, two admonitions and incorrigibility) are ascertained, the superior general of the institute with his council, having considered all the circumstances, shall deliberate whether the case be one for dismissal.

If the majority of the votes are for dismissal:

1.° In *diocesan institutes,* the whole matter must be referred to the Ordinary, in whose diocese the religious house of the professed is located, and it rests with him to decide on the dismissal according to his discretion, conformably to the terms of can. 647;

2.° In the case of *papal institutes* the superior general issues the decree of dismissal; but to become effective it must be ratified by the Apostolic See. This latter text is taken from " *Conditae* " (II, 1), which says that the superior general, in dismissing professed members, must follow the rules of the institute and the pontifical decrees. But these constitutions should now be modelled upon the new law.

§ 3. The religious has the right to freely expose his reasons, and his replies must be conscientiously reported in the acts, which are to be forwarded to the S. Congregregation of Religious. In order to obtain this result, it will be best to make an abstract of the papers proving the offences, admonitions, and reasons stated by the religious and hand it over to the religious himself for his signature.

Can. 651

§ 1. Etiam ad dimittendas religiosas professas a votis perpetuis sive sollemnibus sive simplicibus exiguntur graves causae exteriores una cum incorrigibilitate, experimento prius habito ita ut spes resipiscentiae evanuerit, iudicio Antistitae.

§ 2. Praescriptum can. 650, § 3 etiam in religiosarum dimissione servandum est.

Also for the dismissal of *religious women* who have made profession of perpetual vows, whether solemn or simple, grave external reasons are required, together with incorrigibility, experience having proved, in the judgment of the superioress, that there is no hope of amendment. The Sister, too, according to can. 650, § 3, must be allowed to defend herself, and her reasons must be faithfully inserted in the documents to be sent to Rome.

Can. 652

§ 1. Si agatur de religiosis iuris dioecesani, Ordinarii loci in quo sita est sororis professae domus, est causas dimissionis expendere et decretum dimissionis ferre.

§ 2. Si de monialibus, Ordinarius loci omnia acta et documenta transmittat ad Sacram Congregationem cum suo et Superioris regularis voto, si monasterium regularibus sit subiectum.

§ 3. Si de aliis religiosis iuris pontificii, suprema religionis Moderatrix rem totam ad Sacram Congregationem pariter deferat cum omnibus actis et documentis; Sacra autem Congregatio tum in hoc tum in praecedenti casu quod magis expedire censuerit, decernet, firmo praescripto can. 643, § 2.

§ 1. In the case of *diocesan institutes* the Ordinary in whose diocese the house of the professed Sister is located, must weigh the motives for and issue the decree of dismissal.

§ 2. If there be question of *nuns* with solemn vows, the local Ordinary shall transmit to the S. Congregation of Religious all the acts and documents with a statement of his own judgment and that of the regular superior if the monastery be subject to regulars.

§ 3. For dismissing members of a *papal institute*, the superioress general likewise shall transmit to the S. Congregation the whole matter with all the acts and documents, but without expressing her own opinion; whereupon the S. Congregation shall decide the case, without prejudice to can. 643, § 2, which guarantees a decent material provision.

Can. 653

In casu gravis scandali exterioris vel gravissimi nocumenti communitati imminentis, religiosus statim potest a Superiore maiore cum consensu sui Consilii vel etiam, si periculum sit in mora et tempus non adsit adeundi Superiorem maiorem, a Superiore locali cum consensu sui Consilii et Ordinarii loci, ad saeculum remitti, habitu religioso illico deposito, ita tamen ut res per ipsum Ordinarium aut per Superiorem maiorem, si adsit, Sanctae Sedis iudicio sine mora subiiciatur.

In the case of grave external scandal or of very serious imminent injury to the community, the religious may be dismissed immediately by the higher superior with the consent of his council, or even by the local superior with the consent of his council and of the local Ordinary if there be danger in delay and time does not admit of recourse to the higher superior; the religious must immediately put off the religious habit and the whole matter must, without delay, be referred to the Holy See (S. C. Rel.) either by the Ordinary or by the higher superior, if he be present.

Note the gradation of *grave scandal* and very serious imminent injury to the community. The scandal must be external, *i. e.,* known to outsiders, *e. g.,* the surrounding parish or municipality, and deserving of the name according to sound moral principles. Gossip or mere prejudice is not scandal. Neither is there real scandal if the fact is not notorious,[1] *i. e.,* known to more than two or three persons. A *very serious injury* would threaten a community if a member had misappropriated large sums of money or proved a stumbling-block to other members by seduction or violent outbursts of temper, or caused suspicion of disloyalty[2] by foolish utterances or actions or political intrigues.

The term *consent* supposes strict balloting and involves the obligation on the part of the superior to abide by the vote of the majority. In case of a tie, for instance, two against two, his own vote would be decisive.

---

1 Cfr. can. 2197.

2 A disloyal citizen can hardly be a good religious, because he is lacking in obedience to the natural law.

CHAPTER III

CAN. 654

Vir professus a votis sollemnibus aut a votis simplicibus perpetuis in religione clericali exempta ne
dimittatur, nisi processu instituto, salvo praescripto
can. 646, 668, et revocato quolibet contrario privilegio.

After stating the rules for dismissing members who
have made profession of temporary vows only, whether
in orders or congregations, and for dismissing members
with perpetual vows in non-exempt institutes, including
nuns with solemn vows, the Code now proceeds to establish fixed rules for the dismissal of another class of religious, *viz.*, members of male institutes with a clerical
character, which belong to the category of exempt religious. These institutes, permitting their members to
make profession of perpetual vows, occupy a higher place
in the hierarchic order, and being by reason of exemption withdrawn from the jurisdiction of the Ordinary,
demand special consideration. Note the term *exempt*,
which comprises not only orders of regulars proper, but
all clerical institutes endowed with exemption by virtue
of a papal indult. Hence the Passionists, the Redempto-
ists, the Missionaries of the Sacred Heart of Mary are
included, whereas all female orders or congregations, although they may enjoy exemption, are excluded. A

396

doubt arises as to laybrothers of exempt institutes; for they belong to such and yet are not of the clerical order proper. This doubt can only be solved by the authentic interpreters. Can. 654 says: No male religious, who has made profession of perpetual vows, whether solemn or simple, in an exempt clerical institute, may be dismissed except upon a *canonical trial*, every privilege to the contrary being revoked, save only the case stated in can. 646 and 668. What a canonical trial means the following canons explain. The legislator *revokes* each and every *privilege* which would render this law ineffective. Hence if any order or exempt congregation has obtained a privilege previous to May 19, 1918, concerning dismissal of perpetually professed members without canonical trial, that privilege is now invalid. The Code excepts only two cases from this general rule, *viz.*: the one mentioned in can. 646, which requires no trial, but only a declaratory sentence; and the case of grave external scandal or very serious injury threatening the community. With these exceptions in view the legislator proceeds to outline the canonical trial. A trial requires a judge, a plaintiff, and a defendant, and, in criminal cases, also a crime that is prosecuted. The canon immediately following determines who is the *judge* in such trials.

Can. 655

§ 1. Ad sententiam dimissionis ferendam competens est supremus religionis vel monasticae Congregationis Moderator cum suo Consilio seu Capitulo, quod quatuor saltem religiosis constet; si qui deficiant, eorum loco totidem religiosos eligat praeses de consensu aliorum qui cum ipso tribunal collegiale constituant.

§ 2. Praeses de aliorum consensu promotorem iustitiae nominet ad normam can. 1589, § 2.

In centralized organizations the *superior general* is the competent judge who issues the decree of dismissal; in monastic congregations the *abbot president* is the judge, but both the general and the abbot must have a council or chapter consisting of at least four religious whom they are obliged to consult. In case one or the other of these counsellors be absent, the president may, with the consent of the others, select *ad hoc* other religious, to form the collegiate tribunal. The president with the consent of the other counsellors must appoint a *promotor iustitiae* according to can. 1589, § 2.

Pope Urban VIII, in 1624, outlined the legal procedure to be taken in case of the expulsion or dismissal (which latter term is used exclusively in our Code) of religious. But, as the decree of the S. C. Rel., of May 16, 1911, stated, these formalities could not always be observed, and hence had to be reduced to what is a *summary proceeding*, which contains the essential elements of an ecclesiastical trial without the accidental features that might delay prompt action. It is this summary trial which we find embodied in the Code, following the instruction of May 16, 1911. The latter, therefore, must form the basis of interpretation.

The *persons constituting the tribunal* are the superior general with at least four "definers" or counsellors. The abbot president takes the place of the judge in monastic congregations. But he too must have at least four counsellors. Hence let it be understood once for all that *all monastic congregations must at their general chapter elect counsellors*. These counsellors are not to be the abbots of the single monasteries, but religious who dwell with the abbot president and form a regular or collegiate tribunal with him. The counsellors of the monastery whose abbot acts as president for a certain term, generally three or six years, are not the counsellors of the congregation, nor can they pretend to act as such. Only in case the one or other of the duly elected counsellors is absent, or missing, or dead, may the abbot president appoint other religious in their stead. But in doing so he must have the *consent,* to be given by ballot, of the remaining counsellors, *i. e.,* those who constitute the tribunal. This is a point which should be clearly embodied in the constitutions, and no abbot is allowed to set it aside. The decree of the S. C. Rel., May 16, 1911, adds that if an abbey is not affiliated with any congregation, recourse must in each single case be had to the Holy See. This should remind all superiors of the importance of the enactment stated above.

But the Code also insists upon appointing a prosecuting attorney or *promotor iustitiae.* He is, according to § 2 of our canon, to be nominated by the superior general or the abbot president " with the consent of the others." Who are these others? According to § 1 they would be the counsellors of the regular tribunal, and this explanation may be accepted if the attorney is chosen for each single case of dismissal. However, the decree of the S. C. of Rel., quoted above, would have him elected by the general chapter. And it is certainly more in conformity with the intention of the legislator that his office be permanent or at least for a determined period or term. Hence he, too, would have to be elected by the general chapter. He must be a *religious* of the same order or congregation, says the decree quoted, and his functions are to defend justice and law: " *pro iuris et legis tutela.*"

CAN. 656

Ad processum instruendum deveniri nequit nisi praecesserint:

1.° Gravia delicta externa sive contra ius commune sive contra speciale religiosorum ius;

2.° Monitiones;

3.° Defectus emendationis.

No judicial proceedings may be begun unless preceded by:

1.° Grave external offences either against the common law or against the special law of religious;

2.° Admonitions;

3.° Failure to amend.

CAN. 657

Delicta debent esse saltem eiusdem speciei, vel, si diversae, talia ut simul sumpta manifestent perversam voluntatem in malo pervicacem, aut unum tantum permanens, quod ex repetitis monitionibus virtualiter triplex fiat.

The offences committed must be at least three of the same species or, if they are of different species, of such a nature that when taken together they manifest the perversity of the will resolved on evil, or only one continuous offence which, from repeated admonitions, has virtually become threefold.

A grave external offence presupposes a public violation of some important law, either of the common law of the Church, in which case it comprises the whole range of the Penal Code (Book V); or of the particular statutory law set up by the respective institute. The essential feature of a *delictum* or crime is that it be externally manifest and cause injury to society at large or to the religious community.[1] Thus not to wear the religious habit is against the common law;[2] entering saloons without necessity is against the general law of the church,[3] etc., etc. The special laws of each religious institute are laid down in the respective constitutions, which differ in different orders. A common feature of all, we believe, is the prohibition of stubborn resistance to the injunctions of a superior when he commands in accordance with the rule and constitutions. Thus a Benedictine would act against his special laws by absenting himself without a sufficient reason from choir-service. A mendicant would transgress his rule if, without reason, he would refuse to go begging as enjoined by the rule. A member of a teaching order would transgress if he would refuse to teach.

These offences, the Code says, must be grave and external, *i. e.*, such as constitute a grievous sin, and be perpetrated notoriously. For we believe we are justified if we take *external* as synonymous with *notorious*. Notorious, according to the Code, is an act which cannot be concealed by any tergiversation or contrivance and excused by no pretext of law or right.[4] However, notoriety, as shall be seen from can. 658, may be effected by still other means, though even these suppose a certain measure of public knowledge.

The Code distinguishes (a) *Offences of the same species*, three in number, for instance, drunkenness committed on three different occasions; this is the numerical

1 In secular law " a crime or misdeamor is defined by Blackstone to be an act committed or omitted in violation of a public law, either forbidding or commanding it." Bishop, *Commentaries on the Criminal Law*, ed. 6, Boston, 1877, § 32.
2 Can. 596, can. 136.
3 Can. 138.
4 Can. 2197.

distinction; (b) *Specifically different offences,* for instance, absence from choir, outbursts of ill-temper, refusal to accept appropriate penances, which, taken together, show a lack of good will and no hope of amendment; (c) *One continuous offence, e. g.,* familiarity proscribed by the constitutions; but this must be, as it were, split into three numerically distinct offences by the canonical admonition. Of these the Code speaks in the following canons, 658–661.

CANONICAL ADMONITIONS

CAN. 658

§ 1. Ad monitionem faciendam necesse est ut aut delictum sit notorium aut de eodem constet ex rei confessione extraiudiciali vel ex aliis sufficientibus probationibus quas praevia inquisitio suppeditaverit.

§ 2. In inquisitione peragenda serventur, congrua congruis referendo, praescripta can. 1939 seqq.

CAN. 659

Monitio fieri debet ad immediato Superiore maiori per se vel per alium de eius mandato; sed Superior mandatum ne det, nisi praevia informatione facti ad normam can. 658, § 1; datum vero mandatum pro prima monitione valeat etiam pro altera.

CAN. 660

Duae debent esse monitiones, scilicet singulae pro singulis duobus primis delictis; in delictis autem continuatis seu permanentibus intercedat necesse est inter primam et alteram monitionem saltem trium dierum integrum spatium.

Can. 661

§ 1. Monitionibus Superior addat opportunas exhortationes et correptiones, praescriptis insuper poenitentiis aliisque remediis poenalibus, quae apta censeantur ad emendationem rei et scandali reparationem.

§ 2. Praeterea tenetur Superior reum ab occasionibus relabendi removere etiam per translationem, si opus fuerit, ad aliam domum, ubi facilior sit vigilantia et remotior delinquendi occasio.

§ 3. Singulis monitionibus adiiciatur dimissionis comminatio.

Can. 658 enjoins superiors not to proceed to canonical admonition unless the offence be notorious or manifest either from the extra-judicial confession of the culprit or from other sufficient proofs furnished by previous investigation. This investigation must be conducted according to the prescriptions of can. 1939–1946. The substance of these prescriptions is: a religious should be appointed to make the investigation; he is bound to strict secrecy and exhorted not to believe hostile denunciations, or to accept anonymous information or such offered by untrustworthy persons; he may secretly and confidentially employ helpers and must report the result to the superior, together with his own opinion. A sufficient proof, according to a decree of May 16, 1911, would be the testimony of two sworn witnesses. Authentic statements by a civil court would also be admitted.

Can. 659 says that the canonical admonition must be given by the immediate higher superior personally or by another acting on his mandate. Hence the provincial should give the admonition, or the local superior in virtue of a special mandate or commission of the provincial. But this commission must not be given by the latter until he has obtained information on the facts, according to can. 658, § 1. The mandate given for the first admonition avails also for the second.

Can. 660 says that at least two admonitions must be given: one for each of the first two offences; but in the case of continuous or permanent offences, an interval of at least three whole days must elapse between the first and second admonition.

Can. 661 provides that (§ 1) the superior shall add to his admonitions opportune exhortations and corrections, besides imposing penances and other penal remedies,— for instance, retreats, removal from office,— which are calculated to procure the amendment of the culprit and the reparation of the scandal.

The superior is also bound (§ 2) to remove the culprit from the occasions of relapse, even to the extent of transferring him, if necessary, to another house, where he may be more easily watched and the occasion of offending is more remote.

Lastly (§ 3) each admonition must be accompanied by the threat of expulsion.

LACK OF AMENDMENT

CAN. 662

Religiosus censetur se non emendasse, si post secundam monitionem novum delictum commiserit vel in eodem permanenter perstiterit; post ultimam monitionem sex saltem dies erit expectandum, antequam ad ulteriora progressus fiat.

The religious is considered not to have amended if, after the second admonition, he commits a new offence or perseveres in the old one; after the last admonition, at least six days must elapse before further steps be taken.

Can. 663

Immediatus Superior maior, postquam monitiones et correctiones incassum cesserint, omnia acta et documenta diligenter colligat et ad supremum Moderatorem transmittat; hic autem ea tradere debet promotori iustitiae, qui ea examinet et suas conclusiones proponat.

After the admonitions and corrections have proved inefficacious, the immediate higher superior shall carefully collect all the materials and documents and send the same to the superior general, who shall deliver them to the prosecuting attorney, who shall examine them and propose his deductions. We say, " deductions," for *conclusion* would mean the end of the allegations or proofs together with a renunciation of further investigation,[5] which cannot be the meaning here. The prosecuting attorney is simply to deduce from the materials submitted some opinion and submit the same.[6]

Can. 664

§ 1. Si promotor iustitiae, cui fas est etiam ulteriores inquisitiones, quas opportunas iudicaverit peragere, accusationem proponat, instruatur processus, servatis praescriptis canonum in Parte Prima Libri Quarti, congrua congruis referendo.

§ 2. Ex processu constare debet de delictis patratis, de praemissa duplici monitione et de defectu emendationis.

After the prosecuting attorney, who may demand further investigations to be made if he deems fit, has formu-

---

5 Cfr. Reiffenstuel, II, 19, n. 159.

6 It is evident that the abbot president must not send the material to the Abbot Primate, because the former is the supreme superior in monastic congregations; besides the Abbot Primate has no council or chapter.

lated the accusation, the *regular trial may begin*.　In this trial, the Code says, the prescriptions of the first part of Book IV (concerning ecclesiastical procedure) must be observed.　These are briefly: that the judge be competent, that the plaintiff (who is generally the institute itself) be duly represented and follow the rules prescribed, that the witnesses be beyond suspicion, that the summons be made according to the established rules, that the admonition be served in a proper way, that the necessary time be granted for defence, that exceptions and appeals be admitted, that the sentence be issued properly. All this, of course, requires a knowledge of Canon Law. The trial itself, says § 2 of our canon, must make it evident that the offences were really committed, that the two canonical admonitions were duly given, and that the culprit did not amend his conduct.　These are the principal points to which the prosecuting attorney should devote his attention.　If one of these cannot be proved, the trial comes to naught.

SENTENCE OF THE TRIBUNAL

Can. 665

Tribunal, diligenter perpensis allegationibus tum promotoris iustitiae tum rei, si quidem iudicaverit satis probata esse ea de quibus in can. 664, §2, sententiam dimissionis pronuntiet.

After the tribunal has carefully weighed the allegations or pleas of both the prosecuting attorney and the defendant, it may pronounce sentence of dismissal, provided it has found the three points mentioned in can. 664, § 2, sufficiently proved.　The sentence must be pronounced by the judge, *i. e.*, the superior general or the abbot president, who must be morally certain of the truth

regarding all three points.[7]   The sentence is called defini-
tive because the end of the trial (*viz.*, dismissal) is attained.

RATIFICATION OF THE SENTENCE

CAN. 666

**Sententia exsecutioni mandari nequit, nisi fuerit a
Sacra Congregatione confirmata; ad quam tribunalis
praeses et sententiam et omnia acta processus quam-
primum transmittere curabit.**

The sentence pronounced by the tribunal shall take
effect only after it has been ratified by the S. Congregation of Religious, to which all the *acta* as well as the sentence itself must be forwarded by the president of the
tribunal.   Note that the S. Congregation will handle no
case unless at least a preliminary attempt has been made
by the religious tribunal to bring forward material enough
for a decision.   Hence it would be useless to refer a case
to the S. Congregation without papers and a previous
sentence, simply to shirk the obligation of a trial.   Of
course, if a dispensation is demanded, the case may go
immediately to the S. Congregation.

DELEGATION OF TRIAL

CAN. 667

**Pro dissitis regionibus etiam in casibus ordinariis
supremi Moderatores cum consensu sui Consilii seu
Capituli possunt dimittendi facultatem demandare pro-
bis ac prudentibus religiosis, qui saltem tres esse debent, firmo praescripto can. 663–666.**

For *distant provinces* the superior general may, even

7 Cfr. can. 1868 ff.

in ordinary cases, with the consent of his council or chapter, delegate the power of dismissal to trustworthy and prudent religious, who must be at least three in number and follow the prescriptions of can. 663–666. It is generally understood that the *dissitae regiones* are those beyond the Atlantic Ocean, but even Great Britain is, or was formerly, considered a distant and remote country.[8]

Can. 668

In casu, de quo in can. 653, religiosus statim potest a Superiore maiore, vel si periculum sit in mora et tempus non adsit recurrendi ad Superiorem maiorem, a Superiore quoque locali, cum consensu sui Consilii, ad saeculum remitti, habitu religioso illico deposito; religioso autem dimisso, statim processus, si nondum fuerit institutus, institutuatur ad normam canonum qui praecedunt.

This canon is a rehearsal of can. 653, with the exception of the last clause: after the religious has been dismissed, a trial (if it had not yet begun) must be started according to the preceding canons.

---

[8] Whether the abbots presidents may delegate the power of dismissal to other religious is not plainly stated in the text. However, considering the great distances in our countries, we believe that, at least in extraordinary cases, as the S. C. Super Statu Regul., June 12, 1858, n. IV (Bizzarri, *l. c.*, p. 856) says, delegation would be admissible and certainly valid.

CHAPTER IV

CAN. 669

§ 1. Professus qui vota perpetua emisit, a religione dimissus, votis religiosis manet adstrictus, salvis constitutionibus aut Sedis Apostolicae indultis quae aliud ferant.

§ 2. Si clericus est in minoribus ordinibus constitutus, eo ipso reducitur ad statum laicalem.

A dismissed professed religious remains bound by his religious vows, unless the constitutions or a papal indult determine otherwise. A clergyman in minor orders is, by dismissal, reduced to the lay state.

CAN. 670

Clericus in sacris qui aliquod delictum commisit de quo in can. 646, aut dimissus est ob delictum quod iure communi punitur infamia iuris vel depositione vel degradatione, perpetuo prohibetur deferre habitum ecclesiasticum.

A cleric in higher orders, who has publicly apostatized from the Catholic faith, or run away with a woman, or attempted marriage, is forever debarred from wearing the ecclesiastical garb. The same punishment follows him if he is dismissed from his institute on account of a crime which in common law is qualified as infamous, or punished with deposition or degradation.

In these two canons the Code states the general penalties for dismissed religious. Note the title of the chapter: it embraces all religious who have made profession of perpetual vows, because the legislator does not distinguish between clerical and non-clerical, exempt and non-exempt religious. Only the constitutions [1] or a papal indult may absolve them from the obligation of observing the vows. Hence a dismissed religious must observe the *vow of poverty* as far as his condition permits. What he acquires really belongs to the religious community. Here the civil law might interfere, unless the by-laws fix the point. As to the *vow of chastity*, the difference between simple and solemn vows is unchanged, that is to say, the former do not debar valid marriage, whereas solemn vows render an attempted marriage invalid. The *vow of obedience* to the religious superior also remains in force as do the special vows of the institute. However, many reliable authors — the Code does not oppose their opinion — declare such religious free from the obligation of the Breviary and fasts, etc.[2]

Can. 670 singles out the case of a religious cleric in higher orders — those in minor orders, dealt with in can. 669, § 2, lose their clerical rank — who has committed one of the offences mentioned in can. 646, or a crime which is punishable by infamy, whether inflicted by law, or *ipso facto* (see Book V).[3] Another class of crimes is that which the law expressly punishes with degradation [4] or deposition.[5] Notice that infamy by law here mentioned is infamy branded as such by ecclesiastical, not

---

1 This concerns members of the Society of Jesus with simple vows: Greg. XIII, "*Ascendente Domino*," § 7.

2 Piatus M., I, p. 223.

3 Can. 2320, 2343, § 1, n. 2; § 2,

n. 2; 2351, § 2; 2356; 2357, § 1.

4 Can. 2314, § 1, n. 3; 2343, § 1, n. 3; 2354, § 2; 2368, § 1; 2388, § 1.

5 Can. 2314, § 1, n. 2; 2320, § 2; 2353, § 2; 2379; 2394 n. 2; 2401.

civil, law. Some crimes, such as larceny, forgery, perjury, are also declared infamous crimes by our civil laws.[6] On the other hand, the differing views as to the solubility of marriage may cause a difference of procedure between Church and State, although the latter looks upon polygamy as infamous at least by statutory law.

STATUS OF DISMISSED RELIGIOUS

CAN. 671

Si vero dimittatur ob delicta minora iis de quibus in can. 670:

1.° Ipso facto suspensus manet, donec a Sancta Sede absolutioncm obtinuerit;

2.° Sacra Congregatio, si id expedire iudicaverit, dimisso praecipiat ut, habitu cleri saecularis indutus, commoretur in certa dioecesi, indicatis Ordinario causis ob quas dimissus fuit;

3.° Si dimissus praecepto de quo n. 2 non paruerit, religio ad nihil tenetur, et dimissus eo ipso privatus est iure deferendi habitum ecclesiasticum;

4.° Ordinarius dioecesis pro eius commoratione designatae, religiosum in domum poenitentiae mittat, cel eum committat curae et vigilantiae pii ac prudentis sacerdotis; et si religiosus non paruerit, servetur praescriptum n. 3;

5.° Religio, per manus Ordinarii loci commorationis, caritativum subsidium dimisso suppeditet pro necessariis ad vitae sustentationem, nisi ipse aliunde sibimet providere valeat;

6.° Si dimissus vitae rationem ecclesiastico viro dignam non agat, transacto anno aut etiam prius, iudicio Ordinarii, privetur caritativo subsidio, eiiciatur e

6 Bishop, *Criminal Law*, 1877, I, § 974; § 502.

domo poenitentiae eique auferatur ius deferendi habitum ecclesiasticum ab ipso Ordinario, qui statim mittere curet opportunam relationem tum ad Sedem Apostolicam tum ad religonem;

7.° Si vero dimissus praedicto tempore tam laudabiliter se gesserit ut merito haberi possit vere emendatus, Ordinarius eius preces apud Sanctam Sedem commendabit pro absolutione a censura suspensionis, et, ea obtenta, eidem in sua dioecesi permittat, adhibitis opportunis cautelis et limitationibus, Missae celebrationem et etiam, pro suo arbitrio et prudentia, aliud sacrum ministerium, unde honeste vivere queat; quo in casu religio caritativum subsidium intermittere potest. Quod si agatur de diacono aut subdiacono, res ad Sanctam Sedem deferatur.

The legislator now determines the status of one who, having pronounced perpetual vows, is dismissed on account of a lesser offence, *i. e.*, one not mentioned in can. 646, nor entailing infamy, degradation, or deposition. Such a religious (1) remains *suspended* until he has obtained absolution from the Holy See. This absolution must be asked from the S. Congregation of Religious, as the following number insinuates. (2) The S. Congregation may command the religious to stay in a *certain diocese* and indicate to the Ordinary of the same the reasons for which the religious was dismissed. (3) If the *dismissed does not abide by the injunction* just named, the institute is under no further obligation towards him, and the culprit is deprived of the right of wearing the ecclesiastical garb. Formerly it was believed that a religious properly dismissed could claim no support from his former institute. The Code humanely provides that, as long as he abides by the injunction of the S. Congregation, he is entitled to the necessary means of subsistence from his institute, as is evident from n. 5. (4) The Ordinary in whose diocese the dismissed dwells for the time being, shall either send him to a *house of penance* or entrust him to the care and supervision of a pious and prudent priest; if the religious does not heed the Ordinary's command, the rule under n. 3 takes effect. (5) The *institute* shall grant, through the Ordinary in whose diocese the dismissed religious lives, the *necessary livelihood*, unless he possesses other means of subsistence. Therefore a religious with simple vows, who retains the right to own property and is blessed with earthly goods, must provide for himself. Besides, it is evident that, in case one is admitted to the sacred ministry, he does not need this charitable subsidy from the religious institute (n. 7). The intention of the legislator is evidently to keep dismissed religious from engaging in a sordid occupation or begging. (6) If the dismissed *religious leads a life not conformable to the ecclesiastical state*, the Ordinary shall, after one year, or even sooner if he deems it opportune, deprive him of the charitable support granted by his former institute, remove him from the house of penance, and deprive him of the right of wearing the ecclesiastical garb. He should report the case immediately to the Holy See and also inform the religious institute. (7) *If*, however, *the conduct* of the expelled religious has *been praiseworthy* for a whole year, so that he may be considered as having amended his life, the Ordinary may petition to have him absolved from suspension, and, if absolution has been obtained, permit him to say Mass under certain precautions and restrictions, *e. g.*, on certain days only, and in private oratories, in the presence of trustworthy persons, etc. He may then also be admitted to other functions of the sacred ministry, in order to gain a livelihood, and in that case the charitable subsidy [7] from the religious institute may cease. As to deacons or subdeacons, the matter must be referred to the Holy See.

OBLIGATIONS OF DISMISSED RELIGIOUS

CAN. 672

§ 1. Dimissus, votis in religione emissis non solutus, tenetur ad claustra redire; et si argumenta plenae emendationis per triennium dederit, religio tenetur eum recipere; quod si graves obstent rationes sive ex parte religionis sive ex parte religiosi, res iudicio Sedis Apostolicae subiiciatur.

§ 2. Quoties vero vota in religione emissa cessaverint, si dimissus episcopum benevolum receptorem invenerit, sub eius iurisdictione et speciali vigilantia maneat, servato praescripto can. 642; secus res ad Sanctam Sedem deferatur.

The dismissed religious is not free from the obligations of his vows (whether the three substantial or special vows),[8] and as these obligations cannot be fully complied with in the world, he is bound to return to the monastery. The latter, on the other hand, on account of the existence of a bilateral contract, is obliged to receive him back if he gives signs of complete emendation. Should serious reasons, either on the part of the institute or of the expelled member, militate against his being received back, the matter may be submitted to the decision of the Holy See. Such *reasons* according to canonists would

---

[7] Note that the text always speaks of a "charitable subsidy," from which we may conclude that there is no question of a strict right enforcible by civil authority.

[8] Such a special vow is that of the Jesuits to go on missions and that of the Minimi to observe perpetual abstinence.

be : scandal to innocent souls, grave detriment to the good standing of the institute resulting from a grievous crime committed by the religious after his dismissal, or an immoral life led by him and witnessed by trustworthy persons, or an incurable contagious disease.[9]

If the vows have ceased to be effective, through a dispensation granted by the Holy See or by virtue of the constitutions, as is the case with the simple vows of the Jesuits, the dismissed religious may apply to a bishop to be received into his diocese. If he is received, he must live under the jurisdiction and special supervision of the Ordinary, without prejudice to the restrictions of can. 642; otherwise the matter must be referred to the S. Congregation of Religious.

9 Piatus M., I, p. 224.

TITLE XVII

DIFFERENT KINDS OF COMMUNITIES

CAN. 673

§ 1. Societas sive virorum sive mulierum, in qua sodales vivendi rationem religiosorum imitantur in communi degentes sub regimine Superiorum secundum probatas constitutiones, sed tribus consuetis votis publicis non obstringuntur, non est proprie religio, nec eius sodales nomine religiosorum proprie designantur.

§ 2. Huiusmodi societas est clericalis vel laicalis, iuris pontificii vel dioecesani ad normam can. 488, nn. 3, 4.

Every society, whether of men or women, whose members imitate the manner of life of religious by living in community under the government of superiors according to approved constitutions, but without being bound by the usual three vows, is not properly a religious institute, nor are its members properly called religious. Such a society is clerical or lay and must be acknowledged either by the Holy See or by the Ordinary, and therefore be either a papal or a diocesan foundation. The most prominent societies of this class are the Lazarists or

Missionaries of St. Vincent de Paul, the Oratorians of St. Philip Neri, and the Fathers of the Precious Blood.[1]

ESTABLISHMENT AND SUPPRESSION

Can. 674

Circa erectionem et suppressionem societatis eiusque provinciarum vel domorum, eadem valent quae de Congregationibus religiosis constituta sunt.

As to the erection and suppression of such an approved society and its provinces or houses, the same laws apply as are laid down for religious congregations.

GOVERNMENT

Can. 675

Regimen determinatur in uniuscuiusque societatis constitutionibus; sed in omnibus serventur, congrua congruis referendo, can. 499–530.

The government of every such society is determined by its constitutions, but, preserving due proportions, canons 499–530 must be observed by all. The general rule is that they are subject to the Ordinary in whatever pertains to the care of souls, whereas in the administration of their own property, in the internal government of their institutes, choice of confessors and chaplains the societies of men at least enjoy independence. However, the following canon must also be considered.

---

[1] Their institute was recognized and the Constitutions were approved by the S. C. EE. et RR., Dec. 17, 1841. The constitutions contain the " general rule " and a special American observance. They, too, must now accommodate themselves, not to the " Auctis Admodum," but to the new Code.

ADMINISTRATION OF PROPERTY

Can. 676

§ 1. Societas eiusque provinciae et domus capaces
sunt acquirendi et possidendi bona temporalia.

§ 2. Administratio bonorum regitur praescripto can.
532–537.

§ 3. Quidquid sodalibus obvenit intuitu societatis,
eidem acquiritur; cetera bona sodales secundum constitutiones retinent, acquirunt et administrant.

Every society, and its provinces and houses, are capable of acquiring and possessing property. The administration of the property is regulated by canons 532–537.
Whatever property the members acquire with a view to
the society belongs to it; as to other property, the members retain, acquire, and administer it according to the
constitutions.

ADMISSION

Can. 677

In admittendis candidatis serventur constitutiones,
salvo praescripto can. 542.

For the admission of candidates the constitutions are
to be observed, without prejudice to the prescriptions of
can. 542.

STUDIES

Can. 678

In iis quae ad studiorum rationem et ad suscipiendos
ordines pertinent, sodales iisdem legibus tenentur ac
saeculares clerici, salvis pecularibus praescriptionibus
a Sancta Sede datis.

In matters pertaining to studies and the reception of
orders, the members are governed by the same laws as
secular clerics, without prejudice to the particular prescriptions given by the Holy See. Cfr. can. 1365 ff.,
995 ff.

DUTIES

Can. 679

§ 1. Sodales societatis, praeter obligationes quibus,
uti sodales, obnoxii sunt secundum constitutiones,
tenentur communibus clericorum obligationibus, nisi
ex natura rei vel ex sermonis contextu aliud constet,
pariterque stare debent praescriptis can. 595–612, nisi
constitutiones aliud ferant.

§ 2. Clausuram servent ad normam constitutionum
sub Ordinarii loci vigilantia.

The members of a society, besides the obligations to
which the constitutions bind them as members, are bound
by the common obligation of clerics, except it appears
otherwise from the nature of the case or from the context. They shall observe the law of enclosure (set forth
in can. 595–612) according to the terms of their constitutions, under the supervision of the local Ordinary.

PRIVILEGES

Can. 680

Iidem, etiam laici, gaudent clericorum privilegiis, de
quibus in can. 119–123, aliisque societati directe concessis, non autem privilegiis religiosorum sine speciali
indulto.

The members, even lay members, of such societies,
enjoy the privileges of clerics enumerated in can. 119–

123, and other privileges accorded directly to the society, but not the privileges of religious, without a special indult.

LEAVING A SOCIETY

CAN. 681

Praeter proprias cuiusque societatis constitutiones, circa transitum ad aliam societatem vel ad aliquam religionem aut circa sodalium exitum a societate etiam iuris pontificii, serventur, congrua congruis referendo, praescripta can. 632–635, 645; circa eorum dimissionem, praescripta can. 646–672.

Besides the constitutions proper to each society concerning the passing to another society or to some institute, or the departure of members from a society, even though it be approved by the Holy See, the prescriptions of can. 632–635 and 645 are to be observed, due proportion being maintained; and as to their dismissal, the prescriptions of canons 646–672 are to be followed.

PART III

THE LAITY

After determining the distinction between clergy and laity, and establishing the hierarchic order in its general and special functions and degrees, the Code lays down rules for a state which in its essence is neither hierarchic nor clerical, yet partakes more of the clerical than of the lay state. This is the large body of religious of whom this volume has so far treated. Now the legislator turns to a still larger class of members, who form the great bulk of the Church established by Christ, *viz.*, the *laity*, more especially as united or organized into confraternities and pious unions. This at first sight seems like slurring the lay state as such, but the slur is only apparent, for the entire third book is devoted to the reception of the Sacraments, the feasts and fasts, ecclesiastical teaching and other matters preëminently intended for the laity.

CAN. 682

Laici ius habent recipiendi a clero, ad normam ecclesiasticae disciplinae, spiritualia bona et potissimum adiumenta ad salutem necessaria.

As far as ecclesiastical discipline permits, laymen are entitled to receive from the clergy spiritual benefits, especially the means necessary for salvation. The reason for this general principle lies partly in the fact that laymen belong to the Church and must therefore be sanctified, taught, and governed, partly in the fact that the Sacraments are instituted for the salvation of men, and lastly that the clergy is the custodian and dispenser of the treasures of grace. The phrase, *"ad normam ecclesiasticae disciplinae"* means that although all Catholics are entitled to the spiritual benefits, yet certain rules must be observed in the reception and distribution of them. Thus only actual and faithful members are in a condition to receive the spiritual bounties offered by the Church, whereas unworthy and disloyal members are debarred from certain benefits either for a time, or until they have complied with the conditions imposed. From this point of view it will be readily understood that the Sacraments especially may be given only to such members as are neither excommunicated nor unworthy to receive them. Besides, it is a general principle that those who have not been in actual communion with the Church during life shall not be in communion with her after death.[1] This reasonable rule debars certain unfaithful members from Christian burial, as will be seen in Bk. III, Title XII. Lastly, it must be remembered that the right to receive spiritual favors entails the duty to honor and support those by whom these favors are dispensed. This duty not only implies proper material support, but assistance in the administration of church property, as far as the sacred canons permit laymen to share therein as trustees, administrators, tutors, etc. Benedict XIV enjoins especially missionaries and pastors generally to provide for the spiritual welfare of the sick and poor, and to visit them in their distress and need without distinction of person or sex.[2] This precept needs no emphasizing,

[1] C. 1, C. 24, q. 2; c. 12, X, III, 28.

[2] *"Omnium sollicitudinum,"* Sept. 12, 1744, § 14.

since it is but a practical application of Christ's teaching.[3] Above all, the means necessary for salvation must be supplied to all. These are primarily the so-called Sacraments of the dead (Baptism and Confession) and secondarily the other Sacraments as far as they are intended for all. For two of them, Holy Orders and Matrimony, are intended merely for society as such, but not for each individual member. So much about spiritual benefits, omitting the sacramentals, which are not necessary for salvation. Since there is an essential hierarchic difference between laity and clergy, it is but meet that this distinction should also appear outwardly. Hence the following canon:

CAN. 683

Non licet laicis habitum clericalem deferre, nisi agatur vel de Seminaricrum alumnis aliisque adspirantibus ad ordines de quibus in can. 972, § 2, vel de laicis, servitio ecclesiae legitime addictis, dum intra eandem ecclesiam sunt aut extra ipsam in aliquo ministerio ecclesiastico partem habent.

With the exception of seminarists and others aspiring to holy orders (even if they do not live in a theological seminary; can. 972), laymen are not allowed to wear the clerical garb, unless they are legitimately engaged in the service of the Church, in which case they may wear the ecclesiastical garb in church and also outside of it, when taking part in ecclesiastical functions. The clerical garb consists of the cassock and the so-called Roman collar. In Rome and in Italy generally, as elsewhere, the students of petits seminaires usually wear a cossack. This practice the Code permits. It also allows sextons or sacristans, singers, beadles (sometimes called

3 Matt. 9, 12 f.; 28, 19.

" Schweizers "), or ushers to wear their distinctive insignia in church as well as outside of it when they take part in ecclesiastical functions, for instance, processions, dedications, and perhaps also in schools if the function has an ecclesiastical character. Outside these places and ceremonies lay people are not allowed to wear the ecclesiastical garb. There is not much danger of transgression in this country. However, we sometimes hear of bogus priests and even prelates, and hence the warning is opportune even here. The prohibition is based upon the *privilegium canonis* and on that of ecclesiastical immunity formerly accorded to the clergy, when scoundrels like the roaming deacons (*diaconi selvaggi*) often abused the clerical dress.

TITLE XVIII

ASSOCIATIONS OF THE FAITHFUL IN GENERAL

We live in an age of organizations, though it would be wrong to imagine that societies were unknown to former ages. On the contrary, even the Middle Ages had their guilds and confraternities, some of which have left traces of their noble deeds. " Nobles, priests, religious, clerks, sons of the soil who labored at various manual works lived then so to say in common, and they are found continually together in all their daily occupations," says Cardinal Gasquet,[1] and quotes a sentence from Toulmin Smith to the effect that guilds are older than kings in England.[2] Fraternities are as old as the Church. The first Christians, according to the Acts of the Apostles, held everything in common and prayed in common.[3] The *collegium tenuiorum* and the corporation of the *fossores* or grave diggers are well known. We may safely say that the Church has always fostered pious unions and confraternities, as long as they kept within proper limits and acknowledged ecclesiastical authority.

The lack of spiritual guidance or of acknowledgment of ecclesiastical authority has caused no little disturbance in the camps of the Christian Socialists, as the unions or federations of workingmen in Germany have

---

[1] Card. Gasquet, *The Eve of the Reformation*, 1901, p. 309 (Ch. XI).
[2] Id., *Parish Life in Mediaeval England*, 1906, p. 253; cfr. also *Translations and Reprints from the Original Sources of European History*, University of Pa., 1902, Vol. II, No. 1, p. 11 ff.
[3] Acts 2, 44 ff.; 4, 32 ff.

proved.[4] The democratic-idealistic movement in France, known by the name of *Sillon,* also seemed to endanger the progress of true democracy and Catholicity and was therefore disowned by Pius X.[5] Besides social or charitable unions, the Church recommends especially confraternities for young people based on supernatural principles,[6] *i. e.,* the teachings of the Gospel. Two rules should always be observed by laymen in founding pious societies: a specific good work to be undertaken and respect for ecclesiastical authority. If these two essentials are properly safeguarded, the Church will favor a society, whereas if they are not, she will disapprove or merely tolerate.

How much influence may be permitted to laymen in ecclesiastical affairs is a difficult and delicate question, the solution of which depends on the kind of work in hand as well as on individual prudence and zeal. What may be becoming, or even necessary, in one country may be inadvisable in another, where circumstances are different.

CAN. 684

Fideles laude digni sunt, si sua dent nomina associationibus ab Ecclesia erectis vel saltem commendatis; caveant autem ab associationibus secretis, damnatis, seditiosis, suspectis aut quae studeant sese a legitima Ecclesiae vigilantia subducere.

The faithful who enrol in societies organized, or at least recommended, by the Church are worthy of praise; but they should beware of entering secret, condemned, seditious or suspect societies, or such as strive to withdraw themselves from the vigilance of the Church.

4 *Ep. Pii X ad Card. Fischer (A. Ap. S.,* III, 18 f.) etc.
5 Aug. 25, 1910 *(A. Ap. S.,* II, 607 ff.).
6 Letter of Card. Merry del Val to Mons. Bougonier, Nov. 19, 1912 *(A. Ap. S.,* IV, 714 f.).

There are societies for every need in the Catholic Church, but not all are organized by her,— in fact very few. Most were established privately and their constitutions had first to be examined and their work tested. As soon as a society is approved by the Church, the latter may be truly said to have given it her sanction and authority. The Society of St. Vincent de Paul, the Association for Christian Doctrine, the Peter Claver Sodality, and many others may be said to have been organized by the Church. Recommendation in a lesser degree involves a judgment — though not an infallible one — as to a society's soundness. Many such recommendations may be read in the *Acta Apostolicae Sedis,* especially under Pius X, who fully realized the usefulness of Catholic associations.

On the other hand there are societies which the Church disapproves. Five different kinds of them are mentioned in our canon, although we would not assert that the lines are sharply drawn. By *secret societies* are meant principally the *Freemasons.* All their societies or lodges are forbidden, but not all are condemned in the same degree. For condemnation means prohibition or proscription enforced by penal sanction, and is generally made by name. Many ecclesiastical documents, especially the constitutions of Clement XII, "*In eminenti,*" April 28, 1738, and of Benedict XIV, "*Providas,*" March 18, 1731, give the reasons why Freemasons are condemned. These reasons are: because they espouse the principle of indifferentism in religion, envelop themselves in secrecy confirmed by terrible oaths, show repugnance and disobedience not only to ecclesiastical, but also to civil law, and, lastly, because they are shunned and abhorred by good and prudent men. It may be true, as often stated, that the lower degrees are not aware of the real tendencies of the craft as manifested in the higher degrees. But this fact does not lessen the danger. It is safe to say that all secret societies are forbidden; some of them are also condemned for reasons which the student of Freemasonry will easily perceive.[7] *Condemned* are societies which aim at the ruin of Church or State, whether their oath be secret or not (S. O., Aug. 5, 1846). Some (the *Independent Order of Good Templars,* the *Odd Fellows,* the *Sons of Temperance,* and the *Knights of Pythias*) have been nominally forbidden,[8] though the Holy Office would not precisely state whether the members incur censure. To enter such a lodge would be a grievous sin, especially since our Code declares that those who enrol in a Masonic sect are excommunicated.[9] Members who would sustain a great loss if they left one of these societies, on account of insurance, may obtain permission to remain in the lodge, provided they entered it *bona fide,* abstain from participation in any ritualistic ceremony, give no scandal, and suffer no spiritual loss.[10]

Seditious, though not secret societies are the radical Socialists, Communists, Nihilists, and Anarchists, who aim at overthrowing all authority, and subverting the family and property rights.[11]

Questionable are all those societies whose moral and religious principles give rise to doubts as to their sound-

---

[7] Cfr. Arthur Preuss, *A Study in American Freemasonry* (Based upon American Masonic Standard Works), 3rd edition, St. Louis, Mo., 1914.

[8] S. O., Aug. 9, 1893; Aug. 20, 1894; Jan., 1896. S. O., May 10, 1884 (*Coll. P. F.,* n. 1615); Aug. 1, 1855 (*Coll. cit.,* n. 1116) S. C. P. F., Sept. 24, 1867 (*Coll. cit.,* n. 1320),

[9] Can. 2335.

[10] Putzer, *Comment. in Facult. Apost.,* ed. 4, 1897, p. 235 f.

[11] Leo XIII, "*Quod apostolici muneris,*" Dec. 28, 1878. Seditious are also certain societies formed for political purposes, though they may bear a literary title.

ness. Such a one was the *Sillon* in France; such are the societies *which seek to withdraw themselves from the authority of the Church,* no matter how well-meaning they may be. Interconfessional associations are almost compelled to shirk the restraints imposed by ecclesiastical authority.

OBJECTS OF CHRISTIAN ASSOCIATIONS

CAN. 685

Associationes distinctae a religionibus vel societatibus de quibus in can. 487–681, ab Ecclesia constitui possunt vel ad perfectiorem vitam christianam inter socios promovendam, vel ad aliqua pietatis aut caritatis opera exercenda, vel denique ad incrementum publici cultus.

After drawing the line between forbidden and recommended societies, the Code explains for what ends or purposes Catholic societies may be established. Apart from religious institutes and societies dealt with in can. 487–681, the Church permits the establishment of societies for a threefold purpose:

(a) To assist the members to promote a more perfect Christian life (*e. g.,* Tertiaries, etc.);

(b) To encourage works of piety or charity (*e. g.,* confraternities);

(c) To promote public worship (*e. g.,* Eucharistic societies, societies for ecclesiastical music and song, altar societies, societies of acolytes and sextons, etc.).

AUTHORITY FOR ESTABLISHING SOCIETIES

Can. 686

§ 1. Nulla in Ecclesia recognoscitur associatio quae a legitima auctoritate ecclesiastica erecta vel saltem approbata non fuerit.

§ 2. Associationes erigere vel approbare pertinet, praeter Romanum Pontificem, ad loci Ordinarium, exceptis illis quarum instituendarum ius, apostolico ex privilegio, aliis reservatum est.

§ 3. Licet privilegium concessum probetur, semper tamen, nisi aliud in ipso privilegio cautum sit, requiritur ad validitatem erectionis consensus Ordinarii loci scripto datus; consensus tamen ab Ordinario praestitus pro erectione domus religiosae valet etiam pro erigenda in eadem domo vel ecclesia ei adnexa associatione, quae non sit constituta ad modum organici corporis et illius religionis sit propria.

§ 4. Vicarius Generalis ex solo mandato generali, et Vicarius Capitularis nequeunt associationes erigere aut consensum praebere pro earum erectione aut aggregatione.

§ 5. Erectionis litterae ab iis qui ex privilegio apostolico associationem erigunt, gratis concedantur, sola excepta taxa pro expensis necessariis.

§ 1. The Church gives her recognition to no society which has not been organized, or at least approved of, by the legitimate ecclesiastical authority.

§ 2. To erect or approve societies belongs, aside from the Roman Pontiff, to the Ordinary of the diocese, with the exception of those whose institution is by Apostolic concession reserved to others.

§ 3. Even in case a concession has been granted, the

written consent of the Ordinary is required for the valid foundation of a society, unless the contrary is explicitly stated in the concession. The permission of the Ordinary to erect a religious house includes permission to establish in this house or the adjacent church any society that may be customary with the religious institute in question, even though it may not form part and parcel of the institute itself.

§ 4. In virtue of their usual powers, neither a vicar general nor a vicar capitular enjoys the right of establishing any society or of granting the required consent to one already established.

§ 5. With the exception of a nominal fee to cover the necessary expenses, letters of foundation are to be granted gratis.

ECCLESIASTICAL SANCTION

CAN. 687

Ad normam can. 100, tunc tantum fidelium associationes iuridicam in Ecclesia personam acquirunt, cum a legitimo Superiore ecclesiastico formale obtinuerunt erectionis decretum.

In accordance with can. 100, associations of the faithful acquire official recognition as juridical persons only when they have obtained a formal decree of establishment from the competent ecclesiastical superior. This decree is issued in the form of a simple rescript. The time from which the recognition is to be dated, is the date of execution, if an executor is chosen; or let us rather say, the date on which the decree reaches those who asked for it. Before that time members cannot validly be enrolled. Note that the question here is of ecclesiastical acknowledgment only; civil recognition depends entirely on the secular authorities.

CAN. 688

Associatio titulum seu nomen ne assumat quod levitatem aut absonam novitatem sapiat, vel speciem devotionis a Sede Apostolica non probatam exprimat.

No society is permitted to choose for itself any name that savors of levity or novelty, or is connected with any devotion discountenanced by the Holy See.

CAN. 689

§ 1. Quaelibet associatio sua statuta habeat, a Sede Apostolica vel ab Ordinario loci examinata et approbata.

§ 2. Statuta quae non sint confirmata a Sede Apostolica, moderationi et correctioni Ordinarii loci semper subiecta manent.

§ 1. Every society shall have its own statutes, which are to be examined and approved by the Apostolic See or by the Ordinary of the diocese.

§ 2. Statutes which have not been approved by the Apostolic See always remain subject to modification and correction by the diocesan Ordinary.

CAN. 690

§ 1. Omnes associationes, etiam ab Apostolica Sede erectae, nisi speciale obstet privilegium, iurisdictioni subsunt et vigilantiae Ordinarii loci, qui ad normas sacrorum canonum eas invisendi ius habet et munus.

§ 2. Associationes tamen, quae vi privilegii apo-
tolici a religiosis exemptis in suis ecclesiis institutae
sunt, Ordinariis locorum fas non est visitare quod attinet ad ea quae internam disciplinam seu spiritualem
associationis directionem spectant.

§ 1. All societies, even those erected by the Apostolic
See, unless they enjoy a special privilege to the contrary,
are subject to the authority of the Ordinary, who has the
right and duty to watch over them according to the prescriptions of the sacred canons.

§ 2. It is not permissible, however, for diocesan Ordinaries to meddle in the internal discipline or spiritual
direction of societies which exempt religious institutes
have erected in their churches by virtue of an apostolic
privilege.

TEMPORALITIES

CAN. 691

§ 1. Associatio legitime erecta, nisi aliud expresse
cautum sit, bona temporalia possidere et administrare
potest sub auctoritate Ordinarii loci, cui rationem administrationis saltem quotannis reddere debet, ad norman can. 1525, minime vero parochi, licet in eius territorio erecta sit, nisi aliud Ordinarius ipse statuerit.

§ 2. Potest, ad normam statutorum, oblationes recipere, et receptas erogare ad pios ipsius associationis
usus, salva semper offerentium voluntate.

§ 3. Nulli associationi eleemosynas colligere licet,
nisi id aut statuta permittant, aut necessitas postulet,
et loci Ordinarii consensus accedat ac servetur forma
ab eodem praescripta.

§ 4. Ad eleemosynas extra territorium colligendas
uniuscuiusque Ordinarii venia, scripto data, requiritur.

§ 5. **Oblationum quoque ac eleemosynarum fidelis erogationis rationem associatio reddat Ordinario loci.**

§ 1. A society legitimately established may possess and administer temporalities under the direction of the local Ordinary, unless the contrary is expressly stated in the letters of approbation. It must render an account of its property at least annually to the Ordinary, conformably to the prescriptions of can. 1525, but it is not in this regard subject to the parish priest in whose territory it exists, unless the Ordinary legislates otherwise.

§ 2. Such a society may accept donations according to the tenor of its statutes, and use them for any good purpose, with due regard, of course, paid to the will of the donors.

§ 3. No society is allowed to seek alms unless either its statutes permit or necessity demands, and then only with the consent of the Ordinary and in the way prescribed by him.

§ 4. For soliciting alms elsewhere than within their own territory, the written permission of the respective Ordinary is required.

§ 5. The society must render an account to the local Ordinary of the alms and other offerings received.

RIGHTS AND PRIVILEGES OF MEMBERS

CAN. 692

Ad fruendum associationis iuribus, privilegiis, indulgentiis, aliisque gratiis spiritualibus, necesse est et sufficit ut quis in eam valide receptus sit, secundum propria associationis statuta et ab ea legitime non expulsus.

To enjoy the rights, privileges, indulgences, and other spiritual favors accruing to a society, it is required and sufficient for one to be validly received into the same, according to the statutes, and not expelled from it.

QUALIFICATIONS FOR MEMBERSHIP

Can. 693

§ 1. Acatholici et damnatae sectae adscripti aut censura notorie irretiti et in genere publici peccatores valide recipi nequeunt.

§ 2. Eadem persona potest adscribi pluribus associationibus, salvo praescripto can. 705.

§ 3. Absentes ne adscribantur associationibus ad modum organici corporis constitutis; praesentes autem, nonnisi scientes ac volentes adscribi possunt.

§ 4. Salvo praescripto can. 704, religiosi possunt piis associationibus nomen dare, exceptis iis quarum leges, Superiorum iudicio, cum observantia regulae et constitutionum conciliari nequeant.

§ 1. Non-Catholics and members of a condemned sect, those laboring under notorious censure, i. e., one they cannot hide by any artifice, and, in general, public sinners, cannot be validly received.

§ 2. Without prejudice to can. 705, one and the same person may be enrolled in several societies. The exception regards Tertiaries of religious orders, who may not belong to several orders without a special indult; thus, for instance, an oblate of St. Benedict may not at the same time be a Franciscan tertiary.

§ 3. Absent persons may not be enrolled as full-fledged members of a society; those who are present may be received only with their knowledge and consent.

§ 4. Without prejudice to can. 704, religious may join pious associations, except those whose laws, in the judgment of the superior, cannot be reconciled with the rule and constitutions. Can. 704 forbids professed religious to become tertiaries of any order.

FORM OF RECEPTION

CAN. 694

§ 1. Receptio fiat ad normam iuris ac statutorum uniuscuiusque associationis.

§ 2. Ut autem de receptione constet, inscriptio in albo associationis fieri omnino debet; imo haec inscriptio, si associatio in personam moralem erecta fuerit, est ad validitatem necessaria.

§ 1. Reception into any society must be effected according to the laws and statutes of the same.

§ 2. To insure certainty in the matter of reception, the name of each member must be inscribed on the roster of the society; if the society enjoys the status of a *persona moralis,* registration is necessary for validity.

NO SPECIAL RECOMPENSE

CAN. 695

Occasione receptionis in associationem nihil directe vel indirecte exigatur, praeter id quod in statutis legitime approbatis designatum sit, aut ab Ordinario loci, ratione specialium circumstantiarum, expresse permissum in associationis favorem.

On the occasion of reception into a society no fee may be exacted beyond that determined in the lawfully approved statutes, or what the Ordinary of the diocese, by reason of special circumstances, has expressly permitted in favor of the society.

DISMISSAL

Can. 696

§ 1. Nemo, legitime adscriptus, ab associatione dimittatur, nisi iusta de causa ad normam statutorum.

§ 2. Qui in casum inciderint, de quo in can. 693, § 1, expungantur, praemissa monitione, servatis propriis statutis et salvo iure recursus ad Ordinarium.

§ 3. Etiamsi in statutis nihil expresse caveatur, etiam loci Ordinarius quod ad omnes associationes, et Superior religiosus quod ad associationes ex apostolico indulto a religiosis erectas attinet, possunt socios dimittere.

§ 1. No one who has been lawfully enrolled in a society, may be dismissed from the same, except for a just cause, according to the statutes.

§ 2. Whoever falls under can. 693, § 1, may be expelled after due warning, with due regard to the respective statutes and without prejudice to the right of appeal to the Ordinary.

§ 3. Even though nothing be expressly stated in the statutes, the Ordinary of the diocese may dismiss any member of any society. The religious superior enjoys the same right in respect to societies erected by his subjects in virtue of an Apostolic indult.

MEETINGS AND OFFICERS

Can. 697

§ 1. Associationes legitime erectae ius habent, ad normam statutorum et sacrorum canonum, celebrandi comitia, edendi peculiares normas quae ipsum sodalitium respiciant, eligendi administratores bonorum, officiales et ministros, firmo praescripto can. 715.

§ 2. In iis quae convocationem ad comitia et electiones respiciunt, serventur ius commune, quod prostat in can. 161-182 et statuta iuri communi non contraria.

§ 1. Societies legitimately established enjoy the right, according to the rules laid down in their statutes and in the sacred canons, of convoking meetings, promulgating special by-laws pertaining to their society, electing administrators for their property, and other officials necessary for the well-being of the society. Can. 715 must not be overlooked in this connection.

§ 2. In all meetings and elections the common law, as outlined in can. 161-182, must be observed, as well as the statutes not opposed to the common law.

MODERATOR AND CHAPLAIN

CAN. 698

§ 1. Nisi privilegium apostolicum aliud expresse caveat, nominatio moderatoris et cappellani pertinet ad loci Ordinarium in associationibus ab ipso vel ab Apostolica Sede erectis aut approbatis, et in associationibus a religiosis vi apostolici privilegii erectis extra proprias ecclesias; in associationibus vero erectis a religiosis in propriis ecclesiis requiritur tantum Ordinarii loci consensus, si a Superiore moderator et cappellanus e clero saeculari eligantur.

§ 2. Moderator et cappellanus possunt, durante munere, benedicere associationis habitum seu insignia, scapularia, etc., eaque adscribendis imponere; quod vero ad conciones attinet, serventur praescripta can. 1337-1342.

§ 3. Moderatorem et cappellanum revocare ex iusta

causa possunt qui illos nominaverunt eorumque suc-
cessores vel Superiores.

§ 4. Idem potest esse moderator et cappellanus.

§ 1. Unless an apostolic privilege provides otherwise,
the appointment of a moderator and chaplain belongs to
the Ordinary in societies established or approved either
by himself or by the Apostolic See and in societies erected
by religious outside their own churches by virtue of an
Apostolic privilege; but in societies established by religious in their own churches, the consent of the Ordinary
only is required in case the moderator and the chaplain
are appointed by the religious Superior from among the
secular clergy.

§ 2. During their term of office, the moderator and the
chaplain are empowered to bless the habit or insignia,
scapulars, etc., of the society and to invest candidates
with them; regarding sermons, canons 1337-1342 are to
be observed.

§ 3. Those who possess the power of nominating mod-
erators and chaplains, as also their successors or Superiors, can revoke the nomination for a just cause.

§ 4. One and the same person may act as moderator
and chaplain.

SUPPRESSION OF SOCIETIES

CAN. 699

§ 1. Ob graves causas et salvo iure recursus ad
Apostolicam Sedem, potest loci Ordinarius supprimere
non solum associationem a se vel a decessoribus suis
erectam, sed etiam associationem ex apostolico indulto
a religiosis erectam de consensu Ordinarii loci.

§ 2. Associationes vero ab ipsa Apostolica Sede
erectae nonnisi ab eadem supprimi possunt.

§ 1. For grave reasons, and with due regard to the right of recourse to the Holy See, the local Ordinary may suppress not only a society established by himself or his predecessors, but also a society erected by religious in virtue of an apostolic indult requiring the consent of the Ordinary.

§ 2. Societies erected by the Holy See itself can be suppressed only by the same.

TITLE XIX

DIFFERENT KINDS OF ASSOCIATIONS

CAN. 700

*Triplex distinguitur in Ecclesia associationum spe-
cies: tertii Ordines saeculares, confraternitates, piae
uniones.*

There are three kinds of associations in the Church:
secular tertiaries, confraternities, pious unions.

PRECEDENCE

CAN. 701

§ 1. Inter pias laicorum associationes, ordo prae-
cedentiae est qui sequitur, firmo praescripto can. 106,
nn. 5, 6:
  1.° Tertii Ordines;
  2.° Archiconfraternitates;
  3.° Confraternitates;
  4.° Piae uniones primariae;
  5.° Aliae piae uniones.

§ 2. Confraternitas sanctissimi Sacramenti, si agatur
de processione in qua defertur sanctissimum Sacramentum, praecedit ipsis archiconfraternitatibus.

§ 3. Omnes autem tunc solummodo ius praeceden-
tiae habent, cum collegialiter incedunt sub propria
cruce vel vexillo et cum habitu seu insignibus associationis.

§ 1. Without prejudice to the regulations laid down in can. 106, nn. 5 and 6, the order of precedence among pious lay associations is the following:

First — Tertiary Orders;

Second — Archconfraternities;

Third — Confraternities;

Fourth — Primary organizations for pious purposes;

Fifth — Other organizations for pious purposes.

§ 2. In processions in which the Blessed Sacrament is carried, the Confraternity of the Blessed Sacrament enjoys the right of preceding even the Archconfraternities.

§ 3. The right of precedence belongs to these organizations only when they march in a body under their own cross or banner and with the garb or insignia of their society.

CHAPTER I

CAN. 702

§ 1. Tertiarii saeculares sunt qui in saeculo, sub moderatione' alicuius Ordinis, secundum eiusdem spiritum, ad christianam perfectionem contendere nituntur, modo saeculari vitae consentaneo, secundum regulas ab Apostolica Sede pro ipsis approbatas.

§ 2. Si tertius saecularis Ordo in plures associationes dividatur, harum quaelibet legitime constituta dicitur *sodalitas tertiariorum.*

§ 1. Secular Tertiaries are those who live in the world under the direction of an Order, and endeavor to attain Christian perfection according to its spirit, in a manner compatible with secular life. They have a moderator of the same order and rules approved by the Apostolic See.

§ 2. If the secular Tertiaries of any Order are divided into several bodies, each of them is called a sodality of Tertiaries.

The first category of Catholic associations is that of the Tertiaries, a name derived from the organization formed by St. Francis of Assisi, most probably in 1221, near Portiuncula,[1] as an order of penitents. However, though the widespread influence of this particular organization is due to the founder of the Franciscans, similar institutes had been in existence before the XIth century. The Clunians admitted laymen to a share in their

---

1 Cfr. *Cath. Encycl.,* XIV, 641.

spiritual benefits.　In the diocese of Treves, in the well-known abbey of Prüm (erected in the eighth century in honor of our Holy Redeemer), Abbot Stephen (988–1000) "instituted a confraternity in honor of St. Benedict in which many noble men were enrolled."[2]　This, perhaps, is one of the first instances where the Oblates of St. Benedict are referred to as a fraternity or sodality. The eleventh century produced the *Oblates of St. Benedict,* who have been reorganized by Leo XIII.[3]　The Order of St. Dominic and the Carmelites (1273) followed this example and admitted seculars among their Tertiaries.　But, as we have said, the best known organization of this kind is that of the Tertiaries of St. Francis. Note that, although they are called an Order of Tertiaries, they cannot be properly styled religious.　On the other hand these societies of Tertiaries are more than confraternities or sodalities, and the rules of confraternities do not simply apply to them.[4]　The division into sodalities of which can. 702, § 2, speaks, is made for the sake of facilitating administration, but each sodality must be affiliated with the Order of Secular Tertiaries or it can have no legal standing in the Church.

POWERS OF SUPERIORS AND OF THE ORDINARY

CAN. 703

§ 1. Firmo privilegio nonnullis Ordinibus concesso, nulla religio potest tertium Ordinem sibi adiungere.

§ 2. Dato etiam apostolico privilegio, Superiores religiosi possunt quidem personas particulares tertio Ordini adscribere, sed nequeunt sodalitatem tertiario-

---

[2] Schorn, *Eiflia Sacra,* 1889, II, p. 351.

[3] Cfr. *Statutes and Prayers for the Oblates of St. Benedict,* Conception, Mo., 1917.

[4] Cfr. Beringer, *Die Ablässe,* 1906 (ed. 13), p. 200 f.

rum valide erigere sine consensu Ordinarii loci, ad
norman can. 686, § 3.

§ 3. Nec sodalitatibus a se erectis possunt concedere
usum particularium vestium, in publicis sacris functionibus deferendarum, sine speciali eiusdem Ordinarii licentia.

§ 1. With the exception of such Orders as have been
accorded the privilege, no religious institute is allowed to
establish a Third Order. Hence only *orders of regulars*,
but no congregations, even though exempt, may establish
a third order of their own, and even these orders need a
special privilege to that effect.

§ 2. Although religious superiors may enroll particular persons as Tertiaries, they may not validly establish a
sodality of Tertiaries, although their order has an apostolic privilege to that effect, without the approval of the
diocesan ordinary, according to can. 686, § 3.

§ 3. Neither are they permitted to allow the sodalities
which they — the religious superiors — have erected, to
wear a special garb at public sacred functions without the
special permission of the Ordinary. This special garb
must not be confounded with the insignia of the Tertiaries, which consist of a scapular of smaller size and a
girdle of hemp or wool, which they may wear at processions without special permission.[5]

RELIGIOUS CANNOT BE TERTIARIES

CAN. 704

§ 1. Qui vota nuncupavit vel in perpetuum vel ad
tempus in aliqua religione, nequit simul ad ullum ter-

---

[5] " *Veste uniformi induti, vulgo
sacco*"; S. C. E. et RR., April 6,
1900; Beringer, *l. c.*, p. 800, p.
805 f.; a *sacco* means a sack or
dress covering the whole body, even
the face, such as some confraternities wear in Rome at funerals.

tium Ordinem pertinere, etsi eidem antea fuerit adscriptus.

§ 2. Si solutus a votis ad saeculum redierit, antiqua
adscriptio reviviscit.

§ 1. Whosoever has pronounced vows, whether perpetual or temporal, in any religious institute cannot simul-
taneously belong to any Third Order, even though he was
once enrolled in such a one.

§ 2. If one is freed from his vows and returns to the
world, his former status as Tertiary revives.

Note the term " has pronounced." It means that a
novice enjoys the privileges of a Tertiary during his
novitiate (S. C. Indulg., Jan. 31, 1893). This canon
binds *all* Tertiaries and the Oblates of St. Benedict
(S. C. Indulg., Jan. 15, 1895).

NO ONE MAY BE A TERTIARY IN TWO ORDERS

CAN. 705

Nulla tertiariorum sodalitas, sine apostolico indulto,
adscribere potest sodales alius tertii Ordinis in eodem
remanentes; singulis tamen sodalibus licet iusta de
causa transire sive ab alio ad alium tertium Ordinem,
sive ab alia ad aliam sodalitatem eiusdem tertii Ordinis.

No sodality of Tertiaries is allowed, without an Apostolic indult, to enroll members of another Third Order;
for a just cause, however, it is permissible for Tertiaries
to transfer themselves either to a different Third Order,
or to a different sodality of the same Third Order.

This rule dates back to Jan. 31, 1893, but has retroactive force, as the S. C. Indulg. declared, June 21, 1893.
Therefore, as a rule, no one may belong to two different
orders as a Tertiary. Nor is there any necessity for this,

as the purposes of all third Orders are practically about the same.

CAN. 706

Publicis processionibus, funeribus aliisque ecclesiasticis functionibus tertiarii possunt, sed non tenentur, collegialiter interesse; at si intersint, cum suis insignibus sub cruce propria incedant necesse est.

At public processions, funerals, and other ecclesiastical functions Tertiaries may, but are not obliged to, attend in a body. If present in a body, they must march under their own cross and wear their proper insignia.

If the first Order, for instance, of the Franciscans march in procession, their Tertiaries may march under the same cross (S. Rit. C., June 30, 1905).

CHAPTER II

CAN. 707

§ 1. Associationes fidelium quae ad exercitium alicuius operis pietatis aut caritatis erectae sunt, nomine veniunt *piarum unionum;* quae, si ad modum organici corporis sint constitutae, sodalitia audiunt.

§ 2. Sodalitia vero in incrementum quoque publici cultus erecta, speciali nomine *confraternitates* appellantur.

§ 1. Associations of the faithful founded to further some work of piety or charity, are known as pious organizations; if they enjoy a quasi-corporate status, they are called brotherhoods (*sodalitia*).

§ 2. Brotherhoods that have for their object the enhancement of public worship are called confraternities.

Such confraternities may be traced to the fourth century. But the climax of the guild and fraternity movement was witnessed in the XIIIth century, when the *Gonfalieri,* or banner-bearers, were founded and recommended by the Church.[1] The most renowned confraternities to-day are those of the Holy Rosary and the Scapular.

ESTABLISHMENT

CAN. 708

Confraternitates nennisi per formale erectionis decretum constitui possunt; pro piis autem unionibus

---

[1] Cfr. Beri..ger, *l. c.,* p. 514.

448

sufficit Ordinarii approbatio, qua obtenta, ipsae, licet morales personae non sint, capaces tamen sunt obtinendi gratias spirituales ac praesertim indulgentias.

Confraternities may be established only by a formal decree of erection; but for pious organizations, the approbation of the Ordinary suffices, though it does not constitute them moral persons, but enables them to gain spiritual favors, especially indulgences. The S. C. of Indulgences (Jan. 8, 1861) issued two formularies, one for confraternities erected by religious superiors, the other for archconfraternities established by an apostolic indult.[2] These formularies are based on the Constitution of Clement VIII, " *Quaecumque,*" Dec. 7, 1604.

SACRED FUNCTIONS

CAN. 709

§ 1. Confratres nequeunt sacris functionibus operam praestare, nisi confraternitatis habitum seu insignia deferant.

§ 2. Mulieres confraternitatibus adscribi tantum possunt ad lucrandas indulgentias et gratias spirituales confratribus concessas.

§ 1. Male members are not allowed to take part officially in any sacred function, unless vested in the garb or insignia of their confraternity.

§ 2. *Women* can be enrolled in confraternities only to gain indulgences and other spiritual favors granted to the members.

The S. C. of Indulg. wishes that the male members should wear the special garb of the fraternity, but this is not a condition strictly required for gaining the indulgences.[3]

2 *Ibid.,* p. 538 ff.   3 Beringer, *l. c.,* p. 572.

Can. 710

Titulus seu nomen confraternitatis vel piae unionis desumatur vel a Dei attributis, vel a christianae religionis mysteriis, vel a festis Domini et Beatae Virginis Mariae, vel a Sanctis, vel a pio opere ipsius sodalitii.

The title or name of a confraternity or pious organization is to be taken from the attributes of God, or the mysteries of the Christian religion, or the feasts of our Lord and His Blessed Mother, or from the Saints, or from the specific work of piety pursued by the brotherhood.

Can. 711

§ 1. Plures confraternitates vel piae uniones eiusdem tituli ac instituti, nisi id eis specialiter concessum sit aut iure cautum, ne erigantur neve approbentur in eodem loco; si vero agatur de magnis civitatibus, id licet, dummodo inter ipsas intercedat conveniens, iudicio Ordinarii loci, distantia.

§ 2. Curent locorum Ordinarii ut in qualibet paroecia instituantur confraternitates sanctissimi Sacramenti, ac doctrinae christianae; quae, legitime erectae, ipso iure aggregatae sunt eisdem Archiconfraternitatibus in Urbe a Cardinale Urbis Vicario erectis.

§ 1. Unless the contrary be specially conceded or provided for by law, several confraternities or pious organizations bearing the same name, or founded under the same auspices, may not be erected or approved in the same place. In large cities, however, this may be done, provided a sufficient distance intervenes between the respective confraternities according to the good judgment of the Ordinary.

§ 2. It is the duty of the diocesan Ordinaries to see to it that the confraternities of the Blessed Sacrament and of Christian Doctrine be established in every parish. Once legitimately erected, these confraternities are *ipso iure* aggregated to the Archconfraternities of the same name established by the Cardinal Vicar in the city of Rome.

Pius V [4] as well as Benedict XIV,[5] and again Pius X, insisted upon religious instruction to be imparted by laymen well versed in Christian doctrine. The Confraternity of the Blessed Sacrament was founded in Rome in 1538, and exceedingly favored by the Pontiffs.[6] Both are warmly recommended to the Ordinaries. Among students, the Sodality of the Blessed Virgin has justly been favored and produced splendid results.[7]

ESTABLISHMENT

CAN. 712

§ 1. Confraternitates vel piae uniones ne erigantur, nisi in ecclesia aut oratorio publico vel saltem semipublico.

§ 2. Ne instituantur, sine Capituli consensu, in ecclesia cathedrali aut collegiali.

§ 3. In ecclesiis vel oratoriis religiosarum Ordinarius loci permittere potest erectionem associationis mulierum tantum, aut piae unionis quae nonnisi precationibus incumbat et gratiarum dumtaxat spiritualium communicatione gaudeat.

4 " *Ex debito*," Oct. 6, 1571, § 2.
5 " *Etsi minime*," Feb. 7, 1742, § 7.
6 Beringer, *l. c.*, p. 593.

7 Cfr. Elder Mullan, S. J., *The Sodality of Our Lady Studied in the Documents*, New York, 1912 (a very thorough work).

§ 1. Confraternities or pious organizations may be erected only in public or semi-public churches or oratories.

§ 2. They cannot be established in cathedral or collegiate churches without the consent of the chapter.

§ 3. In churches or oratories of religious women, the diocesan Ordinary is allowed to erect associations for women only, or pious organizations, the scope of which is to gain spiritual favors by means of the apostolate of prayer.

Leo XIII, July 7, 1883, granted permission to erect confraternities of the Sacred Heart of Jesus for the conversion of sinners in such oratories, and this privilege is now extended to all societies engaged in the work defined above, not only to the alumnae of female religious institutes, but also to other lay persons of both sexes.[8]

RELIGIOUS SUPERIORS

Can. 713

§ 1. Religiosi cum confraternitatibus piisve unionibus a se erectis possunt et debent communicare omnes et solas gratias spirituales, quae in facultatibus a Sede Apostolica receptis specifice et nominatim communicabiles declarentur, eaeque in actu erectionis manifestandae sunt singulis, servato praescripto can. 919.

§ 2. Confraternitatibus, ab iisdem erectis, non licet vestem propriam seu insignia, quae in publicis processionibus aliisque sacris functionibus deferenda sunt, assumere sine speciali Ordinarii loci licentia.

8 Beringer, *l. c.*, p. 593; Mullan, *l. c.* n. 1925; sodalities of the Bl. Virgin for women only may be erected in the chapels of Sisters if the Ordinary permits them, Mullan, *l. c.*, n. 1932; even sodalities or pious organizations of both sexes the Ordinary could permit according to S. C. EE. et RR., Jan. 18, 1907, Mullan, *l. c.*, n. 1933.

§ 1. Religious who have erected Confraternities or organizations for pious purposes, can and should impart to them all and only those spiritual favors that have been explicitly specified as communicable in the faculties received from the Apostolic See. Without prejudice to can. 919, said favors shall be communicated to all sodalities in the act of erection.

§ 2. Without the special permission of the diocesan Ordinary it is not permissible for confraternities to assume a garb or insignia to be worn in public processions or at other sacred functions. The indulgences are not given by the fact of erection, but communicated by the Apostolic See. But as soon as the superiors have obtained the necessary faculties, they must communicate the spiritual favors in detail to their respective confraternities as soon as these are erected. In doing this they must follow the rules imposed by the Apostolic See, otherwise the favors are null and void.[9] As to the dress, it is hardly necessary to add that the *sacci* or sacks seen in Rome are not worn in our country.

CHANGE OF DRESS

Can. 714

Confraternitas proprium habitum vel insignia, sine licentia Ordinarii loci, ne dimittat neve immutet.

No Confraternity is allowed to abolish or modify its garb or insignia without the permission of the diocesan Ordinary.

POWER OF THE ORDINARY

Can. 715

§ 1. Comitiis confraternitatum, etsi in regularium

9 Beringer, *l. c.*, p. 535.

ecclesiis et oratoriis celebrandis, per se vel per delegatum praeesse sine iure tamen suffragii, dignos et
idoneos officiales et ministros electos confirmare, indignos vel non idoneos respuere aut removere, statuta
aliasve normas, nisi a Sede Apostolica approbatae
fuerint, corrigere et approbare, pertinet ad loci Ordinarium.

§ 2. De comitiorum extraordinariorum celebratione
confraternitas Ordinarium loci eiusve delegatum tempestive praemoneat; secus Ordinario ius est comitia
impediendi vel eorum decreta penitus infirmandi.

§ 1. It pertains to the diocesan Ordinary to preside,
either personally or by proxy, at the meetings of confraternities, even those held in the churches and oratories
of regulars, to confirm the election of worthy and capable officials, to reject or remove unworthy ones, and to
amend and approve statutes and norms that have not the
formal sanction of the Holy See. However, the Ordinary has not the right of suffrage at these meetings.

§ 2. Confraternities shall in due time notify the Ordinary or his delegate of any extraordinary meeting; if
they fail to do so, the Ordinary may impede such meetings or annul their decrees.

PARISH RIGHTS

CAN. 716

§ 1. Confraternitates et piae uniones, in propriis ecclesiis erectae, functiones non paroeciales, servatis
servandis, independenter a parocho exercere possunt,
dummodo ministerio paroeciali in paroeciali ecclesia
non noceant.

§ 2. Idem servetur etiam in casu quo paroecia erecta
sit in ipsa confraternitatis ecclesia.

§ 3. In dubio utrum functiones confraternitatis vel piae unionis noceant, necne, ministerio paroeciali, ad Ordinarium loci spectat ius decidendi, itemque statuendi practicas normas servandas.

§ 1. Confraternities and pious organizations having theii own churches, may exercise non-parochial functions,[10] *servatis servandis,* independently of the parish priest, provided the parochial ministry does not suffer any injury.

§ 2. The same holds good in cases where the parish as such is erected in the church of a confraternity.

§ 3. In case of doubt whether the functions of a confraternity or pious organization injure the parochial ministry, the diocesan Ordinary is to decide and lay down practical rules for guidance.

Can. 717

§ 1. Si in ecclesiis non suis erectae sint, proprias functiones ecclesiasticas in sacello tantum vel altari, in quo sunt erectae, peragere possunt ad norman can. 716 et peculiarium statutorum.

§ 2. Patrimonium confraternitatis et piae unionis, quae erecta sit in ecclesia non sua, aut cuius ecclesia sit simul ecclesia paroecialis, debet esse separatum a bonis fabricae vel communitatis.

§ 1. If established in churches not their own, confraternities may perform their proper ecclesiastical functions only in a chapel or at an altar specially designated

---

10 Parochial functions are only those strictly defined in can. 462; in these the director and members are not allowed to participate or meddle, cf. Mullan, n. 260, n. 967; but besides these associations are dependent on the parish priest if the confraternity is erected in the parish church, Mullan, *l. c.,* n. 948, as can. 717 insinuates.

for their services according to the prescriptions of can. 716 and the statutes.

§ 2. The property of any confraternity or pious organization established in a church not its own, or in a church which serves at the same time as parochial church, must be kept separate from the rest.

PROCESSIONS

CAN. 718

Confraternitates processionibus consuetis et aliis, quas Ordinarius loci indixerit, tenentur collegialiter cum propriis insignibus et sub proprio vexillo interesse, nisi Ordinarius aliud praescripserit.

Unless the local Ordinary determines otherwise, confraternities are obliged to take part in a body in the usual processions, and others ordered by the Ordinary. They march under their own cross and wear their proper insignia.[11]

HEADQUARTERS

CAN. 719

§ 1. **De Ordinarii loci consensu confraternitas vel pia unio de alia ad aliam sedem transferri potest, nisi iure aut statutis a Sede Apostolica probatis translatio prohibeatur.**

§ 2. **Quoties agatur de transferenda confraternitate vel pia unione alicui religioni reservata, Superioris consensus est requirendus.**

§ 1. With the consent of the diocesan Ordinary, any confraternity or pious organization may transfer its quar-

---

11 " In solemn processions, in which the pastor usually takes part, the confraternity can have its chap-lain at its head, apart from the pastor." Mullan, *l. c.*, n. 267.

ters from one place to another, unless such transfer is prohibited either by law or by statutes that have been approved by the Holy See.

§ 2. Whenever there is question of transferring a confraternity or pious organization that belongs to a definite religious institute, the consent of the respective superior is required.

CHAPTER III

CAN. 720

Sodalitia quae iure pollent alias eiusdem speciei associationes sibi aggregandi, *archisodalitia*, vel *archiconfraternitates*, vel piae uniones, congregationes, societates *primariae* appellantur.

Brotherhoods that are empowered by law to affiliate to themselves other associations of the same nature, are termed archconfraternities or archbrotherhoods, or pious organizations, congregations, societies of primary rank.

AGGREGATION

CAN. 721

§ 1. Nulla associatio potest sine apostolico indulto alias sibi valide aggregare.

§ 2. Archiconfraternitas vel primaria unio eas tantum potest confraternitates vel pias uniones sibi aggregare, quae sint eiusdem tituli ac finis, nisi indultum apostolicum aliud ferat.

§ 1. No association can validly affiliate to itself other associations without an apostolic indult.

§ 2. Unless an apostolic indult grants larger powers, archconfraternities or organizations of primary rank are allowed to affiliate with themselves only those confraternities or pious organizations whose title and purpose is the same as their own.

CAN. 722

§ 1. Per aggregationem communicantur omnes indulgentiae, privilegia et aliae gratiae spirituales communicabiles quae associationi aggreganti directe et nominatim a Sede Apostolica concessae fuerint vel in posterum concedantur, nisi aliud in indulto apostolico caveatur.

§ 2. Ex hac communicatione nullum ius associatio aggregans acquirit supra aggregatam.

§ 1. By affiliation, confraternities and pious organizations share equally in all the indulgences, privileges, and other communicable spiritual favors that have been or will be conceded by the Apostolic See to the archconfraternity or pious organization, provided the contrary is not stated in an apostolic indult.

§ 2. The affiliating society does not acquire any right over the affiliated by virtue of this communication of privileges.

Communication of privileges between confraternities is entirely excluded. Only directly granted favors may be communicated to affiliated organizations.

CAN. 723

Ad aggregationis validitatem requiritur ut:

1.° Associatio iam fuerit canonice erecta nec alii archiconfraternitati vel primariae unioni aggregata;

2.° Fiat de consensu Ordinarii loci scriptis dato una cum eius litteris testimonialibus;

3.° Indulgentiae, privilegia et aliae gratiae spirituales quae per aggregationem communicantur, enumerentur in elencho, ab Ordinario loci in quo archiconfraternitas sita est, recognito et societati aggregatae tradendo;

4.° Aggregatio fiat formula in statutis praescripta et in perpetuum;

5.° Litterae aggregationis expediantur gratis omnino et nulla prorsus mercede etiam sponte oblata, exceptis necessariis expensis.

Valid affiliation requires: (1) that the association be canonically erected and not affiliated to any other archconfraternity or primary pious organization; (2) that it is done with the written approval of the diocesan Ordinary and with testimonial letters from him; (3) that the indulgences, privileges and other spiritual favors communicated be enumerated in writing, the list to be inspected by the Ordinary of the diocese in which the archconfraternity exists, and forwarded to the affiliated society;[1] (4) that the affiliation be made according to the form prescribed in the statutes and forever;[2] (5) that, excepting unavoidable expenses, the letters of affiliation be expedited gratis and without recompense, even if such be freely offered.

TRANSFER OF ARCHCONFRATERNITIES

CAN. 724

Archiconfraternitas vel primaria unio de alia ad aliam sedem nonnisi ab Apostolica Sede transferri potest.

Archconfraternities or primary organizations can be

---

[1] The superior of the primary society is not allowed to withold some indulgences and privileges, but must communicate all he has. Mullan, l. c., n. 151.

[2] This is generally called diploma and must be placed in the church or sacristy.

transferred from one place to another only by the Apostolic See.

Can. 725

Titulus **archisodalitii** *vel* **archiconfraternitatis** *vel* **unionis primariae,** etiam honoris tantum causa, potest associationi ab una Sede Apostolica concedi.

The titles " Archconfraternity," " Archbrotherhood," " Primary Organization," may, even as honorary titles, be granted only by the Apostolic See.

APPENDIX

Questions to be Answered in the Quinquennial Report of Religious Superiors (can. 510) [1]

1. Has the congregation obtained the decree of approbation or encouragement, and when was it granted by the Holy See?

2. What is the end or particular scope of the institute?

3. Has the name which the institute took in the beginning, or the scope or habit of the Sisters, undergone any change afterwards, and by what authority?

4. How many members have received the habit since the beginning, or at least in the last twenty years?

5. How many members have left the institute since the beginning, or at least in the last twenty years, and when, whether during the novitiate, after the temporary profession, or after having taken perpetual vows? Have there been any fugitives, and how many?

6. When was the last report sent to the Holy See?

I. About Persons

(a) *About Postulants*

7. How many new members have been received since the last report?

8. Did all of them bring the proper testimonials?

9. Have any special efforts been purposely made to draw members, and especially have the Superiors availed themselves of the newspapers for this purpose?

10. How often and for what impediments or obstacles was a dispensation required, and by what ecclesiastical Superior was it granted?

11. In which house and for how long did postulants or candidates dwell?

1 Translation substantially from Bastien-Lanslots, *op. cit.*, Appendix.

(b) *About Novices*

12. How many houses are there with a novitiate, and was each one founded with the sanction of the Holy See?

13. How many novices have received the habit of the institute since the last report?

14. How many novices are there at present?

15. Are the novices kept apart from the professed Sisters, according to law?

16. Has each of them a complete copy of the constitutions?

17. Have all of them before profession spent a whole and continuous year in the novitiate house under the care of the mistress of novices?

18. Has the time of the novitiate, as established by the constitutions, ever been extended or shortened, and by what authority?

19. Have the novices applied themselves during the first year of the novitiate to works of piety, or have they been put to other work, and to what kind of work?

20. Have the novices been sent to other houses in the second year of the novitiate, where two years are prescribed?

21. Has the Bishop or his delegate made the required examination of candidates before they took the habit or made their first profession?

(c) *About Professed Sisters*

22. How many members are there at present in the congregation: (a) with temporary vows; (b) with perpetual vows?

23. Have the temporary vows always been renewed at the proper time?

24. Have the members been admitted to take perpetual vows at the expiration of the period of temporary vows?

25. How many professed Sisters or novices have died since the last report?

(d) *About Sisters who have left or have been dismissed*

26. How many members have left the institute since the last report? (a) of the novices; (b) of professed Sisters with temporary vows; (c) of professed Sisters with perpetual vows.

27. Have the rules regarding the dismissal of members, as laid down in the constitutions, been always observed?

28. Has a dispensation from the vows always been obtained in cases of dismissal, and from what ecclesiastical Superior?

29. Has, in cases of dismissal of Sisters with perpetual vows, the confirmation of the Holy See always been obtained?

30. Has the entire dowry, however invested, and the furniture they brought, in its present condition been returned to those leaving for any reason whatever?

31. Have those who have left the institute, having no property of their own, been provided with sufficient funds for their safe and decent return to their families?

II. About Property

(a) *About Houses*

32. How many houses does the institute possess, and in which dioceses are they located? Has the institute any provinces, and if so, how many?

33. Have any new houses been opened since the last report, and if so, how many? Has the proper authorization been obtained for all, and has the mode of procedure prescribed by the constitutions been followed?

34. How many members of the different classes are there in each house, and in what works have they been employed (in case the institute has charge of different works)?

35. Has any house been suppressed since the last report, and by what authority?

36. Has each member her own cell, or at least her own bed in the common dormitory, properly separated from the others?

37. Has a place been set aside with all necessary conveniences for the care of the sick?

38. Has a sufficient number of rooms been set aside, as should be, for the reception of guests, apart from the community rooms?

39. Has the dwelling of the chaplain or of the confessor a separate entrance, and has it any communication with that of the Sisters?

(b) *About Finances*

40. What has been the yearly income and expenditure since the last report; (a) of the institute in general, and (b) of each house in particular?

41. Has the institute or any individual house acquired, since the last report, any movable or immovable property, and what is its value?

42. Has the money always been invested profitably, yet honestly and safely?

43. Has there been any loss or damage since the last report; if so, how much and from what cause?

44. Has any immovable or very expensive movable property been alienated, to what value and by what authority?

45. Has any part of the capital been spent?

46. Are there any debts on the property in common, or on any house in particular, and to what amount?

47. Has any new indebtedness been incurred since the last report; if so, how much and by what authority?

48. Has each house a procurator or treasurer other than the local superiors and the treasurer general?

49. Have the procurators, general and local, given a report of their administration at stated times, and have these reports been examined and approved?

50. Are there any lawsuits pending about the property?

51. Has each house a safe closed with three keys, and are the laws bearing on the subject observed?

52. Have money or other valuable been accepted from lay people for safe keeping, and on what conditions?

53. Have the dowries of the Sisters been invested safely and profitably, according to Canon Law? Has any part of them been used; if so, how much, in what manner, and by whose authority?

54. Are any pious legacies or foundations in the institute, either for Masses to be offered or for works of charity; if so, which are they?

55. Have the obligations been faithfully carried out?

56. Has the principal of those foundations been duly invested, and is there an entirely separate account kept of them?

57. Has an account of these foundations been rendered to the Bishop, according to the constitution " Conditae "?

58. How much of the favorable balance of each house has been turned into the common treasury at the end of each year?

59. Have all contributed their share willingly or unwillingly?

60. Have the superior or treasurer any money of which they can freely dispose, even for the welfare of the institute, without rendering an account of it?

III. About Discipline

61. Are the spiritual exercises carefully performed in each house, as prescribed for each day, month, year, or other times?

62. Do all the members hear Mass daily?

63. Can all members be present at the common exercises, and are those who must occasionally be absent from the one or the other on account of domestic work, given time to perform them privately afterwards?

64. Is the decree "*Quemadmodum*" observed, (a) with regard to the manifestation of conscience; (b) with regard to sacramental confession? Is the decree "*Sacra Tridentina Synodus*" concerning Holy Communion observed, and are both decrees read in public at stated times in the vernacular?

65. Is the ordinary confessor changed every three years or confirmed by lawful authority?

66. Are the prescriptions concerning the enclosure in that part of the house especially reserved for the religious faithfully carried out?

67. Are the religious frequently given the privilege of the parlor, and are the constitutions on that point observed?

68. Do the superiors always give a companion to Sisters leaving the house?

69. Are catechetical instructions given, as also pious exhortations to the lay-sisters, to the pupils, to the servants and others living in the house, how and at what times?

70. Are writings on piety, religion, etc., even for the exclusive use of the community, ever printed without the consent of the Bishop?

71. Do the members use any books and which, either ancient or modern, even written by hand, edited with the permission only of the Superiors of the congregation?

About the Observance of Certain Special Laws

72. Are all the regulations concerning the general chapter faithfully carried out: (a) in regard to the letters of convocation; (b) in regard to the election of delegates; (c) in regard to the election of tellers and of a secretary; (d) in regard to the election of the superior general; (e) in regard to the election of general councillors, treasurer, and secretary?

73. Has perfect freedom been given to the members for writing and for receiving letters which are exempted from the inspection of superiors?

74. Has the law concerning the changes of superiors after a certain lapse of time been faithfully observed? Have any dispensations been obtained from the law, how many and for whom?

75. Have the general and provincial superiors rightly performed the prescribed visitation of the houses?

76. Have the superior general and the provincial and local superiors called their councils at fixed times to treat of the business of the congregation, of the province or of the house?

77. Has due liberty been given to the councillors in these deliberations?

78. Have the elections of the general chapter been made freely and according to the laws?

79. Have the superiors with the required motherly care supplied all necessaries to the members, especially with regard to food and clothing? Are there any among the members who procure these things for themselves from outsiders?

80. Is the number of Sisters in any place so inadequate that they are overburdened with work to the serious detriment of their health?

81. Is due provision made for the comfort of the sick, and are their corporal and spiritual needs charitably attended to?

82. Have the pontifical decrees been publicly read at the appointed times?

About the Works of the Congregation

83. How many persons or classes of persons have been benefited by the works to which the religious devote themselves according to the scope of the institute?

84. If the number of such persons has decreased since the last report, give the reasons.

85. For congregations which collect from door to door:

(a) Do the constitutions clearly and certainly authorize them to collect from door to door?

(b) Has the decree " *Singulari,*" of March 27, 1906, been inserted in the constitutions?

(c) Is this decree faithfully observed in all its details?

86. Have the Sisters in their houses any hostelries or hos-

pitals for all classes of persons, even of the other sex, and if so, with whose permission and with what safeguards?

87. Have the Sisters taken upon themselves the care of the domestic department in seminaries, colleges, and other houses of ecclesiastics, and to what extent?

88. Do the Sisters practice any works of charity (such as taking care of infants, of confinement and surgical cases) which appear improper to virgins consecrated to God and wearing the religious habit?

89. Have the Sisters who wait on the sick in their homes always used the precautions prescribed by the constitutions?

90. Have the superiors ever allowed Sisters to dwell in the houses of lay people and for how long?

91. Has, since the last report, any new work, or kind of work been added to those already existing, and by what authority?

92. Have any abuses crept into the congregation, or into individual houses, and of what nature?

93. Are there any troubles or difficulties existing, (a) with the ordinaries, (b) with the confessors, (c) with the chaplains?

It is evident that this questionnaire is not to be answered by all alike. Besides, it may be reasonably expected that the S. Cong. of Religious will modify and shorten it according to the Code. As it is now, it might prove irksome to the superiors who have to answer all those detailed questions.